Many Globalizations

Many Globalizations

•

CULTURAL DIVERSITY IN THE CONTEMPORARY WORLD

EDITED BY

Peter L. Berger and Samuel P. Huntington

UNIVERSITY PRESS

2002

OXFORD

UNIVERSITY PRESS

Oxford New York
Auckland Bangkok Buenos Aires Cape Town Chennai
Dar es Salaam Delhi Hong Kong Istanbul Karachi Kolkata
Kuala Lumpur Madrid Melbourne Mexico City Mumbai Nairobi
São Paulo Shanghai Singapore Taipei Tokyo Toronto

and an associated company in Berlin

Published by Oxford University Press, Inc.
198 Madison Avenue, New York, New York 10016

Oxford is a registered trademark of Oxford University Press

Library of Congress Cataloging-in-Publication Data
Many globalizations : cultural diversity in the contemporary world /
Tamotsu Aoki . . . [et al.]; edited by Peter L. Berger and Samuel P. Huntington.
p. cm. Includes bibliographical references and index.
ISBN 0-19-515146-1
1. Culture.
2. Globalization.
I. Aoki, Tamotsu.
II. Berger, Peter L.
III. Huntington, Samuel P.
HM621 .M36 2002 306—dc21 2001047454

1 3 5 7 9 8 6 4 2

Printed in the United States of America
on acid-free paper

Contents

———— • ————

Illustrations

————— • —————

Acknowledgments

————— • —————

This book is the principal product of the three-year study on globalization and culture in ten countries conducted under the auspices of the Institute for the Study of Economic Culture (ISEC) at Boston University. The study was codirected by the editors, Peter L. Berger (sociologist, director of ISEC) and Samuel P. Huntington (political scientist, Alfred J. Weatherhead III University Professor, Harvard University). A number of additional monographs and articles are being prepared by several of the country researchers.

The Pew Charitable Trusts provided major funding for the study. The Taiwan research was funded by the Himalaya Foundation, Taipei. The Japan research was funded by the Nippon Foundation and the Suntory Foundation. The administration of the study at ISEC was made possible by the ongoing support of Boston University and the Lynde and Harry Bradley Foundation. Special thanks go to Luis Lugo of the Pew Charitable Trusts, not only for the financial support of his foundation but for his personal interest and encouragement.

An occasion for great sorrow was the death of Seizaburo Sato (political scientist, Institute of International Policy Studies, Tokyo), who began the research in Japan. He was both an esteemed colleague and a personal friend of the editors. Upon his death the Japan research was taken over by Tamotsu Aoki.

As the following list shows, the country researchers who contributed to this volume represented a range of academic disciplines:

Tamotsu Aoki, anthropologist, Graduate Institute of International
   Policy Studies, Tokyo
Ann Bernstein, policy analyst, Centre for Development and
   Enterprise, Johannesburg
Arturo Fontaine Talavera, political scientist, Centro de Estudios
   Publicos, Santiago
Hsin-Huang Michael Hsiao, sociologist, Academia Sinica, Taipei
James Hunter, sociologist, University of Virginia
Hansfried Kellner, sociologist, University of Frankfurt
E. Fuat Keyman, political scientist, Bilkent University, Ankara
János Mátyás Kovács, economist, Institute of Human Sciences,
   Vienna, and Eötvös Lorand University, Budapest
Ergun Özbudun, political scientist, Bilkent University, Ankara
Hans-Georg Soeffner, sociologist, University of Konstanz
Tulasi Srinivas, anthropologist, presently at ISEC, during the
   research affiliated with the National Institute of Advanced
   Studies, Bangalore
Yunxiang Yan, anthropologist, University of California, Los Angeles
Joshua Yates, sociologist, University of Virginia

During the period of the research a monthly seminar on the topic of
cultural globalization was conducted at the Harvard Academy for International and Area Studies under the direction of Samuel Huntington.
The discussions at this seminar were helpful in sharpening the focus of
the research. The contributions of Don Posner and Tim Snyder should
be particularly mentioned. Colleagues at ISEC contributed ideas and
criticisms throughout the same period, both informally and at the bi-
weekly ISEC colloquium. Thanks are specifically due to Marilyn Halter,
Robert Hefner, Mariano Plotkin, Adam Seligman, and Robert Weller.
Thanks are also due the Rockefeller Foundation for making available its
Bellagio Center for one of the team meetings.

Finally, special thanks are due to Laurel Whelan and Amy Simmons,
of the administrative staff at ISEC, and to Donald Halstead for a skillful
job of copyediting this volume.

The three years of the study provided a rich experience for all concerned, both in terms of intellectual stimulation and agreeable personal
interaction. It is a great pleasure to welcome this book as the most tangible result of their joint endeavor.

---— • ——---

Introduction

THE CULTURAL DYNAMICS OF GLOBALIZATION

Peter L. Berger

The purpose of this introduction is not to summarize the rich and diverse contents of this book, but to present a picture of the cultural dynamics of globalization as seems plausible to me at this point. Most of the data making this picture possible has come from the research project on which the book is based; however, given the fact that the chapters on the various countries studied in the project are here within the same covers, I have refrained from tedious cross-references to these chapters.

A somewhat cynical colleague once remarked that the goal of every scholarly enterprise is to blow someone's theory out of the water. In this instance that someone was me. While it would be a wild exaggeration to say that I had a theory of cultural globalization, I did have a picture of it, and I succeeded, more or less, in convincing Samuel Huntington, the codirector of the project, and the international research team to accept my picture as a starting point for the investigation (or, if you want to be properly *wissenschaftlich*, as a set of hypotheses). Not surprisingly, over the more than two years of the project, most of them kept hacking away at this picture and, at the end of the day, I had to agree with most of the criticisms. In my own mind, at any rate, the basic features of the original picture have remained unscathed, but it has also become considerably more complicated. As I often tell my students, one of the pleasures of being a social scientist (as opposed to, say, a philosopher or theologian) is that you can have as much fun when you are proven wrong as when you are proven right.

The initial picture that the project had was a Toynbee-like one of challenge and response. The challenge is supposed to come from an emerging global culture, most of it of Western and indeed American provenance, penetrating the rest of the world on both elite and popular levels. The response from the target societies is then seen as occurring on a scale between acceptance and rejection, with in-between positions of coexistence and synthesis. I think that this picture still holds up; however, one must add to it a much more variegated set of reactions by the target societies, including those initiated by governments.

I will make some further preliminary observations before I begin to describe this more complicated picture. The term "globalization" has come to be emotionally charged in public discourse. For some, it implies the promise of an international civil society, conducive to a new era of peace and democratization. For others, it implies the threat of an American economic and political hegemony, with its cultural consequence being a homogenized world resembling a sort of metastasized Disneyland (charmingly called a "cultural Chernobyl" by a French government official).

It is clear to me that both the promise and the threat have been greatly exaggerated, and this insight owes much to the complicated picture coming out of our research. Furthermore, there can be no doubt that the economic and technological transformations that drive the phenomenon of globalization have created large social and political problems such as the bifurcation between winners and losers, both between and within societies, and the challenge to traditional notions of national sovereignty. These problems cannot be dealt with here, though of course they must be taken into account as an ever present background. The present topic is the *cultural* dimension of the phenomenon, and "culture" is understood here in its conventional social scientific sense: as the beliefs, values, and lifestyles of ordinary people in their everyday existence.

What everyone assumes is not always wrong. There is indeed an emerging global culture, and it is indeed heavily American in origin and content. It is not the only game in town, as I shall try to make clear, but it is the biggest game going and it will likely stay that way for the foreseeable future. The Chilean historian Claudio Veliz has called it the "Hellenistic phase of Anglo-American civilization," a phrase that is meant to dissociate it from explanations in terms of imperialism. The then-relevant world became Greek at a time when Greece had virtually no imperial power; today, though the United States does have a great deal of power, its culture is not being imposed on others by coercive means.

Then as now, language is a crucial factor in this cultural diffusion. The principal vehicle of Hellenism was Koine, the basic and rather vulgar Greek in which, not so incidentally, the New Testament was written. Today, the English language, in its American rather than British form, is the koine of the emerging global culture. Regardless of the future of American imperial power, no rival is on the horizon. The millions of people all over the world who increasingly use English as their lingua franca do so mainly for practical reasons. Young Chinese who importune tourists to let them practice their English do so because they want to get on the Internet and improve their job prospects, not to read Shakespeare or Faulkner.

But people do not use language innocently. Every language carries with it a cultural freight of cognitive, normative, and even emotional connotations. So does the American language, even apart from the beliefs and values propagated through the American mass communication media. Just think of seemingly innocuous terms like "religious preference" or "sexual orientation," or phrases like "I cannot express myself in this job," "I need more space in this relationship," or "You have the right to your opinion."

The emerging global culture is diffused through both elite and popular vehicles. Arguably the most important elite vehicle is what Samuel Huntington has felicitously called the "Davos culture" (after the annual World Economic Summit meeting in that Swiss mountain resort), an international culture of business and political leaders. Its basic engine is international business, the same engine that drives economic and technological globalization. But it would be misleading to think of this culture only in terms of those few likely to be invited to Davos; there are millions who *would like* to be invited and who engage in what sociologists have nicely called "anticipatory socialization."

There is, for instance, a global network of ambitious young people in business and the professions who have popped up in every country studied in our project: a sort of yuppie *internationale*, whose members speak fluent English and dress alike and act alike, at work and at play, and up to a point think alike—and hope that one day they might reach the elite summits. However, one must be careful about assuming that this apparent homogeneity embraces their entire existence. It clearly does for some of them; for better or for worse, they are cosmopolitans all the way. But others manage an art of creative compartmentalization, seeking to combine participation in the global business culture with personal lives dominated by very different cultural themes. It will always be an empirical question which of these two options one ascribes to a particular group.

A comparison between eastern Germany and India is interesting in this regard. After unification, a horde of business consultants descended on the former German Democratic Republic, teaching and advising on how to behave in the new economy—essentially, how to become Wessies. There has been a good deal of sullen resistance to this (including the so-called Ossie nostalgia), but the cultural resources to maintain or construct alternative personal lifestyles have been very meager. By contrast, despite a multitude of business schools and training courses to teach Indians how to behave as participants in the global economy, many of the computer professionals in Bangalore succeed in combining such participation with personal lifestyles dominated by traditional Hindu values.

There is another elite sector of the emerging global culture, sometimes merging with the business culture, sometimes in tension with it. That is the globalization of the Western intelligentsia; I have called it, not so felicitously, the "faculty club culture." It is carried by a variety of vehicles: academic networks, foundations, nongovernmental organizations (NGOs), some governmental and intergovernmental agencies. It too seeks and actively creates markets throughout the world, but the products it promotes are not those of multinational corporations but the ideas and behaviors invented by Western (mostly American) intellectuals, such as the ideologies of human rights, feminism, environmentalism, and multiculturalism, as well as the politics and lifestyles that embody these ideologies.

Just as would-be East German and Indian participants in the elite business culture must learn the appropriate behavior and acceptable opinions of this culture, so, mutatis mutandis, must those who want to be successful in the elite intellectual culture. In addition, since the latter culture is by definition much more ideological than the pragmatic business world, the price of admission to faculty club culture is higher in terms of its impingement on personal life. Put simply, a successful businessman in Eastern Europe may act like an American in the boardroom but go home and, in the best indigenous tradition, beat his wife and order the children about. The Eastern European intellectual who wants to have a good relationship with the Ford Foundation, however, will have to be more careful if he wants to keep a comparable compartmentalization going. The two cultures often interpenetrate. Thus corporations hire longhaired academics to teach intercultural or gender "sensitivity" to their employees (in the possibly mistaken belief that this will enhance productivity); on the other hand, human rights and environmentalist activists attack corporations for this or that alleged misbehavior. The two cultures then find themselves in conflict.

What may be broadly called the "health ideology," which has its origins in the American intellectual class, has spread beyond it to affect much wider masses of people in their values and behavior and has led to global political activism. The business culture has absorbed much of this by instituting "wellness" programs and encouraging "fitness." At times, though, there has been conflict, as in the assault of the antismoking movement on the tobacco industry. The story of the antismoking legislation in South Africa is instructive in this regard. With the demise of the apartheid regime a government came into power that was dominated by people with a long and positive relationship with Western NGOs. The antismoking legislation (proudly announced as the most stringent anywhere in the world) was the direct result—a bizarre one in a country on the verge of a catastrophic AIDS epidemic. This action was clearly not the result of a pragmatic assessment of the country's most pressing health needs, but of the influence of the Western-dominated faculty club culture.

It is intriguing to look at the two elite cultures in the light of the old neo-Marxist dependency theory. The Davos and the faculty club cultures have their "metropolitan" centers, with a "periphery" dependent on them. But the centers of the former culture are no longer exclusively Western. There are also powerful centers in Tokyo, Hong Kong, and Singapore, with Shanghai and Bombay as potential additions. The "metropolis" of the globalized intelligentsia is much more exclusively Western, indeed American. Thus, when the term "cultural imperialism" is used, it is probably more applicable to East 43rd Street, where the impressive headquarters of the Ford Foundation are located, than to the corporate bastions of Wall Street and Madison Avenue. I might add that this is a descriptive statement, not necessarily a value judgment. One may deplore *or* welcome the influences emanating from any of these Manhattan addresses.

Be this as it may, the preponderant position of the United States in both elites is not open to doubt. It follows that the most important "globalizers" are Americans. James Hunter has provided a picture of this group, whom he calls "parochial cosmopolitans": people who move with the greatest of ease from country to country while remaining in a protective "bubble" that shields them from any serious contact with the indigenous cultures on which they impinge. The bubble also shields them from serious doubts about what they are doing. Hunter finds this type of person in both corporations and NGOs, with the possible exception of those engaged in evangelical missionary enterprises.

Hunter's depiction of these "globalizers" has been criticized; it may have left out more sophisticated members of both elites. However, it plausibly describes an important segment of American businesspeople and intellectuals engaged in global activities. They are reminiscent of Arthur Miller's famous salesman, who rides "on a smile and a shoeshine"—a prototypical American figure. Compared with earlier "civilizing missions" (say, the British or French ones, not to mention the unlamented Soviet one), this American "cultural imperialism" has about it a quality of (not necessarily endearing) innocence. It comes out clearly when these people are genuinely surprised by hostile reactions to their efforts.

By far the most visible manifestation of the emerging global culture is in the vehicle of popular culture. It is propagated by business enterprises of all sorts (such as Adidas, McDonald's, Disney, MTV, and so on). Although control of these enterprises is exercised by elites, popular culture penetrates broad masses of people all over the world. The vast scope of this penetration can hardly be overestimated. Just take one statistical indicator: In 1970, 10.3 percent of Chilean households had televisions; in 1999 the figure was 91.4 percent. Although some of the programs carried by Chilean television originate from within the country, an enormous number of the contents came from abroad, mostly from American media.

Much of the consumption of this popular culture is arguably superficial, in the sense that it does not have a deep effect on people's beliefs, values, or behavior. In principle, an individual could wear jeans and running shoes, eat hamburgers, even watch a Disney cartoon, and remain fully embedded in this or that traditional culture. However, an inhabitant of a Chilean shantytown wearing a T-shirt with the inscription "Make Love Not War" may be expressing a more significant change. Nor is it likely that young Chilean people dancing frenetically to rock music are engaged in the consumption of a cultural import with no significant consequences on outlook and behavior (as the official guardians of traditional values are rightly aware).

I would suggest a differentiation between "sacramental" and "nonsacramental" consumption. Anglican theology defines a sacrament as the visible sign of an invisible grace; mutatis mutandis, the definition applies here as well. Some consumption of the globalizing popular culture is quite "nonsacramental." To paraphrase Freud, sometimes a hamburger is just a hamburger. But in other cases, the consumption of a hamburger, especially when it takes place under the golden icon of a McDonald's restaurant, is a visible sign of the real or imagined participation in global modernity. The research on McDonald's restaurants in East Asia by the Harvard anthropologist James Watson and his team (to which Yunxian Yan belonged) suggests that there is a switch from "sacramental" to "nonsacramental" consumption as this type of fast food becomes commonplace over time. In Beijing, as in other places, when McDonald's was a newcomer, people went there not just to eat hamburgers but to participate vicariously in American-style modernity. In Tokyo or Taipei, where McDonald's had been around for a long time, going there was just one consumer option among many: the hamburger was just a hamburger. Needless to say, there is no way of deciding a priori which type of consumption prevails. It will always be a matter of empirical inquiry.

Finally, the emergent global culture is carried by popular movements of one kind or another. Some of them are linked to faculty club culture, such as the feminist and environmental movements, or what the French sociologist Daniele Hervieu-Leger called the "ecumenism of human rights." Sometimes the efforts of their Western sponsors fail to produce genuine popular movements, in which case, to use the language of dependency theory, the indigenous activists constitute a "*comprador* class" in the service of "metropolitan" agencies. At other times, though, the missionary outreach is successful and popular movements with a broad appeal eventuate. Again, only careful empirical research can determine which of these two possibilities is in play.

I have long argued (and have not changed my mind) that evangelical Protestantism, especially in its Pentecostal version, is the most important popular movement serving (mostly inadvertently) as a vehicle of cultural globalization. It is a movement of astounding scope—in large areas of East and Southeast Asia, in the Pacific islands, in sub-Saharan Africa, and most dramatically in Latin America. The British sociologist David Martin, who has devoted many years to the study of this phenomenon, estimates that it involves at least 250 million people worldwide. And, as Martin has shown, it brings about a dramatic cultural revolution. The Chilean and South African data, for example, show how conversion to this type of religion transforms people's attitudes to family, sexual behavior, child rearing, and, most importantly, to work and general economic attitudes.

Not to put too fine a point to it, now as in an earlier period in Britain and North America, this is a religion that promotes what Max Weber called the "Protestant ethic"—a morality singularly appropriate for people seeking to advance in the nascent stage of modern capitalism. While this form of Protestantism is clearly of Anglo-Saxon origin (modern Pentecostalism originated in the United States some one hundred years ago), it has been successfully indigenized everywhere it has penetrated. It does not typically use the English language, and its worship (especially in its music) takes over many indigenous forms. However, the "spirit" that is expressed here has unmistakably Anglo-Saxon traits, especially in its powerful combination of individualistic self-expression, egalitarianism (especially between men and women), and the capacity for creating voluntary associations. Thus it not only facilitates social mobility in developing market economies (that, of course, was the gist of the Weberian thesis) but also facilitates actual or anticipated participation in the new global economy. To this must be added the fact that among the leaders of this movement there is a consciousness of being part of a global movement, with increasing cross-national contacts between them and with the centers of evangelicalism in the United States.

As observed earlier, there are both tensions and convergences between the different sectors of cultural globalization, both on the elite and popular levels. If there is one theme that all have in common, it is individuation: all sectors of the emerging global culture enhance the independence of the individual over against tradition and collectivity. Individuation must be seen as a social and psychological process, manifested empirically in the behavior and consciousness of people regardless of the ideas they may hold about this. In other words, individuation as an empirical phenomenon must be distinguished from "individualism" as an ideology (though, of course, the two are frequently linked).

This insight is useful because it helps explain why the new global culture is so widely attractive. It has been understood for a long time that modernization undermines the taken-for-granted authority of tradition and collectivity and, therefore, by default, makes the individual more self-reliant. This is a "liberation," but it may also be experienced as a great burden. "Individualism" as an ideology legitimates the "liberation" and, if necessary, helps alleviate the burden. In either case, the new global culture has a built-in affinity with the modernization process; indeed, in many parts of the world today it is identical with it.

For people caught in the early stages of the modernization process, there is above all a new sense of open possibilities and an aspiration for greater freedom—the sense of burden usually comes later. Thus the emerging global culture is attractive to all those who value the individuation they have already experienced and aspire to an even greater realization of it. It is noteworthy that in this sense the global culture resembles Hellenism, which also celebrated the individual and his striving for "excellence," thus freeing him from the constraints of tradition (Veliz's metaphor holds up).

We now have a picture of a cultural earthquake affecting virtually every part of the world. When the earthquake hits, different people respond differently. There are cases of supine acceptance—the yuppie *internationale* mentioned before is a case in point. Then there are attempts at militant rejection, be it under banners of religion (Taliban) or nationalism (North Korea). Since total isolation from the global culture necessarily requires near total isolation from the global economy, the costs of this posture are very high indeed. But there are less totalistic forms of rejection, typically practiced by governments trying to balance global economic participation with resistance against global culture—China is the most important case of this. It is a difficult balancing act. More intriguing are the cases in-between acceptance and rejection.

There is almost everywhere what James Watson called "localization": the global culture is accepted but with significant local modifications. As Watson points out, McDonald's in America has an implicit contract with its customers: it provides clean, inexpensive food; they eat it and leave promptly. That, after all, is the meaning of *fast* food. In East Asia this contract had to be modified because customers *linger*. Two groups especially do this: housewives relaxing in the restaurant after shopping or other errands and schoolchildren before going home. The attractions are clean premises, accessible restrooms, and (for the housewives) protection against inopportune advances. This localization is particularly interesting because it has obvious economic consequences to which McDonald's management has had to adapt.

But the localizations can have more far-reaching aspects. For example, Buddhist movements in Taiwan have taken on many of the organizational forms of American Protestantism to propagate a decisively non-American, non-Western religious message. For another example, a peculiarly German institution, the Love Parade, took over the form of the American gay pride march but made it into a pan-erotic festival marked by a distinctively German methodical seriousness (thus, perhaps, falsifying the thesis that "German orgy" is an oxymoron).

Impinging global influences can also lead to a revitalization of indigenous cultural forms. Thus the inroad of Western-based fast food chains in India and Japan has led to the development of fast food outlets for traditional foods, and the invasion of Western fashions in Japan has led to the development of an indigenous fashion industry marked by distinctively Japanese aesthetics.

Localization shades over into another response, best described by the term "hybridization." This is the deliberate effort to synthesize foreign and native cultural traits. Japan, ever since the Meiji Restoration, has been a most successful pioneer of this response, but there are many other examples. The development of an overseas Chinese business culture, combining the most modern business techniques with traditional Chinese personalism, is a very important case of this, given the great economic success of the Chinese diaspora throughout the world. However, as mainland China becomes integrated into the global economy, very similar hybridizations can be observed, as in the newly fashionable notion of the "Confucian merchant." The case of software engineers in

Bangalore who garland their computers in Hindu ceremonies is a particularly dramatic example of the same thing. On a much less sophisticated level, the synthesis of Christianity and traditional religions in the so-called African indigenous churches (AICs) is another fascinating case. All these cases make it abundantly clear that the idea of a mindless global homogenization greatly underestimates the capacity of human beings to be creative and innovative in the face of cultural challenges.

Yet there are differences between cultures in the capacity to adapt creatively. The distinction between "strong" and "weak" cultures suggested by Samuel Huntington is useful in this connection (though it is important to stress that these are descriptive categories, not value judgments). The cultures of eastern and southern Asia—notably Japan, China, and India—have been notably "strong," while African cultures and some in Europe have been relatively "weak."

The German case is particularly interesting. One would intuit that one is dealing with a "strong" culture here, but it turns out not to be. The reasons are clear. Sensitivity to the charge of revived nationalism in the wake of the Third Reich has weakened the willingness to assert German cultural self-esteem and has brought about a relatively passive posture in the face of impinging influences from abroad. This becomes clear when Germany is compared with other European societies (notably France) and goes far in explaining why Germany (more precisely, Germany to the west of the former Iron Curtain) seems to be the most "Americanized" country in Europe.

Some of the concepts developed in the 1970s by Brigitte Berger, Hansfried Kellner, and myself in the context of modernization theory are surprisingly applicable to the phenomenon in question here. We said that modernity comes in "packages" containing patterns of both behavior and consciousness. Some of these packages can be taken apart and reassembled without arresting the modernization process, such as the package of Christianity and modern medicine brought by Western missionaries. We called these linkages "extrinsic." Other packages cannot be taken apart without stopping the modernization process, such as the linkage between modern medicine and a scientific conceptualization of causality. These we called "intrinsic" linkages. When packages are diffused from one societal sector to another, we spoke of "carryover"—as when economic costs/benefits thinking is carried over into family life (marriage as a contract, children as investments, and so on). And when the attempt is made to limit the diffusion, we called this "stoppage"—as when individuals behave one way at work and then behave very differently when they come home (the Japanese businessman takes off his navy blue suit, puts on a *yukata*, and practices his calligraphy). I think these concepts remain useful as one tries to understand different responses to the emerging global culture.

The above series of responses to the challenge of the emergent global culture do not provide the whole picture. There is also the increasingly significant phenomenon of *alternative globalizations*; that is, cultural movements with a global outreach originating outside the Western world and indeed impacting on the latter (in her discussion of India's hoped-for new "tryst with destiny," Tulasi Srinivas uses the term "emissions" to refer to the same phenomenon). This is important, not only because it corrects the notion that non-Western and non-American cultures are simply reacting to the forces of cultural globalization, but because it implies that there may be more than one path to modernity. This too is not an altogether new idea. In recent years it has been revived in the writings of the Harvard Sinologist Tu Weiming, the Israeli sociologist Shmuel Eisenstadt, and others. In other words, alternative globalizations intend the possibility of alternative modernities.

These movements can also be found on both elite and popular levels. On the elite there have been both secular and religious movements of alternative globalization. While this particular appeal has diminished in recent years (to be precise, since the recent Asian economic difficulties), Western business and policy circles were for a while eagerly striving to emulate Japanese industrial policy and management techniques. A good religious example is Opus Dei, arguably the most influential Catholic organization in the world today.

Opus Dei began in Spain but is now very influential in Latin America (including, notably, Chile), the Philippines, and other Catholic communities. It is militantly conservative in its theology and morality but very positive in its attitude to modern global capitalism. Opus Dei was very active politically in the waning years of the Franco regime and was instrumental in the transition to a market economy (and later, at least indirectly, in the transition to democracy in Spain). The two most prestigious business schools in Spain are run by Opus Dei. What is involved here is more than an intelligent accommodation with social change. There is the deliberate attempt to construct an alternative modernity—capitalist, democratic, but at the same time resolutely loyal to Catholic religious and moral traditions. (And this, incidentally, explains why Pope John Paul II has been so favorably disposed toward Opus Dei, in contrast with his skepticism toward the Jesuits, who used to be the elite cadre of militant Catholicism but whose traditional loyalties have become somewhat shaky in recent years.) In Latin America there has also been the conscious effort to posit an "integral" Catholic culture against the "Americanizing" force of evangelical Protestantism.

On the popular level, but sometimes reaching into more elevated social strata, India has "emitted" a number of highly influential religious movements. The Sai Baba movement is a good example, claiming two thousand centers in 137 countries; the claim may be exaggerated, but there is no doubt that there are many such centers in Europe and North America. This movement is starkly supernaturalistic, clearly an alternative to a modern scientific worldview. The Hare Krishna movement is an even more visible case of an Indian cultural "emission." Similarly successful in the West have been a number of Buddhist movements, such as Soka Gakkai, which comes out of Japan. The "Buddhist renaissance" in Taiwan intends a global outreach as well; thus the Tzu-Chi Foundation has branches in forty countries.

Islamic movements in Turkey and all over the Muslim world clearly intend an alternative modernity: not rejecting modernity in the style of the Taliban in Afghanistan or even the militant factions in the Iranian regime, but rather seeking to construct a modern society that participates economically and politically in the global system but is animated by a self-consciously Islamic culture. A comparable Islamic movement in Indonesia—procapitalist, prodemocratic, tolerant of religious pluralism, but decisively committed to the Muslim faith—was an important factor in the demise of the Suharto regime and the election of its own leader, Abdurrahman Wahid, to the presidency. Throughout the Muslim world today, even in Iran, such visions of an alternative Islamic modernity are gaining influence.

Arguably the most important cultural influence coming from Asia into the West is not carried by organized religious movements but arrives in the form of the so-called New Age culture. It has affected millions of people in Europe and America, both on the level of beliefs (reincarnation, karma, the mystical connections between the individual and all of nature) and of behavior (meditation, yoga, shiatsu, and other forms of therapeutic massage; tai-chi and the martial arts; generally, the use of alternative medical traditions of Indian and Chinese provenance). Given its nonorganized, broadly diffused character, New Age is more elusive than the religious movements mentioned above, but it is being studied by an increasing number of scholars of religion. It remains to be seen to what extent New Age will permanently influence the "metropolis" of the emerging global culture and thus modify the shape of the latter. The British sociologist Colin Campbell has tellingly described the New Age phenomenon as "easternization."

As far as popular culture is concerned, Japan has been the most successful "emitter." Japanese automotive and electronic products have earned their reputation for reliability, and in consequence Japanese notions and techniques of quality control have greatly influenced European and American industry as well as consumer behavior. The case of Shiseido cosmetics is interesting, like that of the Japanese fashion and design industries, in combining modern products with traditional Japanese notions of aesthetics and finding that this has an appeal beyond the borders of Japan. In all of this, incidentally, the analogy with Hellenism is again instructive. In the late Roman period, in circles dissatisfied with what Greco-Roman civilization had to offer, there was a turn toward the East in terms of behavior and ideas—*ex oriente lux*. In the end, the West Asian movement of Christianity was the greatest beneficiary of this cultural development.

A further complication must be added to our picture, as there are also what could be called *subglobalizations*—movements with a regional rather than global reach that nevertheless are instrumental in connecting the societies on which they impinge with the emerging global culture. "Europeanization" is probably the most important case of this, especially in the countries of the former Soviet bloc. German and Austrian influences in Hungary and other ex-communist countries, Scandinavian influences in the Baltic states, and Turkish influences in Central Asia serve both to "Europeanize" and to globalize. There is also the ideological project of a distinctively European version of modern capitalism, seen of course in contrast to what is perceived as the Anglo-Saxon version. The linkage of Europeanization and secularization is a particularly interesting aspect of this. As countries are absorbed into the "European project," a distinctive "Euro-secularity" seems to be part of the deal—it can be observed most dramatically today in Poland and Ireland.

There are other cases: the diffusion of Hong Kong and Taiwan media in Southeast Asia and mainland China, and of Japanese popular culture in Taiwan; Mexican and Venezuela media penetrating other Latin American countries and the Hispanic population in the United States. There are also African American influences in South Africa, sometimes with ironic effects: dashikis, colorful shirts with African motifs worn by men, come from western Africa and were never seen in South Africa during the apartheid period. They became popular among African Americans as part of a new black self-consciousness, were introduced into South Africa via the United States, and are now sold as "Mandela shirts" in fashionable boutiques in Johannesburg and Cape Town. None of these cultural items are part of the emerging global culture as such, but they *mediate* between the latter and the more parochial cultures on which they impinge.

Under certain political conditions, it is clear, tensions between global and indigenous cultures can give rise to what Samuel Huntington has called a "clash of civilizations." But there are also sharp cultural conflicts within societies (if you will, an internalized "clash of civilizations"). The conflict between a secularized elite and religious revitalization movements is an important case in point—dramatically visible in Turkey, other Muslim countries, Israel, and India. The cultural tensions between Wessies and Ossies in the wake of German reunification were mentioned before. Furthermore, Western "culture wars" are exported as part and parcel of the globalization process. Thus a Hungarian, for instance, looking west for cultural inspiration, comes on free market ideology versus environmentalism, freedom of speech versus "politically correct" speech codes, Hollywood machismo versus feminism, American junk foods versus American health foods, and so on. In other words, "the West" is hardly a homogeneous cultural entity, and its conflict-laden heterogeneity is carried along by its globalization.

Cultural globalization is a turbulent affair, very hard to control. Some governments, of course, make the attempt. "Managed globalization" (as Yunxiang Yan calls it) by the Chinese regime is the most important case, but similar efforts can be seen in both authoritarian and democratic regimes. France is a case of the latter, as is Quebec and Canada as a whole. The Mbeki government in South Africa speaks of an "African renaissance," the ingredients of which are somewhat vague at this point, but the intention is also to "manage" the globalization process through state actions. This case is interesting because it is an effort to carve out an alternative modernity from rather "weak" cultural resources—any successes here would be very interesting (and cheering) indeed.

Here the problems of cultural globalization link up with the problems of economic and social globalization—notably, the problem of how to "manage" the losers in the global system. Social resentments can be channeled into cultural resistances, the "Seattle syndrome" legitimated in cultural terms. The campaign against McDonald's in France is a good example of this: the economic worries of French farmers elevated into a defense of French civilization against American barbarity. With the (perhaps temporary) demise of Marxism, there is here a fertile field for a renascent left, in Europe as elsewhere. The old left themes of anticapitalism and anti-Americanism obtain a new lease on life. It is too early to tell how widespread this new constellation will be.

The picture that I have presented here is, as announced, quite complicated. It resists easy summations, except for the not unimportant conclusion that cultural globalization is neither a single great promise nor a single great threat. It also suggests that globalization is, *au fond*, a continuation, albeit in an intensified and accelerated form, of the perduring challenge of modernization. On the cultural level, this has been the great challenge of *pluralism*: the breakdown of taken-for-granted traditions and the opening up of multiple options for beliefs, values, and lifestyles. It is not a distortion to say that this amounts to the great challenge of enhanced freedom for both individuals and collectivities. If one values freedom, one will be very reluctant to deplore this development, despite its costs. One will then be most interested in the search of middle positions between endless relativization and reactive fanaticism. In the face of the emerging global culture, this means middle positions between acceptance and militant resistance, between global homogeneity and parochial isolation. Such a search has its difficulties, but, as the data of our project show persuasively, it is not impossible.

PART ONE

———————— • ————————

Globalization and Alternative Modernities

1

Managed Globalization

STATE POWER AND CULTURAL TRANSITION IN CHINA

Yunxiang Yan

In a sharp-toned essay on the impact of American hegemony on Chinese society, a Chinese commentator noted that during the 1999 student demonstrations against the NATO bombing of the Chinese embassy in Belgrade on 7 May 1999, many young protestors were drinking Coca-Cola as they chanted "down with American imperialism" in front of the U.S. embassy in Beijing. The irony goes much further. When some young activists sent messages over the Internet calling for a resistance movement to the invasion of Western culture, they seemed unaware that the messages they were writing were in English and signed with English personal names such as "Joan" and "Frank." Others went to eat at a KFC outlet immediately after posting anti-McDonald's slogans on the streets.[1] Similarly, when China Central Television Station (CCTS) canceled its scheduled broadcast of National Basketball Association (NBA) games as a protest gesture in June 1999, a large number of viewers called in to complain, insisting that sports events should have nothing to do with politics.

During the latter part my field research, in the summer of 1999, I was fortunate to interview a college student who was both a team leader of the student demonstrations in front of the American embassy and one of those who called in to complain about the cancellation of the NBA broadcast. When asked why he had acted so contradictorily, he seemed quite surprised and replied, "No, there were no contradictions. Yes, I hate American hegemony, and I love the NBA games. But they are two different things. NBA games belong to the world, and everyone has the right to enjoy them." Looking directly into his eyes, I saw his sincerity and innocence. I suddenly realized that, at least for youths like him, there might actually be a truly global culture that can be enjoyed and appropriated by people from different cultural backgrounds, while they are politically nationalistic at the same time.

This chapter consists of two sections. First, I examine the four faces of cultural globalization (as outlined by Peter Berger) in the Chinese context: business elite, faculty club, popular culture, and social movements.[2] It was not difficult to detect the presence of the four globalizing forces by the end of the 1990s, but their influence on Chinese social life varies in both degree and kind. In general, the globalizing force of popular culture seems to be the strongest, while social movement tends to vary from case to case; however, both have directly influenced the everyday lives of ordinary people. By contrast, the influence of transnational scholarship and the transnational business elite are limited to development within the relevant social strata. The party-state has made great efforts to take control of all four globalizing forces, but more often than not, it has not been successful as it planned to be.

In the second section, I analyze the agents and social context of the process. By the end of the 1990s, both the majority of ordinary Chinese citizens and the country's elite had accepted the view that globalization represented an inevitable stage in China's modernization as well as an opportunity to catch up with the developed countries. To take advantage of this opportunity, the Chinese state has been playing an important role in forming a national consensus, facilitating China's participation in the globalization process, controlling the direction of economic integration, and balancing the pros and cons of cultural globalization—a complex role that in many ways resembles that of a firm manager. Hence the title of this chapter, "Managed Globalization."

MAPPING THE FOUR FACES OF
CULTURAL GLOBALIZATION

Davos Culture or Confucian Merchant?

Is a transnational business elite and associated Davos culture emerging in China? As shown in the following two examples, this question cannot be answered with a simple yes or no. During my 1998 fieldwork I met a successful businesswoman in her late thirties. She owns real estate companies in two mainland cities and an import-export firm in Hong Kong; she also owns a house in Connecticut and several years ago became a U.S. permanent resident, though she often has to travel in and out of China to manage her businesses. She told me that she basically spends an equal amount of time in all four locales, but she only has the feeling of being at home when she is at her American residence, where she can retreat completely from her work. "I think I am a world citizen" *(shijie gongmin),* she once told me quite matter-of-factly.

The second example concerns another successful businesswoman, Ms. Wu, who was Microsoft's chief executive officer in Beijing until June 1999, when she resigned for what were reported as unspecified personal reasons. However, through a close friend who had been working with Ms. Wu on her autobiography, I learned that the real reason behind her resignation was her dissatisfaction with the ways that Microsoft had taken over the Chinese market. She thought that some of the strategies that Microsoft had used to compete with Chinese companies were immoral and thus unacceptable. She had been torn between being a good CEO and a good Chinese citizen and chose to quit after her superiors at Microsoft's headquarters heard her complaints and protests. "After all," she told my friend shortly after her resignation, "I am Chinese."

By the end of my field research in 1999 I was convinced that it was still too early to see a distinctive Davos culture in Chinese business circles. It is true that some individuals in business circles do indeed live very westernized lifestyles, are familiar with Western culture, and, when at work, behave similarly to their counterparts in New York or London. At the same time, it remains to be seen how far this Davos culture can penetrate Chinese social life and whether these business elites can actually act as part of a transnational capitalist class (in Sklair's terms) when there is a conflict between company interests and national or cultural traditions.[3] Particularly in regard to the latter, I met a number of successful businesspeople who showed a strong interest in promoting an indigenous *rushang*, or "Confucian merchant" type, of business elite—a phenomenon I shall address shortly.

The entire question of a specifically Chinese business culture may arise because of the multiple forms of business ownership and the incomplete market economy during the transition period of socialism. A company can be state owned, collectively owned (by a local community), privately owned, a joint venture, or an independent foreign enterprise. People in different kinds of companies have different degrees of access to the outside world, different work ethics, and different values and behavioral patterns.

In general, those who work in state-owned companies tend to be more conservative and less sensitive to changes in the outside world; this does not necessarily apply to those who hold high positions in these companies, however. In fact, due to the intimate, sometimes kinship-based connections between state-owned companies and the government, the CEOs and managers of these companies have a strong sense of being part of the political as well as the business elite. Many of them regularly travel to Europe and North America, and some have studied abroad. Mr. Li, for instance, is a vice president in a company owned by the Chinese Academy of Sciences, which is both a research institute and a branch of the government within the science community. Mr. Li is quite successful and travels back and forth between Los Angeles and Beijing, as his wife and daughter live in Santa Monica, California. He insists, however, that although he likes the value system and lifestyle in the United States, his career remains in China and he has to maintain Chinese ways of doing business.

The managerial elites in joint venture and foreign companies are more westernized than their counterparts in state-owned companies, and many of them have obtained MBAs or other graduate degrees from abroad. It is interesting that these people actually promote Western culture in the workplace; for example, in terms of an institutionalized management system or communications and socializing skills. (The most extreme case I encountered was one in which Western dress codes were imposed on all employees, while additional rules regarding the use of

makeup were imposed on female employees.) In their private lives, however, many of these elites remain rather traditional, especially in the way
they deal with gender relationships, the education of children, and in-
terpersonal relations. They referred to themselves as a new type of
"Confucian merchant" (here the word "merchant" refers to all types of
businesspeople), and several were strongly opposed to what they perceived as the total acceptance of "superficial aspects of Western culture"
among younger professionals.

Age plays an important difference in China. The young professionals
(marketing, technical, and scientific personnel in their twenties) who
make up the majority of the newly emerged social group of "white col-
lars" tend to embrace Western values and lifestyles enthusiastically. Having grown up in the more open environment of the late 1980s, these
yuppies readily enjoy Western pop music, movies, and moral values,
such as personal freedom, independence, and a strong sense of entitlement to enjoy better lives. They also take the lead in new trends in fashion, sports, entertainment, and other consumer activities. Because they
are young and in most cases single, they have the power and privilege to
explore new things.[4]

An interesting development among the yuppie professionals is that
women tend to perform better and are more satisfied with their current
jobs than their male counterparts. As a result, a large number of women
aged twenty-five to thirty-five now hold midlevel managerial positions
in many joint venture and foreign companies. In addition, an increasing
number of female professionals are experiencing difficulties in finding
acceptable mates due to their higher status and salaries in the workplace
and their more westernized lifestyles in the private sphere.[5]

Most of these young professionals work at the lower levels of management, marketing, and technical support in both foreign and state-
owned companies. As they become more senior in both biological and
professional terms, however, the tendency has been for them to become
more conservative and traditional. Eventually many prefer to become
"Confucian merchants," or successful scholar-businesspersons, similar
to the scholarly officials in imperial China. Here the term "Confucian
merchant" implies that a businessperson is also a scholar who has mastered the essence of traditional Chinese culture, is devoted to the promotion of scholarship and cultural affairs, and maintains close ties with

the political elite. According to Mr. Chen Tiansheng of Beijing, who is himself a well-known member of this class, it is incorrect to define "Confucian merchant" merely as a scholar who has become a businessperson. "Cultural background alone cannot make someone a Confucian merchant. More importantly, a person's behavior must conform to Confucian norms, such as benevolence, righteousness, propriety, intelligence, and sincerity."[6]

The unique features of the business environment in China seem to be a major reason why so many of the business elite hold up the ideals of Confucian merchants. Despite two decades of market-oriented reforms, the Chinese market is still characterized by a dual-track system, in which the state controls strategic market resources, owns most of the large enterprises and firms, and can to a great extent determine the fate of private companies through the implementation of specific policies and regulations. In most cases, special connections to key people who are in charge of relevant government agencies are the key to business success. The newly emerged business class therefore relies on the support of both the state (central or local) and its agents (the cadres), a phenomenon termed "symbiotic clientelism" by David Wank. Moreover, personal networks based on kinship and friendship ties *(guanxi)* are also extremely important in the business world.[7]

Consequently, as several interviewees pointed out to me, Western-style management and business skills are, in practice, only secondary to the success of many private entrepreneurs, although in public many attribute their success to modern management and technology, in order to fit the widely accepted official narrative of modernization. It is no wonder, therefore, that so many Chinese business elite and managerial professionals hold substantially localized views of the world, regardless of their Italian-made shoes, Swiss wristwatches, and fluent English.

Learning from the West and the Sinification of Scholarship

As already indicated, one of the major reasons why the Chinese business elite do not feel the drive to become westernized is that the Chinese way of doing business helps them to survive and succeed in China. This, however, does not apply to intellectuals and researchers in the social sciences and humanities who have found that the best way for them to succeed is to import Western theories and research methods. It seems to me that in the second domain of cultural globalization—faculty club culture—the Chinese case captures some features of the Hellenistic phase of Western intelligentsia.

It is widely recognized that the hegemony of Marxist ideology and the planned economy serve as the two pillars that sustain the power base and the legitimacy of the Chinese Communist Party (CCP). However, when CCP leaders decided to reform the economy, they also hoped to keep the old ideology intact. Although Deng Xiaoping introduced pragmatism into economic development, he also insisted that the party-state uphold the four basic principles: the socialist road, dictatorship of the proletariat, leadership of the Communist Party, and Marxist-Leninist-Mao Zedong thought. These four principles have been held sacrosanct by the CCP since they were first put forward in 1979, and they remain the core of the old ideology as well as the symbol of Communist rule. The party-state severely punishes anyone who dares to challenge them.

The best strategy for intellectuals who do not openly challenge the party-state but want to achieve more intellectual space and freedom is to avoid the Marxist discourse by constructing other discourse systems. This means importing Western theories and research paradigms and using them to critique contemporary society and culture. Hence the so-called new Enlightenment movement of the 1980s, during which time all kinds of Western thought and a large number of translated books and articles flourished. Freedom, democracy, and the market economy were introduced to China as the magic spells of modernity, and the names of such Western thinkers as Weber, Freud, Sartre, and Levi-Strauss were part of the most frequently used vocabularies among intellectuals and college students.

A strong pro-West trend clearly took shape during the 1980s, culminating in the six-part TV documentary *River Elegy*, which was aired in 1988–1989. This TV series completely discredited traditional Chinese culture and called for an unconditional embrace of Western culture. During this period the majority of Chinese intellectuals believed in the universality of the Western model of modernization. For them, the only way that China could modernize itself was to learn from the West. This trend was put to an end by the Tiananmen Square incident on 4 June 1989.

In the 1990s, while some scholars tried to rediscover useful resources from tradition (hence the renewed interest in Confucianism), the most active scholars were those who used deconstructionism, postcolonialism, and other postmodernist theories to critique the modernization project. Michel Foucault, Edward Said, Pierre Bourdieu, and Jacques Derrida became new cultural heroes among Chinese postmodernists, and there was a new wave of translating foreign (mostly English and French) books. Parallel to the postmodernist trend was the translation and promotion by new liberal intellectuals of works by Jürgen Habermas and Friedrich Hayek. This was accompanied by a heated debate after 1997 regarding the role of global capitalism in China between the so-called New Left and the new liberals, with each side accusing the other of mindlessly applying Western theories to Chinese realities.

Another factor contributing to the "globalization of scholarship" derives from more mundane origins—financial support. As there is virtually only one state-sponsored foundation for the social sciences and humanities, which accordingly only offers grants to politically correct projects, many independent and open-minded scholars must find research funding abroad, either by collaborating with foreign scholars or by applying directly to foreign foundations. Some funding agencies with branch offices in China have shown a strong interest in more direct involvement. For instance, the Ford Foundation funded a research project on migrant peasant workers in Chinese cities and was able to line up eight research teams to carry it out. Interestingly enough, six of the eight research teams were from state-sponsored research centers; only one was from Peking University, while the other was from the Chinese Academy of Social Sciences.

Receiving foreign aid is, as Chinese scholars point out, by no means free. In order to compete for grants, researchers have to design their projects in accordance with Western academic norms and make inquiries in line with the interests of the funding agencies. As a result, Chinese scholars have ended up following Western scholarship in terms of both theory and method, including the work of the most radical postmodernists, who, in the eyes of the more old fashioned liberal intellectuals, may be considered the worst copycats of Western scholarship.

A related development is that transnational companies have begun to establish various scholarships and fellowships at China's top universities, thus exerting a great influence on students. According to a 1997 news report, more than 70 percent of the 4 million-plus scholarship funds at Peking University were offered by transnational companies, while at neighboring Qinghua University, 50 percent of the scholarships came from foreign sources. As these two elite schools are regarded as China's Harvard and MIT respectively, many began to worry about the long-term influence of foreign scholarships on science and intellectual circles in China.[8]

As many of my interviewees noted, this presents a twofold dilemma for Chinese scholars who uphold independence and freedom of speech. At the economic level, they have to choose between the party-controlled government foundations and the foreign funding sources that are themselves by no means apolitical when spending money for Chinese scholarship; at the political level, they want to oppose the oppressive authoritarian political regime (which means welcoming capitalism and the market economy and capitalism), but they also want to defend Chinese culture from the sweeping power of global capitalism, without slowing down the speed of reforms that will open the country to the outside.

In response to the increasingly strong influence of Western scholarship in China (it should be noted here that even researchers of ancient Chinese literature are required to take an English test when they come up for promotion), a trend to Sinify the social sciences has become popular in recent years, and a debate on scholarly norms and academic rules has been ongoing for more than two years in all major academic circles. A number of scholars attribute the situation to China's weak position in the world economy and to politics. They argue that once China reaches its goal of modernization, its academic traditions will be widely accepted by the global scholarly community.[9]

The Triumph of Big Mac and Hollywood Blockbusters

Popular culture is clearly an area in which global influence is dominant. TV sitcoms from both the West and neighboring countries, Hollywood blockbusters, pop music from Hong Kong and Taiwan, Japanese cartoons, and the NBA Finals and World Cup soccer matches are among the hot items of cultural consumption sought by a majority of ordinary consumers. When Michael Jordan retired in 1999, many Chinese fans were very upset, and stories about him ran for weeks in the Chinese print media.[10]

Take the growth of McDonald's in Beijing as another example. As one of the ultimate icons of American culture and the king of the fast food industry, McDonald's has been successful ever since it entered the Chinese market in the early 1990s. In Beijing, McDonald's opened its first restaurant in April 1993; by the summer of 1998, it boasted thirty-seven restaurants scattered throughout the city. As I argue elsewhere, what attracted customers to the McDonald's restaurants was by no means only its hamburgers, but the cultural elements that are associated with Americana and the special social space it provides, where ordinary consumers can enjoy both American food and a Chinese version of American popular culture.[11]

Several new developments in the domain of popular culture are particularly noteworthy. First, consumerism now serves as the ideological backdrop for popular culture, and popular culture in turn encourages mass consumption. Since the early 1990s consumerism has become a new cultural ideology in Chinese society, silently replacing both Marxist ideology and traditional Chinese values. Unlike the mass consumption of the 1980s that concentrated on household appliances such as refrigerators and TV sets, consumerism in the 1990s featured a newly emerged interest in a variety of leisure activities, many of which lie at the core of popular culture, such as sports, body building, MTV, karaoke bars, and so on. At the same time, hedonistic values and the desire for material goods are blatantly expressed in sitcoms, pop music, movies, and other forms of mass media, encouraging people to consume more and more. This change has in turn further shaped the development of popular culture.[12]

Second, the rapid development of popular culture has to a certain extent helped create a new kind of social space—one that is highly commercialized but lies outside state monitoring and control. Among many other things, this includes the rapid growth of private publishing businesses, nonofficial periodicals and newspapers, and privately funded movies and TV series. By 1997 there were more than 5,000 newspapers and 9,175 periodicals in China. The majority of them are dependent on market returns, and in order to survive, they generally have to position themselves in the market for popular culture.

Third, Western influence is not the only globalizing force in the domain of popular culture. Soap operas and pop music, for instance, are mainly influenced by Hong Kong, Taiwan, Singapore, and Japan. As Thomas Gold notes, popular culture manufactured in Hong Kong and Taiwan, including pop songs, musical extravaganzas, martial arts films, soap operas, and romance fiction, is particularly appealing to consumers in the greater China region (and in South Korea as well). Its soft content, escapist perspective, and Chinese language make it more accessible to the vast majority of Chinese audiences, as opposed to Western popular culture, which has to undergo a process of localization.[13] Nevertheless, this cultural-proximity argument cannot explain the equal popularity of Japanese cartoons and Hollywood movies in Chinese society.

Individual Rights and Social Movements

RELIGIOUS MOVEMENTS

Social movement, and religious movement in particular, is an area that is under the careful watch of the party-state, because it has the potential of developing opposition forces. For instance, Christianity has developed rapidly in Chinese society during the past two decades, but only the state-endorsed Protestant and Catholic churches are allowed to exist and develop—those that refuse to cooperate with the state are regarded as subversive and are prohibited. A 1993 survey shows that there were more than 6 million Protestants and nearly 4 million Catholics in China, but these figures are incomplete because they include only officially registered believers. Underground and/or nonregistered church activities likely involve many more believers; some scholars estimate the total number of Protestants and Catholics in China to be between 30 and 40 million.[14]

The recent crackdown on Falun Gong shows once again that the party-state will not tolerate any independent organizational forces in society. Beginning in the early 1990s as a popular movement that combined breathing exercises, faith healing, and a millenarian message, Falun Gong had attracted 70 million believers in China by 1999, plus another 30 million or more elsewhere in the world. This figure exceeds the total number of Communist Party members (about 62 million) and is cause for fear among CCP leaders. It has been reported that Falun Gong's founder, Master Li Hongzhi, was forced to move to New York under government pressure. When several leaders of the sect were arrested in April 1999, more than ten thousand practitioners assembled in front of Zhongnanhai, the office compound and residence of the China's top leaders, to stage a sit-in. The protest quickly ended after the government negotiated with the group's leaders, but the gathering, which occurred very close to the tenth anniversary of the Tiananmen Square incident, sent a strong signal to CCP leaders and the outside world. A nationwide state-sponsored campaign against Falun Gong was launched in late July 1999, with the party-state mobilizing virtually all media and organizational resources to attack the practice of Falun Gong, and using the legal system to punish a number of the sect's leaders.[15]

SECULAR MOVEMENTS

Let us now examine three secular social movements—consumer protection, environmental protection, and feminism—that are related to the globalization process in various ways.

While the consumer protection movement started spontaneously, with no clear connection to Western resources, the party-state played a strong role in leading it from an early stage. The country's first consumer protection organization was established in a county in central China in 1983. One year later, the China Consumer Association (CCA) was founded with strong support from the party-state. By 1998, the CCA had established a nationwide network with more than three thousand branch associations at provincial, municipal, and county levels, plus a reported forty-five thousand grassroots organizations below the county level. The government pays all CCA employees above the county level, and operational funds are derived from the relevant government agencies. Although the association is registered as a "mass organization" at the Ministry of Civil Affair, the president and vice president at each level must be party cadres who have transferred from the Bureau of the Administration of Industry and Commerce.[16] In addition to official support for the association, the party-state has also pushed for more legal regulations in the consumer market, such as the Law of Protection of Consumer Interests and Power, which was implemented in 1995.

The CCA official backing generates the power necessary for it to deal with manufacturers and service providers regarding customer complaints. Thus far, it has had a 90 percent success rate in obtaining compensation for consumers. Encouraged by this, the number of complaints by consumers increased from fewer than eight thousand in 1985 to more than 700,000 in 1997, which in turn led to an increase in public awareness regarding both consumer rights and individual identity (i.e., the consumer as an individual). Inspired by the CCA's success, greater numbers of individuals have begun to defend their rights, and consumer lawsuits have increased rapidly.[17] Nevertheless, official support for the consumer protection movement also strengthens citizens' dependency on the government. As the CCA is a semiofficial agency, the filing of complaints with the association has become a way for consumers to lodge petitions to the government, a practice that can be traced back to ancient China.

If the consumer protection movement is only tangentially related to outside influences (importing some ideas and perspectives), China's environmental movement has been nurtured and, to a certain extent, even directed by a variety of global forces ranging from private foundations to the United Nations. Furthermore, due to their heavy reliance on external support for both theory and funding, Chinese environmental organizations seem to be more independent from government control and thus bear some features of voluntary associations. The largest environmental group is the Beijing-based Friends of Nature; by 1998, it had more than four hundred individual members and several group members. Its activities include educational programs, tree planting, animal protection, and media monitoring. Another environmental organization, Global Village, focuses only on educational activities. Both groups receive regular funding from foreign foundations, and their leaders frequently travel abroad (it should be noted that these leaders speak English fluently, which is probably a necessity for their jobs).

These groups have recently been criticized for their excessive interest in media exposure and their reliance on foreign support. As one scholar pointed out to me, although there are a lot important issues to be addressed in neighborhoods in and around Beijing, Friends of Nature always carries out projects in remote and exotic places, such as Yunnan or Tibet, which catch the attention of the foreign press and environmental agencies, such as the Society for the Protection of Endangered Species.

Nor has the third secular movement, feminism, yet expanded beyond a small circle of scholars, journalists, artists, and other cultural elite. It is interesting to note that Chinese feminist scholars have tried to distance themselves from the field of women's studies, indicating that they view feminism as different from women's liberation—a much politicized term used by the party-state. In the past several decades, women's studies in particular and women issues in general were supposedly dealt with by the All-China Women's Association (ACWA), which, like other semiofficial organizations, has branches at all levels of the administrative system.

According to some feminist scholars, it was the 1995 UN Women's World Conference in Beijing that broke the ice and introduced a genuine feminist perspective to China. At the time, the party-state was eager to host the 1995 conference because it wanted to restore an open, reform-oriented image in the wake of the Tiananmen Square incident. As a result, it accepted a whole set of notions commonly used in feminist discourse in the West, such as the theory of gender and gender study, which were completely new to those who had been involved in women's work or women's studies under ACWA leadership. Through its representatives in the women's association, the party-state also accepted the idea that a gender perspective should be incorporated into mainstream policymaking, without noting that this theory, which had originated in the West, was in many respects in conflict with the Marxist theory of women's liberation.

The party-state's recognition of the theory of gender has, according to some feminist scholars, led to a breakthrough in both conventional women's studies and the feminist movement in China, because it grants a legitimate status to feminist theories and opens up new space for the movement's growth. From 1993 (during preparations for the UN conference) to 1998, more than thirty research institutes were established, more than one hundred seminars or conferences were held, and more than 150 books and nearly two thousand articles were published. Several feminist scholars argue that these activities might not have possible without the 1995 UN World Women's Conference. At the same time, ACWA scholars and officials, with ideological and practical support from the party-state, made efforts to promote a Marxist perspective on women's studies.

Feminist scholars tend to receive grants and scholarships from abroad, while scholars in conventional women's studies are supported by the official ACWA. This creates even more distance between the two groups, further complicating the relationship between global influence and local resistance. According to a senior scholar affiliated with the

ACWA, well-known feminist scholars have on several occasions encountered difficulties in obtaining permission to go abroad, because their rivals in the local women's associations were unhappy with their outward-oriented research and foreign contacts. Furthermore, some scholars who were trained in the West have also been accused of trying to monopolize gender studies in terms defined by Western feminist scholars. According to several interviewees, competition and conflict between internal and external forces in the field of gender studies are still unfolding.

"CHINA TO THE WORLD": AGENTS AND AGENCY OF CULTURAL GLOBALIZATION

As described above, by the end of the 1990s, the strong presence of Western (mostly American) culture was obvious in all four aspects of the cultural globalization process in China, although its influence on Chinese culture varied across different groups, genders, and social domains. The trend of westernization was also clearly exhibited in changes of everyday life, such as the rising demands for romantic love and sexual freedom, the escalating divorce rate and the emergence of single-parent families, the triumph of consumerism and commodity fetishism, the fever for MBA degrees and the English language, the popularity of American fast food chains, and the competition among urban youth to be "cool."

Do we see a process of cultural convergence here? The answer could be yes if one merely counted the number of Western cultural items imported into China and consumed by local people. But a closer look shows that, more often than not, the imported culture is transformed and localized, as in the case of McDonald's in Beijing. More importantly, we need to pay close attention to the agency of local people because, in many cases, they do not share the same perspective as outside observers.

Ownership and Agents

The key issue here is the ownership of the emerging global culture. In other words, do cultural values and cultural products that originate in the West always belong to the West, even after they are imported to a non-Western society? Anthropological studies of transnationalism have shown that the emerging global culture is marked by diversity rather than uniformity because local cultures, as Richard Adams notes, "continue to yield new emergent social entities, new adaptive forms brought into being in order to pursue survival and reproduction both through and in spite of the specific work of capitalism."[18] Daniel Miller's analysis of an American soap opera in Trinidad, for instance, reveals that the local audience managed to appropriate this foreign cultural product into their social life. The geographic origin of the imported culture has become increasingly less relevant. Miller points out that what really matters are its local consequences.[19]

Indeed, the localization of foreign culture and the indigenous approach toward imported culture are key to understanding the current process of cultural globalization in China, as the majority of Chinese have taken an active and positive approach toward the imported foreign culture. This is officially reflected in the 1990s slogan, *Zhongguo zouxiang shijie, shijie zouxiang Zhongguo* (China to the world, and the world to China), which contains a twofold message. At one level, the emphasis is on the two-way, equivalent process in which China is actively reaching out to the world while the world is reaching out to China. At a deeper level, the slogan indicates movement toward a foreign culture, as revealed in the verb *zouxiang,* which means "walking/marching toward."

At the societal level, many intellectuals, business elites, and professionals have positively appropriated cultural values and cultural products from the West, as described above. For them, ownership of Western culture is neither immutable nor nontransferable; on the contrary, they feel a sense of entitlement in claiming the localized foreign culture as their own, or as part of the emerging global culture in which they too play a role.

A good example is the college student I cited at the beginning of this chapter. As he put it, NBA games, Coca-Cola, Hollywood movies, and the Declaration of Independence all belong to the new world to which he feels a sense of entitlement. In scholarly jargon, "the emerging global culture transcends national boundaries"; or, as a prominent writer bluntly states, if a culture can help improve the economic development and living standards of other nations, that culture should be shared by all human societies and be called "a shared culture of the human race."

There is no need to ask whether the elements of this shared culture of the human race belong to socialism or to capitalism, to the West or to the East.[20] Such a positive claim to imported culture clearly shows the centrality of agency in China's choice of cultural globalization.

Four social groups, or agents, are particularly noteworthy for their active role in promoting cultural globalization: (1) transnational companies and other foreign agencies that produce and/or export cultural products to China; (2) the Chinese state that manages the influx of foreign culture by controlling the cultural market; (3) Chinese intellectuals and other cultural elites, who function as both the commentators and practitioners of cultural globalization; and (4) Chinese youth, who constitute the most loyal and enthusiastic consumers of the imported culture. While all four groups exert their agencies in the cultural globalization process, the globalizer/exporter and the main consumers of the emerging global culture (categories 1 and 4) seem to play a less important role than the other two agents, Chinese intellectuals and the Chinese state.

Briefly speaking, a common concern of the globalizer/exporter is how to enter the Chinese market and quickly reap profits. For this purpose, localization seems to be the major strategy adopted by transnational companies. As a high-ranking manager at Beijing McDonald's told me, McDonald's is not a multinational company but a multilocal company, and Beijing McDonald's is committed to making hamburgers a part of the local culinary culture. After Kodak purchased seven Chinese film companies and became one of two major film companies in China, its top CEO told Chinese audiences that the China Kodak Company aimed to become "a first-rate Chinese company."[21]

Interestingly, although they are the most enthusiastic consumers of the imported culture, the current generation of youths seems to be more nationalistic than those born in the 1950s and 1960s. As indicated above, most urban youths enjoy Western values, such as personal freedom and independence, prefer to consume imported goods whenever they can afford to, and also are eager to learn English and to study abroad, preferably in the United States (e.g., the TOFEL exam remained popular among college students throughout the 1990s).

At the same time, a large number of youths have negative opinions about the United States because it is a hegemonic superpower, as indicated by two surveys conducted among urban youths in 1994 and 1995.[22]

In May and June 1999, *Beijing qingnianbao* (Beijing Youth Daily), one of the two most popular newspapers in China, published a series of articles and discussions that reexamined issues of human rights, freedom of speech, American blockbuster movies, and Western culture in general. A central theme of these discussions, which won popular support among young readers, was criticism of American hegemony.[23] What should be noted here is that cultural globalization does not necessarily imply the disappearance of political nationalism—under certain circumstances, the two may well coexist.

The most important agents of cultural globalization in China, however, are intellectuals and the state, whose interactions constitute a two-decade long discourse on China's strategies and efforts to reach out to the world.

How Chinese Intellectuals Perceive Cultural Globalization

By the 1990s, the subject of globalization was no longer new to Chinese scholars and policymakers, who had been engaged in such discussions since the early 1980s. More importantly, Chinese discourse of globalization presents itself as a continuation of the grand narrative of the modernization project, as opposed to most Western discussions that treat globalization as a postindustrial, postmodern phenomenon.

Most intellectuals and policymakers regard globalization as a historical trend that is both inevitable and unavoidable—with a strong flavor of historical teleology, in other words. For instance, according to some globalization advocates, the entire modern history of China can be viewed as a series of attempts to meet the challenges of the outside world and to regain its status in the global community of nation-states. During the first stage (1840–1949), the Chinese state became a vassal of Western powers during the process of globalization. The second stage (1949–1978) was marked by the Chinese Communist Party's efforts to resist Western dominated globalization by its socialist road, which was modeled after the Soviet Union. And while resistance to globalization secured China's political independence, it also caused China to fall farther behind in terms of its economy and culture. It is only during the current third stage that China has positively participated in all aspects of the globalization process, for which the reform efforts of the party-state, among others, should be credited.[24]

Cultural globalization was first put forward as an important issue in the 1980s, during a debate on China's status in the contemporary world. It began with an article published in 1987 warning that unless China were to speed up its reform process, the country would likely be left behind again in the new postindustrial era. Should this occur, China would eventually lose its membership in the emerging global village (*qiuji* in Chinese, or global membership). The article immediately caught the attention of the mass media and led to a discussion of global membership in academic and other elite circles. Underlying the discussion was an urgent call for a more radical reform and greater openness in Chinese society, as well as a strong pro-West tendency, calling for Western culture to be introduced more aggressively into Chinese society (or learning from the West, as some advocates bluntly put it).[25]

Since the early 1990s, the issue of globalization has once again become a focus of debate between two opposing groups. According to liberal intellectuals and reformers in official circles, globalization is a new stage in the modernization process, and a developmental opportunity that China cannot afford to miss. Some maintain that globalization can bring permanent peace to the world, eliminate the inequalities between the developed and developing countries, and lead to further development and prosperity. Others argue that cultural globalization will spread universal values, such as freedom, democracy, and human rights to Chinese society and may therefore be politically beneficial to Chinese people.[26]

Thus far the dominant attitude among Chinese intellectuals is to warmly welcome and actively join the globalization process. Their key argument is that globalization represents the highest state of modernization and human development. A critique of globalization in China, therefore, must also confront the issue of modernization, which is why criticism of globalization mainly comes from a small group of intellectuals who have been labeled the New Left or Neo-Marxists. According to their view, global capitalism will eventually do more harm than good to China, and the Western model of modernization is not the proper path for China. They are more concerned with the increasing social inequalities caused by the rapid accumulation of capital and the accelerating social-cultural-environmental degradation caused by the blind economic development promoted by the party-state and the influx of foreign capital.[27]

In relation to the debate on China's role in the process of globalization, the issue of nationalism was also a central concern among Chinese intellectuals in the 1990s. China's failed bid to host the 2000 Olympics games, the prolonged negotiations over China's entry into the WTO, the tensions across the Taiwan Straits in 1996, and, more recently, NATO's accidental bombing of the Chinese embassy in Belgrade in 1999, were major sociopolitical events that triggered much heated debate over nationalism during the past decade. One of the landmark nationalist writings during this period was the 1996 publication of *Zhongguo keyi shuo bu* (The China That Can Say No), a provocative book written by several radical young authors who claim to have awakened from their pro-West illusions and worship of American culture. The book was an instant success and more than two million copies were sold. In the following year, the book *Yaomohua Zhongguo de beihou* (Behind the Scene Of Demonizing China) was published, and the fact that all eight authors had earlier studied in the United States made the book more credible to ordinary readers in China. Then, in 1999, in response to the NATO bombing incident, there was yet another wave challenging Western hegemony and calling for nationalism.[28]

It seems to me that the majority of Chinese intellectuals have shown tremendous self-restraint in facing the dilemma of dealing with Western hegemony on the one hand and fighting for freedom and democracy in China on the other. Among other concerns, they are mostly worried that the party-state could manipulate nationalistic emotions among the younger generation and utilize political nationalism as a means to maintain its authoritarian regime. They have thus made efforts to prevent the surge of narrow-minded nationalism.[29]

The consensus among most intellectuals is to keep China open to the world and to push China to participate actively in the ongoing globalization process. Radical nationalism has been rejected by the majority of Chinese intellectuals because it has the potential to hinder China's active participation in the globalization process. This development-modernization-globalization thesis is also shared by CCP leaders, but the party-state always presents itself as the embodiment of the nation's will and thus demands the loyalty and support of the Chinese people to achieve the nation's ultimate goal, the modernization of China.

The Party-State and Management of Cultural Transition

In his study of the economic relationship between China and the United States, Phillip Saunders tries to solve an empirical puzzle: Despite

China's fear of economic vulnerability and the danger of Western hegemony, over the past decade China's economic dependence on the United States has increased significantly. After examining the strategies that the Chinese state employed during the 1990s, he concludes that "Chinese leaders accepted the necessity of increased integration into the international economy, but they have sought to manage this process on their own terms in order to maximize benefits and minimize vulnerabilities."[30]

This observation can also be applied to the party-state's role in the cultural domain. As the late "paramount leader" Deng Xiaoping put it, "When you open the window, flies and mosquitoes come in." The flies and mosquitoes that Deng was referring to are the inevitable influx of Western thought and cultural values that accompany the foreign investment, technology and management skills, and which could pose serious challenges to the Communist regime through "peaceful evolution." Despite their fear of and repeated attempts to fence off Western thought and cultural values, however, CCP leaders have maintained the open-door policy, and the party-state has gradually retreated from many areas of social life.[31] As a result, the influence of foreign cultures has become increasingly stronger over the past two decades.

The key to the strategies of the Chinese state is to understand that the political survival of the Communist regime depends on the state's capacity to maintain rapid economic growth and to create more employment opportunities for the large population of unemployed young laborers. This is particularly true since 1989 and the Tiananmen Square incident, and it is by no means an accident that China participated even more actively in both economic integration and cultural globalization in the 1990s. The best example of the state's determination to catch the globalization is certainly its ongoing efforts to enter the World Trade Organization, which can be traced back to the 1980s.[32]

As far as the four aspects of cultural globalization are concerned, the party-state has thus far taken different approaches and strategies to maintain control, and at the same time to facilitate growth. The business elite culture seems to be the least worrisome for CCP leaders, and the official media has been crucial in promoting a Western-style management system and corporate culture. Popular culture is another area that the state has seemingly decided to leave aside, because it can be used to lessen the social tensions of the post-1989 era and to create an image of prosperity and happiness. In contrast, the state has always closely watched and

tightly controlled areas of intellectual development and social movement because the former poses a direct challenge to communist ideology, while the latter may lead to collective action on a large scale, a
source of great fear to the party-state.

How the Chinese state controls and manages the cultural market in
the era of cultural globalization is a complicated topic that requires a
full-scale study; suffice it to mention here only several strategies that the
party-state has employed. First, ideological campaigns against the increased influence of foreign culture, mostly from the West, remain its
main weapons. Political-ideological attacks, such as the state campaigns
against "spiritual pollution" in the 1980s and "bourgeois liberalization"
in the early 1990s, have been frequently launched against liberal intellectuals and other elites.

Second, the party-state has never loosened its control over key organizations in cultural affairs and important sectors of the cultural market, such as publishing, the movie and television industries, and the
news media. During a short period of commercialization in the early
1990s, for instance, several influential newspapers in Taiwan and Hong
Kong attempted to enter the mainland market, but they were rejected by
the party-state. According to a senior editor, at least one Hong Kong
newspaper group bought several magazines in China, hoping to make
its way into the Chinese market. However, once central government authorities became aware of this, the magazines were immediately closed.

In another case, the journal *Dongfang* (The Orient) served as a key
forum for liberal intellectuals, publishing debates on virtually every important social issue, including globalization, since 1993. The party-state
allowed the journal to flourish until 1996, when a group of scholars tried
to publish a reexamination of the Cultural Revolution on its thirtieth
anniversary. The state decided the journal had gone too far and ordered
it closed. As my interviewees pointed out, similar cases have occurred
every year and in every field of the cultural industry—there are always
books, journals, or movies closed down by the state for ideological
and/or political reasons.

The third and probably more "advanced" strategy used by the state to
control the cultural sector is what my interviewees referred to as *liyi
daoxiang*, which can be translated as "railroading with interests." This
means the state rewards those who uphold the party line with economic

or political awards and punishes those who defy the party by depriving them of lucrative opportunities.

Take the mass media as an example. As a result of learning from their Western counterparts, the Chinese media underwent systematic management reforms. By the late 1990s, most newspapers and television stations were mainly relying on revenues generated from commercials, and many journalists worked on temporary or project-based contracts, as opposed to being hired as permanent government employees. By 1998, two-thirds of the employees at China Central Television Station, arguably China's most important media organization, were working on contract, and most of its programs were being produced by project leaders who did not need to report on everyday production activities to the party leaders.

When I first learned of these changes, I regarded them as signs of loosening state control of the ideological fortress. However, after participating in the production of a TV program, I realized that commercialization actually did little to undermine the power of the state, because most if not all producers and directors were state employees—in many cases, high-ranking cadre. They could greatly benefit from the programs they produced, but only if they did not make political mistakes that offended the party-state. As a result, these producers and/or directors were extremely conservative politically and careful in practice, making every effort to sell their products without challenging the party-state. Censorship is thereby self-imposed, and the party-state does not need to intervene.

Because the state still controls many important resources and, more importantly, access to the Chinese cultural market, foreign companies and cultural agencies also have to be careful not to challenge the state's authority and power; otherwise they will be denied opportunities to conduct business in China. During my fieldwork in 1998 and 1999, I consistently heard stories of how foreign companies had made concessions to the Chinese government simply in order to enter the vast cultural market. I previously mentioned that McDonald's rapid development in the Beijing market had a great impact on both the local fast food industry and fast food culture. It should also be noted that Beijing McDonald's is a joint-venture enterprise in which the Chinese partner holds 51 percent of ownership and that the company contains a branch organization of the Communist Party (it was reported that when a labor dispute occurred in

1993, the Party organization in McDonald's helped restaurant management to deal with dissatisfied employees).

Although its strategies may vary from time to time depending on changes in the domestic and international environment, CCP leaders have always had an immutable goal: to remain the sole leader-manager of the modernization project and, through the project, to maintain its overall power and authority in China. This is clearly stated in the above-mentioned "four basic principles" put forward by the Deng Xiaoping at the beginning of the reform era. Any attempt to challenge the leadership and power of the party-state has always been severely punished; the crackdown on Falun Gong is just a more recent example. From the party-state's perspective, cultural globalization is no exception: it must remain under the leadership of the Communist Party. This is also why China has shown less flexibility regarding the cultural market in its WTO negotiations, such as insisting on limits to imported foreign movies and restrictions on private publishing.[33]

The party-state also wants to protect the national and local cultural industries from the powerful impact of foreign and transnational companies. For instance, in order to prepare for the challenge of the foreign media after China's entry into the WTO, the central government encouraged the formation of large corporate groups in the print media sector by merging several newspapers in 1998. Similar strategies were adopted in the publishing, movie, television and fast food industries during 1998 and 1999.

One of the latest examples of the party-state's role in protecting the Chinese cultural industry from the overwhelming power of transnational forces is the banning of the travel abroad of a basketball superstar. In recent years the state has actually been quite flexible in terms of sports exchanges, with many foreign athletes and coaches working in China and a large number of Chinese athletes playing abroad. However, when the NBA first tried to recruit Yao Ming, a seven-foot, four-inch basketball star, the Chinese authorities said no and ordered that he stay with his home team to prepare for the upcoming Olympic workouts. The NBA management was disappointed, but according to my telephone interviews with several informants in Beijing, most people in China welcomed the state's decision.[34] Since them the party-state has apparently reconsidered, and Yao Ming was drafted by the Dallas Mavericks in April 2001.

The party-state was also credited for taking other similar actions in the cultural sector. Among the media professionals and other experts whom I interviewed in 1998, more than 70 percent that, at the current stage of China's economic development, a certain degree of state control and protection is essential for the growth of a national and local cultural industry.

However, it should also be noted that the Chinese party-state is no longer a monolithic entity. There are various interest groups within the CCP and government that are involved in the competition, negotiations, and political struggles among leaders and different government agencies. The development of the auto industry, for instance, has been a recent focus of debate, because it obviously does not fit the overall long-term interest of the Chinese people, given the rapidly deteriorating environment. Nevertheless, the industry was able to line up allies in its lobbying efforts from both within the government and outside China for a radical development plan. Similarly, when dealing with foreign culture imports, there are inherent conflicts of interest between government agencies, such as the CCP's Propaganda Department and the Ministry of Culture on the one hand, and the China Central Television Station and the China Film Administration Bureau on the other.

Moreover, the Chinese economy has developed unevenly in terms of geography over the past two decades, creating a huge gap between the more developed provinces of the southeast coast and the inland provinces. In recent years it has become common for local governments to compete with one another in attracting foreign investment by offering special deals to foreign investors, such as lower rents, tax exemptions, and labor controls. A recent example is that on 19 May 1999, less than two weeks after the NATO bombing of the Chinese embassy in Belgrade, the Beijing municipal government formally invited the top CEOs of seventeen transnational companies to serve as international advisers. Other provinces quickly followed suit.[35] Similarly, local cultural affairs and entertainment industry authorities have also made concessions to attract foreign investment in local cultural markets. As a result, the central government's efforts to manage the process of cultural transformation have been frequently challenged at the local level.

CONCLUSION

The China case of cultural globalization bears several interesting features. (1) Globalization has been reinterpreted as part of the modernization effort, an important component of the goals of the party-state; (2) the majority of the cultural elite promote reaching out toward the process of globalization and have been the key to cultural translation and localization; (3) the Chinese party-state has been playing an active leadership role in almost all aspects of the process, and by so doing it intends to secure its legitimacy and power; and (4) the populace has also demonstrated a strong appetite to accept, localize, and eventually appropriate elements of imported foreign culture.

All these points indicate that the West-centered, challenge-response paradigm of global-local interactions may not be universally applicable. The Chinese case demonstrates a new type of cultural globalization: a managed process in which the state plays a leading role, and the elite and the populace work together to actively claim ownership of the emerging global culture.

NOTES

This chapter is based on field research conducted in 1998 and 1999 in Beijing and documentary data collected over the past two years. I owe special thanks to Peter Berger, Samuel Huntington, Liang Xiaoyan, Robert Weller, and the participants of the Cultural Globalization Project for their comments on earlier drafts of the paper.

1. Li Guoqing, "Kanbujian de baquan" (The invisible hegemony), *Xinzhoukan* (New Weekly), June 1999, pp. 13–16.

2. See Peter Berger, "Four Faces of Global Culture," *National Interest* 49 (1997): 23–29.

3. See Leslie Sklair, *Sociology of the Global System* (Baltimore: Johns Hopkins University Press 1991), pp. 62–72.

4. See Pan Wenlan, "Zhongguo chengshi bailing de zhoumo" (The weekend of white collar in urban China), *Haishang wentan* 6 (1998): 22–27.

5. Zhou Yiqian, "Shanghai: Nuxing fazhan de fudi" (Shanghai: The blessed place for women's development), *Shanghai wenhua* (Shanghai Culture) 6 (1998): 55–57.

6. See He Li and Dong Naijia, "Rushang shuo zhi" (Confucian merchant on intelligence), in He Li, ed., *Yu 100 laoban duihua* (Dialogue with one hundred CEOs) (Beijing: Jingji Guanli Chubanshe, 1998), p. 79.

7. For an excellent study of the relationship between businesspeople and government officials, see David Wank, "Bureaucratic Patronage and Private Business: Changing Networks of Power in Urban China," in Andrew Walder, ed., *The Waning of the Communist State: Eco-*

nomic Origins of Political Decline in China and Hungary (Berkeley: University of California Press, 1995), pp. 153–183. For the role of personal networks in Chinese business world, see, among others, Alan Smart and Josephine Smart, "Transnational Social Networks and Negotiated Identities in Interactions between Hong Kong and China," in Michael Smith and Luis Guarnizo, eds., *Transnationalism from Below* (London: Transaction, 1998), pp. 103–129.

8. See Zhang Ying, "Waiqi jiangxuejin denglu xiaoyuan" (Scholarships by foreign enterprises landed at campus), *Beijing Youth Daily*, 6 November 1997, p. 7.

9. Jiang Xiaoyuan, "Xueshu qiangshi libukai shehui jingji zhichi" (Strong scholarship depends on social and economic support), *Dongfang* (Orient) 4 (1994): 19–22 (1994).

10. For instance, *Beijing Youth Daily*, one of the most popular newspapers, published reports and news on Jordan's retirement almost daily from 13 January to 27 January 1999. Other print media also covered the event extensively.

11. See Yunxiang Yan, "McDonald's in Beijing: The Localization of Americana," in James Watson, ed., *Golden Arches East: McDonald's in East Asia* (Stanford: Stanford University Press, 1997), pp. 39–76; and Yunxiang Yan, "Of Hamburgers and Social Space: Consuming McDonald's in Beijing," in Deborah Davis, ed., *The Consumer Revolution in Urban China* (Berkeley: University of California Press, 2000), pp. 201–225.

12. See Linda Chao and Ramon Myers, "China's Consumer Revolution: The 1990s and Beyond," *Journal of Contemporary China* 7, no. 18 (1998): 351–368; for case studies regarding the impact of consumption on social life in Chinese cities, see Deborah Davis, ed., *Consumer Revolution in Urban China* (Berkeley: University of California Press, 1999); for a more critical analysis of the trend of mass consumption and its impact on children, see Bin Zhao, "Consumerism, Confucianism, Communism: Making Sense of China Today," *New Left*, March 1997, pp. 43–59; for the political implications of consumerism, see Yunxiang Yan, "The Politics of Consumerism in Chinese Society," in Tyrene White, ed., *China Briefing 2000* (Armonk, N.Y.: Sharpe, 2000), pp. 159–163.

13. See Thomas Gold, "Go with Your Feelings: Hong Kong and Taiwan Popular Culture in Greater China," *China Quarterly* 136 (1993): 907–925.

14. See Li Liang, "Zhongguo Jiduojiao xianchuang de kaocha" (A survey of the current situation of Chinese Christianity), *Dongfang* (Orient) 2 (1995): 53–58; and Wu Fei, "Zhongguo noncun shehui de zongjiao jingying: Huabei moxian nongcun Tianzhujiao huodong kaocha" (The religious elite in rural China: A survey of Catholic activities in a north China county), *Zhanlue Yu Guanli* (Strategies and Management) 4 (1997): 54–62.

15. See reports in the *Economist*, 1 May 1999; and *Los Angeles Times*, 2 November 1999, p. A4.

16. For more details, see China Consumer Association, ed., *Zhongguo xiaofeizhe yundong shinian* (Ten years of consumer movement in China) (Beijing: Zhongguo Tongji Chubanshe, 1994).

17. For more detailed reports on the development of consumer protection, see Beverly Hooper, "From Mao to Market: Empowering the Chinese Consumer," *Harvard Asian Pacific Review* 2, no. 2 (1999): 29–34; Leslie Pappas, "Shoppers of China, Unite!" *Newsweek*, 5 April 1999; and Yunxiang Yan, "The Politics of Consumerism in Chinese Society," in *China Briefing 2000*, pp. 159–193.

18. Richard Adams, "The Dynamics of Societal Diversity: Notes from Nicaragua for a Sociology of Survival," *American Ethnologist* 8, no. 2 (1981).

19. Daniel Miller, "The Young and the Restless in Trinidad: A Case of the Local and Global in Mass Consumption," in Roger Silverstone and Eric Hirsch, eds., *Consuming Technologies: Media and Information in Domestic Spaces* (London: Routledge, 1992), pp. 163–182.

20. Liu Xinwu and Jiu Huadong, "Queli renlei gongxiang wenming guannian" (Toward a notion of the shared culture of human race), *Dongfang* (Orient) 6 (1996): 21–25.

21. Two managers in Beijing McDonald's, personal interview by author, 1994 and 1998. As for Kodak's decision to become a Chinese company, see Zhang Ke and Dai Lan, "Keda: Zuo yiliu Zhongguo gongsi" (Kodak: To be a first-rate Chinese company), *People's Daily*, 24 November 1999, p. 2, overseas ed.

22. See Yang Dongping, "Qiguai de minjian yizheng" (The strange civil debate of politics), in Xiao Pang, ed., *Zhongguo ruhe miandui xifang* (How China faces the West) (Hong Kong: Mirror, 1997), pp. 206–217.

23. See special reports and articles published in *Beijing Youth Daily*, 15–20 May 1999, 24 May 1999, and 12 June 1999.

24. See Yang Xudong and Wang Lie, "Guanyu quanqiuhua yu Zhongguo yanjiu de duihua" (A dialogue regarding globalization and China studies), in Hu Yuanzi and Xue Xiaoyuan, eds., *Quanqiuhua yu Zhongguo* (Globalization and China) (Beijing: Zhongyang Bianyi Chubanshe, 1998), pp. 1–21. Similar arguments can be seen in a number of essays collected in this edited volume and its sister volume, Yu Keping and Huang Weiping, eds., *Quanqiuhua de beilun* (Antinomies of globalization) (Beijing: Zhongyang Bianyi Chubanshe, 1998).

25. For a comprehensive collection of essays in this debate, see Lu Yi, ed., *Qiuji: Yige shijixing de xuance* (Global membership: A choice of the century) (Shanghai: Baijia Chubanshe, 1989).

26. See, for example, Li Shenzhi, "Quanqiuhua shidai Zhongguoren de shiming" (The mission of the Chinese people during the age of globalization), *Dongfang* (Orient) 4 (1994): 13–18; Yang Chaoren and Han Zhiwei, "Quanqiuhua, zhidu kaifang, yu minzu fuxing" (Globalization, institutional openness, and the renaissance of the nation); and Cai Decheng, "Quanqiuhua shidai de shichang, kexue, yu minzhu" (Market, science, and democracy in the era of globalization), in Yu Keping and Huan Weiping, eds., *Quanqiuhua de beilun* (Antinomies of globalization) (Beijing: Zhongyang Bianyi Chubanshe, 1998), pp. 137–147, 181–193; Wang Yizhou, "Quanqiuhua guocheng yu Zhongguo de jiyu" (The globalization process and China's opportunity); Liu Junning, "Quanqiuhua yu minzhu zhengzhi" (Globalization and democratic politics); and Liu Li, "Jingji quanqiuhua: Fazhanzhong guojia houlaijushang de biyou zhi lu" (Economic globalization: The inevitable path that developing countries can catch up); all three essays are in Hu Yuanzi and Xue Xiaoyuan, eds., *Quanqiuhua yu Zhongguo* (Globalization and China) (Beijing: Zhongyang Bianyi Chubanshe, 1998), pp. 37–46, 67–71, 136–146.

27. See Wang Hui, "Guanyu xiandaixing wenti dawen" (Questions and answers regarding the issue of modernity), *Tianya* (Frontiers) 1 (1999): 18–24.

28. Some authors of *The China That Can Say No* put together a third "say no" book in the early 2000, entitled *China's Path under the Shadow of Globalization*. Thus far, the book has not attracted much public attention. For a detailed review of the development of nationalism among Chinese intellectual circles in the post-1989 era, see Suisheng Zhao, "Chinese Intellectuals' Quest for National Greatness and Nationalistic Writing in the 1990s," *China Quarterly* 152 (1997): 725–745; see also Geremie Barme, "To Screw Foreigners Is Patriotic: China's Avant-Garde Nationalists," *China Journal* 34 (1995): 209–238.

29. For instance, to criticize *The China That Can Say No*, a group of liberal intellectuals published a collection of essays entitled *Zhongguo ruhe miandui xifang* (How China faces the West), ed. Xiao Pang (Hong Kong: Mirror, 1997). Due to the political environment in China at that particular time, the book had to be published in Hong Kong and was thus limited in circulation.

30. Phillip Saunders, "Supping with a Long Spoon: Dependence and Interdependence in Sino-American Relations," *China Journal* 43 (2000): 55–81.

31. For a detailed study of the decline of state power, see Andrew Walder, ed., *The Waning of the Communist State: Economic Origins of Political Decline in China and Hungary* (Berkeley: University of California Press, 1995).

32. For the latest official views promoting China's entry into the WTO, see, for example, He Meizhong, "Zhongmei jianshu woguo jianru shijie maoyi zuzhi shuangbian xieyi de zhongyao yiyi" (The significance of the agreement between China and the U.S. on China's entry to the World Trade Organization), *People's Daily*, 17 January 2000, p. 1, overseas ed.; and Guo Yan, "Zhengjue renshi jiaru WTO de li yu bi" (Correctly understanding the pros and cons of China's entry into the WTO), *People's Daily*, 29 February 2000, p. 4, overseas edition.

33. See, for example, Jonathan Peterson, "Cultural Issues Color Movie Export Picture," *Los Angeles Times*, 31 October 1999, p. C1.

34. See Brook Larmer, "Boxed Out by Beijing," *Newsweek*, 10 April 2000, pp. 40–41.

35. See, for example, the news about the Beijing case in *People's Daily*, 20 May 1999, p. 1, overseas ed., and another news report on similar action taken by the Guangdong provincial government in *People's Daily*, 15 November 1999, p. 1, overseas ed.

2

Coexistence and Synthesis

CULTURAL GLOBALIZATION AND LOCALIZATION
IN CONTEMPORARY TAIWAN

Hsin-Huang Michael Hsiao

This chapter analyzes the interplay between the cultural globalization and localization forces in contemporary Taiwanese society. Globalization has gradually become the focal point of attention in the social sciences since the late 1980s and has emerged as a powerful paradigmatic concept in explaining many far-reaching economic, social, and cultural transformations taking place in many parts of the modern world. The debate about globalization as a world process and its consequences has also been going on in different fields of intellectual work. However, it is commonly agreed that the trend toward greater internationalization of the economy, rooted in transnational capital, mass production, and powerful communication technology, is readily observable in global mass consumption.

As a concept for analyzing the worldwide process in various aspects of modern life, globalization is an important theoretical reflection on both the liberal modernization theory and the radical world system theory. Though globalization theorization also recognizes the origins and consequences of contemporary globality, it is much less directed and predetermined in its causal reasoning than the two previously mentioned theories.

Tomlison (1991, 175) points out that globalization suggests the interconnection and interdependence of all global areas, though not as part of any deliberate design. Giddens (1990, 64) also formulates globalization neutrally, as "the intensification of worldwide social relations which link distant localities in such a way local happenings are shaped by events occurring many miles away and vice versa." Put another way, globalization refers to all the processes by which the people of the world are incorporated into a single world society (Albrow 1990, 9) and should be regarded as a multidimensional process that unfolds in multiple realms of existence simultaneously, going beyond economy, finance, markets, technology, communication, and politics, into the realm of culture and identity.

In this connection, Robertson's view that globalization is both an objective process of the compression of the entire world and a subjective process of the intensification of the consciousness of the world as a whole is therefore quite instructive (Robertson 1992, 8). Globalization means an increase in global interdependence along with the awareness of that interdependence; its essential character is actually the rise and expansion of individual consciousness of the global situation and of the world as an arena in which we all participate.

However, this does not suggest that globalization involves massive forces of homogenization or global sameness, under which local and national identities, cultures, and traditions are inevitably profoundly threatened or even obliterated—far from it. Globalization also involves the promotion or facilitation of local difference and diversity—the rise of local heterogenization. Nor is it completely paradoxical to talk about an emerging global tendency in which civilizations, regions, nation-states, nations within states, nations that cut across states, and indigenous peoples are in fact being pressured or inspired to reconstruct or reappropriate their own histories, identities, and traditions (Robertson 1998, 28, 30). Local response to the global can take different forms: resistance and denial are certainly not the only possibilities.

To acknowledge the globality of locality as a possible outcome of globalization may sound ironic, but it is true that discourse and ideas concerning the local, the indigenous, are promoted and advocated by global and transnational movements. It is therefore possible to discover that the result of the negotiations between globality and locality is the creation or invention of cultural authenticity. In this sense, local cultural responses really matter for the way globalization finally ends up, just as globalization matters for the manner in which local cultures eventually transform.

The notion of cultural globalization as elaborated by Waters (1995), Berger (1997), Held (1999), and Tomlison (1999) has become a legitimate field for research on globalization. It is not that there is simply a cultural dimension to globalization. Culture is an intrinsic aspect of the entire process of complex connectivity at globalization's core. Globalization offers alternate ways of managing everyday life, and it alters the context of meaning-construction and interpretation for most individuals in localities affected by it. In short, cultural globalization involves changes in both the way routine life is handled and in the way the meaning of life is interpreted. Furthermore, the forces and impacts of cultural globalization, as well as local responses to them, can be observed at both the micro-individual level and the macro-institutional level.

Berger has formulated four distinctive processes and phenomena of cultural globalization. These occur simultaneously, are related to each other, and interact with the indigenous cultures on which they have impinged (Berger 1997, 24):

- Davos culture, or international business culture
- McWorld culture, or global popular culture
- Faculty club international, or world intellectual culture
- New religious movements, or popular religious culture

Berger has also formulated a typology with four possible consequences for the intersection of globalizing forces and indigenous culture:

- Replacement of the local culture by the globalized culture
- Coexistence of the global and local cultures without any significant merging of the two
- Synthesis of the global universal culture with the particular indigenous culture
- Rejection of the global culture by powerful local reaction

Overall, the above four globalizing forces have indeed been prevalent in Taiwan since the 1980s and have brought Taiwanese cultural patterns closer to the "imagined" global culture. However, this has not eliminated Taiwan's cultural diversity; in fact, it has promoted much greater cultural heterogeneity. Cultural globalization in Taiwan can be regarded as a profound process that has shaped the structural framework within which diverse cultural reflections are developed. As will be shown in the following sections, Taiwan cultural patterns, as manifested in the explicit conduct of everyday life as well as the implicit construction of symbolic meaning for individuals, are now virtually coproduced by globalization's impacts and indigenous responses.

DAVOS CULTURE

Without doubt, Taiwan's capitalist, outward-looking industrial development, with significant international trade and foreign investment since the 1960s, has already integrated Taiwan's economy into the world market. Among the different sectors of Taiwan's business enterprises, a very high percentage is in one way or another connected to the global business community. Over the last three decades, their contact with international businesses and their CEOs, managers and technicians has been intense. The learning and exchange of each other's business-cultural patterns between Taiwanese businessmen and foreign buyers and investors has been constant, although in most cases it was Taiwanese businessmen who had to learn from their American or Japanese counterparts, especially in the decades prior to the 1990s. At the same time, however, many of the international businesses that have established corporate networks in Taiwan have learned to adapt their business practices to fit local circumstances.

At the individual behavioral level, it is no surprise to observe an almost universal trend among Taiwanese businessmen and the managerial class in modern industrial and service sectors to dress, talk, and act like their counterparts around the world. Business English is the common language, and having English first names is almost a required practice. They have also developed a globalized pattern of life with similar tastes. In Taipei, Kaoshiung, and the other big cities, it is easy to find this globalized business class working in many of the larger high-tech and financial firms, as well as the in sectors related to international trade.

It is also interesting to note that many local Taiwanese managers employed by international firms have developed dual behavioral patterns. In the workplace, they usually behave exactly like any other members of the globalized managerial class; in the local communities in which the foreign firms have located, however, they not only shift from English to the local Minnanese or Hakka, they also change their mind-set. To many of them, doing business or managing enterprise is one thing, but there are other aspects to life, and business is not everything. To act like an international businessman or manager is a learned behavior for the workplace—a newly adopted code of conduct that is an "addition" rather than a "replacement" of what has been learned about life and living from the local culture.

On the other hand, local small business owners and self-made entrepreneurs in most of the traditional businesses, as well as some of those in the export manufacturing sector, have successfully run their businesses all along without having learned to dress, talk, or act like members of the world business class. Although they might not know how a Davos-like businessman should behave, they know very well how to deal with the trade agent and exactly when to deliver their order. These small businessmen, who have made the "Taiwan miracle" known to the world, have separated their learned business know-how in dealing with world markets from the patterns of everyday life learned from the indigenous culture. To them, the two cultures that guide their two different life domains coexist without much conflict.

At the business organizational level, it is in multinational companies' best interests to adapt to the local social conditions and business culture. This can be found in marketing strategy and/or management style, and many multinational managers have made real efforts to adapt to Taiwanese ways of doing business, either by decentralizing decision making to local managers or by indigenizing high-ranking personnel. Despite the globalizing of Taiwan's economy and its businesses over the past few decades, it is clear that neither American nor Japanese management models have supplanted Taiwan's indigenous business practices. Instead, there is significant fusion in management styles in many of the multinationals operating in Taiwan as well as in many of the local companies that compete in world markets. As a result, there is no pure American, European, Japanese, or Taiwanese-Chinese management model that can best characterize the actual business culture of today's Taiwan.

From our interviews with executives of German, American, and Japanese financial service companies in Taiwan, it is clear that foreign executives and top managers have to localize their so-called international business culture into the local reality. This is particularly crucial when they are seeking to determine a client's credit for approving a loan, as the local concept and criteria of "credit" are different from what they are in the West, where a bank's computer can automatically print out the record of client's credit line. In Taiwan, however, no such information is readily available in the local banking system. Therefore, the credit check must be done in a different way, and this will rely heavily on the local manager's judgment as to the client's credit, trust, reliability, and trustworthiness. Even in the high-tech industries, the so-called globalized pattern of management prevalent in the West still needs to be adapted to Taiwan's social milieu.

In addition to the above examples of organizational adaptation to globalization and localization in management practices, it is important to note that traditional practices still prevail in Taiwan's business world, and that Taiwanese businessmen still conduct much of their business through *guanxi* (a network of personal relationships and connections) and *xinyong* (personal reliability, trustworthiness). This personalized business culture is not limited to developing business connections and partnerships; it also contributes to Taiwanese entrepreneurship and management style.

Regardless of size or scale, Taiwanese enterprises cannot be separated from the family: the latter is always the foundation of the former, and the Chinese family still has a strong effect on how contemporary Taiwanese businesses are initiated, organized, and expanded. In this sense, the enduring organizational form of Taiwanese enterprises is the family business, which is something else that economic globalization has not fundamentally altered. Just the reverse, in fact: under globalization, there is growing recognition of family business as a unique and effective organizational form and management setting (Donckels and Frohlick 1991).

Since family is still the prevalent feature of Taiwanese business in which there is a close overlap of ownership and control, familial hierarchical status, authority patterns, and obligatory relationships are taken as models of business organizational roles. There is a strong paternalistic organizational climate inside these businesses, especially in decision making and personnel management, and there is always one dominant executive, the father figure, who makes the final call. While trust is the key to Taiwanese family business operations, it lies predominantly within the family circle. Here again, the core family is still the most important locus of security and identity for many of today's Taiwanese business establishments.

In most cases, corporate leadership is passed on to the sons—only under special circumstances can sons-in-law or daughters be given key positions. As in traditional Chinese families, the succession question can often become a structural source of tension for modern Taiwanese businesses. Although succession from one generation to the next inevitably brings about some changes in business development strategies, these are usually managed cautiously by the heirs, in order to maintain family business traditions.

As mentioned earlier, personalism is still the key to understanding Taiwanese business operations, and it extends to employer–employee relations: family-like harmony, unity, loyalty, and emotional commitment are treated as necessary means to bond employees to the business. This personalism also goes beyond the internal realm of enterprises and extends to interbusiness practices. Nevertheless, it cannot be mistaken for simply an emotional commitment, as it always involves a sophisticated, rational calculation of short- and long-term business interests (Hsiao 1994).

Globalization, however, has certainly helped accelerate the transformation of some aspects of these family businesses. Furthermore, the above characterization of this local business culture is not static and should not be regarded as evidence of local resistance to managerial globalization. Though the resilient local business culture is still not fully comprehended or appreciated by many foreign business executives, most take doing business in Taiwan as a challenge and have already formulated strategies for dealing with the Taiwanese family business culture.

In sum, this analysis so far clearly demonstrates that the coexistence of the Taiwanese family business model with globalized Fordism from the United States and Toyotism from Japan does not necessarily cause much tension or conflict between multinational corporations and local businesses. Nor do differences in business culture appear to be cultural barriers to international companies doing business in Taiwan or for local Taiwanese enterprises expanding their business links around the world.

MCWORLD CULTURE

Besides the evident presence of an internationalized business environment, Taiwan today is a society ornamented by various globalized popular cultures and lifestyles. "Popular culture" refers to both a specific culture with symbolic objects and to "a whole way of life" (Michael 1996). Here in Taiwan, popular culture is commonly defined as the cultural pattern of life produced for the people (consumers, in other words) and is distinguished from folk culture in that it is mass-produced for mass consumption. International business has indeed created global consumer needs via the very powerful mass media, and has then fulfilled them with its cultural products.

In essence, global popular culture is pretty much media based, and the producers of advertising, television, cinema, pop music, and other branches of the mass communication industry manage it. These multinational media and communication industries have played a crucial role in shaping Taiwan's popular culture and public tastes. In many of the big cities, residents can watch more than forty cable-television channels in their living rooms. More than 68 percent of Taiwanese households subscribed to cable television in 1998, a significant increase from 43.4 percent in 1994, while more than 3 million Taiwanese were using the Internet in 1999, forming what is called an "Internet tribe."

A 1999 survey found that the Taiwanese have very diverse tastes in media-driven popular culture, and that pop music, soap operas, TV dramas, and films were available in the local languages of Minnanese and Mandarin, as well as in English and Japanese. An average of 50 percent to 63 percent of the survey's respondents who were interviewed expressed a fondness for different local and foreign dramas and films. Significantly, the popularity of Japanese popular culture among the Taiwanese has been increasing in the recent years, especially Japanese TV dramas and film: about 36 percent of Taiwanese indicated a liking for them in 1994, and this increased to 51.3 percent in 1999 (Chang 2000).

It is the infrastructure of the cross-national television industry, made up of media and communications companies, multinational capital and internationalized languages, that has made the globalized culture of Taiwan possible, just as it is Coca-Cola, McDonald's, Disney, Levi's, Calvin Klein, Nike, CNN, Polygram, EMI, Toyota, Microsoft, Starbucks, and Marlboro that have contributed to the making of globalized taste, fashion, language, ideas, dreams, and value judgments in contemporary Tai-wanese society. These homogenous-seeming tastes and lifestyles are still more or less an urban middle-class phenomenon, but to young urban-ites they are more than just new life choices: they represent new symbols and new meaning in life. In contrast, as much as older and rural resi-dents and members of the working class enjoy the new American and Japanese things in their lives, they have not internalized them into their symbolic and value worlds. In other words, the prevailing McWorld cul-ture still has class boundaries in Taiwan, and its symbolic and interpre-tive impacts are most evident among the urban middle class.

As mentioned above, Japanese pop culture has increasingly domi-nated Taiwan's cultural scene in the last decade. One of the main reasons for this is that in 1993 the government finally lifted its 1972 ban on show-ing Japanese TV programs, which was originally enacted when the Japanese government officially recognized the People's Republic of China. By the mid-1990s, however, the term *ha-ri-zu* ("tribe of Japanese infatuation") had come to be associated with the idea of a mindless be-sottedness with anything Japanese.

The *ha-ri-zu* might not know much about Japan's history, economy or politics, and they do not have the profound nostalgia towards that country still felt by some members of the older generation who grew up during Japanese rule. Instead, they are the products of Japanese pop cul-ture and media manipulation. Not surprisingly, they are also big fans of Japanese pop cultural objects and symbols such as food, toys, cosmetics, cartoons, TV shows, idols, videos, CDs, clothes, and fashion magazines, and they collect all these items too. Hello Kitty, for example, has created a collection fever among *ha-ri-zu* and many other consumers: sales of its key chains, appliances, credit cards, cell phone accessories, and other items amounted to US$35 million (NT1.2 billion) in 1999.

"Japanese fever" has been particularly evident in the popularity of Japanese melodramas among the younger generation. Japanese TV shows have already taken over many local cable television stations, and most viewers can now watch five Japanese cable TV channels. In a way, the success of Japanese melodramas has also renewed the popularity of modern Japanese culture. According to Iwabuchi (1998), this has been made possible by the cultural proximity between Taiwanese and Japan-ese perspectives on the experience of modern life. Japanese melodramas have successfully localized and indigenized modern American and European lifestyles and culture, and the Taiwanese have in turn found this Japanese mode easy to digest. In other words, the Japanese have localized American dreams and transmitted them to Taiwan via pop media programs, and these depictions of the modern Japanese life experience have provided young Taiwanese with a perfect reference for modernization and globalization.

This identification with modern global culture via Japanese pop culture can also be observed in many other societies in Northeast and Southeast Asia. However, the popularization of U.S. and Japanese popular culture in Taiwan has not enhanced a deeper public understanding of the two "model" societies and cultures. No profound cultural exchanges or learnings have come about; nor has it inspired reflection on Taiwan's own society and culture.

Side by side with the Americanization, Europeanization, and Japanization of lifestyles and popular culture here, there has also been a rise in "repackaged" cultural localization and indigenization, in which many local cultures and traditional lifestyle elements, including traditional Taiwanese cuisine, opera, puppet shows, antique collecting, tea houses, and tea drinking, as well as Taiwanese rock music and modern art, have been revitalized and reinvented. Furthermore, several cultural performing arts groups have been established with a great public enthusiasm and state support, and the creation, development, and revitalization of these groups and art forms, including Cloud Gate (dance), *Little West Garden* (puppet show), *Min-Hua Garden* (Taiwanese opera), New Formosa (Taiwan rock music), and Han-Tang Yuefu (classical Chinese court music and dance), can be seen as a local response to globalization.

Since the 1980s, Taiwan has entered the world's third wave of political democratization, and a new national identity has also been constructed and developed along with it. This changing political landscape has greatly facilitated and inspired Taiwan's cultural reconstruction and revitalization—a move to establish the cultural foundation for the new nation-building process. One such important and typical example over the last decade is the rewriting and reinterpretation of Taiwanese history among political and academic circles, where there is a movement toward "de-Chineseness" and "re-Taiwaneseness" in the effort to reread the last four hundred years of Taiwan's history, since the Han Chinese first emigrated there. In Academia Sinica, Taiwan's most prominent academic institution, a new institute of Taiwan history was established in 1994 under much "politically correct" pressure, despite the fact that it already has two institutes that have history as their research focus.

This cultural and political atmosphere of Taiwanization has also led to the establishment of many government-sponsored cultural institutions, including the National Traditional Arts Center, the National Center for Research and Preservation of Cultural Properties, the National Museum of Prehistory and Archaeology, and the National Museum of Traditional Theater. This has also been reflected in the reorganization of the central government with the creation of two culture/ethnicity–related bureaucracies: the Council of Aborigine Affairs and the Council of Hakka Affairs. Furthermore, many localized and grassroots cultural organizations and NGOs have been created to help deepen indigenous cultural identity, and the preservation of local cultural heritage has gained importance as an "identity redeemer," thanks to the preservation movements advocated by local cultural groups.

In an island-wide survey conducted by Academia Sinica in 1999, 57 percent of those interviewed felt that the cultures of all the nations in the world would become increasingly similar—a clear sign of the consciousness of the global homogeneity and sameness. But in the same survey, 65 percent responded that despite world cultural convergence, Taiwan needed to keep its own cultural characteristics—a call for cultural authenticity.

In short, under the impact of McWorld, Taiwanese society has responded with both the rise of indigenized commercial consumer culture and conscious efforts toward the reconstruction of Taiwanese national and local cultural identities. Even though the globalization forces of popular culture prevail in contemporary Taiwanese cultural life, they not only coexist with localization forces but have facilitated the growth of cultural diversity and the search for cultural authenticity in Taiwan.

FACULTY CLUB INTERNATIONAL

Globalization is certainly occurring not only in the realms of trade, business, technology, popular culture, and media communication, but also in ideas, concepts, and thoughts. While it is obvious that the international mass media has played an important role in bringing those new ways of thinking into Taiwan, it is the intellectuals who have actually served as "carriers" of these emerging ideas from abroad. This "reverse brain drain" began to take place in Taiwan in the late 1970s and early 1980s, when more and more young, talented Taiwanese returned with advanced academic degrees from American universities and began to take on different jobs. These returned intellectuals have since become the "carriers" and "localizers" of many Western/global values.

They have even formed a "new knowledge class" in Taiwan's academic, social service, media, and other cultural institutions and have "diffused" what they learned overseas throughout their workplaces and the public sphere. They have been teaching or writing about these new ideas and thinking in university classrooms, newspapers, and journals, and many have translated important works into Chinese. It is thus no surprise that, since the 1980s, Taiwan's publishing industry has grown very rapidly, with large numbers of newly translated books on almost every conceivable subject filling the shelves. These trends continued through the 1990s and beyond, although with even more speed and in a more systematic fashion.

In the 1990s, both Taiwan's new and long established publishing companies began to systematically publish influential and popular bestsellers from abroad in Chinese. Established publishers like China Times, Linking Publishing Company (United Daily News Group), and Commonwealth, as well as new publishing houses like Rye Field and New Century, have all produced a vast number of newly translated books and series under an array of fancy titles such as *Next, New Age, Global Citizen, Global Perspective, History and Culture, Classics, Knowledge,* and *Inspirations.* One can see from these headings that new titles in the social sciences— mainly psychology, sociology, history, economics, and political science, as well as business and philosophy—have been the favorite subjects.

The works being translated into Chinese include both serious academic writings and popular readings. English is the most popular international language, followed by Japanese and, to a lesser extent, German and French. Noticeable themes include the global democratization issue (*The Third Wave, The Clash of Civilizations and the Remaking of World Order, The Third Way*), the environment and sustainable development

(*The Club of Rome Reports, World Watch Reports, The El Niño Phenomenon*), gender equality (a new translation of *The Second Sex*), modern capitalism (*The Crisis of Global Capitalism, False Dawn, Trust, Was Ist Globalisierung?*), the postmodern discourse (*Postmodern Theory, Postmodernism*), and pop psychology (*EQ*, the *Chicken Soup* books, *New Passages*).

Public reception of these translated works has been very positive. Many U.S. bestsellers also top the list in Taiwan, and the literary sections of many major newspapers often carry book reviews of translated titles, which certainly helps their promotion. Though the quality of the translations has always been an issue, there has been great improvement in recent years, as the translators have become much more professional. Nowadays a lot of the translators have received advanced degrees abroad and, beyond the language skills, they now have the expertise necessary to creating quality translations.

In addition to the growing availability to the general public of literature in translation, there has been another "institutionalization" of important Western thinking and discourses, involving both the globalization and localization of foreign ideas, values, and ideologies. Through the mobilization and organization of many grassroots social movements, many Western discourses on society and culture have been initiated and posed to the public. As a result, more than twenty new social movements have emerged in Taiwan's civil society since the 1980s.[1] The respective social movement organizations took these new Western/global values and discourses as their guiding principles and their frame of reference to legitimate their causes, and activists quickly learned to draw on Western discourses to persuade the general public to support the new social movements. Taiwan's intellectuals have always been the most influential social class in leading new social thinking and reform, and they have awakened the public's awareness of environmental issues, human rights, and gender equality through discourses that were adopted straight from the West and then localized. Many social activists are returning intellectuals who have studied abroad, and sympathetic journalists have also played a role in raising and shaping public awareness of these issues. In short, through grassroots mobilization, local social movements have globalized Taiwan with discourses that originated in the West, though these have been localized so as to be acceptable to the Taiwanese—a dynamic interplay of cultural globalization and localization.

To take the environmental movement as an example, it is unmistakably Taiwanese in culture and social organization, though it has directly borrowed its philosophical roots from the West (Weller and Hsiao 1998). It has successfully raised public concern over environmental problems by inventing a "cultural action frame" that combines Western environmentalism, Taiwanese folk religion, and Chinese traditional familism (Hsiao 1999).

Localization or indigenous responses to Western cultural ideas and discourses have been present in Taiwan's literature and social sciences since the 1970s and 1980s. The "indigenous literature movement" in the mid-1970s was the first deliberate effort by many young writers to search for an indigenized literary idea and identity, a conscious indigenous rejection of the Western modernism that had dominated Taiwan's literature since the 1960s. This movement has since successfully established social realism as the mainstream in Taiwanese literature.

In the 1970s and 1980s, indigenization extended to other cultural fields like music, the performing arts, and film. During the same period, social scientists also began a journey of self-discovery and self-criticism and called for further indigenization of the social sciences, as many felt the need to develop Taiwanese social sciences that would celebrate their own cultural and intellectual identities. At the same time, it was made clear that this indigenization was not aimed at halting learning from Western social sciences and did not advocate the creation of nationalistic social sciences—on the contrary. Through indigenization, Taiwan's social scientists hoped on the one hand to uphold the universality of the social sciences, while reflecting cultural and national relevance on the other. They also hoped that Western social science would be reinvigorated by new elements stemming from diversified cultures. In this way, the social science movement too involved a combination of both indigenization and globalization.

The Taiwan experience of the globalization as well as the localization of Western thinking and discourse in literature, social science, and social movements since the 1970s and 1980s demonstrates the diverse local reactions to cultural globalization. In literature, it has taken the form of resistance; in the social sciences, it has involved the coexistence of globalization and localization. In new social movements, it has further "synthesized" the relevant Western discourses into something culturally more acceptable to the Taiwanese public.

In conclusion, the importation and acceptance of new thinking from the West since the 1980s can be seen as a process of cultural globalization through which Taiwanese culture has been brought closer to the imagined world intellectual culture. This process has also brought about cultural localization, and the interplay of globalization and indigenization further facilitated Taiwan's cultural heterogenization in the 1990s and will likely continue to do so for decades to come.

NEW RELIGIOUS MOVEMENTS

Though Taiwan cannot be called a "religious supermarket," by the end of 1999 its religious scene could at least be described as a "window of world religions." Though the Ministry of Interior recognizes only eleven "conventional" and "legitimate" religions, there are in fact about 250 religious sects of all sorts in existence today. Terms like "new religions," "new religious phenomena," and "new religious movements" all refer to either the rise of many newly emerging religious sects from abroad or the revitalization of local traditional Buddhism.

Many of the new religious groups in the first category are transplants from countries such as India, Japan, Vietnam, and France. Some of the more noticeable new religious sects include New Age, Osho, Krishnamurti, and Transcendental Meditation (India); Nichiren Shoshu, Soka Gakkai, and Aum Shinrikyo (Japan); the Supreme Ching Hai (Vietnam); and Raelian Religion (France). Taiwan also has new religious sects transplanted from America such as Scientology and ISKCON, but they seem to operate with a much lower profile.

These new religious groups were introduced in the new political climate of democratization that followed the lifting of martial law, which had lasted for nearly forty years (1949–1987). Under the very strict authoritarian rule of the 1960s and 1970s, all religious activities were monitored by the state. In the post–martial law era, however, government no longer had absolute control over social associations and religious groupings, and new religions were brought into Taiwan in a variety of organizational forms, including scholarly associations, study groups, and membership associations.

The second category of new religious movements came as a result of the rejuvenation of traditional Buddhism. In comparison with the stalled development of Catholicism and Protestantism, local Buddhism has entered a new era known as the "new religious renaissance," in which there has been a phenomenal increase in its followers over the past decade: from 800,000 in the mid-1980s to more than 5 million by 2000. The number of registered Buddhist temples has multiplied as well, from 1,157 to more than 4,500, while the number of monks and nuns has increased from 3,470 to more than 10,000 during the same period. Among the revitalized Buddhist groups, the most high-profile religious leaders and their temples are Master Cheng-Yen of Tzu-Chi on the east coast, Master Sheng-yen of the Dharma Drum Mountain in the north, Master Hsin-Yun of Foguangshan in the south, and Master Wei-Chieh of Chung-Tai Temple in central Taiwan.

The most striking difference between this newly revitalized Buddhism and its traditional form lies in their philosophical stands, in which the new groups have adopted a hands-on approach in reaching out to society through charitable works and social causes. These new Buddhist groups are involved in social welfare and medical services, education, publications, and environmentalism, and their worldly approach has dramatically changed the way religion has been practiced in Taiwan for centuries.

Religious philosopher Huei-Nan Yang put it this way in an interview: "Instead of staying passively behind temple walls chanting and meditating, monks and nuns are now traveling the streets to publicize their religion. You see them giving speeches, teaching meditation, and publishing books." Yang also points out that when the dynastic emperors favored Chinese Buddhism, it too made direct contributions to society. The current "new" trend in Taiwanese Buddhism under globalization, therefore, is a "renewal" of the lost tradition. Yang has termed this a "Buddhist renaissance."

The popularization of both the new imported religions and a newly revitalized Buddhism can be seen as a religious response to meet the spiritual needs of the Taiwanese people who are under great pressure from over-modernization. In a sense, these two streams of the new religious movements are similar, in that they are both more or less counter-modern in nature, though their approaches to dealing with modernity are quite different. Most of the imported foreign religious sects have focused their "religious practices" on taking care of individual followers' mental and emotional needs. They very much emphasize mysticism, meditation, and scientific explanation and engage in psychological counseling, psychoanalysis, healing, and health food promotion.

A similar approach was also found among the many indigenous semireligious Chi-Gun groups, the most noticeable one being the Tai-Chi Gate group. One common characterization of these new religious sects is that they take an inward-looking, individualistic, and self-healing response to modernity. Through private meditation, followers are expected to develop self-assertion and self-identity and to restore order and value to their personal lives: an alternative path of resacralization.

On the other hand, the new Buddhism has taken a rather collectivist approach to modernity's consequences by getting followers involved in various types of philanthropic and social welfare work. It is also important to stress that the involvement of these Buddhist groups in charity and welfare is modeled after Western Christian notions of church welfare. These groups have also gotten involved in higher education by building colleges and universities—again, an emulation of the Western Christian tradition.

In a sense, the new Buddhism has further secularized Taiwan's religious life. The Tzu-Chi, Foguangshan, and Dharma Drum Mountain groups have even extended their religious activities to other countries by setting up international branches. They have also established the Western organizational form of the foundation to advocate and promote cultural, welfare, and reform causes. In fact, the Tzu-Chi Foundation has initiated very active social relief programs in more than forty countries around the world: a unique example of the globalization of Taiwan's new Buddhism.

This comparison between the two camps of Taiwan's new religious movements has revealed that they have taken different views and approaches to the consequences of modernity: the sacred search for self-identity and the secular path to the development of a collective conscience. Both religious cultures have expanded Taiwan's religious territories and made its religious landscapes more heterogeneous. Their coexistence since the 1990s has separately fulfilled the diverse needs of the different classes that follow them. No significant or obvious synthesis has ever been observed.

CONCLUSION

The analysis in this chapter indicates that the Taiwanese experience in the interplay of globalization and localization has clearly demonstrated a form of "multiple coexistence" in all four cultural domains. In the globalization of international business culture and world intellectual culture, the Taiwanese case has even revealed various degrees of "synthesis" between cultural globalizing forces and organized local responses. Overall, there is no evidence that the encounter of globalization and localization has ever resulted in serious cultural conflict or clash. The global culture has neither taken over local Taiwanese culture, nor has it faced severe rejection. In this context, the Taiwan experience further illustrates the possible nonconflictual character of the cause and effect of cultural globalization.

It is also clear that the international business and popular cultures have been rapidly developing in parallel with Taiwan's ever deepening capitalist development. The existence of these two global cultures has further incorporated Taiwan into global capitalism and capitalist culture. Local responses to the two global cultures are also capitalist in nature. However, both world intellectual culture and popular religious culture counter capitalist forces and their developmental logic. These two global cultures, as well as local reactions to them, can thus be described as global antisystemic forces that challenge or alter the "reproduced" capitalist cultures that have taken hold in Taiwan over the past decades. It is important to note, therefore, that globalization has its own inner dialectics, and that capitalist driving forces and anticapitalist forces do simultaneously coexist. Localization responses and their consequences have revealed a similar inner dynamism, which has had significant ramifications for Taiwan's cultural scene.

The role of the state in all this has varied. On the one hand, it has played a key role as a "facilitator" and a "promoter" in globalizing Taiwan's local businesses and local popular cultures. On the other hand, the state has held rather ambivalent attitudes toward bringing world intellectual culture and new religious sects into Taiwan. In contrast to the state, sectors in the civil society—intellectuals, the cultural industry, religious entrepreneurs—have played a much more active role in promoting cultural globalization and responding to it by means of localization. Nor has the state taken a dominant position in localization the four cultural globalization forces under study; rather, it has pretty much gone along with the demands from the various localization forces in the civil society.

The Taiwanese case of cultural globalization and localization points to the very nature of Taiwan as an open, plural, ever changing, and self-adapting modern society.

NOTES

1. They are the consumer movement, the antipollution movement, the nature conservation movement, the women's movement, the student movement, the New Testament Church Protest, the labor movement, the farmers movement, the teachers' rights movement, the disabled welfare movement, the veterans movement, political prisoners movement, the mainlanders home-returning movement, the Taiwanese exile returning movement, the antinuclear movement, the Hakka cultural identity movement, the non-homeowners housing movement, the judicial reform movement, and the freedom of the press movement.

REFERENCES

Albrow, M. 1990. Introduction to *Globalization, Knowledge, and Society*. Edited by M. Albrow and E. King. London: Sage.

——— . 1997. *The Global Age*. Stanford: Stanford University Press.

Berger, Peter. 1997. "Four Faces of Global Culture." *National Internet* 49: 23–29.

Chang, Ying-Hwa. 2000. *Taiwan Social Change Basic Survey, 2000*. Tapei: Institute of Sociology, Academia Sinica.

Donckels, Rik, and Erwin Frohlich. 1991. "Are Family Businesses Really Different? European Experiences from STRATOS." *Family Business Review* 4, no. 2: 142–160.

Featherstone, Mike, Scott Lash, and Roland Robertson, eds. 1995. *Global Modernities*. London: Sage.

Giddens, Anthony. 1990. *The Consequences of Modernity*. Stanford: Stanford University Press.

Held, David, et al. 1999. *Global Transformations: Politics, Economics, and Culture*. Cambridge, U.K.: Polity.

Hsiao, H. H. Michael. 1994. "Chinese Corporate Philanthropy in East and Southeast Asia: A Typology." In *Evolving Patterns of Asia-Pacific Philanthropy*, edited by K. H. Jung, pp. 79–95. Seoul: Institute of East and West Studies, Yonsei University.

Hsiao, H. H. Michael, et al. 1999. "Culture and Asian Styles of Environmental Movements." In *Asia's Environmental Movements*, edited by Y. S. Lee and Alvin So, pp. 210–229. London: Sharpe.

Hsiao, H. H. Michael, and Hwa-Pi Tseng. 1999. "The Formation of Environmental Consciousness in Taiwan: Intellectuals, Media, and the Public Mind." *Asian Geographer* 18, no. 1–2: 99–109.

Iwabuchi, Koichi. 1998. "Japanese Culture in Taiwan." *Contemporary* 125: 14–22. In Chinese.

Michael, Payne, ed. 1996. *A Dictionary of Cultural and Critical Theory.* Cambridge, U.K.: Blackwell.

Robertson, Roland. 1992. *Globalization.* London: Sage.

Robertson, Roland, and Habib Haque Khondker. 1998. "Discourses of Globalization: Preliminary Considerations." *International Sociology* 13, no. 1: 25–40.

Tomlison, John. 1991. *Cultural Imperialism.* Baltimore: Johns Hopkins University Press.

——— . 1999. *Globalization and Culture.* Cambridge, U.K.: Polity.

Waters, Malcolm. 1995. *Globalization.* London: Routledge.

Weller, Robert, and H. H. Michael Hsiao. 1998. "Culture, Gender, and Community in Taiwan's Environmental Movements." In *Environmental Movements in Asia*, edited by A. Kalland and G. Persoon, pp. 83–109. Richmond, U.K.: Curzon.

3

Aspects of Globalization in Contemporary Japan

Tamotsu Aoki

Japanese society has been undergoing continuous change since the end of World War II. It has been particularly sensitive to developments in Western Europe, the United States, and other parts of Asia, and there has been a tendency for Japan to look for the way it should be with reference to these external developments. However, this adaptation to external change is only one aspect of the matter. Japanese eating habits, fashion, business activities, and the concerns of intellectuals demonstrate a great variety of patterns of change. While many of these are indeed direct reactions to changes in the international situation, there are also changes that are better understood as multicentered processes arising from cultural interactions in two or more directions.

This investigation of the effects of globalization on Japan focuses on a number of specific areas, such as the activities of intellectuals, the overseas expansion of Japanese business, and the transformation of lifestyles (food and clothing in particular). In each case, developments in these areas related to globalization are examined, as well as what they show about the particular form globalization has taken in Japan.

THE "FAST-FOODIZATION" OF DAILY LIFE

Japan entered the era of postwar economic growth in 1955, but it was only in the 1970s that this growth was manifested in the daily lives of ordinary people and brought about a certain kind of general prosperity. The term "fast-foodization" is entirely appropriate to a discussion of the changes in Japanese eating habits and fashion that began in the 1970s. We will examine this phenomenon here as one aspect of the linkage between the transformation of Japanese society and globalization.

McDonald's Japan Corporate Strategy and the Fast-Foodization of Eating Habits

"CHEAP, QUICK, AND TASTY"

It has been said that popular food culture in Japan today is dominated by the three qualities of "cheap, quick, and tasty,"[1] which reach their ultimate realization in fast-foodization. All the major fast food chains began business in Japan in the 1970s, following the complete liberalization of the restaurant market in 1969.

The custom of eating out rather than in the home has existed in Japan for a long time, but it was only in the 1970s that it became widespread. Up until the early 1970s, the top ten companies with the highest sales in the restaurant business were conventional restaurants, where customers sat together at tables and had food brought to them by waiters (the top names were Fujiya, Nihonshokudo, Yoronotaki, New Tokyo, Restaurant Seibu, and the like). This changed after 1976, when McDonald's Japan became number seven. In 1977, it rose to third place, where it remained until 1979. In 1980 and 1981, McDonald's was in second place, before attaining overwhelming dominance as number one in 1982. Other foreign fast food chains began to appear in the top ten in the 1980s. KFC entered the top ten in 1980; in 1990, it ranked second only to McDonald's.

The figures for 1996 show how greatly the fast food chains have penetrated the market: McDonald's was number one (with sales of 298.3 billion yen),[2] KFC was in fourth place, Moss Burger was fifth, and Mister Donut was sixth. The growth of McDonald's is particularly remarkable: from five stores (and sales of 200 million yen) in 1971, to 2,439 stores (and sales of 333.7 billion yen) in 1998. By 1996, McDonald's had already attained a more than 100 billion yen lead in sales over its nearest rival (Hokka Hokka Tei So-Hombu, with 164 billion yen).

On 8 March 1998, McDonald's Japan recorded a total sales figure of 1.696 billion yen in just one day. The number of McDonald's hamburgers sold during the year was 674 million. This means that, on average, every Japanese eats 5.4 McDonald's hamburgers a year. In 1994, the year in which the bubble economy collapsed and the deflationary spiral began, McDonald's Japan adopted an astounding price-cutting strategy, reducing the price of a hamburger from ¥210 to a mere ¥130. This move lies behind the company's recent success, and it is part of the consistent policy of the Fujita Shoten company and its founding president, Fujita Den, who manages McDonald's Japan. (McDonald's Japan is a consortium in which the capital is shared equally between Fujita Shoten and the American parent company.)

THE ATTENTION TO "CULTUREDNESS"

In its market strategy for establishing McDonald's in Japan, Fujita Shoten was more conscious of introducing new eating patterns than of entering the restaurant business. How could Japanese consumers be persuaded to adopt the American style of hamburger eating, holding it in their hands and munching it while standing (as some do)? The basic strategy was to establish this "new Western culture" as a fashion. At the time, in 1976, banks and other sponsors showed little appreciation for this approach, labeling it a ridiculous entertainment industry. But the reason for Fujita Shoten's success was that they appreciated the "culturedness" of the hamburger. They realized that its introduction would mean changing the Japanese public's eating habits, and that they had to establish a new food culture based on meat and bread within an existing culture based on rice and fish.[3] Of course, the Japanese were already familiar with meat and bread, but the combination of meat and bread in the hamburger, and the whole way of holding it with the hands, as well as eating it while standing on the street, meant importing a new food culture.

TARGETING CUSTOMERS

McDonald's Japan did not target the low-income strata as their initial market, as the parent company did in the United States. Instead, they built up their popularity with the higher-income middle classes first, and then expanded downward to the general population. Fujita Shoten prevented the hamburger from acquiring the reputation of being cheap junk food and tried as much as possible to give it the image of a classy foreign product.

This strategy of expanding from the top to the general public is reflected in their choice of location for their first store. Instead of first setting up at a suburban roadside and expanding into the city center, as McDonald's had done in America, they began with their store in Tokyo's Ginza Yonchome. According to the thinking of the time, the Ginza was the focal point of Japanese consumer culture. The department stores concentrated in this district sold reliable high-class goods, and it was generally believed that they were setting the trends for future developments in consumer culture. The second McDonald's to open in Japan was located close to Shinjuku station. The locations of both these stores reflect the strategy of starting in the commercial center and then expanding outward, a highly effective strategy for establishing the McDonald's hamburger among Japanese consumers in the 1970s. The high-class appeal of Ginza and the youth culture of Shinjuku became McDonald's strategic base. This approach succeeded very well.

LOCATION SELECTION

The business strategy of McDonald's Japan was to target both the high-income strata and younger people. The vibrant central districts in which they set up their stores were areas in which both these social groups congregate. Even in the provincial cities, McDonald's deliberately chose locations like department stores close to railway stations, where wealthy people and the young could be enticed to spread the new food culture of hamburger eating. This contrasts with the approach of KFC Japan, which followed the American pattern by starting from a store in the suburbs of Nagoya. As a result, KFC penetration of the Japanese market was much slower. The strategy based on the idea that new things start from the center worked well for McDonald's Japan. Within Fujita Shoten, central points that attract customers, such as department stores close to stations, are called TGs (traffic generators). The strategy of combining wealthy strata and the young is referred to as a "customer-catching structure," and the mode of location selection is called "TG logic."

THE DIVERSITY OF FAST-FOODIZATION

In the overwhelmingly successful business strategy of McDonald's Japan, the predisposition of modern Japanese toward Western culture fits well with the idea of introducing a new food culture. The strategy succeeded against the background of a general transformation of lifestyles in the 1970s, and the tendency toward the formation of a uniform middle-class society. However, it would be dangerous to look only at the success of American fast food companies and draw the too easy conclusion that this represents Americanization (or globalization).

At about the same time that American fast food companies began setting up in Japan, a simultaneous process of fast-foodization of traditional Japanese foods was occurring. Until the 1980s, Kozo-zushi Honbu, which mostly sold simple takeout sushi meals, held a position close to the top in the sales ranking of restaurant companies. It was also in the 1970s that "revolving sushi" (a restaurant in which customers selected dishes of sushi from a revolving conveyor belt) established itself in the fast food market. Yoshinoya Gyudon expanded its business at the same time, and Chinese-style noodles entered the Japanese culinary lifestyle as *ramen.*

There are four main types of food in the Japanese fast food market: hamburgers, sushi, *gyudon* (a bowl of rice topped with beef), and *ramen.* It was in the 1970s that all of these entered the restaurant market as fast foods and came to be widely consumed by Japanese people.

McDonald's and KFC entered as foreign companies. They did not initially target the mass market, and their entrance to the scene coincided with a trend toward the fast-foodization of Japanese eating practices. Thus globalization cannot be equated with Americanization or cultural importation. In the 1970s, changes took place in the food, drink, and restaurant businesses, and consumer tastes changed in accordance. However, there were both external and internal aspects to these changes, which should not be viewed as constituting a one-directional wave of globalization.

Various factors were behind the rapid move toward fast-foodization: the urbanization of Japanese society beginning in the 1960s; the shift toward the nuclear family; the easing of lifestyles as a result of economic growth; the tendency toward eating out rather than in the home (associated with home ownership and the new view of the household); the movement of women away from housework; and changes in the concept of time linked to new lifestyles, in which everything is speeded up (e.g., the average length of a customer visit to Yoshinoya is as little as seven minutes). All four types of fast food listed above are characterized by simplicity, ease of preparation, and uniformity (a guarantee of the same quality in every store). Above all, the customer does not have to wait. Since the profit margin is small, a high customer turnover is essential.

The globalization of food culture must be considered in the context of economic growth, social change, the development of convenience products, the growth of the urban middle class, the changing social role of women (including the reduction of the housework burden thanks to mechanization and increased participation in the labor market), the development of a common cultural consciousness through the mass media (particularly television), home ownership, and the establishment of the custom of eating out. The causes are both internal and external.

The Fast-Foodization of Clothing

The 1970s were also the decade in which T-shirts and jeans came to prominence as a clothing style of the Japanese; this phenomenon can be called the fast-foodization of clothing. In clothing too there is a tendency toward simplicity and ease of use. T-shirts and jeans are no longer a fashion confined to the young and are gradually becoming the everyday clothing of the middle-aged men and women as well.

In modern Japan, clothing has been overwhelmingly influenced by Western culture. Japanese-style clothing is now very much the exception, while Western-style clothing is the general rule. Japanese clothing, worn by men or women, is gradually disappearing from the home. Yukata and Japanese nightgowns are sometimes worn in the home, and some men wear Japanese dress at rites of passage, such as coming-of-age ceremonies, weddings, and funerals. Japanese clothing is still relatively common among women, but even so, many brides wear Western-style wedding dresses.

T-shirts and jeans are analogous to fast food. Just as fast food is cheap, quick, and tasty, so T-shirts and jeans are easy, casual, and robust. This style is of course completed by the addition of sports shoes or sneakers.

The Orientation toward High Culture

At the same time that economic growth in Japan gave rise to the massification tendencies outlined above, it also brought about a strong orientation toward high culture. In the area of food culture, there was a gourmet boom, which led to the appearance of every kind of high-class restaurant (e.g., French, Japanese, Chinese). In the area of clothing, Western-brand goods, tailored clothing, and formal attire came to prominence.

This polarization between fast-foodization and high-culture orientation was not expressed in the form of a social division between classes, as it was in Europe, the United States, and the rest of Asia. With the growth of a large social "middle mass" in Japan, high culture became something that anyone can do. This is a peculiar characteristic of Japanese society.

Globalization is a phenomenon that has occurred in accordance with the changes going on within Japanese society itself. Although the extent of development differs, the same phenomenon, caused by industrialization, economic growth, the burgeoning of the urban middle class, the expansion of education, and the spread of information and knowledge throughout society, can be observed in parts of China, most of Southeast Asia, South Korea, and Taiwan. Globalization progresses in accordance with the degree of development in each society, and the traditions and culture of each country and society are reflected in the process.

Furthermore, globalization is far from being a uniform process. Although Japanese eating habits have been penetrated by fast-foodization, they have not succumbed to total domination. Since the 1970s, the process of fast-foodization has advanced in Japanese food culture, just as it has in the area of clothing and fashion. At the same time, however, a strong orientation toward high culture has emerged, involving the laborious work of artisans. As a result, there has been a process of polarization; however, it is manifested in the lives of single individuals and has not resulted in a polarization between social classes.

In the above, I have outlined the phenomenon of the fast-foodization of daily life as one aspect of globalization. The following examination of the overseas expansion of Japanese companies will illuminate further aspects of the process of "change in accordance with the degree of development of different societies" and the "stratification and diversification of cultural change."

GLOBALIZATION FROM THE PERSPECTIVE OF JAPANESE OVERSEAS BUSINESS EXPANSION

The Penetration of Japanese Mass Culture and Japan's Image in Asia — Suntory

SUNTORY'S EXPANSION

Suntory is a large Japanese company producing and selling alcoholic beverages, soft drinks, and food products of various kinds.[4] It began exporting liquor and other products to Korea and Southeast Asia in 1931, but until the middle of the 1970s its overseas operations had brought little success. There were both domestic and external reasons for this. Until the mid-1970s, whisky and other types of "Western liquor" were selling well in the domestic market, leaving little room for expansion overseas due to production and managerial capacity limitations. Furthermore, the overall standard of living in Asian countries had not yet reached the necessary level for mass consumption of beverages like whisky, so there was not yet sufficient market potential for expansion in Asia.

However, in the 1990s, Suntory's sales in the Asian market increased greatly. In China's Jiangsu province, the local Suntory branch attained top-brand status in the beer market. In Shanghai, the two brands of beer that Suntory began selling there in 1996 obtained a market share of more than 30 percent. In 1997, Suntory also began producing and selling oolong tea in China. Sales of this product have risen rapidly, and there are plans to expand production.

Long-term employees working for Suntory in China and Southeast Asia point out the similarities between the changes in consumption patterns that occurred in Japan in the 1970s and those now taking place in other parts of Asia. It is not just that the number of potential consumers has increased due to greater prosperity, nor is it simply a matter of the diversification of tastes. According to these employees, the most significant change is that consumers have come to use certain products as "tools" for the expression of "their own personal style," independent of any image the seller of the product might attach to it.

An example of this can be seen in the sales success of both canned and bottled oolong tea in China. Tea is, of course, China's most traditional beverage, and the success of cold canned or bottled tea in a country where cold tea was virtually unheard of is remarkable. The advertisements for the product featured the slogan "Our Age," and walking around town carrying a bottle of oolong tea became something of a fashion. In fact, it has become a symbol for a new generation, expressing an alternative style of tea drinking in contrast to the traditional one.

This phenomenon is related to the economic development and urbanization of Asian countries and to the formation of an urban middle class. Why it is that Japanese products that have sold particularly well as lifestyle and consumption patterns have undergone change? An answer to this question requires looking at other factors that play a role.

JAPAN'S IMAGE

There are at least two reasons for the growth in sales experienced by Suntory and other Japanese beverage manufacturers. The first reason has to do with Japan's image. According to people who have been responsible for sales and management in overseas localities, the reputation for high quality and reliability already established by Japanese automobile and domestic appliance manufacturers was very helpful to companies entering the market later with other types of products, for example, beverages. Even though factors such as ease of use and efficiency are irrelevant in the case of beverages, the promise of high quality still had a great effect on sales.

Furthermore, beginning in the 1980s, Japanese *manga* (cartoon books), animation, and dramas (melodramas, soap operas, etc.) become widely appreciated in Asia. Japanese drama in particular is said to be "closer to home" and more "realistic" than European or American dramas and has become extremely popular. This gave Japanese products a vague aura of just "looking good," and many people came to feel a "yearning" for them. One could not say that this was the immediate cause that allowed Japanese beverage manufacturers to increase their sales, but consumer tastes have not only become more diverse, there has been a clear tendency to favor Japanese products, which was surely helped by the general image of Japan.

MARKETING AND THE COMMON EXPERIENCE OF SOCIAL CHANGE

While it is true that the image of products has a great influence on how well they sell, great effort is also required in order to build up distribution networks and find retail outlets. Another reason Suntory employees cite for their success in Asia is that the "Japanese way of selling products suited the locality." For example, securing a market for a product does not end with signing a contract, but involves building up personal relationships through repeated visits and socializing with business partners. This style of doing business is characteristic of Japanese companies. When Suntory tried to enter markets in Europe and America, this approach was met with total incomprehension, leaving Suntory's employees at their wit's end. But in Asia the personalized approach to business not only resembled the Japanese way, it proved to be the only way anything could be achieved.

Furthermore, the way in which products enter a new market is unrelated to the associations derived from their original creation and mode of use. In postwar Japan, products originating in Europe and America were given new associations and images in accordance with local conditions as they became established as elements of a new lifestyle. This experience was a great advantage to Japanese companies in their expansion into the Asian market, as Japan's prior experience of social change and the promotion of new products to fit new lifestyles, formed a common basis on which sales activities in Asia could be built.

This examination of Suntory's overseas expansion, especially its recent activities in Asia, shows that its economic activity is greatly affected by the spread of Japanese popular and mass culture, and by the image of the country resulting from this. Experience of specific types of social change and the business mode of building up human relationships are also important factors. Although global patterns of consumption have become evident throughout Asia too, the distinctive regional histories and cultural backgrounds that are involved in the selection and adoption of products must not be ignored.

Globalization by Cultural Fusion: Shiseido

SHISEIDO'S EXPANSION

In contrast to Suntory, which used the penetration of mass culture in its overseas expansion, the Japanese cosmetics manufacturer Shiseido has attained global brand status by an entirely different route.[5] In 1997, Shiseido's sales in European markets ranked number one in Italy, number two in Germany and Holland, number eight in Belgium and Austria, number nine in Switzerland, and number eleven in France and the United Kingdom. Considering that modern cosmetics were first developed in Europe and that the cosmetics market there was already crowded with super brand names like Lancôme, Chanel, and Clarins, Shiseido's success in Europe is all the more remarkable.

Shiseido's overseas business had not always been so successful. The turning point was the internal company debate and rethinking of the company's overseas strategy, as well as subsequent organizational reform, which began in 1975. This debate was not so much about the material aspects of the business, such as the development of new products and retail outlets, as it was about the company's basic principles and identity. After two years of discussions, the following three points, which formed the basis for its subsequent image making and expansion in France, were adopted as defining the company's identity:

- Shiseido is a cosmetics company that originated as a pharmacy.
- Shiseido is a cosmetics company that aims to combine an Oriental medical approach with the most advanced technology.
- Shiseido is a cosmetics company that has created a hybrid sense of beauty by fusing Japanese culture with the Western sense of beauty.

THE GENEALOGY OF SHISEIDO'S CULTURE

Shiseido's more than one hundred years of history will not be detailed here. However, it is important to understand the relevance of the company's "cultural genealogy" to its success in France.

Shiseido was founded in 1872. The aim of its founder, Fukuhara Arinobu, was to promote the new values and culture of Western pharmacology in a country still dominated by Chinese medicine. He was succeeded by Fukuhara Shinzo, who had studied pharmacology at Columbia University and later spent much time in Europe. While in Paris, Shinzo had contacts with Japanese artists practicing Western techniques of painting, such as Kawashima Riichiro and Fujita Tsuguharu. The contacts cultivated during this period were very important in the later establishment of what the company calls "Shiseido design."

The Shiseido Design Department began in 1916, and the "Shiseido style" it developed was modern, combining elements of art nouveau and art deco with traditional Japanese art. One of its principle creators, Yamana Ayao, was attracted to the art nouveau style of the English artist Aubrey Beardsley and was stunned by the reflection of his own Japanese identity in Beardsley's art, which was in turn influenced by Japanese art, especially *ukiyoe* (woodblock prints). Thus a whole history of mutual interactions and influences is implicated in the development of the Shiseido style: art nouveau developed mostly in France from the influence of Japonism at the end of the nineteenth century, and this in turn rebounded and influenced Japanese designers. Clearly, the Shiseido image and corporate identity developed by the company in France are directly related to the history of Shiseido design.

THE CREATION OF A NEW CORPORATE IMAGE

In the creation of a new, richly symbolic Shiseido image expressing the company's identity in the 1980s, the role of one individual, the image creator Serge Lutens, has been very great. Lutens created a new art nouveau style, building on the Shiseido style of the 1920s. Instead of being directly influenced by Shiseido style, however, Lutens based his creation of an image linked to Japan on Roland Barthes's *The Empire of Signs*. Despite the absence of any direct linkage, Lutens continues the lineage of the Shiseido sense of beauty, admirably combining Eastern and Western elements in a new form. His works have succeeded in impressing on French consumers Shiseido's image as "Japanese and not Japanese, Western and not Western." Fukuhara Yoshiharu, the present chairman of Shiseido, describes Lutens's relationship with Shiseido as one of "emotional kinship."

Shiseido's success in the French market is due to not only its image strategy but also its efforts in product development and organization. In order for its products to attain market acceptance, however, a corporate identity and an image expressing that identity was absolutely essential—without this, there could have been no penetration of the market. Thus Shiseido's overseas development was indeed a process of culture contact and of gaining cultural acceptance.

GLOBALIZATION AS THE FUSION OF DIFFERENT CULTURES

We will now consider the phenomenon of globalization from the point of view of Shiseido's international development. As already indicated, the turning point in Shiseido's international development was the acceptance of the Shiseido image in France. Underlying this acceptance was more than a century of mutual influence between Japan and France in the arts. A fundamental commonality in their respective sensitivities to beauty made this interaction possible.

Shiseido's international expansion, therefore, does not amount to one-directional penetration or the influence of one culture on another. Shiseido's success in France, the center of the cosmetics world, is linked to its later success in the rest of Europe and the United States. Shiseido is now doing business in fifty-nine countries, covering most of the world except Africa. Its activities are therefore global; however, contrary to the image of globalization as something homogenizing and mechanical, this is a fusion of cultures resulting from creative development involving the interaction between different identities.

In the case of Suntory described earlier, globalization was supported by the penetration of a new image of Japan based on mass culture. The case of Shiseido shows a globalization different pattern made possible by a process of cultural hybridization through artistic exchanges over the course of more than a century.

JAPANESE CORPORATE GOVERNANCE

As overseas expansion by Japanese companies progressed, these companies naturally underwent internal change. In this section, we examine, among other things, how the employment system of Japanese companies and the consciousness of business executives have changed, paying particular attention to what has come to be known as Japan's unique system.

Until the 1980s, the Japanese-style management system was often highly praised. It has since come to be seen as needing major transformation. In view of the recession that has been ongoing since the beginning of the 1990s and the inability of Japanese companies to deal adequately with the wave of internationalization and information technology, there are now calls for the introduction of a corporate system more in tune with global standards. The Japanese system of lifetime employment, promotion according to seniority, and company-based labor unions has been indicted as inefficient and irrational in the context of global competition.

However, what has been seen as an unchanging system distinctive to Japan is in fact the product of a synthesis between distinctive premodern business practices and technological and managerial-organizational elements introduced from Europe and America. It is also a system that has been gradually built up over many years, altering its form in accordance with changes in the world order and Japan's position within it, as well as domestic social and lifestyle changes. The idea of the Japanese system as a static entity, therefore, needs to be reconsidered, as well as how the system will, or should, change in the current period of globalization.

The System of Lifetime Employment and Promotion According to Seniority

The term "lifetime employment" was probably first used by J. C. Abbeglen, whose book *The Japanese Factory* (1958) was translated into Japanese.[6] Lifetime employment came to be widely used as a term describing a central feature of Japanese-style management and entered the consciousness of people both within and outside the country.

Strictly speaking, it is not really lifetime employment, but rather long-term employment that has been characteristic of Japanese companies. Actual job termination rates show significant variation among different types of industry. For example, among electricity and gas companies, the rate was an average of 4.9 percent between 1987 and 1997, while in the service sector it was 16.6 percent during the same period.[7] There has always been considerable movement of personnel within companies and between related companies. However, comparing the overall 10–15 percent job resignation rate for all types of industry in Japan with the 20–30 percent rate of the United States[8] shows that the guarantee of stable, long-term employment has been a central feature of the Japanese system.

The system of long-term employment in Japan has its origins in the premodern employment practices of merchant households. However, the process of development up to the present day has been a discontinuous one. In the early Meiji period, until about 1890, the "westernization" of employment relations proceeded in accordance with the aim of modernizing business organizations. With the development of light industries after the Sino-Japanese War (1894–1895) and heavy and chemical industries after the Russo-Japanese War (1904–1905), this process went even further. However, following the post–World War I depression and the severe labor strife of the twentieth century, labor movement leaders such as Uno Riemon advocated the establishment of a more paternalistic style of management favoring employment stability. Thus the system of long-term employment became established in Japan after a long period of instability.[9]

According to top managers in the Toyota automobile company, long-term employment has much merit from the point of view of management as well. It enhances the quality of the labor force by making long-term training possible and increases employee loyalty to the company. Toyota had its ranking downgraded by Moody's Investors Service because of the long-term employment system, but the company plans to challenge this.[10] With the exception of certain fields that are said to be institutionally backward, such as banking and insurance, and product technology businesses, where technological innovation is vital, it seems unlikely that the system of long-term employment will break down rapidly, considering the advantages of productivity and efficiency it brings and managers' attachment to the system.

The system of promotion according to seniority too is a well-established custom in Japan and has roots going back to the employment practices of the Edo period (1603–1867). By the 1920s, it was already institutionalized to nearly the same extent it is today. However, this does not mean that it has not been changed. Adjustments were made around 1944 to correct an overemphasis on seniority, and again in about 1960. Since the latter half of the 1990s, a third period of reevaluation has taken place.[11]

As a result of these changes, the age allowance paid to white-collar workers has in some cases been entirely eliminated, most notably in the restaurant business and in the product development divisions of companies in the electrical industry. In many companies, the system of promotion according to seniority is valued as a means of meritocratically rewarding the differences in ability that arise from length of service. In the private sector, it is impossible to award pay raises and promotions uniformly to employees in their forties or older, and there is naturally some personnel evaluation according to achievement and ability. Even in the civil service, which is considered the sector most resistant to change, the promotion of people from their mid-thirties onward is based on individual achievement and ability, leading to a diversification of career tracks.

The system of promotion according to seniority is based on the idea that the experience and knowledge gained from long service contributes to productivity. It is a system favorable to continuous technological innovation. Considering that it already contains an element of evaluation according to individual ability, it is unlikely to be eliminated entirely, even as the business environment undergoes change. However, in sectors highly sensitive to information technology, there is a need to obtain strategic personnel, and reconsideration of the system is becoming quite active.

Instead of leading to a wholesale abandonment of the systems of long-term employment and seniority-based promotion, however, globalization has become the occasion for the continuation in a modified form of these customary practices.

THE INFLUENCE OF GLOBALIZATION AMONG THE INTELLECTUAL ELITE

Finally, we consider the relation between Japanese intellectuals and globalization. This will involve a consideration of what Peter Berger has called "faculty club culture" and "Davos culture."

Faculty club culture and Davos culture do not necessarily conflict with the existing culture of Japanese intellectuals; in some respects, they overlap. For example, concern with such topics as human rights, the environment, and feminism was comparatively high in Japan even before the arrival of globalization, and these issues have contributed to the development of a distinctive context and framework of consciousness. Since a "modernism" based on Western European and American models has long formed the mainstream in Japanese academia, an intellectual culture resembling faculty club culture had already taken shape before globalization emerged. At the same time, there are differences among countries in the degree to which these topics have been influential, especially in Japan.

Human Rights, the Environment, and Feminism

The issue of human rights in postwar Japan developed in close relation to the "problem" of people of Korean nationality (both North and South) living in Japan. Beginning in the mid-1970s, there was a shift to a concern centered on policies toward resident aliens of other nationalities. In particular, the problem of receiving Vietnamese refugees emerged in 1975. In the same year, the G7 summit met for the first time, forcing Japan to realize its own international position. From the mid-1980s on, the number of foreign "trainees" and workers began to increase rapidly. As a result of the 1985 Plaza Accord, the value of the yen rose sharply, and large numbers of migrant laborers entered the country from Asia and the Middle East, along with people of Japanese descent from Brazil, Peru, and other Latin American countries.

However, the number of illegal migrants rose even more, which brought forth two contrasting reactions from the intellectual community. On the one hand, the "Closed Country" *(Sakoku)* faction, concerned with the rise in crimes committed by foreign workers and the emergence of discrimination problems, advocated a cautious approach to accepting foreign labor. On the other hand, there were those, particularly economists, who believed that labor liberalization and internationalization were inevitable and demanded that foreign labor be actively recruited. This "Open Country" *(Kaikoku)* faction advocated the necessity of globalization as the basis for introducing foreign labor. It goes without saying that this view also reflected the interests of a corporate world suffering from a severe labor shortage.

In addition to these two factions, there was another that demanded that the human rights of foreign workers, whether legal or otherwise, be respected. This group advocated the abolition of discrimination toward foreigners and the right of resident aliens to participate in local politics. This stream of thought was nurtured by faculty club culture and was part of an international movement for human rights.

Concern for environmental issues emerged and developed in Japan from the problem of pollution, the underside of modernization. Although there were some influences from the environmental movement in Europe and the United States, environmental issues in Japan have tended to be seen as continuous with issues of government and industry versus residents. Marxist-influenced intellectuals have played a particularly significant role in the environmental movement. Intellectuals in Japan have not responded much to the problems of wild animals and the natural environment, despite the altered environmental consciousness growing out of the global environmental movement that emerged in the 1980s. With respect to the environmental movement, the influence of globalization has been comparatively weak, and the distinctive context of Japan has continued to be the most significant factor.

By contrast, the direct influence of faculty club culture is clearly present in the feminist movement, where intellectuals with experience studying or doing research in Europe and the United States have played the leading role in the diffusion of feminism, women's studies, and gender studies.

In sum, we can see that the worldwide growth in concern for such topics as human rights, the environment, and feminism has certainly extended to Japan. There are, however, disparities between the different topics in the extent of influence, ranging from environmental issues, which shows little faculty club influence, to feminism, on which its influence is strong and direct.

The Economic Globalization Debate

In intellectual discourse, globalization's greatest influence is probably in the debate about economic globalization. From the 1960s until the early 1970s, it was generally believed in Japan that the country's management style was an encumbrance left over from an earlier age; in fact, the dominant economic opinion was that the existing system and customs were outdated and should be done away with. This view was a product of modernism, which was then the dominant paradigm in the postwar Japanese social sciences. However, in the late 1970s and early 1980s, Japanese-style management came to be positively viewed both at home and abroad, as the American economy declined and the performance of Japanese companies gained much acclaim.

Things began to change again in the late 1980s. After the Plaza Accord of 1985, international cooperation was presented as the cure for trade imbalances and the tide turned against Japan, as globalism became dominant. Criticism of Yamatoism (Japanese xenophobic nationalism) came from intellectuals in Europe and America. At the same time, cultural relativism came under attack, especially among some U.S. intellectuals, while the criticism of Japan developed by James Fallows, Chalmers Johnson, Karel van Wolferen, and others was not only directed against Japanese economic organization but concerned itself with *Nihonjinron* (Japanese cultural nationalism) and *Nihonbunkaron* (Japanese culture discourse).

The tone of Japanese economic discourse eventually changed in response to a number of things, including foreign criticism, the World Bank/IMF structural adjustment talks taking place at the time, and the reevaluation of the relationship between Japan and the United States thirty years after the 1960 redrafting of their mutual security treaty. Protectionism then became a legitimate basis for advocating economic structural reform in Japan. Thus the issue of economic globalization was first discussed among Japanese economists against a background of economic friction between Japan and the United States. From the U.S. side, this was seen as a demand for the opening of markets—and indeed, many of the features that have come to be known as "global standards" are in fact distinctive characteristics of the American economic system.

The debate about economic globalization later developed into a debate about the role of the market and the state, deepening to a discussion of social philosophical issues. Generally speaking, advocates of globalization in Japan see the market as a universal and rational mechanism and believe that the system should be reformed to allow the market a greater role. Those who are skeptical of this view tend to argue for a reconstruction of traditional communities, including the state, which is being eroded by globalization. A characteristic feature of this debate is that many of the advocates of globalization on the American economic model were once business school students in the United States. This mode of thinking, of course, reveals a strong affinity with Davos culture.

The positions of Japanese intellectuals with respect to the issue of economic globalization can be categorized roughly as follows:

- Globalism: a position demanding the loosening and abolition of restrictions in order to allow the greatest possible scope for the operation of market mechanisms
- Regionalism: a position advocating the conception of a regional community transcending the nation-state to counteract the power of the market

- Nationalism: a position emphasizing the significance of existing nation-states as the basis for individuals' sense of identity, and advocating the preservation and strengthening of the nation-state against the market
- Localism: a position seeking to devolve many of the existing functions of the state to local organizations, and to revive regional society by promoting decentralization

This shows that only a certain group of intellectuals in Japan hold a position close to the Davos culture (those falling into category 1), whose ideas and habits have not at the present time come to dominate the intellectual elite in Japan.

CONCLUSION

The term "global standards" has recently gained much currency in Japan and is often cited as a basis for the necessity of reform by advocates of economic globalization. However, the actual meaning of the term is unclear, even in the field of economics. Postwar Japanese society has always paid close attention to what was going on "outside" and has successively attempted to reform itself under the slogans of "modernization," "westernization," and "internationalization." Even though the slogan has now shifted to one of globalization, the underlying structure of asserting the necessity and legitimacy of "reform" while comparing Japan abstractly with the "outside" has remained unchanged. This is another aspect of the globalization discourse in Japan.

However, in regard to lifestyle and mass culture, as well as actual business practices and the ideas of the intellectual elite, globalization is not a process in which some existing "standard" spreads and covers the whole. Rather, it is a dynamic movement in which a loose commonality takes shape spatially and temporary, and at different levels.

The fast-foodization of lifestyles can be seen as an aspect of globalization in the sense that it is part of the worldwide move toward rationalization. At the same time, however, it is also a product of the social and cultural transformation of Japanese society itself. The global lifestyle comes into being as a result of the compound effect of both internal and external changes. Globalization is itself a multilayered and multicentered process, as can be seen in of the spread of Japanese mass and popular culture in Asia and the formation of hybrid cultures from the fusion of different high cultures. In Japan, therefore, globalization has not resulted in homogenization but has developed in a dynamic fashion, giving rise to significant diversity and multipolarity.

NOTES

Dedicated to the memory of the late Professor Seizaburo Sato, site director for Japan.

This chapter is a report on the work carried out by the research group in Japan, which was organized under the leadership of the late Seizaburo Sato. Since the latter's sudden death in December 1999, leadership of the research group has passed to Tamotsu Aoki. Therefore, this report combines the results of the research carried out by each member of the group (Kiyotada Tsutsui section 4, Masako Okamoto section 2, Eiji Takemura section 3, and Tamotsu Aoki section 1), with Tamotsu Aoki taking overall responsibility.

1. Yasuhiko Nakamura, *Convenience Stores, Family Restaurants, Rotating Sushi* (Tokyo: Bunshunbunkoi, 1998).

2. Figures are quoted in U.S. billions: 1 billion = 1,000,000,000.

3. I would like to acknowledge the kind advice and assistance provided by the Fujita Institute of Future Management Research, particularly the invaluable support of Nobuhiro Nakabayashi, in relation to our research concerning the spread of fast food in Japan from the 1970s to the present day. I would also like to thank them for allowing me to use their research reports, including *Twenty Years of McDonald's in Japan*.

4. I would like to express my sincere thanks to the international department of Suntory Ltd., which gave unstinting support by providing the necessary research material and assistance with interviews. "Ninety Years of Suntory," International Department pamphlet, 1990.

5. I would like to express my sincere thanks to the Information Department of Shiseido Ltd. for their continued support of my research by providing the necessary documents and assistance with interviews. The following materials relate to Shiseido's overseas expansion: Kazuyuki Komiya, *The Challenge of International Brands in Paris for Shiseido* (Tokyo: Jitsugyou no nihonsha, 1993); *Shiseido Legends*, vol. 3 (catalog); *120 years of Shiseido* (Tokyo: Kyuryudo, 1990); *Ayao Yamano Exhibition,* Meguro Art Museum, 1998 (catalog).

6. J. C. Abbeglen, *Japanese Factories* (Tokyo: Diamondsha, 1958).

7. Ministry of Labor, Research Department, *Research on the Direction of Employment, 1998*; and Ikumi Arabe, *Keieigaku Nyumon* (Introduction to business management) (Tokyo: Chuo Keizaisha, 1997).

8. Kazuo Koike, *The Japanese Employment System* (Tokyo: Toyo Keizai Shinhousha, 1994).

9. Hiroshi Hazama, *Research on Japanese Labor Management* (1964).

10. *Asahi Shimbun*, 28 November 1998.

11. Mr. Tsunehiko Yui, interview by author.

4

"A Tryst with Destiny"

THE INDIAN CASE OF CULTURAL GLOBALIZATION

Tulasi Srinivas

The phrase "a tryst with destiny" has great historic resonance for most Indians. These are the words spoken by Jawaharlal Nehru, the first prime minister of a free India, at midnight on 14 August 1947, heralding a new dawn of Indian freedom and independence after two hundred years of British colonial rule. I would like to believe that what is happening in India today with regard to economic liberalization and cultural globalization is in fact yet another tryst with destiny for India, one that gives India the chance to enter the global stage—an opportunity that many Indians feel must not be missed this time around.

The point of departure for this chapter, indeed this entire book, was Peter Berger's deceptively simple essay, "The Four Faces of Globalization,"[1] which appeared in the fall 1997 issue of the *National Interest*. Berger wrote that if a "dialogue of cultures"[2] were to take place, the processes of cultural globalization and the resistance to it would need to be understood far more clearly than they are today. Berger described four "carriers" of cultural globalization: an international business elite called "Davos culture," a term originally coined by Samuel Huntington to describe members of the Davos business summit of Europe; an international intellectual elite that Berger called "faculty club culture"; "McWorld," a term for popular culture coined originally by Benjamin Barber;[3] and "evangelical Protestantism," or any large-scale popular (generally religious) movement. Berger concluded that cultural globalization is the movement of goods and ideas (cultural freight) from the West to the rest of the world.[4]

I, however, am interested in examining cultural globalization as a two-way process, and I focus on non-Western, primarily Indian, contributions to the process of cultural globalization.[5] While cultural globalization forces do enter India, cultural models are also increasingly emitted *from* India. What are commonly called New Age practices, which include meditation, yoga,[6] spiritual healing, massage, and Tantrism, are popular in the West today. Lifestyle gurus Deepak Chopra and Shri Sathya Sai Baba have large followings in New York, Santiago, and Munich. In Kassel, Germany, one can undergo an eight-day Ayurvedic getaway,[7] including Ayurvedic cooking, herbal teas, massage, and individual treatments that include frequent dips in the Kurhessen hot springs. In Birmingham, England, one can eat authentic *masala dosa* and chicken curry.

In fact, Indian cultural artifacts are consumed all over the world: silk sari bedding is advertised at Bloomingdale's, Indian jewelry and dress, henna tattoos, Darjeeling tea, and toe rings are all bought every day by Europeans and Americans. These consumer objects are sometimes mediated through American marketing, but their cultural provenance is indisputable. This chapter seeks to examine India's role as a cultural emitter and the questions that this raises for India and for the process of cultural globalization as a whole.

Cultural globalization in India is difficult to discuss, as differences exist across region, religion, ethnicity, sect, class, and caste.[8] It is not possible to speak for the whole of India with a single voice. India is a civilization with great cultural density—what Samuel Huntington refers to as a "strong culture"—and as such may provide us with a template of a working alternate modernity. Though discussions of "alternate" or "multiple" modernities[9] raise fears of Islamic fundamentalism or Singapore-style "Asian values," I hope to extend our understanding of the process of cultural globalization by showing that other plural and democratic alternatives may exist.

The ethnographic data for the study was collected primarily in the southern city of Bangalore, though researchers made frequent trips to other parts of the country to collect data.[10] Indians consider Bangalore one of the most globalized cities in India, and we therefore assumed that it would show the strongest globalization dynamic.

In order to identify the areas of study that would best examine the paradoxes, problems, and possibilities that cultural globalization presented, we first conducted four focus groups among Bangalore professionals, businessmen, and intellectuals. We also examined the local newspapers for material identifying key areas of study and spoke to people in Bangalore and Delhi about their concerns for themselves and the country. The problem was to choose from the wealth and complexity of the material we found, but we finally settled on three subjects to study: (1) the food industry in India and its response to the entry of global food giants; (2) the religious and social phenomenon of a local godman called Sai Baba who has a global following; and (3) the computer software industry in India and its work culture. This chapter will discuss data from each of these studies and the questions that they raise.

In any Indian city, and especially in Bangalore, the force of globalization is difficult to miss: giant advertisements for Coca-Cola, MTV, Hyundai motors, Intel-based PCs, and Sunrise coffee all jostle for visual space.[11] Globalization in its most visible form is the culture of conspicuous consumption as promoted by the international media. The two most recognizable globalizing forces in India are multinational companies and MTV-style popular culture, both of which appeal to the English-speaking, westernized, urban middle classes.[12]

We found that most middle-class families in Bangalore had a family member in the West. Popular topics of conversation included time differences across the globe, the complications and inconveniences of airplane travel, the American political system, and the European Union's monetary problems. Indians are familiar with the West and its cultural influences, and so the responses to cultural globalization in India take different forms, ranging from hybridized acceptance to total rejection. I will describe particular instances of both these positions.

Popular culture as carried by the media influences urban Indian youth a great deal, dictating their choice of how to dress, where to be seen, what music to listen to, and what opinions to adopt. Hindi films, the Bombay-based franchise of MTV, and Rupert Murdoch's Hong Kong–based Star TV play a large part in setting trends, encouraging consumption, and creating a marketing dynamic conducive to youth culture. But the global culture carried by the media is not derived only from the West. Hybrids of Western and Indian cultural types are routine,[13] and it appears that some level of localization is essential for success in the Indian market.[14]

For example, a pastiche of Indian-inspired dress styles and American-style banter conducted in Oxbridge English, interspersed with Hindi film–style dialogues, is the norm for Indian TV hosts. "Bhangra pop," which draws from the folk music of rural Punjab and West Indian reggae, is brought to Indian youth via the younger generation of the Indian diaspora in Birmingham and London. So cultural fusion models that successfully mix Western influences with culturally familiar Indian types are readily accepted.[15]

While there is still significant poverty in India,[16] we found that the urban poor became insiders to cultural globalization through imitation of middle-class consumption patterns. For example, whereas maids in middle-class Bangalore homes used to wash their hair with indigenous soap-nut powder, they have now started using shampoos bought from local stores. They also have regular TV-watching schedules and save money to buy "foreign" consumer items. Cultural globalization does in fact trickle down from the middle classes to the poor.

On the other hand, the Indian middle class is rejecting certain types of global cultural forces. One of the less appealing but increasingly visible forces of cultural globalization in India is the evangelical Christian movement. Missionary activity in India is growing at a rapid pace as these movements become increasingly "Fordist," or assembly line, in character.[17] Missionaries, primarily from America and Europe, spend a month or so in Indian cities forming and training "cell groups" of individuals who in turn proselytize. This in turn has led to tension between missionaries and pro-Hindu groups and has resulted in the killing of seven missionaries. These deaths were spotlighted by the national media and led to national debate about the position of religious minorities in India. The middle classes were vocal in expressing their distress at the changing nature of missionary activity in the country, as well as the intolerant response to it.

India is the largest and the *only* plural, working democracy in South Asia, and it is surrounded by nondemocratic countries—China to the north, Burma to the east, and Pakistan to the west. As Khilnani puts it, "The longevity and persistence of Indian democracy is the single most remarkable fact of postcolonial India, distinguishing it from nearly all other Asian countries."[18] In the 1940s and 1950s it was widely held that democracy in India would not survive, as the seeds were sown in a "poor and largely illiterate" country. But democracy has not just lasted, it has flourished and taken over the public political imagination. In Khilnani's words, "The principle of authority for the country now irrevocably rests in the modern nation-state."[19]

Economic liberalization and globalization occupy a central place in all economic discussions in India today.[20] Globalization raises hopes that the Indian economy can grow and reduce the poverty of its many millions of citizens; however, it also raises fears that the economic growth may prove to be too expensive in other ways. Over the past ten years the Indian government has demonstrated remarkable flexibility in dismantling archaic economic laws that hindered growth, which has led to a spurt of economic growth. The economy has reached a growth rate of about 5 percent, while inflation fell to below 2.8 percent in November 1999, the lowest point in the decade.[21] The latest Asian Development Bank figures report India's potential growth at over 7 percent, a rate at which it would catch up with China in another two years,[22] something that has not occurred since 1990. But the fear I heard expressed repeatedly by globalization pundits is whether the Indian government can sustain economic growth and dismantle the existing trade laws fast enough. These fears are heightened by the popular understanding that countries that do not leap onto the globalization bandwagon seemed doomed to live in economic backwaters.

On the other hand, the primary concern expressed by potential foreign investors seems to be political stability. Four years ago, when the Bharatiya Janatha Party (BJP) came into power, the fear both in India and abroad was that the BJP would yield to the right-wing faction within the party. But over the past three years the BJP has shown no signs of yielding to the Rashtriya Sevak Sangh[23] or any other fundamentalist subgroup. The BJP has managed to maintain a steady government presence, in spite of factional fighting and attempts from within to topple the government.[24]

The BJP has indicated that India wants to be a player on the global stage. Its successful nuclear testing, though the source of much concern to the United States and other developed nations, was seen by most Indians as a source of national pride. Although there has been much hand-wringing over the issue in local and national papers by Indian intellectuals, most Indians feel that the nuclear testing demonstrated Indian sovereignty, power, and scientific ability. Most also view India's refusal to sign the U.S.-based Comprehensive Test Ban Treaty as yet another sign of the ability of the Indian state to take a strong stand, while the government's handling of negotiations during the 1999 Kashmir crisis was seen as a diplomatic coup.[25] That Britain and the United States supported India's view only underlined the government's strong moral position.[26]

India is already an acknowledged South Asian power. The challenge for the government is how to parlay its position as regional power into a position of global power. But for India's citizens, the question is what kind of opportunities the global marketplace will provide for them. The government's main concern is successfully treading the razor's edge between opening the economy to free trade at the request of its impatient citizenry, while retaining some policies that will protect the people.

DIGESTING GLOBALIZATION: THE INDIAN FOOD INDUSTRY

Two food booms are taking place in India simultaneously: the boom in multinational brand-name foods and the indigenous food boom. The entry of multinational food companies has been widely reported by the media, but the concurrent boom in local foods and indigenous cuisine has been ignored. This latter boom is also significant, but its signs are subtler, and it is often missed. We will first discuss the multinational food corporations and their presence in India.

The first multinational food company to enter the Bangalore market was Kentucky Fried Chicken, or KFC as it is popularly known. In 1996 it bought out an old and beloved clothing store on Brigade Road in the center of the commercial area of colonial Bangalore. The old building was torn down and replaced by a sparkling two-story, red and white facility. Soon after it opened, passersby were entertained by the sight of local farmers in cotton dhotis and turbans picketing the restaurant. The Karnataka Rajya Raita Sangha (Karnataka Union of Farmers), led by Dr. Nanjundaswamy and local leader Mr. Vatal Nagaraj, organized a series of protests against KFC, which subsequently demanded police protection and operated for a year with a police van parked outside its plate glass windows.[27]

KFC had targeted specific suppliers for a special breed of chicken that would give them the "best" product, so local farmers were convinced that KFC would put local poultry farmers out of business. The farmers objected to KFC on two counts: it would encourage nonvegetarianism in south India and, compared with *nati* (native fowl), the multinational corporation (MNC) chicken had no taste. Local newspapers ran several stories about KFC, which often fueled anti-MNC feelings. However, the protests served to open up discussion about MNCs, and it became evident that Bangaloreans had mixed feelings about the entry of a foreign multinational companies in the arena of food production. They were fairly comfortable with MNCs that built software, but when it came to food and food production, antiglobal sentiments were rife.

The KFC example becomes more informative when it is compared with the trajectory of other brand-name foods in India, such as McDonald's and Pizza Hut. McDonald's, the world's premier fast food restaurant, has been unsuccessful in India, despite the company's employment of strategies that it has developed and tested successfully in many other parts of the world. McDonald's attempted to invent a need for the hamburger among the urban middle classes through a fourfold strategy—creating a demand for the product through advertising, capturing a niche market, localizing through hybridized food products, and employing local food suppliers.

But McDonald's has a product that poses certain marketing problems in a country like India, and the idea of a beef patty on a bun is not one that appeals to the majority of Hindu Indians, even among the very westernized. Indians were already familiar with the hamburger from countless Indian restaurants that served the dish, but it was rarely the item of choice. It is significant that after four years in India, McDonald's had sold only 7 million burgers. In comparison, over 7 million *dosas*[28] are made in India every day and 75 million movie tickets are sold every week. Amit Jatia, of the company's Mumbai (Bombay) headquarters, states that McDonald's will take at least five to six years to break even in India.[29]

McDonald's has spent a great deal of time and money building double kitchens in every restaurant to prevent the mixing of vegetarian and nonvegetarian foods. Purity and pollution are very important to Indian consumers. Although McDonald's has made a valiant effort, consumers associate the company with their brand-name product, the beef burger. We found older members of families surreptitiously sniffing plates for meat smells in a McDonald's in south Delhi; more aggressive customers have insisted on inspecting both kitchens to make sure that all the utensils were kept separate. Still others have subjected employees to long questionnaires about the care taken to keep meat products away from the vegetarian kitchens.

McDonald's has also attempted to localize, that is, Indianize, the menu. They replaced their signature hamburger, the ubiquitous Big Mac, with the Maharajah Mac, a so-called Indian hamburger, and they've also introduced several vegetarian items. But the lack of spice in the meat lost it many customers. Even teenagers and young adults preferred the taste of the mutton patty in the corner Indian restaurant to those at McDonald's. Nor did its set meal of burger, fries, and a Coke appeal to the Indian consumer the same way it does to those in other parts of the world.[30]

McDonald's parent company has spent considerable time and money distributing information about the sourcing of its raw materials within India, and it wants to be seen as a company that encourages the Indian food industry.[31] According to a press release, McDonald's is supplied with iceberg lettuce from Ootacamund in the south, cheese from Dynamix Dairy products in Pune, dehydrated onions from Jain Foods in Jalgaon, sesame seeds from Ghaziabad in Uttar Pradesh, and so on. However, rumors about McDonald's among middle-class consumers focus on the company importing potatoes that have the right specific gravity for its famous fries.[32]

Multinational food companies have found it difficult to penetrate the Indian market. The standout exception is Pizza Hut, which entered India in 1997 and opened its first facility in Bangalore. Bangaloreans were familiar with pizzas prior to this. When I was going to college in Bangalore in the early 1980s, snack shops and westernized restaurants served pizzas and pasta. The basic structure of the pizza, with its *nan*-like bread topped with tomato sauce and vegetables, is both familiar and reassuring to the Indian consumer. When Pizza Hut initially entered the industry, it did a brisk business, and its outlet on Cunningham Road in central Bangalore was crowded with families and young businessmen who wanted a casual lunch.

In 1998 competing global chains owned by Singaporeans (Pizza Corner) and Indians in other parts of India (Pizza World) also entered the Bangalore market. The research shows that Pizza Hut lost customers to these rival chains for two reasons: Pizza Corner's pizzas were cheaper, were considered tastier, and could be delivered everywhere in the city. We found that Bangaloreans have become adept at using delivery services, which allow family members of different age groups and food needs to eat together in the comfort of their own home. Older family members can have home-cooked Indian food and youngsters can eat takeout. Pizza Corner capitalized on its understanding of the Indian family's different generational needs; its success rests on competitive costs, familiar taste, convenience, and accessibility.

But the Indian food market is flooded with many types of indigenous food that are far tastier and less expensive than brand-name foods, so multinationals who want to do business there have to adapt to interstices in the food market. But large brand-name companies are not flexible in the true sense of the word. The local variations that McDonald's introduces in various countries are in themselves highly standardized and regularized, and if a company like McDonald's or Pizza Hut sets itself up as separate for distinct reasons, it becomes even less flexible and adaptable.[33]

In fact, the iconic visibility of a McDonald's or a Pizza Hut—its brand name—reduces its effectiveness in a plural food market like India's. McDonald's, Pizza Hut, and other American-owned multinational corporations are based on the American ideal of standardization and predictability—the point of any multinational food company is to be able to replay this miracle of standardization all over the world, and it is standardization that its consumers enjoy.[34] But the Indian consumer does not want standardization in food products. Because of the country's ethnic plurality, Indians are used to a plurality of many different types of food within a single small geographical area: there is no pan-Indian cuisine. To attempt to standardize and homogenize the food product is to misunderstand the needs of the Indian consumer.[35]

The Indigenous Food Industry

The indigenous fast food boom has grown apace with the multinational boom, but it is rarely discussed in India or elsewhere. The indigenous food industry includes food products for immediate consumption, as well as what are called pre-prepared foods, such as snacks, spice powders, lentil wafers, pickles, and chutneys. The industry takes Indian recipes, simplifies them for quick production, and decreases time and cost to the consumer.

In 1989 there was only one company in Bangalore, MTR,[36] that made pickles and powders used in home cooking; today over three hundred companies do business in local markets, and MTR is a global exporter. Middle- and lower-middle-class housewives rely on these mixes and snacks to provide food for the family. Pre-prepared foods cover a wide array of products, and they are constructed to appeal to the taste buds of certain ethnic and caste groups. *Authenticity is valuable to the Indian consumer.* I have seen women throw out packets of powders or chutneys because "It did not taste correct. It has preservatives."

Preparation of these indigenous foods has become a local cottage industry. Local entrepreneurs, many of them women, often employ poor women from the targeted caste or ethnic group to prepare the product so it has an authentic taste. These entrepreneurs often form cooperatives and sell their products to larger companies for marketing. The local boom in food products has led to older women finding secure jobs in these cooperatives, and the rise of the housewife entrepreneur.

This study showed that when urban middle classes eat out, they mainly favor two types of restaurants. The first are small stand-up eateries that serve Indian food at reasonable prices, and which have adapted their menus to a linguistically mixed consumer base by displaying large color photographs of the food items over the service counter. There are no seats, and patrons eat their food standing at long counters. Prices are reasonable, with a plate of *idlis* (made from rice and *dal*) costing less than ten rupees, or about forty cents. These restaurants are always full and noisy, and people of every class, from laborers[37] to businessmen, seem to visit them for a quick snack.

The second type is the neighborhood restaurant. These are family restaurants with and extensive menus featuring over a hundred dishes, divided into popular categories: south Indian, north Indian, and Chinese. Some even serve what they call a "continental" menu, primarily consisting of American dishes such as pizza. There are many versions of these restaurants, with varying prices. They usually have pleasant decor and are loud and noisy; they are not only packed on weekends, but often on weekdays, well into the night. These neighborhood restaurants offer a menu for all members of the typical Indian family at an affordable price. Our research showed that the most popular dishes were the north Indian curries and breads combined with Chinese fried rice or noodles. In contrast to the McDonald's burger, local Indianized Chinese food is highly popular among the urban middle classes.

Chinese food was brought to India through Calcutta's expatriate Chinese community. India's Chinese population has kinship networks in all the major metropolitan centers, and Chinese restaurants were built one at a time as family businesses over several decades. Though Chinese food is in fact just as "foreign" as the burger, it has been localized and hybridized to suit the Indian palate. We decided to call this the "lone infiltrator" model cultural globalization.[38] Not only is the lone infiltrator faster, more flexible, and less visible than the larger MNC model, it is also quickly accepted by the local population because of its lack of iconic branding.

Westernization or Sacramental Consumption?

Peter Berger defines the term "sacramental consumption" as the eating of food that carries with it the cultural freight of freedom, democracy, human rights, and so on. He uses the example of a McDonald's hamburger consumed in the former Soviet Union as carrying with it the freight of freedom and capitalism. While this may be true for American burgers in former communist countries, I find that the concept of sacramental consumption cannot be extended to the Indian case. I believe that Indians do not make these kinds of links between the political reality of the source country and a food, because they live in a plural democracy; hence, they do not imbue food with this cultural freight.

They may, however, invest the burger with other symbolism. For example, the young adults who do eat at McDonald's in New Delhi are apparently demonstrating their status, wealth, and upward social mobility. But Western material culture can easily be borrowed without the West's social and political institutions, and sacramental consumption in India appears to be subordinate to the process of westernization. Nevertheless, the consumption of burgers may eventually pave the way for greater westernization.[39]

If we examine cultural globalization as a linear process, with the emphasis on a later stage of globalization, the positive cultural value attached to American or Western food is reduced the further one is exposed to global culture.[40] Those who know what to eat at KFC are considered "insiders"; those who do not are "outsiders" who are forced to consume the myth through consumption of the product. The instant one becomes an insider to global culture, the incentive to consume diminishes. At that point, the incentive to consume a product can only be located in the innovation of newer and more interesting products.

GLOBAL GODMAN: INCLUSION, SALVATION, SYNCRETISM

The international Sai Baba movement claims to have 70 million devotees and two thousand centers in 137 countries, though 20 million followers would seem to be a more accurate number.[41] The Sai organization's overseas centers are grouped into fifteen different regions. Even so, very little is known about the sect, its transnational devotee base, or its leader, the charismatic godman Shri Sathya Sai Baba. Although he only speaks Telugu and a smattering of other local Indian languages, "Baba," as he is popularly known in India, has been able to successfully translate his message for cultures as diverse as those of Chile, Singapore, Germany, and Kenya.

The seventy-four-year-old Shri Sathya Sai Baba is believed to be *bhagwan* (God) by his devotees, and he is referred to by this name. His mythicized life story follows the typical structure of most mystics and godmen, with revelation occurring at an early age following a traumatic event. In typical hagiographic style, he claims mythic descent from both Shiva and Vishnu,[42] as well as Shirdi Sai Baba, a respected godman and saint.

The debate in India about Sathya Sai Baba has centered on his ability to materialize objects such as rings, necklaces, and sacred ash.[43] His detractors claim that these materializations are magic tricks; his devotees believe that these powers are evidence of his sacredness. He is also known for his divine ability to heal the sick, read people's worries before they are articulated, and release devotees from their earthly pain. This divinity is associated strongly in the minds of his devotees with that of Jesus Christ and Krishna.[44] His devotees surrender themselves completely to him, which is a facet of sectarian belief in India, and his physical presence makes the relationship between the divine and the devotee approachable and intimate. What makes Shri Sathya Sai Baba so different from other godmen and religious philosophers is his assertion of divinity in a human form. He emphasizes a nonintellectual love of God and rejects the abstract religious theorizing of other Indian godmen, scholars, and philosophers.

Baba's spiritual empire extends globally, but the physical center of the movement is in Prashanthi Nilayam, his ashram at Puttaparthi, a dry and dusty town in the rural hinterland of Andhra Pradesh, approximately one hundred miles from Bangalore. Puttaparthi plays host to Baba's global following and has grown to include specialty restaurants, tourist bungalows, hotels and villas, gift shops, all-night pharmacies and restaurants, and gymnasiums on wide, paved roads. Banners in twenty-four languages fly all over Puttaparthi, welcoming international devotees to the "home of Baba."

I will digress briefly to describe the symbol of Shri Sathya Sai Baba, as I think that it is directly related to the concept of creating a global following. The Sai logo is based on a flower consisting of two rows of five petals each. The inner ring of five petals contains the symbols of the major world religions: the Hindu *om*, the Christian cross, the Zoroastrian fire, the Islamic crescent, and the Buddhist wheel. Each traditional religious symbol is accompanied by creative new transcultural readings. For example, the exhortation for the Christian cross is, "Cut the 'I' feeling clean across and let your ego die on the cross, to endow on you Eternity." For the Islamic crescent it is, "Be like the star, which never wavers from the crescent but is fixed in steady faith." And so on.

The incorporation of traditional symbols into the larger Sai logo enables Sathya Sai Baba's international devotees, who are part of an existing structured religious community, to relate to the movement on a symbolic level. For those who are disenchanted with their traditional religions, the reinterpretations of the symbols allow them freedom to pick portions of the religion they are comfortable with and weave them into the larger structure of Sai faith to create a lifestyle. Furthermore, the incorporation of these symbols into the Sai logo gives prospective devotees the impression that Sai Baba has created a universal faith outside the sphere of any single religion. To emphasize this universality of Sai devotion, under the logo are words attributed to Sathya Sai Baba: "Let the different faiths exist, let them flourish, and let the glory of God be sung in all the languages and in a variety of tunes. That should be the Ideal. Respect the differences between the faiths and recognize them as valid as long as they do not extinguish the flame of unity."

The Global Village of Sai Devotion

We found that Sai devotees flocked to Puttaparthi and Whitefield from all over the globe to meet Baba, as he is reluctant to travel outside India. Groups of devotees struggling with unwieldy luggage in the Bangalore airport can be seen at any time of the year—they are easily recognizable by their white or saffron T-shirts with the Sai Baba logo, and their necklaces with his photograph.

On the various occasions that we visited the Sathya Sai summer ashram in Whitefield, the number and ethnic diversity of his devotees repeatedly impressed us. We visited on relatively normal days as well as festival days. On normal days there were over five thousand people present to seek his blessing at five in the morning;[45] on festival days half a million to a million seek his blessing. We were told there were tour groups from different countries that regularly came once a year to visit Baba. I saw groups from Japan, Norway, the Netherlands, Germany, Indonesia, Malaysia, Singapore, Russia, the United States, and England. They were easy to pick out, as members all wore uniforms with designated colors or banners identifying them by nationality.

The central ceremony of the visit to a Baba ashram is Baba's daily *darshan*, which occurs twice in a given day on any day of the week: once at 6:00 A.M. and again at 4:00 P.M. Thousands of devotees from all over the world brave the heat, mosquitoes, and hours of waiting to get a glimpse of Baba. Our data revealed that over 60 percent of the people present were non-Indian. *Darshan* lasts about fifteen minutes. After Baba leaves, the crowd disperses in complete silence. We were told that this was the regular routine for most of the year.

The Devotees

We conducted one hundred interviews with devotees from all parts of the globe while they were at Puttaparthi. Extracts from these interviews underline the fact that they come from different religious traditions and different cultures, yet they appear to find no contradiction in being a devotee of Baba and claiming to be a Christian, a Buddhist, or what have you. We asked devotees about their religions, how they met Baba, and their attitudes before and after meeting him. We also asked them about themselves and their families, jobs, and lives in their own countries. We received a variety of responses, and the following sample indicates both their wide cultural base and their singular depth of devotion to Baba.

Grace, a nurse from Zanzibar, has been a self-proclaimed Baba devotee since 1995. For her, Jesus is "omnipresent." She told us that "being a Christian and being a devotee of Baba are not mutually exclusive positions. Belief in Baba does not mean I am not a believing Christian. Baba is Christ. He speaks my language and reads my mind. He told me to serve humanity and spread love."

Joule heads a Sai center in Holland and told us that there are over three thousand Dutch devotees of Baba. She believes that people of faiths other than Christianity are not respected in Holland, so she keeps her faith in Baba a secret from others when in Holland, only sharing it with other known Baba devotees. She believes that the holy trinity is Christ, Mother Mary, and Baba.

Chan, an eighteen-year-old student from Singapore, is a Puttaparthi tour guide for other East Asians. His mother and brother visit Baba at least twice a year and have been devotees for the past twelve years. His mother is divorced and owes her success in business to the blessings of Baba. She gives Baba at least 15 percent of her yearly income yearly and feels that his intervention will remove all problems from her life. Chan told us that his family was originally Buddhist, but they now believe in Baba as well.

Murthy is an Indian electronics engineer. He has his own business in steel fabrication and has been a Baba devotee for the past ten years. Problems in his business, which he could not solve, made him turn to Baba. His family now prefers to have marriage alliances with other Baba devotees, "as it is easier for them to understand us and vice versa."

Chithra Kishore is a nonresident Indian living in New York. She and her husband are both physicians and have been Baba devotees for eleven years. Chithra met Baba through friends in Hyderabad and turned to him when she had problems in her marriage. She has faith in his divinity and respects Baba for using the resources that he gets through his divinity to do charitable works. Chithra admitted that she is "disturbed" by his tendency to do magic but assured us that "he does them [manifestations] much less now."

After interviewing Baba devotees from many parts of the world, the two questions that occurred to us were, How is this relationship sustained between Baba and the devotee? and What is in Baba's message that it appeals across so many cultures?

Devotion by Long Distance

Since both transnational devotees and those from other parts of India can visit Puttaparthi only once or twice a year, they rely on visual images of Baba—videos, photographs, and sculpted images—to cement their relationship to him. Photographs of Baba are available everywhere in Puttaparthi and in the Sai centers around the globe. The one in Winnipeg, Canada, does a brisk business in Sai ephemera, as do the centers in Sydney and Munich.

Photographs of Baba often include a lithographic collage image referencing his mythic origin, and they trace the changing nature of his origin over the past twenty years. Earlier collages made visual links to Vishnu, Shiva, or his proclaimed "ancestor," Shirdi Sai Baba.[46] more recent ones superimpose pictures of a serene and smiling Baba over that of Jesus Christ. When we asked one of the poster vendors in Puttaparthi about his clients, he told us that he always displayed the Jesus posters to "foreigners" but saves the Shiva/Vishnu posters for Indian tourists.

The photo collages and other Sai ephemera are at the crux of globalization: how to maintain a recognizable locally based tradition while simultaneously connecting to a global community of devotees. The Sathya Sai Baba organization has been one of the most successful in walking this cultural globalization tightrope.

Unorganization as Alternate Organization

There is no central administration of the movement from India; the Sai organization in India does not connect with the regional centers worldwide, except when the devotees come to visit Baba. It is an informal organization based on devotee needs, and overseas centers are established according to those needs. We were told that the Sai center in Amsterdam originally operated from a devotee's garage but now rents a church basement on Thursdays to hold their meetings. Dutch devotees told us that they hoped to gather enough money to build a center of their own one day, and we heard similar stories from devotees in Perth, Santiago, and Munich.

Seemingly, globalization of the Sai Baba movement would require a vast network of organization and involve many people at various levels in the hierarchy, which is how most international religious movements are organized. However, the Sai Baba movement relies in large part on the initiative of the devotees to form the overseas centers, and the central Sai organization is not involved in the management of the overseas branches in any significant way. The overseas branches are managed from within, and connections between branches occur through members' personal friendships or over communication through the Internet. Sociologists and anthropologists claim that this lack of organization can only be a phase and that the movement will have to become organized and "rationalized" in order to function; nevertheless, the organization has remained in this state of creative unorganization for the past fifteen years and is growing everyday.

Syncretism by Inclusion

It appears from our study that the Sai movement is successful because it encourages syncretism and creates a community of shared belief through inclusiveness. Sathya Sai Baba encourages his devotees to stay within their own religious tradition, and in this he is unique. For example, Baba says, "I affirm all the names that Man uses for the adoration of the divine. . . . Continue your worship of your chosen God along the lines familiar to you. Then you will find that you are coming nearer and nearer to ME. . . . For all the names are mine and all the forms are mine."

Devotees therefore do not feel that they have to choose between different faiths: devotion to Baba is presented as a lifestyle choice, one that in no way threatens the devotee's original religious affiliation. Thus devotion to Baba is *merely added on to* the devotee's religious identity as an *enhancing* characteristic; religious identity becomes deeper and more layered, and the devotee can choose devotional patterns based on his or her environment—religious identity is fluid and is framed according to context and the need of the moment. Joule, the Dutch devotee, can therefore go to church on Sundays and worship Baba on Thursdays without feelings of guilt or anxiety.

This principle of syncretism by inclusion is in fact a fundamental characteristic of Hinduism.[47] The Baba movement derives its central meaning structure from Hinduism, and inclusion is a typical Hindu method for promoting ideas. Baba's syncretism structures the encounter between various religions in the minds of his devotes, and it enables them to create meaning within the encounter. It is an old argument that Hinduism engulfs and transforms every religion, philosophy, or idea that threatens it. Even so, it remains true in the case of the Baba movement.

Scholars of India may argue that India has exported religious thought to the West for the past several centuries in the form of new philosophies new sects and so on, and I would agree. What makes the Sai Baba movement different is the scale of the movement, and its centrality. Seventy million people joining a voluntary global movement cannot be ignored—this is no longer a marginal phenomenon.

Cultural Emissions and Emitters

The Sai Baba study revealed to us that India provided a rich civilizational base with resources for being what we termed a "cultural emitter." Technically, cultural emissions could be spread outward, regardless of the economic power of the country. But if the emitter country is poor and underdeveloped, as in the case of India, a mediator (usually an economically powerful country) assists the diffusion of the emission. However, when the emitter country achieves some sort of economic stability, the mediator is no longer necessary, and the emitter country gains self-consciousness as a potential cultural emitter. This emitter self-consciousness usually results in a restructuring of cultural concepts and institutions, incorporating the global and modern with the traditional and local. This is India's situation today.

The current state of globalization assumes a primary cultural emitter in the United States, surrounded by several receptor countries. However, it is crucial to the discussion of globalization to examine countries like India that, we believe, are in a position to become emitter countries.

THE INDIAN SILICON VALLEY

Though India's software industry[48] constitutes only 1 percent of the total world software industry, it is a case study of a single industry growing to an international standard[49] and being seen as a model to be emulated by other developing countries. The growth of the Indian software industry, whose exports topped $US2 billion in 1998 and are expected to be over $US6 billion by the year 2001,[50] raises some interesting questions regarding the nature of business in modern India: Is there anything "Indian" about business in India? Does being Indian help or hinder in the global business world? Lastly and perhaps most importantly, Can India convert this opportunity into a meaningful leap onto the world economic stage?

The industry is centered in Bangalore, with 55 percent of both international and Indian software firms headquartered in the city. The Bangalore cluster of industries has been the subject of special editions of the *London Financial Times,* the *Economist, Newsweek,* and the *Times of India.* It officially employs over five thousand engineers,[51] though unofficially over thirty-five thousand engineers are believed to live and work in there. We found it an ideal environment for studying a global industry with local effects.

Though Bangalore had become the center of high technology in India over the past decade, essential city services remained very poor. The city's infrastructure could not absorb the sudden growth the software cluster created, so everyday life in Bangalore is miserable, with frequent power cuts, traffic jams, and breakdowns in the water system. By 1996 fewer industries were locating in Bangalore, and Hyderabad, the capital city of the neighboring state of Andhra Pradesh, began challenging Bangalore's software industry dominance. The location of the Indian software industry is now seen as a regional prize, and south Indian states do battle, promoting their capital cities as cleaner and greener, in efforts to attract international capital.

One of the most famous and successful software companies in India is Bangalore-based Infosys Technologies. In 1999 it became the first Indian company to be traded on Wall Street and has been successful ever since. Issues relating to the Indian software industry will be discussed primarily in reference to the example of Infosys Technologies, an Indian-owned and operated business.

David and Goliath: The Local Hero in a Global Industry

Infosys of Bangalore is the industry leader in India and all, or nearly all, software engineers dream of being as successful and well liked as its founder and managing director, Narayan Murthy. We found that Infosys has a strong hold on India's public imagination and that Murthy was a highly admired role model for young businessmen, so it was one of the software companies we studied in detail.

Infosys began in 1980 with an initial investment of about $US300. The company based its structure on four main modules: education, technology, human resources, and infrastructure. Its original purpose was to train and use India's large pool of talented English-speaking engineers to provide cheap labor for the U.S. software industry's growing needs, a process called "body shopping." There is a twelve-hour time difference between Bangalore and California's Silicon Valley, and with improved communications technology, software could be produced on a twenty-four-hour basis at a significantly lower cost. Accordingly, Infosys became an offshore development center for the U.S. software industry, and over the next decade its revenues grew to over US$23 million.

But Infosys was quick to realize that other developing countries could and would provide increased competition to the Indian software industry if it continued to be based on body shopping. It therefore decided to begin developing its own software that it would sell globally, and the Indian software industry followed that lead. Infosys then changed its name to Infosys Technologies and built a campus-like corporate headquarters outside Bangalore in Electronics City. It has also bought many U.S. subsidiary companies and at the time of this writing was planning to buy several more. Infosys revenues grew from $2.64 million in 1991 to $39.59 million in 1997, at which time the company's net worth was approximately $500 million, and it had sixty-five hundred shareholders. It has grown even larger since then.

Infosys is an industry leader in not only growth and income but also management decisions and policies. At Infosys the emphasis is on the employee, who is fondly referred to as an "infoscion"—a marked contrast to what is seen as the typically corrupt, overbearing, and ineffectual Indian businessman. Narayan Murthy would be the first to admit that his policies are standard successful business policies around the world. However, Indians do not see his interest in employees' long-term loyalty and overall health and happiness merely as an effective business strategy, but as a modern extension of the old Indian patron–client relationship. Many parents, regardless of whether they know anything about modern business practices or the software industry, urge their children to apply for jobs: I have heard more than one tell their children, "Join

Murthy. He will take care of you. With him you will have nothing to worry about."

People in Bangalore see Narayan Murthy as a "local hero." Educated in Mysore and settled in Bangalore, he seems to take pride in his regional roots, and his interest in local affairs and his concern about Bangalore is very deep seated. For example, when a series of traffic accidents occurred on the Hosur road leading to his company, he donated several expensive jeeps and motorcycles to the city's police. He has also repeatedly told me that in spite of traveling all over the world, he is always happy to get back to Bangalore, a sentiment that is echoed by all his employees at Infosys. He has recently become mayor of Electronics City, and he advises the Karnataka and Indian governments on creating effective policies for technology development.

We interviewed non-software Bangalore professionals (e.g., lawyers, doctors) and asked them what they knew about Narayan Murthy's life and about his company. We found that they knew a great deal and took pride in his many accomplishments. They repeatedly told us that he was a multibillionaire in U.S. dollars but chose to live a middle-class life, retaining his two-bedroom home in a Brahmin suburb of the city. Reports that he is a teetotaler and a vegetarian and works long hours beside his employees have added to his mythical stature, even though the values of deferred gratification, hard work, and thrift, combined with an entrepreneurial spirit, are commonly associated with Protestantism in the West.[52]

When we interviewed him, the conversation drifted to his refusal to pay bribes to Bangalore customs to release new software or to pay protection money to the police. He is very proud of the fact that Infosys has "never paid a rupee in bribe and will never do so." But he told us that he felt that as a Bangalorean and an Indian he must do more for the city and the country. "It is not business as usual. We must see that our country moves forward."

The rooting of his identity in India and in Bangalore makes him an icon of Indian success: many young entrepreneurs look at him and feel a sense of pride in being Indian. Out of the one hundred Indian engineers we interviewed, over half told us they have chosen to stay in the country and contribute to growing India's economy because of his example. The careful maintenance of a local identity enables him to act as a spokesperson for the local, in spite of his also being part of a global industry.

The Next Generation: Migration, Money, and Marriage

Prior to 1989, it was common for Indian youngsters to try to "go abroad," either to study or to work. This was considered a valid ambition that would lead to upward social mobility, and in the early 1980s it seemed that every family in Bangalore had at least one family member in Dubai or the United States. But today, Indians prefer to stay in India. As one software engineer told me, "Twenty years ago, if you wanted to make it you had to go to the U.S.; now, you can stay at home and be a millionaire. So why would we go there? No family, no friends, no good food, nothing there for us."

Since 1982, the upper-income groups in the city have grown considerably. The wealth of these classes is not based on traditional land or bureaucratic office but on professional services.[53] The middle class is prominent in the city and is vociferous in demanding better services and goods and commodities, and software engineers are at the forefront of these groups. Young men and women with cell phones, laptops, and new cars are conspicuous. More than three hundred pubs in the central business district are packed on evenings and weekends with loud and noisy discussions of the latest change in management in Sunnyvale, Chicago, or Bangalore.

In addition, more and more women are finding employment in the software industry. As a result, software companies have become endogamous units, with the traditional intracaste marriages being replaced by intercaste and interreligious marriages. Of the hundred software engineers interviewed for this study, most stated that they would allow their parents to pick their partner, but in the same breath they confessed to liking a colleague and trying to work it out with their parents. Parents now have to deal with love marriages and office romances.

These changes do not, however, indicate that Indians are becoming more global in all aspects of their lives. For example, I visited several computer companies on Saraswati Puja Day, when Hindus traditionally worship the tools of their trade—their scissors, machines, cars, buses, and so on—for protection and prosperity. And I found that the computer terminals in these companies were in fact being worshiped. They were garlanded with flowers, and incense was placed before them. When I asked executives about this they told me, "It keeps the staff happy," but I frequently found that they too were wholeheartedly participating in the ritual. Indian software entrepreneurs have decided that they can remain culturally Indian and at the same time achieve economic success in the global marketplace. This has given them a sense of security about being Indian that they did not possess earlier.

Many scholars of India have commented on the Indian ability to shift between many different paradigms with no conflict. Wendy O'Flaherty refers to this as the "tool box mentality," in which the appropriate paradigm is used for the appropriate occasion. This layered thinking, along with a deep and abiding faith in God, seems to help Indians resolve the contradictions Westerners seem to face when encountering the same situations and choices. Milton Singer refers to this as the "dividual" (divided) self. Indians are used to a culturally plural society in which many different codes of conduct, values and belief systems coexist. They may not all be viewed equally, but they form part of the matrix of cultural templates. Indians therefore have access to many alternate cultural paradigms from within their own culture.

CONCLUSION

Two important examples of cultural globalization that were not mentioned in this chapter are the suicide of twenty-three cotton farmers in North Karnataka state after a crop failure and the international patent battle over the spice turmeric.

Globalization and Agriculture

Twenty-three cotton farmers in northern Karnataka committed suicide between December 1997 and May 1998.[54] They were deeply in debt to local moneylenders and had taken an "honorable" way out. Lured by the promise of higher yields and more money, the farmers invested in "foreign" seeds[55] and fertilizer, but their lack of specialty knowledge, combined with the failure of the monsoon, resulted in the total ruin of the crop and the farmers alike. The farmers committed suicide in the hope that government compensation would pay off the moneylender's debts and so prevent their children from having to become bonded laborers.

Small farmers within a forty-mile radius around Bangalore no longer want to grow rice or vegetables, only the cash crops of the global market: scented flowers for the French perfume industry, pickle gherkins, and cut tropical flowers for the European and U.S. flower markets.[56] New methods of agriculture, hybrid seeds, fertilizers, and an emphasis on productivity have displaced traditional, indigenous methods. But indigenous agricultural methods are tied into the local farmers' culture, so such displacements translate into shifts in the local culture. Globalization is changing the culture of agriculture, and for marginal farmers the consequences are disastrous.[57]

Biopiracy

Late in 1998, the *Times of India* (Delhi edition) reported that India was locked in an international patent battle over turmeric.[58] As background to the turmeric case, a Texas biologist four years earlier had created a laboratory strain of basmati rice that yielded more grains per seed head, which was patented internationally by the United States under the brand name "Texmati."[59] Indians were outraged by this American engineering and patenting of what was acknowledged to be a product of Indian culture. Following this, when the U.S. Patent Office granted a patent for the medicinal use of turmeric in 1995, the Indian government was determined not to lose the battle and hired a panel of ecological and biogenetic legal experts to fight "bio-piracy" in the international law courts. Since then, the patent has been withdrawn, but a new culture of international legal expertise that transcends national boundaries and deals with the ownership rights of civilizations and cultures has emerged to negotiate these issues.

Final Reflections

How, then, are we to think about cultural globalization? The predictions of a rise of a global underclass bear uncomfortable similarities with the old dependency theory debates. But the problems of the underclass continue to be the reality that policymakers in developing countries face.

This study suggests that we need to examine the current assumptions relating to cultural globalization. The first assumption is that cultural globalization is somehow inevitable and those who attempt to resist or reject it are fools. Other assumptions are that cultural globalization is inherently "good" and "desirable," and that the changes it brings in its wake must be accepted. We need to rethink what is meant by cultural globalization as a whole and view the process of cultural globalization critically.

Second, the data highlights the relationship between the global and local, and the hybrids that are created to bridge the gap. Are the two categories in a dialectical relationship to one another? Is this merely a reformulation of the old tradition and modernity debate?

Third, the study suggests that countries like India, with rich and deep civilizations, have potential cultural emissions, as well as potential alternate structures of modernity. But for a nation or civilization to become a cultural emitter, it appears that a cultural self-consciousness must be developed. The civilization must be made aware of its potential as an emitter country and must also view itself in relation to other civilizations. On the other hand, it appears that the movement toward certain cultural emissions, or certain emitter countries, is dictated by a complex system of factors: the political power of the emitter country in the global power balance, the economic power of the emitter country, the availability of human labor and technology, the aesthetic that is popular at the time, and the emitter country's cultural resources.

Furthermore, all cultural emitters will not be regarded equally, so a hierarchy of emitters may emerge, with "primary emitters" such as the United States operating on a global level and "secondary emitters" operating in the parts of the world they dominate culturally.

Finally, the study leaves us with some questions: What are the implications for understanding the process of cultural globalization? What does it mean when certain cultural emissions are accepted, and the social, political, and religious structure in which they are embedded is ignored? Is cultural globalization a cumulative, linear process, or will there be setbacks? I ask these questions to stress the need to view the process of cultural globalization carefully, completely, and critically.

NOTES

I am grateful to M. N. Srinivas for his selfless sharing of ideas and his gentle advice. To G. K. Karanth (Institute for Social and Economic Change, Bangalore) for ably guiding me. To M. N. Panini (Jawarhalal Nehru University, Delhi) for sharing his data on agribusiness in and around Bangalore. To Narayan Murthy, chairman, Infosys Technologies, for his time and help. To Roddam Narasimha, director of the National Institute of Advanced Studies, Bangalore, and his colleagues, especially Ms. Hamsa Kalyani and Mr. Aithal, for making me welcome and helping me in every way possible. To the research assistants, Mr. Srinivas, Ms. Dhanu Nayak, and Mr. Panigrahi, for their work. I am particularly grateful to Ms. Vijayalakshmi (ISEC) for her untiring work on Sai Baba and his devotees, and I gratefully acknowledge the many useful suggestions and comments received from Peter L. Berger, Samuel P. Huntington, Robert P. Weller, Lakshmi Srinivas, Michael M.J. Fischer,

Ann Bernstein, James Davison Hunter, Yunxiang Yan, Dr. Aoki, Hansfried Kellner, Arturo Fontaine Talavera, Michael Hsaio, János Kovács, and Fuat Keyman.

1. Peter L. Berger, "Four Faces of Global Culture," *National Interest,* Fall 1997.

2. Samuel P. Huntington, *The Clash of Civilizations and the Remaking of the World Order* (New York: Simon & Schuster, 1996).

3. Benjamin R. Barber, *Jihad versus McWorld: How Globalism and Tribalism Are Reshaping the World* (New York: Ballantine, 1995).

4. More recent conceptualizations of globalization and global culture have also tended to equate the process with homogenization of culture linked to Western, primarily American, economic and political domination.

5. S. N. Eisenstadt, ed., "Multiple Modernities," *Daedalus,* December 1999.

6. "Over Ten Million Americans Practice Yoga," *Los Angeles Times,* 20 August 2000.

7. The Ayurvedic Clinic in Kassel offers *abhyanga,* (harmonizing massage with herbal oils), *shirodhara* (oil applied to the forehead for vegetative harmonization), *ushnasnana* (Ayurvedic sweating cure), *basti* (regulation of intestinal system), *virechana* (harmonization of entire digestive system), and *padabhyanga* (simple Ayurvedic foot reflex zone massage, harmonizing, and regenerating). See *www.ayurveda-klinik.de.*

8. M. N. Srinivas, *On Living in a Revolution and Other Essays* (Delhi: Oxford University Press, 1992), pp. 76–77.

9. The current literature on modernity and globalization takes one of two positions: Fukuyama's "end of history" idea or Huntington's "clash of civilizations."

10. Researchers of food traveled to Delhi, Bombay, and Madras. Frequent trips were made to the Sai Baba ashram in Puttaparthi and to North Karnataka and Goa to examine the nature of global agribusiness.

11. Emma Duncan, "The Tiger Steps Out; A Survey of India," *Economist,* 21 January 1995.

12. The Indian middle class numbers approximately 250 million and is growing. The Indian middle-class consumer is being courted by global companies, a situation that was unthinkable ten years ago.

13. "Think Globally, Program Locally," *Business Week,* bonus issue on twenty-first-century capitalism, 1994, pp. 186–189.

14. Ulf Hannerz: "My sense is that the world system rather than creating massive cultural homogeneity on a global scale, is replacing one diversity with another; and the new diversity is based relatively more on interrelations and less on autonomy." In James Clifford, *The Predicament of Culture* (Cambridge: Harvard University Press, 1988), p. 17.

15. James Watson, ed., *Golden Arches East: McDonald's in East Asia* (Stanford: Stanford University Press, 1997), pp. 36–37; Yunxiang Yan, "McDonald's in Beijing: The Localization of Americana, in *Golden Arches East,* pp. 56–61.

16. "While the Indian economy grew at over 7.5 percent a year in the mid-1990s, the proportion of Indians living in poverty dropped just one percentage point between 1993–1994 . . . ages for unskilled workers rose by 2.5 percent in real terms during the 1990s." See "Indian Poverty and the Numbers Game," *Economist,* 29 April 2000.

17. See James Hunter's chapter in this volume.

18. Sunil Khilnani, *The Idea of India* (Harmondsworth, U.K.: Penguin, 1997), p. 10.

19. Khilnani, *Idea of India*, p. 60.

20. In 1947, when the British left India, they bequeathed to India a large bureaucratic system, which grew to gigantic proportions under Nehru's Soviet-inspired five-year economic plans. In the 1980s, with the Iran-Iraq war and the slow collapse of the Soviet market, India fell into a foreign exchange crisis and the government was close to bankruptcy. This economic impasse led to urgently needed economic reforms. Then finance minister Manmohan Singh instituted a slow but steady liberalization of the Indian economy. The caution of Singh's gradual opening of the Indian economy enabled India to avoid the recent economic downturn that affected the rest of Asia.

21. By May 2000, inflation had crept up to 5.8 percent. *Economist*, 13 May 2000.

22. *Economist*, 13 May 2000.

23. Rashtriya Sevak Sangh (RSS) is a right-wing pro-Hindu organization with links to the BJP.

24. The most recent attempt was the coalition formed by Sonia Gandhi and the Tamil Nadu opposition leader J. Jayalalitha, who passed a no-confidence motion in the ruling coalition government headed by the BJP in 1998, forcing the entire country to go to the polls. The BJP coalition was reelected.

25. "Ever More Dangerous Kashmir," *Economist*, 19 June 1999, p. 32.

26. "During Mr. Clinton's six-day tour of Asia, most of it spent in India, the United States came closer than ever before to endorsing India's view of the region's main conflict." See "Will Pakistan Get Any Closer to Clinton?" *Economist*, 1 April 2000, p. 37.

27. *Deccan Herald*, June 17, 1997.

28. Lentil crepe eaten with chutney as a popular breakfast snack.

29. Malini Goyal, "Big Mac versus Indian Pop Tates," *Economic Times*, 27 March 1998.

30. Watson, *Golden Arches East.*

31. "It's Mac, the Desi Snack," *Outlook*, 20 July 1998.

32. Bacchi Karkeria, "Mac Maharaja," *Times of India*, 10 November 1998, Bangalore ed.

33. I am indebted to Lakshmi Srinivas for this argument.

34. Watson, *Golden Arches East.*

35. Peter Fuhrman and Michael Schuman, "Now We Are Our Own Masters," *Forbes*, 23 May 1994.

36. Over the past decade MTR has become a global brand of food products. Initial preparation takes place in the factories in and around Bangalore, and the products are shipped to over forty countries where Indians in the diaspora live.

37. In a survey of three *Darshinis* in different parts of the city, we found roadwork gangs, auto-rickshaw drivers, housewives with children, teachers, students, and shopkeepers eating there.

38. I am indebted to Robert P. Weller for this phrase.

39. M. N. Srinivas, *Essays on Modernisation of Underdeveloped Societies* (Bombay: Thacker, 1971), p. 153.

40. Watson, *Golden Arches East.*

41. The 70 million number, which I doubt, was given to me by the Sathya Sai Baba organization in Puttaparthi. The 20 million number is from a 27 November 2000 *India Times* article on the Sai Baba movement.

42. Two of the gods of the Hindu trinity. Shiva is the god of destruction and Vishnu of creation.

43. Since the 1970s, Indian scientists and other rationalists have tried to expose Sai Baba as a charlatan.

44. Sophie Hawkins, "Bordering Realism: The Aesthetics of Sai Baba's Mediated Universe," in C. Brosius and M. Butcher, eds., *Image Journeys: Audio-Visual Media and Cultural Change in India* (New Delhi: Sage, 1999), pp. 142–156.

45. Baba can be seen early in the morning and at four o'clock in the afternoon. In between he receives private visitors.

46. A Muslim mystical fakir who was believed to be the lost son of high-caste Hindu parents.

47. I am grateful to Adam Seligman for sharing with me a chapter entitled "Inclusivism and Tolerance" by Wilhelm Halbfauss in *India and Europe: An Essay in Understanding* (Albany: SUNY Press, 1981). Halbfauss quotes a scholar by the name of Paul Hacker who used the term "inclusivism" to describe the rationale of tolerance in Hinduism.

48. Bangalore was first named "the Indian Silicon Valley" in a *Time* magazine article, 14 March 1994, p. 32.

49. Edward A. Gargan, "India among Leaders in Software for Computers," *New York Times,* 29 December 1993.

50. The industry expects India's software exports, now growing at an annual clip of 50 percent, to top $6.3 billion in the financial year to March 2001, up from $4.0 billion last year. Global consultants McKinsey and Company said last year that, aided by appropriate initiatives, infrastructure, and policies, the software and allied services sector would account for 2.2 million jobs by 2008, exceeding the current level by over 340,000.

51. V. N. Balasubramaniam and Ahalya Balasubramaniam, "Bangalore Is Where the Action Is" (unpublished manuscript).

52. Max M. Weber, *The Protestant Ethic and the Spirit of Capitalism* (London: Tavistock, 1993).

53. Sunil Khilnani, *The Idea of India* (Harmondsworth, U.K.: Penguin, 1997).

54. A. R. Vasavi, "Agrarian Distress in Bidar: Market, State, and Suicides," *Economic and Political Weekly,* 7 August 1999, 2263–2268.

55. Multinational seed companies such as Monsanto and Cargill have been in the Indian market since the early 1980s, but their presence has been highlighted recently due to the emphasis on agribusiness.

56. All the data on agriculture and agribusiness is drawn from "From Agriculture to Agribusiness: A Sociological Study of the Impact of Economic Liberalization," by M. N. Panini of Jawaharlal National University Delhi (unpublished manuscript).

57. A. R. Vasavi, "Hybrid Times, Hybrid People: Culture and Agriculture in South India," *Man,* June 1994, pp. 283–300.

58. Turmeric is a root that has been used in Indian cooking and medicine for several hundred years.

59. Texmati and its family of rice, Jasmati and Kasmati, are all genetically engineered products of Alvin Rice Technologies, Inc., in Texas.

PART TWO

Globalization and Regional Subglobalization

5

Cultural Globalization in Germany

Hansfried Kellner and Hans-Georg Soeffner

Foreign visitors to the western part of the Federal Republic are frequently amazed by the degree to which Germany's political, economic, and social cultures resemble those of the United States. It appears to many that Germany, more than any other Western society, is in the vanguard of an emerging global order, and that one has to make special efforts to discover cultural and social traits peculiar to an older Germany. Though one can still identify remnants of the brisk, orderly, but nevertheless cozy ways in which German life was conducted in the past (people are often tempted to compare it to a well-tooled and smoothly running Swiss clock), the new overlay of global gloss and high technology makes it difficult to identify what is uniquely German today.

To foreigners and Germans alike the trademark "Made in Germany" continues to signal high standards, reliability, and solid workmanship, all qualities that are held to be the traditional hallmark of Germanness. Yet there is an awkward mixture of the old and the new. The image of Biedermeier furniture placed in Le Corbusier structures of steel and glass suggests itself here. Nevertheless, tourists still find the traditional regionally designed pieces of folkloristic styles: the Bavarian lederhosen and Oktoberfest, the Rhenish carnival and wine villages, the Saxonian Christmas loaf, and so on. However, the local and regional peculiarities, relics of former small states and princedoms and equally part of the modern German federal system, are changing their faces under the impact or the rejection of globalizing cultural patterns. In this respect, regionalization trends are present, as almost anywhere else in the European Union, albeit not as strong as in France, Spain, or the United Kingdom.

Independent of this general trend, a specific German cultural borderline of the "old states" (the "old" Federal Republic of Germany—FRG) and the "new states" (the "former" German Democratic Republic—the DDR or GDR) can still be observed, even though the cultural differences between these two regions are constantly decreasing. Visitors who ventured into the eastern part of Germany after the country's reunification in 1990 were struck by the conspicuous differences between the two on all levels of society, and after forty-five years of existence in the Soviet orbit, the contrast between the Federal Republic and the former German Democratic Republic was pronounced and disquieting to many. In the West everything appeared to be high gloss, ultramodern, and dynamic; in the East everything was rundown, drab, and stagnant. Despite these "mildewed" qualities, however, older, more nostalgically inclined West Germans found the East to be "a Germany without America." And indeed, this non-American Germany carries on its own life; for instance, in old sentimental films idealizing traditional regional settings from the 1930s up to the 1950s, which are broadcast by MDR, the leading East German TV channel.

The contrast between the two Germanys dramatically brings to the fore the degree to which the country has changed over the past five decades. When international structural data are used to compare the Federal Republic before 1990 with other European countries, it becomes clear that at the turn of the millennium Germany is a "lead" society in every imaginable way. In the indexes of modernization, for instance, Germany competes with Japan for second place after the United States. The forces of modernization and globalization have undoubtedly been particularly virulent in their work here, and after the transfer of massive capital sums and technological know-how they have even begun to make inroads into the eastern part of Germany as well. Visually at least, the German East is beginning to resemble the West.

There can be no doubt that German culture has been open to the forces of globalization to a particular degree. Although Germany has been in the forefront of technological and scientific modernization since the turn of the nineteenth century, its extraordinary receptivity to global forces is of a more recent standing. Since the end of World War II giant waves of globalization have washed over the Federal Republic, serving to transform all levels of German society perhaps even more radically than those of other comparable European nations. This peculiar German openness to the forces of globalization can only be understood against the background of the trauma of the Nazi era and the collapse of the country at the end of the disastrous war that it waged against its neighbors.

Politically, the western part of the country, the Federal Republic of Germany, had to reconstruct itself from the ground up. After factious internal debates it opted to take Western liberal democracy, particularly in its American form, as its guiding model. Renouncing all manifestations of a dangerously corrupted nationalism that a growing number of Germans believed were responsible for the country's demise, the new German constitution tried to safeguard the Western-style democratic understandings of the role of the state. Domestically, it promoted the rights of the individual, the rule of law, and the practice of justice on all levels of society; internationally, it moved the Federal Republic toward the adoption and promotion of supranational political conceptions and political mechanisms.

It is a well-established historical fact that as of the mid-1950s the Federal Republic defined itself as a major carrier of the principles underlying the Atlantic Alliance, and in subsequent decades it emerged as the chief promoter of the European Community. This course of action firmly established the politics of democracy in the Federal Republic, which, with all their ups and downs, have served the country well for close to fifty years. It also propelled the FRG toward reconciliation with its neighbors and embedded its foreign policy in a network of multilateral institutions. In fact, the Federal Republic sees itself today as the model of liberal democracy that, with its promises for a safer and more rewarding political future, deserves to be emulated by other countries.

Economically, at the end of World War II, Germany had to start from scratch. With the country divided, its chief industries destroyed and masses of refugees from the east flooding into its domain, it was compelled to act quickly and efficiently. Yet the destruction of its former industrial enterprises and the dismantling of entire industrial complexes to pay reparations to countries that had suffered from Germany's irresponsible expansionism necessitated a fundamental reconstruction of the German economy. This emphasis on the development and installation of more advanced and highly productive industries provided Germany with a competitive edge vis-à-vis its European neighbors in subsequent decades.

Much of the reconstruction was kicked off by the infusion of Marshall Plan funds, and the country benefited from the support and supply of U.S. technical know-how in the early years after the war. Within a decade after the end of the war it was already possible to speak about "the German Economic Miracle" (das Wirtschaftswunder). The restructuring of the economy was designed along lines of pure economic efficiency, and the soziale Marktwirtschaft (social market economy), the long cherished hallmark of the German economy, put into place a union-sponsored economic model that allowed for workers' participation in matters of industrial relations and guaranteed that they would share in the profits.

It is this fusion of free enterprise, social participation, and sharing that distinguished West Germany from the realities produced by the command economies of the socialist East. It also greatly helped inoculate West Germans against the promises of messianic communism. Their astounding economic success provided Germans with a new confidence and helped change Germany's pariah status among nations, while an objectified "quasi-sacrilized" Deutschemark served the country as a surrogate for a politically eroded nationalism.

Culturally, the prototypical openness of German culture to the forces of globalization must be explained against the background of tortured confrontations with the country's political and military past. On the cultural level as well, the trauma of the Nazi past induced a quest for a new national self-understanding and an intensified search for cultural forms that could provide legitimate foundations and expressions of new cultural styles. Intellectual elites, for their part, tried to locate such foundations in supranational principles guided by an ethic of a philosophical universalism. The motto Nie Wieder ("Never Again": nationalism, militarism, racism, Holocaust) emerged as a collective imperative and soon resounded through all available forms of communication, be it party platforms, institutions of education, and in all sorts of intellectual discourses and events.

It is precisely in this respect that the crimes, riots, and parades of the comparatively small, radical right-wing groups and skinhead gangs that have recently occurred (particularly in East Germany) are highly irritating to the representatives of the intellectual discourses and the wider political public. These right-wing movements, however, are organizationally and ideologically different from historic forms of Nazism and have to be regarded as expressions of newer trends in the rejection of modernization and globalization. Even so, most public reactions culminate in a helpless surprise and lead to the befuddled question, How could this relapse into barbarism occur, in spite of all the educational efforts in schools, universities, and the mass media? Viewed soberly, however, a resurgence of German Nazism cannot really be spoken of.

The specific role and development of postwar mass media in both parts of Germany constituted the background of these reactions. State-owned broadcasting and television understood their activities as "educational tasks." Many media representatives considered themselves advocates of "the" public conscience and their media as "the stage as moral institution," following Schiller's motto. Even when the state monopoly in broadcasting and television was replaced by a system of both private- and state-owned channels (FRG 1984), the moral and educational attitude of media representatives with respect of how to cope with the Nazi past on the whole did not change. In recent years, questions of "Europeanization" and "globalization" in some ways seem to provide an antidote against nationalist fundamentalism and thus are strongly supported.

On the more popular level, modern means of communication found an astoundingly fertile ground for the promotion of global cultural products that began to flood the countries of the West in the postwar era. West German youth were distinguished by an aversion to the appearance of being "provincial hicks" mired in antiquated and suspect German cultural styles. Slogans such as the demand to leave the *Muff von tausend Jahren* (the German mildew) were very popular among the young. In this sense it can be argued that the imperative to be cosmopolitan became an integral part of the cultural physiognomy of the new West German citizen. In addition, the presence of an extraordinarily large number of foreign guest workers made necessary by the country's burgeoning economy greatly enhanced Germany's emerging polyglot multiculturalism.

In Germany as elsewhere, "ethnic neighborhoods" and "cultural ghettoization" increasingly characterize urban centers. Both were caused by continuous waves of immigrant labor, civil war refugees, and asylum seekers. No other European society in the latter half of the twentieth century faced the kind and magnitude of population movements experienced by the Federal Republic of Germany.[1] This fact remains mostly unknown abroad and is glossed over by conservative politicians' claims that Germany is "not a country of immigration." Germany's growing multiculturalism was driven even further by the well-known love of Germans for trips abroad.

A comparison with cultural developments in the German East again reveals the extent and depth of the cultural transformation that has occurred in the Federal Republic since the end of World War II. The the wall erected between the two Germanys kept East Germans in place and also protected them—for better and for worse—from the forces of globalization. The citizens of the German East were compelled to adapt themselves to the downside of the political and economic divide, while West Germans greatly benefited from the upside.

Twelve years of Nazi dictatorship followed by forty-five years of life under a communist regime made for an uneasy continuation of the centralist norms and values of Germany's authoritarian past. In East Germany there was an apparently seamless transition from the war command economy of the Nazi regime to Easy Germany's socialist command economy and from one form of totalitarianism to the next. Though the mass media were able to transcend political borders and whetted the East German desire and taste for Western products and, to some degree, for cultural expressions and notions, the East German command economy in collusion with its centralist authoritarian politics prevented East Germans from acquiring them.

Thus East Germany was turned into a culturally inward-looking society absorbed primarily by itself. The agitprop (ideological bombardment) typical of communism helped produce an odd cultural mix in which global desires for material goods competed with a romanticized rejection of the same. Deprived of the benefits of globalism, so-called small life world and economic niche existences (accompanied by gray market syndromes) developed on the level of everyday life. A general withdrawal from the dynamism of global modernism was its most distinctive feature. The term *innere Emigration,* which characterized parts of German bourgeois life under Nazism, applied to what occurred in East Germany under communism, only this time on a much broader social scale.

Though the reunification of the country appeared to open up long waited new opportunities for the citizens of the German East, the cultural forms that had gained a foothold during the communist era prevented them from making skillful use of them. The habits and cognitive styles they had acquired during these long and difficult years could not easily be translated into those required for flourishing in the new global cultural order. While East German cultural habits now, after painful conflict, appear to have started to slowly approximate those of West Germany, all the data indicate that considerable differences remain between the two, despite the massive transfer of money to the East that undoubtedly helped speed up the process of economic adaptation.

In addition to the already mentioned economic and political differences between West and East Germany, there are four other reasons for the emergence of a particular East German cultural mentality, including the lack of immigration from abroad, the lack of freedom of the press, and the lack of possibilities for tourism during the communist period.

The fourth reason continues to exert an impact today: the religious agnosticism caused by the socialist educational system and the equally antiecclesiastical and antireligious official policy over a period of forty-five years, in which a generational religious lag occurred.[2] Only 10 percent of East Germans consider themselves religious, which is unique for Europe if not for the entire world. In consequence, neither everyday life nor the life passages of East German citizens are associated with church or religion as they used to be in the "old Germany." Other traits of old Germany, however, have been retained, such as traditional choral societies; *Schrebergärten* (allotment gardens), disguised during GDR times as *dadcha* culture, and all sorts of homeland sentiments. These flourish much more strongly in East Germany.

Leaving the continuing cleavage between East and West Germany aside, it can be concluded that there is an understanding and a vision of global modernity in the German Federal Republic today that is based on constitutional democracy, trust in the superiority of a socially responsible free market system, and a pronounced respect for human rights. As a matter of fact, this understanding has taken on measures of a unanimous "civil religion" among the intellectual, political, and economic elites of Germany and the wider public beyond.

However, these pillars of the postwar German cultural creed have come increasingly under fire in recent years. What moves the German public today are passionately expressed concerns for the need to reconcile, or balance out, the benefits of global markets and modern technology with its real or assumed losses. Added to these growing concerns are preoccupations with the custodial care of nature and the environment, which to many appear to be endangered by the uncontrolled expansion of industries responsible to no one but themselves.

Two separate though connected sets of issues dominate present-day public debates about the German future. In the first set are society-level issues that revolve around the need to find a cultural identity that does not easily dissolve into the homogenized mass of globalism, though a multicultural way of life is embraced by many. The second set revolves around such questions as (1) how to guarantee and further issues of human rights, (2) how to channel and control a socially responsible free market, (3) how to develop mechanisms for the responsible care of the environment, and (4) how to promote ethically responsible technological innovation.

As already pointed out, Germans, who are well aware of the burdens of their troubled past, have long tried to map out their international agenda within a European context, and their concerns have taken on a heightened significance in recent years. To implement an emerging European vision, mostly with Germany and France at its core, Germany has been seeking to rally potential partners. What unites them is the task of devising a course of globalization that is not entirely dominated by the overshadowing power of America. Their overarching aim, however vaguely and even contradictorily defined, is to carve out a distinctly European cultural identity. To this end, it will be necessary to establish institutions that are strong and enduring enough to foster the process in an institutionally controlled way. Many hope that already existing European institutions can be used for this purpose, though in some cases new ones may have to be designed.

Although the political unity of Europe—in contradistinction to its economic unity—may be some time in coming, it is strongly hoped that the existing web of distinctly European institutions will be able to take over the capacity to steer and guide that that the individual nation-states have lost in the globalization process. Therefore, if the question of the role of the state is placed in the global context, visions of a political and institutional unity going beyond the economic are the central issue of the German future and, by extension, that of Europe as well.

GLOBALIZATION EXAMINED

In order to delineate the contours of globalization in some detail, the German research teams decided to conduct three separate research efforts.[3] The first sought to identify and describe the existence of a Davos culture by examining the dispersion of the global managerial lingua franca among German business managers. The second addressed questions of German intellectual elites with respect to their traditions, current perspectives, and visions of the future. The third focused on the emergence of forms of cultural self-representation in German mass events and the media.

The Diffusion of the Lingua Franca of Global Business among Managers in West and East Germany

The linguistic structure of the German business elite was studied in considerable detail in order to determine the degree to which a conceptually global framework in business has emerged and how it has interpenetrated managers' daily use of language and their understanding of how to conduct business in the emerging global order. The contours of the constitutive features of this framework and their embodiment in language form the model of a lingua franca for global managers. Its emergence and forms of acceptance in the German West and the German East highlights not only the intricate shifts of meaning in doing business in the global order over the past decades but also the differences between the two Germanys on this level.

From the outset it is important to note that the phenomenal globalization of business has engendered the emergence of a distinctive communicative world among business managers and entrepreneurs. Whether managers are of U.S. or German origin, they are united by very distinctive understandings of what it means to conduct business in the global context. In all likelihood, this now applies to all top business managers all over the world.

The use of English, mostly in its American form, is a basic element of the global communicative world and hence of Germany. It would be a mistake, however, to regard English as *the* lingua franca of the modern global world solely on the basis of its overt lexical structure. The use of this language, by Americans or Germans, refers to the application of an arsenal of particular technological terminologies (often of American origin as well), and, more importantly, it implies acquisition of shared schemes of understanding and interpretation of the purpose of management itself. Our study found that although contemporary English and German business-language usage are superficially distinct, on the structural level of their semantic meanings they are astoundingly similar.

During the past decades, the language basis of business communication in the United States and in Germany has gone through distinct phases of development that can be traced through shifts in meaning that have led to common forms of understanding. For instance, terms such as "success," "effort," "achievement," "contribution," and so on, and their German equivalents *Erfolg, Anstrengung, Leistung,* and *Beitrag,* continue to be used in long established ways, yet the schemes of their meaning and interpretation no longer signify the same things. An example here may illustrate the degree of the shift that has taken place.

Whereas in the l950s and l960s the themes of business, particularly in Germany, leaned heavily toward the more administrative aspects of management, in more recent decades the themes have shifted toward entrepreneurship. For instance, in the earlier period, the management vocabulary (and this applies to many terms beyond those given above) was geared toward an understanding that saw the purpose of business in the optimization of existing resources; in the later period, however, the emphasis is on the redirection of given resources away from present yields (regardless of whether they are flourishing, diminishing, or low) toward new areas of activities deemed to have a potential future. This redirection implies that present-day business managers are encouraged to make existing resources obsolete in favor of measurable promising future results. As our study found out, this shift is strongly reflected in both the ordinary and technical language they use.

To apprehend what is involved in the new understanding of doing business, it is important to realize that old strategies for doing business have been replaced by mind-sets that require a focused attempt to use available resources for the purpose of uncovering new fields of actions for doing business. To be sure, important aspects of the older, established strategies have not been abandoned completely (after all, the business of business is business), yet the emphasis now is on the need to stake out objectives that allow for the expansion of already available and efficiently operating business ventures.

These business ventures may themselves relate to the management of finance, production, design, services, and so on, yet the way they are managed is now geared toward potential future demands. This implies, therefore, that more than a simple identification of customers is at issue. The innovative aspect of doing global business comprises the identification of factual customers as well as the assessment of the viability of the imagined needs attributed to them.

In this context the utility of brand names gains a great deal of importance. The manager's objective is to prompt customers to associate their potential (frequently yet to be stimulated) needs with a specific brand name and to rationally assess whether a "critical mass" can be created to do business on a large scale. The importance of the use of brand names in doing business today implies that that competition is less about price than about the triumph of images.

Here the trade wars between different brand names of blue jeans come to mind. Selling what is essentially the same garment means selling an image. In the shopping arena it is less price differences that compete than the images they signify for the customer. Though the engineered quality of a given product remains important, its quality in the global market is increasingly derived from the need horizon of the customer. The "trick" of the manager is to see the quality of the product within the context of that market. "Effective" marketing in the global arena requires the manager to fuse the two—the engineered and the imagined—and to stimulate large groups of customers to do the same, ideally on a global scale.

The "need" for upscale Gucci bags, for instance, is similar today in Hong Kong, Paris, Cairo, New York, Munich, and Rome. The Italian-based House of Gucci apparently has uncovered a need in individuals that make their bags globally attractive. Furthermore, since Gucci bags are quite pricey, many attempts are made to pirate the Gucci label and sell imitation bags at considerably lower cost worldwide.

Clearly, marketing has become *the* important dimension of the global business culture. Accordingly, modern business language is highly fused with marketing terminology on all planes. Issues that were once important in successfully selling on the market, such as export-import ratios, are no longer the foremost concern of today's managers. What matters in the global market is the emergence and acceptance of a customer's identification with a given product and the recognition of its diverse qualities in different regions of the world. Modern marketing on the global level is not merely a matter of the art of salesmanship. Though it is still important, the task now is to target the creation of markets themselves. In other words, "global" managers are expected not to be creatures of markets but their creators.

Another fundamental transformation of doing business on a global scale that has occurred in recent decades, be it in Germany, the United States, or any other aspiring competitive country, relates to the shift of managerial standards of organizational and self-evaluation. The term "synergy," massively used in contemporary business language, aptly describes the synchronization of the diverse elements involved in the organization of a firm and its personnel if a company wants to become successful on the global market.

Yet synergy does not fall from heaven. It has to be created and managed organizationally, and effectively synchronizing the various activities and divisions of a firm is the major task of modern global managers. Instead of organizing management in long tested hierarchical ways, which was particularly the case in Germany in previous decades, the management of synergy requires that top managers today cut across hierarchical lines and organize the company's activities along horizontal lines. This implies that the various aspects of a business venture have to be managed in novel ways that include the cross-fertilization of ideas and new levels of communication, cooperation, and network synchronization. The aim is to speed up both managerial and creative processes and to establish high overall standards of performance.

Furthermore, the pride and allegiance of professionals—frequently referred to as the "knowledge workers" in recent literature—should no longer be primarily determined by the standards of their profession. Rather, these should be tuned to and fused with the objectives, tasks, and allegiances of the firm. The contributions of individual professionals, therefore, have to be increasingly considered in terms of their overall performance for the firm. This shift also implies that it no longer suffices for managers to evaluate the contributions of their professional staff in terms of the quality of their work. Their contribution to the firm's overall performance and objectives must be analyzed. Again, the contemporary use of common terms like "success," "effort," "achievement," and "contribution" reflect this shift in meaning.

In this connection, it has to be pointed out that firms operating in the global market are making use of new strategies and measures of personnel development. Such procedures have little to do with the issues personnel departments have traditionally been charged with handling. What is at stake for firms and managers today is to recognize what is subsumed under the term "synergy" and to act in line with its imperatives.

One managerial task and bit of conceptual rhetoric that is writ large in this context are the terms "team" and "teamwork development." What is aimed at here are clusters of teams that follow a product from the beginning of its development to its end in the market and the integration of their energies into a well-functioning whole; that is, the "synergizing" all levels of actions involved. Teamwork development tasks of this kind demand high-level, simultaneous intertwining of the capacities for designing, planning, scheming, engineering, and organizing. The ability to create an organizational environment for the purpose of encouraging such inspired forms of collaboration has now become a precondition for success. In fact, the "teamwork development" concept stands at the core of what is commonly referred to as "corporate culture" and "corporate identity." In sum, being a successful corporate manager today means being a virtuoso performer of all these required tasks at the same time. This holds true for all global managers, and German managers operating on a global scale are no exception to this rule.

After the reunification of Germany in 1990, one of the foremost tasks for the united country was to reconstruct the East German world of firms and their economic culture along the lines of the global standards already governing business in the West. This required transforming a command economy into a market economy or, to put it more concretely, dismantling Soviet-type *Kombinat* structures and reorganizing them into entrepreneurial corporate enterprises. Needless to say, this process encountered numberless difficulties and produced a high degree of frustration and lingering grievances on the part of all involved.

This task of reconstruction was organized on the governmental as well as the private level. Our studies of the transformation process of the East German management culture brought a wealth of information to the fore, and from the data gained by means of experience and research the following key points stand out.

From early on, the need to retrain former East German *Kombinat* managers arose as a central task. To operate in a market economy obviously requires some knowledge of how a modern market operates. East German managers, directors, and engineers, however, had little and frequently erroneous knowledge about how markets function. Their abilities had been honed in terms of administrative/bureaucratic skills, and they were accustomed to operating in hierarchically organized command structures. The professional side of work in East Germany was measured by standards of professional quality, and these professionals—in particular the engineers and scientists—took great pride in being highly qualified professionals. As a matter of fact, on the level of professional standards, East German engineers and scientists commanded professional know-how that was equal to that of their Western counterparts. At the same time, however, they were blissfully ignorant of what it takes to operate successfully in a market economy.

Training programs organized by West German managers and professionals, channeled through West German firms, banks, and governmental agencies, were set up to familiarize East German managers and professionals with the knowledge required for doing business in a market economy. It soon became evident that while the trainees were certainly "efficient" in the sense of administration and engineering, they had great difficulties in translating their skills into the market "effectiveness" described above.

For instance, engineers typically assumed that the quality of a product is all that matters—that quality in and of itself is all that was required to conquer a market. Even after East Germans had been trained in the use of sales techniques, they continued to be seriously wanting in marketing savvy. Beyond the acquisition of the necessary terminology, the requirement of identifying customers, locating them, and reaching them, or, heaven forbid, developing customer needs, left East German professionals helpless. What they were still lacking after massive efforts of training was precisely the forms of conceptualization, scheming, fantasizing, and so forth that have been found to be essential for becoming "effective" players in the market and in the global market a fortiori. As matters stand today, the marketing divisions of East German firms still have to be heavily staffed by West Germans. Here as elsewhere, it has become evident that modern management cannot be learned in the schoolroom, even though the instruction may be the most inspired yet. That practice and experience matter holds particularly true when the tasks to be performed require the "whole" person.

East German professionals and managers were found to be generally resistant to training programs that sought to impart knowledge and skills for the development of synergy. In particular, the imperative to communicate and synchronize horizontally, which is so essential for teamwork effectiveness, met with a high degree of suspicion. They often argued that Western-style personnel development programs were simply another version of the ideological bombardment they had been compelled to endure under communism: "Work brigade devices of the communist command economy have already acquainted us with similar strategies" was the typical reaction to such attempts.

East German professionals working in the economic arena had become accustomed to delivering "solid" work during their working hours and withdrawing into their private world afterward. The demands of an emerging global business culture to energize one's efforts beyond the boundaries of the world of work, to internalize the habits of "effective" global management, and to think in strategic terms of the synergy required at this level of business remain a difficult challenge for East German business managers, at least the older generation, to master. All of this will take time, as these new dimensions of doing business in the modern era can only be acquired in an experienced, living reality. There are signs, however, that the younger generation of East Germans is catching on quite rapidly.

German Intellectual Elites: Between Tradition, Europeanization, and Globalization

Seen from a historical bird's-eye view, the development of intellectual elites and their influence on German national culture demonstrates how decisive the events in 1945 were, even if their consequences only surfaced toward the end of the 1960s. The nineteenth and the beginning of the twentieth centuries saw both the conservative and reform-minded elites in Germany recruiting themselves from the ranks of the educated bourgeoisie and the nobility. Corporate executives, military elites, and civil servants in essence came from the same social origins, as well. The advancement and integration of German Jews formed part of this structure. With the exception of a few "internationalisms," such as the socialist workers movement being part of the Socialist Internationale and the religious denominations adhering to ecumenical institutions, the German elites pursued national visions. This in principle was as true for the reform movements (like the *Wandervögel*, the youth movements, and the *Reformpädagogik*) that originated in German Romanticism as it was for nationalist, conservative circles. Though the former and the latter had different philosophical views and visions of society, their concepts were nevertheless framed by the idea of the nation.

The Third Reich simultaneously unified and put an end to these visions. The führer's plans and racial theories, and the dream of a greater German Reich, merged into a contradictory and destructive entity that absorbed parts of the reform movements. The youth movement turned into the *Hitlerjugend* and the *Bund Deutscher Mädel*, the socialist workers organizations were transformed into the *Volkswohlfahrt* and the *Reichsarbeitsdienst*, and the churches saw the formation of the *Deutsche Christen*. The führer acted in a similar manner when he reorganized and incorporated old conservative elites and professional trade organizations into the National Socialist associations that he subsequently held under firm control. The persecution, arrest, and murder of political and religious opponents, the annihilation of "inferior races" and those "unworthy of life" all left the nation with a horrifying legacy of its crimes, a national disgrace, and a deep mistrust in any kind of German national sentiments. This enormous gap in German spiritual and cultural life gradually diminished after the war, but its legacy is still felt today.

The new Federal Republic of Germany (today referred to as "old West Germany") regarded the Third Reich and the Holocaust as not only a collective trauma but a sort of negative founding principle whose motto and collective imperative, as mentioned before, were "Never Again!" This founding principle, created from the war trauma, transformed the injured nationalism into supranational ideologies. The political and economic orientation to the West, the reconciliation with France and the rest of the neighboring countries in the West, and later with Poland, all played a role in this process.

Two cultural orientation patterns emerged that sometimes paralleled and sometimes contradicted each other: the European idea and the paradox of the Western-founded universalism. The two patterns were characterized by the fusion of a new universalism and scenarios of a "second," "third," or at any rate "new" modernism on the one hand and on the rejection of global patterns, insofar as these were felt to be more American than global, on the other. A pronounced form of a "European perspective" emerged, but both developments were based on a deep suspicion of former German nationalism.

At the same time, people took great pride in successful democratization, in the German version of a free and socially responsible market economy, the rule of law and the constitution. This pride was more than a constitutionalist patriotism à la Habermas: it was proud in seeing Germany applying a universalistic program of progressive modernism. On careful inspection of important German political party platforms, one finds at the core a German vision of globalization that is environmentally sustainable, respects human rights, underscores the social responsibility of free markets, and measures technological progress by ethical parameters.

In this process it is the Europeans, the German Michel and the French Marianne, in collusion with other member states of the "European core" who, as our studies of the German cultural elites discovered, deem themselves trustworthy of implementing a globalization vision other than an American one. The latter still enjoys respect and is viewed as having similar values, but its conjectured imperial pretensions and pursuit of its own political and economic interests are seen as excessive. Lincoln, Jefferson, Martin Luther King, Herman Melville, Mark Twain, William Faulkner, Ernest Hemingway, George Gershwin, Leonard Bernstein, jazz, rock, rap, Hollywood, jeans, and Coca-Cola are all "just fine." But trade barriers, military dictates, and media multinationals are less so.

As our studies show, German cultural representatives abroad (e.g., those with the Goethe Institute) see themselves as representatives of national and European culture. They cooperate with their colleagues from

England, France, Italy, and the Benelux countries and aim at arriving at a common understanding that Europe as a whole provides the "better" cultural globalization program. The new German intellectual and cultural elites have helped shape the new Europeanized universalist program of progressive modernism to a considerable degree.

These postwar cultural elites originated in the educated middle classes, until a wave of sweeping education reforms in the late 1960s cleared the way for the advancement of the lower classes. Meanwhile, more than a third of the twenty- to thirty-year-olds have now completed secondary education, a fifth of this group has attained postsecondary degrees, and half of all university and college students are women.[4] Accordingly, German intellectual, administrative, and business elites have never been so diverse.

The "peacetime" elites of the 1960s and 1970s (the successors to the postwar elites) were raised surrounded by Western thinking, consumption, and work patterns. Their life philosophies are defined by an amalgamation of Western economic, environmental, and lifestyle ideologies. Prewar mentalities have no place in this environment. The sentiments of the peacetime elites do not derive from the cultural horizons of Germany's postwar economic miracle; their spiritual home is the Federal Republic after 1968. It is they who insistently remind the nation of its Third Reich past and vigorously demand a course of politics beyond German nationalism. For them, Germany's home is in the middle of Europe, and Europe should itself become the center of a new kind of supranational political understanding. A European nationalism seems to be a way out of the German trauma.

In recent decades different social movements in Germany have undergone a process of change that has led them from the representation of discrete group interests (e.g., democratic, liberal middle class, intellectuals, artists, women's movement, socialists, the younger labor movement) to the representation of overlapping goals and universal/global ideas. Initially, their topic was the observance and respect of general human rights on the national scale or at the level of "enlightened" cosmopolitans; more recently it has based itself on the universal and apparently self-sufficient core value of modern "Western" industrialized societies: the autonomous, self-determined, "emancipated" individual, living in harmony with himself or herself and his or her nature. This agenda has beyond doubt become the numerically smallest and yet spiritually the largest fundamental common denominator of all social movements in contemporary Germany. It seems to be the ultimate authority of determination and evaluation, the one "institution" that measures all other social institutions.

This view of an "emancipated subject" is in its origin a child of the Enlightenment. Originally, the idea of the autonomous individual lived close to its siblings *(liberté, égalité, fraternité)* before it isolated itself and became self-sufficient. Now, as a collectively (!) shared view and collective lifestyle of individualization, this consensually accepted self-interpretation is the answer to a society that is "multicultural" and "mass cultural" at the same time. In fact, this individuation is one of its most significant characteristics. It should also help to clarify this that the (intellectual) middle class in present-day German society turns economic necessities (e.g., full employment, division of labor, equality of men and women, mobility, changing workplaces, and "partners") into some sort of a desired goal. This type of wishful thinking does not correct the current social system but is its direct offspring and guarantor.

Accordingly, the German (European) concept of individuality is often seen by its protagonists as very different from what it signifies in Asia and even in the United States. What seems to be a fusion of different global views and what appears to be the same terminology is held as distinctly European and not quite overlapping with what is usually termed "the Western notion of the subject." The small differences in U.S. and European semantics suggests that this notion is a myth. Nevertheless, German intellectuals, the faculty club, believe that they represent universal—global—values. They see themselves as belonging to a democratic economic system and value canon that is bound to prevail globally in the long run and will eventually determine "global culture."

As our studies discovered, this collective intellectual belief lies at the core of the new social movements initiated and supported by new intellectual elites in Germany. Trusting in the force of their vision, leaders of these movements, however, are repeatedly taken by surprise at the relatively weak response their intellectual agendas elicit in the wider public. This has sociostructural reasons.

In Germany, new social movements are supported by and draw their members from middle-class intellectuals. However, in terms of economic and political power, they are outsiders or, at best, exist on the margins of the economic and political decision-making centers. Literati, artists, journalists, writers, film producers, commentators, teachers, ministers, and professors all constitute the reasoning bourgeois public (*räsonierende Öffentlichkeit*), but they do not wield the central powers of social action. Though intellectuals dominate the visible public fields (media, advertising, and education), they notoriously tend to overestimate their importance. They present and at the same time mistake themselves as pivotal actors and directors of society solely in running a public stage that they themselves do not finance are not taken into account by those who do.

Although intellectuals are powerless and cannot effect things like real "doers," they are quite influential as an interpretative authority, however. Intellectuals in Germany, notably sociologists, impart an explanatory voice to social issues, developments, and political conditions, as do, for instance, Ulrich Beck in Germany and Anthony Giddens, a friend of Beck's, in Great Britain. The German faculty club, just like its international associates, confers value-laden collective meaning propositions to social incidents, persons, and topics and provides the public with an explicit or implicit world outlook accordingly.

However, the faculty members are more the interpreters and prophets of their society than its educators. By applying even more meaning to an already "meaningful" world, in dissecting it into value hierarchies, by highlighting certain issues and neglecting others, stressing certain priorities and dismissing divergent possibilities, they form and give rise to collective lines of thought one can barely escape from. The European value hierarchies in the vision of German intellectuals, for example, are typically thought of in philosophically universalistic conceptions and political global terms that are projected on this basis without considering other value options.

As in other countries, the branches of NGOs in Germany (e.g., Greenpeace, Amnesty International, Medecins sans Frontières, World Wildlife Fund) view themselves, unlike governmental organizations, as actively pursuing and implementing the agenda of human rights and environmental protection. Their philosophies and activities are deeply rooted in the German public consciousness and their programs, as German donations figures point out,[5] find themselves next to church charities in receiving the strongest support. Nearly 80 percent of adult Germans contribute money to charities: since 1985 the conservatively estimated amount donated each year was at least DEM 4 billion—the upper limit is a matter of speculation. Some 30 percent of all these benefactors are supporting NGOs, and these trends are increasing.

In this connection it is interesting to note that environmental and human rights organizations have found a strong foothold in both the Lutheran and Roman Catholic national church conventions. This demonstrates how closely the (inter)national faculty club and the NGOs are connected in Germany in terms of both ideas and organization. Just as regionalists and nationalists are absorbed by globalization nightmares bemoaning the loss of tradition, the faculty club and the NGOs are preoccupied with the deficiencies of the (often yet to be fulfilled) world order and see their purpose as exposing the weaknesses, mistakes, and failures of political and economic globalizing developments, along with human rights violations and environmental shortcomings.

Those who presume an immanent confrontation between the elites of the faculty club and Davos culture and suppose no contacts worth mentioning between the two—and perhaps even assume a deliberate avoidance of each other outside the political arena and other battlefields—had better consider the German situation and think again. Both of the major churches with their academies, as well as the most important political foundations (the Christian Democratic Konrad Adenauer Foundation, the Social Democrats" Friedrich Ebert Foundation, the Liberal Naumann Foundation) and cultural organizations (the Goethe Institute and the Humboldt Foundation among others) all provide, by means of conferences, congresses, and expert hearings, a constant dialogue between politics and business on the one side and environmental and human rights organizations on the other.

Viewed culturally, the sociopolitical system of the Federal Republic of Germany has to be regarded as an arranged marriage of Davos culture and the faculty club, however controversial this may appear. This marriage enables all family members to switch from one group scenario to the other; furthermore, this situation mirrors itself in the political parties. After all, the environmentalist Greens are part of the country's current coalition government headed by a Social Democratic chancellor, who is in turn considered a strong ally of corporate Germany.

Cultural Self-Representation in Mass Events and the Media

Modern societies present themselves primarily through their mass media, particularly through their television systems. They are media societies in that they are provided with a system of electronic looking-glass boxes that reach their audiences in every household. The materials presented in the boxes are tracked down and staged by the seemingly omnipresent television cameras. They stretch out like tentacles to ensure that just about any kind of socially relevant activity is not only put on screen, but that is also presented like a performance.

Every ordinary person therefore has to count on the possibility of being shoved onto the media stage at any given moment in his or her everyday life. As our extended studies of the TV media have found out, the awareness of the fact that one could nowadays suddenly find oneself in the spotlight belongs to a common understanding. As a consequence, *performance* has become a central category in social life, and the ability to perform is imperative for individuals. In this respect there are no structural differences between pop culture, political presentations, or church events.

On the basis of this pattern, social movements in Germany developed in the early 1970s as a form of organization that not only helped enact mass events but also offered the participants a mix of educational entertainment and self-portrayal, delectation, and participation concocted into a "collective performance." Pop bands, popular and politically active entertainers, politicians, ecclesiastical dignitaries, and unionists shaped, often on intertwining stages, an agenda that was not only seized by their audiences, but was channeled purposefully to the media to ensure the significance of these mass events. Mile-long marches, human chains, and huge motorized parades are, in Kracauer's phrase, forming new "ornaments of the masses." Helicopter camera crews are recording these ornaments in their entirety to relay a message to the nation and perhaps the world beyond and to give the participants of the occasion the opportunity to marvel at their "work" from their living rooms afterwards.

An interaction between entertainment (pop music, cabaret) and performed collective sentiments has entered into the structure of mass gatherings, from small downtown parades to events of scale. All involved have to invest effort into the occasions to make them event- and meaningful. A synchronization of emotions for a period of time (a few hours or a weekend) is to be enacted. As a matter of fact, our studies found that this has become the structuring principle of modern movements as such: Mass rallies have to be *events* and everyone involved, whether famous or not, is obliged to *perform* to nourish the collective spirit of the occasion.

In this direction, a new type of social movement or "moving masses" has recently emerged. Its purpose is to demonstrate a "new" politics, a politics of being decidedly nonpolitical yet highly meaningful (e.g., Love Parade, raves, Christopher Street Day). These movements cannot be understood any longer in terms of traditional political scenarios such as "extraparliamentary opposition" or "left" or "right"—they are a phenomenon of globalization. Whereas Love Parade is a genuine German invention that also attracts more than a million international participants, Christopher Street Day parades, as an American "import," have become events whose popularity goes beyond the boundaries of the gay subculture.

These mass events and their corresponding forms of musical expression (hip hop, techno, rap) are the stage on which, independent of any political preferences and affiliations, "lifestyle groupings" based on leisure time and special-event aesthetics are created. People belonging to these lifestyle groupings do not choose their respective styles to declare a membership in concrete, local or rigid ideological groups; instead, they try to live a philosophy by means of which they identify with other people of the same style, people they most often don't even know. They use everyday aesthetic practices and accessories—clothing, consumer habits, leisure time activities, cultural preferences—as means of identifying with their own and dissociating themselves from other groups.

Global distribution of brand-name goods associated with "prominent" fashion designers (e.g., Armani, St. Laurent, Versace, Ferre, Boss, Sander, Joop), sport articles (e.g., Nike, Adidas, Reebok, Helly Hansen), and furniture manufacturers (e.g., Thonet, Collani, Le Corbusier, Gropius) provide identification vehicles for forms of self-emblematization and stylization. Local events become an emblem for their participants' global sense of belonging. The traditional boundaries that ran along the lines of party loyalties, world outlooks, and ethnic origins are supplanted by others. Rather than integrate into the regional or the national, they "play into" the global video clip—the parameter and measure of everything. This is less a merger of global and domestic presentation patterns than a new global media-driven principle of self-representation: a performance aimed at both the camera lens and fellow participants.

The rules of media presence (if you are not in the media, you do not exist socially) dictate in particular the behavior of VIPs and those aspiring to such status. It does not suffice to display one's viewpoint, expert knowledge, or world outlook on only one stage: what is needed is being "present" anytime and everywhere, on talk shows, mass rallies and, if at all possible, in the news.

Consequently, the media feature an itinerant circus of VIPs whose faces appear in midnight talk shows, street parades, academies, universities, and even church events. The "circus artists" consist of real or aspiring national bigwigs who leave the impression of being part of a regional phenomenon. However, the structure of media presentation and performance is global, and people can claim worldwide prominence if national channels forward their "catch" to CNN or NTV—a contribution to cultural globalization in an almost complete fashion. To this end, Germany does indeed belong part and parcel to a culturally globalized world.

CONCLUSION

While we were studying cultural globalization from various angles and in various areas, nothing stood out as being more important for cultural change than language. Goods, techniques, and fashions can be imported by a society without necessarily leaving deep marks in the sediment of its inner cultural-meaning structures. Not language, however. As long as a foreign language is used solely as a means of communicative exchange between members of different societies, this amounts to not much more than a question of translation. However, once the vast vocabularies and semantic references of a foreign language start to invade and become incorporated into the everyday vernacular of a society, the situation changes radically, and the cultural-meaning structures of the importing society are then thoroughly affected. Wittgenstein's famous dictum, "The limits of my language are the limits of my world," comes to mind here. People don't use language innocently, and the "language games" (to use another central image of Wittgenstein) brought in from abroad carry with them mind-sets whose traits penetrate the local cultural.

As we found in our studies, modern "language games" of Anglo-American origin are highly important to the question of cultural globalization in Germany. Beyond its widely referenced status as the lingua franca of modern times, the English language has entered by bits and pieces into the everyday colloquial forms of communication in various German areas of life. Terms like "event," "performance," groove," "happy," and "cool" now belong to the contemporary standard German vernacular, particularly among the young. What is even more significant is that they carry a highly globalized American semantic load that the conventional German vocabulary cannot easily find substitutions for.

The "invasion" of anglicisms into the semantic fields of contemporary German becomes fully apparent in distinct areas of everyday German life, for example, the widespread use of computer- and electronics-related terms and phraseologies that have come to pervade the technical as well as everyday fields of action. The abundance of electronic devices (e.g., computers, e-mail, Internet) in almost every household has put Microsoft and Apple terms on the "mental hard drives" of ordinary citizens, and the respective vocabularies have become a prerequisite for the daily and global communications they are involved in. The consequences of this form of acculturation are immensely important to questions of cultural globalization. Furthermore, there are the anglicisms that pervade the media arenas from pop music, politics, economy, science, sports, and fashion to everyday communication, which we have dealt with.

Even to an outside observer with some flair for matters linguistic, the rhetorics of "performance" and "events" often seem to be a lofty-sounding gibberish between German and English. Finally, there is the area of management and business consulting in which, as we have shown, English is not only a widespread technical lingua franca but an arena where the semantic deep structures and mind-sets of the "global players" are permeated by conceptions that belong to the German and English business language in a similar if not identical fashion.

Against this fusion of anglicisms into the vernaculars of German culture and language, there are in Germany today some observable reluctance and protests. Next to cultural traditionalists, they are particularly voiced, as we have pointed out, by cultural policy officials and the representatives of German cultural institutions abroad (e.g., Goethe Institute, DAAD-German Academic Exchange Service, political foundations). They argue that English should not be considered innocently as a lingua franca on equal terms with that of Latin in medieval times. They point out that no political superpower stood behind Latin as the United States stands behind the English language in our times. They further argue that Latin could not therefore be used, even in a latent fashion, as a vehicle for promoting political and cultural aspirations. With respect to the all-pervading contemporary use of (American) English they perceive some danger of this being the case in our day. They share this view, as expected, with their fellow European colleagues (from the Institute Française and the Societá Dante Alighieri, for example). As official representatives, their concern is the implementation of a European culture that can hold its own as a "player" on the global scene. The future will have to show, however, whether this will indeed turn out to be a realistic vision.

NOTES

1. For a general overview, see Bernhard Schäfers and Wolfgang Zapf, eds., *Handwörterbuch zur Gesellschaft Deutschlands* (Opladen: Leske & Buderich, 1998), p. 81.

2. See Statistisches Bundesamt, ed., *Datenreport 1999*, Bundeszentrale für Politische Bildung, no. 365. According to the census data given here, 73 percent of East Germans declare that they do not to belong to any religious denomination.

3. The final findings of the Frankfurt research team's study of the global managerial lingua franca will be published under the title "Die Sprachwelten der Manager im Zeitalter der Globalisierung" in either an anthology, *Kulturelle Globalisierung in Deutschland: Mythos, Ideologien, und Beobachtungen* (Constance, Germany: Universitätsverlag Konstanz, 2001) or in a separate monograph. Use has been made of two recently completed studies: K. F. Bohler and H. Kellner, *Unternehmensberatung in der ostdeutschen Wirtschaft* and *die Beratung ostdeutscher Betriebe durch Ostdeutsche* (Frankfurt, 2000).

The compete findings of the Constance research team on the German intellectual elites and the emerging forms of cultural self-representation in mass events and the media, as well as further studies on German cultural institutions, ecclesiastical academies, and practices of German companies in the field of the "global players," will be published in the anthology *Kulturelle Globalisierung in Deutschland: Mythos, Ideologien, und Beobachtungen* (Constance, Germany: Universitätsverlag Konstanz, 2001).

Hansfried Kellner wishes to acknowledge and extend his gratitude to the members of the Frankfurt research team: Karl Friedrich Bohler, Anette Zenker Sebastian Kansy, and Engelbert Peters.

Hans-Georg Soeffner wishes to acknowledge and extend his gratitude to the members of the Constance research team: Anne Honer, Thomas Lau, Bernt Schnettler, and Markus Hablizel.

4. Schäfers and Zapf, *Handwörterbuch zur Gesellschaft Deutschlands,* pp. 85ff., 167ff.

5. Andreas Voß, *Betteln und Spenden* (Berlin: de Gruyter, 1992), p. 2ff.

6

———— • ————

Rival Temptations and Passive Resistance

CULTURAL GLOBALIZATION IN HUNGARY

János Mátyás Kovács

An earlier version of this chapter was entitled "Turbulence in the Vacuum," which is nonsense in physics, of course.[1] Nevertheless, the metaphor reflected two essential components of cultural change in my country during the postcommunist period: a void left by Soviet civilization that, as if under the influence of *horror vacui*, attracted foreign cultures to Hungary and offered a chance for the revival of indigenous ones, and fierce competition among these cultures to fill that void.

While I would still subscribe to the thesis of turbulence, my belief in a post-Soviet cultural vacuum has slowly faded. As our first case studies[2] were completed in Budapest, it became clear that in a great many fields of cultural transformation, the notion of vacuum has to be replaced (or complemented) by notions of path dependency, friction, resistance, and compromise. In other words, there is an awful lot of handwriting on the allegedly blank sheet of postcommunist culture—handwriting that is extremely hard to erase.[3] What follows is meant to be a study of this hardship.

I will begin by presenting a stereotypical view of the unhampered globalization of culture, revealing the implicit assumptions constituting its core. These assumptions will then be simultaneously contrasted with the real world of cultural change in Hungary and the standard concepts of cultural globalization offered by various branches of Cultural Studies literature to consider local resistance. The chapter ends with a couple of suggestions for fine-tuning these concepts to match the "cultural carnival" of postcommunism in Hungary.

A MIGHTY COMMONPLACE

Let us first admire a notoriously unambiguous image of cultural change in the former Eastern bloc. No thorough library search is needed; it is more than enough to open a newspaper in any corner of the world and read the first "analytic" report sent from under the "ruins of the Soviet empire." According to journalistic (and to a large part of scientific) wisdom, Eastern Europe is rushing through a process of cultural globalization that is contingent upon the collapse of communism. Although in certain countries globalization may be disturbed by the tendency of Balkanization (this is the counternarrative of similarly low quality), it is tantamount to an irresistible, mass culture–based Americanization of newly reviving national cultures that have barely gotten rid of communist control.[4]

A symbolic embodiment of this process in Hungary would be a former communist apparatchik in national costume riding a wild horse on the Puszta (the Hungarian steppe) with a hamburger in his dirty hand. This image usually suggests the final destination of the ride as well. After having replaced the party card with a credit card,[5] our hero will establish his own firm and substitute the horse for a car and his traditional dress for blue jeans or a designer business suit. The dirt (that is, primordial traditions) may partly disappear, but the hamburger will remain.

So will the hatred of antiglobalization activists and the condescending smile of distinguished Western liberals witnessing the Eastern newcomers, who seem to be proud to take part in a "catching-up revolution" (to use Jürgen Habermas's unfortunate phrase) and to be "globalized into capitalism" thereby. These freshmen allegedly display the tragic irony of nouveaux riches.[6] Caught up in an assimilation mania, they tend to forget their mother tongue in acquiring pidgin English, and they mistake American sitcoms, musicals, and wellness fashions for high culture, and fast food, huge limousines, and suburban housing projects for unparalleled modernity.

These newcomers' demands for cultural commodities of dubious quality and taste are insatiable. From their savings made in the brave new world, the first trip of the happily globalizing Hungarian family leads to Disneyland. The parents believe in Scientology, their son and daughter (while sweating in a fitness club) dream about becoming a talk show host or a cover girl, and the grandfather curses the Yalta Agreement which, for more than forty years, prevented him from gambling his forints in the Baden, Austria, casino. To take revenge on the communists, he has already applied for admission to the Rotary Club.

Besides the recurrent themes missed by no observer (e.g., 1989 as a caesura, the United States as the chief seducer, mass consumption as the main carrier of acculturation, globalization as an iron law), the analogy of the horseman rests on a series of implicit propositions of equal significance. Let me mention three of them.

From Sovietization to Americanization

What happened throughout Eastern Europe in 1989 may have been an innocent opening up to the world and to the indigenous cultural traditions of the peoples in the region. However, according to this thesis, the 1989 revolution also marked the beginning of global homogenization. Depending on the analyst's ideological taste, this process is usually described in two ways: either under the spell of liberal triumphalism, as spiritual integration in the free world through promoting, by the West, the weak but talented and industrious in the East; or, using postcolonial discourse, as cultural impoverishment and annexation of an entire region. Deep down, however, the two diagnoses are not dissimilar: both can easily be deduced from an elementary doctrine of colonization. Accordingly, given the huge power of foreign cultures, they inevitably conquer, eradicate, or at least marginalize their indigenous rivals, while the natives eventually surrender to the occupants or even fall in love with the civilizers.[7]

As regards the region and Hungary in particular, this is a mere replication of the old dogma of sweeping Sovietization and the story of how a majority of the natives found a relatively comfortable place under the reform-minded communist leaders after the 1956 revolution was crushed. Nevertheless, the fact of reform communism hints at a peculiar metamorphosis of the culture of invaders. If in the past the *Ruskies* could not help but adjust to local cultures instead of annihilating them entirely, why should one suppose that it will be any different for the *Yankees*?

Colonization: Lucky and Smart

This assumption provides an easy answer to the above question: Soviet culture was alien ("Asian") and weak in terms of its corruption force, which are more or less compulsory an the top, whereas the American culture seems to be closer to the hearts and minds of the citizens of Eastern Europe, is economically and (geo)politically invincible, and— seemingly—optional. The emphasis here is on the word "seemingly." In the past you *had to* cram Russian; today you *can* learn English (but you'd better do it if you want to get a good-paying job)—once upon a time, you heard on the radio that your country had become a member of the Warsaw Pact; nowadays you are asked in a referendum whether you agree on joining NATO (but you'd better, if you don't want capital fleeing your country).

According to this thesis, on the demand side of the equation, all the important prerequisites for a successful colonization drive are in store. The invader (or, to put it in technical terms, the exporter of culture) is lucky because what is being offered by him, and the way in which the offer is being made, are congruent with the cultural needs of the importer. Furthermore, demand for the cultural commodities of the West has accumulated in the region through the forced abstinence and negative indoctrination exercised by the communist regimes, so delayed consumption is now erupting like a volcano all over Eastern Europe.

From the supply side's point of view, the competition among international cultural producers is not very strong. Given an Americanized structure of demand, customers in the ex-communist countries prefer U.S.–type free markets to continental social market economies, Hollywood to Cinecitta, and Coca-Cola to Perrier. And even if they think they're choosing a European cultural good, a German soap opera, or a French rap song, for instance, these turn out to be variations of the American original. Even the pizza cannot be regarded as a masterpiece of Italian culinary culture if one of its main carriers in Eastern Europe is Pizza Hut.[8]

The lucky exporter must keep only one single maxim in mind: Do not remind the natives of the previous colonizer.[9] The smart new ruler does not provoke the locals with odd ideologies and brutal force; he corrupts them, primarily through consumption and entertainment.[10]

Weak Resistance

The colonizer is lucky in another respect as well: he does not run the risk of facing powerful counterattacks by indigenous forces. According to this thesis, Soviet culture evaporated overnight, and national traditions could not be sufficiently mobilized before the new invaders inundated the postcommunist cultural desert. Globalization is essentially a two-person game. On the one side, we find the West dominated by the "one and only" American civilization, which is omnipotent and unambiguous; on the other, a uniform group of actors appears, the Eastern European societies *ohne Eigenschaften.*

To use the terminology of the Hungarian populist extremists, the "moral backbone" of our society was cracked by the Bolshevik liberals (a code name for the Jews) and their American principals. We have become a "nation of waiters" serving "foreign vulture capital," just as we used to do for the Soviet Big Brother a decade ago.[11] In other words, much of the cultural legacy of communism—social anomie, moral relativism, lack of self-confidence, helplessness, and so on—not only survived the old regime but is reinforced by the vast difference between the strong identity of the new occupants and the subservience of the domestic agents of culture, let alone the final consumers.[12]

Public resistance to cultural globalization remains rather shallow. Even the "ethnically conscious" administrations in Eastern Europe are too poor to finance cultural self-protection and are under enormous pressure from both within and without to open all gates to international exchange and communication. "Over the past decade, we intellectuals in the ex-communist countries have lost our status as educated opinion leaders and true patriots and have been replaced by political charlatans and ignorant businessmen, the compradors." This is the vicious argument the populists use to compensate for their weakness.

IMMEDIATE OBJECTIONS

The whole story is far too familiar, isn't it? It sounds as if it were told by Lenin, Marcuse, and Le Pen in full harmony. Small pieces of truth wrapped in suspicion and exaggeration, it's a narrative that rests on the iron law of globalization, a moralizing conspiracy theory, and romantic anticapitalism. These dogmas now integrate unreconstructed communists, conservative ethno-nationalists, and neopopulists in Eastern Europe and intimately connect them with many of the antiglobalists in the West. Under communist rule, the words "America" and "imperialism" could only be coupled in the party jargon of communist hard-liners. Today, it's almost as fashionable to make ironic comments on "cultural garbage" of U.S. provenance as it was to laugh at banal Soviet war movies fifteen years ago. Furthermore, this pirouette is even being performed by self-proclaimed liberals in Hungary, one of the most westernized countries of the former Eastern bloc.

Are they true guardians of elite and folk culture, or snobs who dismiss American civilization *en bloc* without being aware of its colorful nature? Do they fear the overkill effects of McWorld and feel powerless witnessing the upsurge of the market in cultural spheres, or do they primarily mourn their own privileges, lost in a bitter competition? Are they hostile to "new harshness" because they are so sophisticated and elevated, or because they are so enervated and apathetic? To be sure, their discontent is essentially sentimental.

Despite the heavy rhetoric favored by nationalist parties,[13] when in government, they tend to refrain from the tedious (and possibly unpopular) work of supporting grassroots initiatives to preserve ethnic traditions. Although the intellectuals around them like to lament over the low number of homemade programs on the television, they are still far from joining forces with Hungary's minuscule group of Seattle-type antiglobalists and launching "Buy Hungarian" campaigns, dismantling fast food restaurants (France), or rallying at the fences around NATO barracks (Germany). But if their organized protests are weak, does that necessarily mean that spontaneous, passive resistance to cultural import cannot be strong?[14] And why resist at all?

As a first reaction let us consider the "chief villain," McDonald's, for a moment. Its Eastern European critics learned (probably from their former ideological supervisors) that capitalism begins with the first hamburger and, as far as quality is concerned, it may end there as well. Nevertheless, in this part of the world hamburgers compete with the successors of fatty pseudo-meatballs that were served by public caterers in canteens of questionable hygiene rather than with French high cuisine. Can one prophesy the inevitable decay of Czech, Hungarian, or Russian civilization, knowing that in the new fast food chains, the quality of meals is stable, the restroom is relatively clean, and the customer is not forced to tip the wait staff? After all, these are achievements that are still unheard of in most local restaurants.

At any rate, would Wiener schnitzel mean Europe-oriented progress as compared to Big Mac? Those who think it would (that is, the new anti-Americans and America skeptics in Eastern Europe) seem to escape into collective amnesia. Demonize U.S. pop culture, magnify and distort the differences between American (i.e., low) and European, including Hungarian, (i.e., high) civilization, and sugarcoat the memory of Sovietization—these three rules may help them disregard most of the cultural advantages offered by the opening up of the communist empire to the world.[15]

Or let us take the example of cyberspace, which is constantly denounced in the East as well as the West as a mediator of cultural trash. In Eastern Europe, however, it is, I believe, much more difficult to condemn Web culture because the citizens of this region still remember that copy and fax machines, not to mention typewriters, were kept under surveillance, and that letters and phone calls were systematically censored by the authorities.[16] Similarly, how can one complain about the stupidity of MTV video clips if not so long ago bombastic communist marching songs, imitation rock and roll (complete with censored texts), operetta and artificial folk music were the main alternatives in many Soviet bloc countries?

DE GUSTIBUS . . .

These comparisons undoubtedly tend to lose their validity as years go by. Again and again, however, official cultural policy in quite a few postcommunist regimes strives to idealize the past by protecting backwardness ("fatty but homemade"), censorship ("tough but iron-handed vis-à-vis criminals too") and national-communist kitsch ("plain but not violent"), just to remain with the above examples. True, one can claim with some justification (and little realism) that the opening up of cultures in the former Eastern bloc could have taken place in a more "decent" way. Why deny that I too sometimes find it hard to suspend my Central European preferences for elite culture and for distinctions between "tasteful" and "tasteless" variants of mass culture?

In this research project, however, our group decided to avoid confronting "high" and "low" cultures and indulging, in a self-conceited way, in an evaluation of cultural performance. Instead, by boring a number of exploratory drills into the depth of cultural evolution in Hungary, we wanted to understand what most observers prefer to interpret a priori.

Our aim was fundamentally apolitical: by presenting our case, we did not want to provide ammunition to any kind of "Global Is Beautiful" campaign. In any event, who wouldn't have second thoughts about the cruel drug dealer from Albania, the stone-headed Brussels bureaucrat, the conceited yuppie, the fanatical sect leader, or the green fundamentalist—just to name some of the new actors of the play called the "cultural transformation in Eastern Europe." Or who could applaud some of its new scenes, such as the shopping mall, the fast food restaurant, the multiplex cinema, and the computer screen, without a sad smile? Finally, who would think that the cultural opening up of the Soviet empire does not imply new power relations between East and West, producing a great number of net losers caught in a grave identity crisis or—in the best case—in various forms of cultural impoverishment?

Yearning for empirical evidence—in what fields, by what means,[17] and via what kind of assumptions?—while remaining within the framework of the initial hypotheses of the overall project,[18] we included an additional—specifically, 1989 related—dimension of research, which I would call "blanket liberalization." This covers all acts of dismantling the old regime and installing the new one, ranging from political amnesty to religious freedom, from patients' rights in health care to currency convertibility, from decriminalizing homosexuality to the dissolution of the workers' militia.[19] Markets and democracies emerged throughout the region in a process of ambitious constitution writing and institution building, which were affected by massive cultural imports from the West. Because of the utmost significance of this dimension in the period of postcommunist transformation (especially in its first, formative years), a whole series of case studies were devoted to it in our Hungarian subproject. Joining NATO, making the first noncommunist law on media, reforming the universities, and establishing the National Cultural Fund are all crucial terrain for observing the fate of the borrowing, reshaping, and/or eventual rejection of Western norms, ideas, and institutions following the 1989 revolution.

The impacts of "Davos culture" were studied in three different fields: in its interaction with the legacy of "network-intensive" (less euphemistically, corrupt) business practices typical under late communism; in the images of Hungary and Eastern Europe in general, developed by CEOs of multinational companies; and in the half victories achieved by mainstream neoclassical economics in Hungarian economic thought.

Various effects of "faculty club culture" were discussed in the papers on media reform, the English language in Hungary, the Soros Foundation, and Hungarian participation at the Frankfurt Book Fair. However, the primary case examined in our research group was feminism, a striking example of failed globalization efforts by the faculty club in most ex-communist countries. Another important carrier of cultural globalization in the proposal of the overall project, evangelical Protestantism, was scrutinized in the larger context of new religious movements in Hungary.

Among the planned research fields only one, McWorld, lacks a deeper analysis. The reason for paying less attention to this crucial issue lies in our fear of repeating conventional truisms about Coca-Cola, blue jeans, and Elvis Presley. In order to bridge this gap, I volunteered to illustrate much of what I would like to say anyway in this chapter with the help of examples taken from the cultural realm of mass consumption.

Because each globalization carrier uses the English language for communication, we thought it absolutely necessary to include a case study on the dynamics of that "carrier of carriers" in Hungary. At the same time, additional research topics were offered by (1) the cultural legacies of Soviet civilization, (2) a large increase in *non-Western* cultural imports after 1989, and (3) the "typically Hungarian" question of whether a small, middle-income country, which is traditionally proud of its cultural talent,[20] is predestined to copying and remodeling foreign cultures, or whether it can also become capable of counter-emission; that is, of marketing some of its cultural produce globally.

The first topic is discussed in a paper on the (de-) Sovietization of Hungarian culture, while the second is examined through the example of Hungary's Chinese community. The third topic appears in a study of exporting Hungarian literature via the Frankfurt Bookfair. Regrettably enough, our research group has not yet had a chance to explore in separate studies the cultural aspects of two major, partly antiglobalizing processes in Hungary: Europeanization and the revival of Central Europe. I try to fill part of this lacuna in this chapter.

ADDITIONAL HYPOTHESES

The peculiarity of the Hungarian case in terms of cultural globalization is often derived from popular stereotypes such as a small country with no relatives, open to the world, situated at the East-West crossroads, European (German) *Kulturkreis*, routine cooperation with the conquerors, legacy of cynical communism (market socialism), moderate nationalism, high level of secularization, lack of Russophobia, no aversions toward the United States,[21] strong cosmopolitan traditions, rapid liberalization after 1989, and so on.

The enumeration of these features at home makes most observers think that if Hungary, with its "weak culture,"[22] is not fatally exposed to Western cultural invasion, then no country in the world can be. Our working hypotheses reflected an inverse logic: How is it possible that even such a "helpless" country, which would seem to be foreordained to become a toy of globalizing forces, displays considerable resistance to them? Let me admit right away that this question is rooted in good old Central European skepticism: If in the past so many things have gone wrong in this region, why would globalization be an exception?

Let us go back to our horseman riding (more exactly, jumping) from communism into capitalism. Clichés like this arouse the reader's suspicion, provided he spent some years in Hungary (or in Poland or Slovenia for that matter) before and after 1989. What happens to the analogy, one might ask, if the communist gentleman had already replaced many of the old cultural requisites, such as the horse and the national costume, under the old regime? What if he decorated his blue jeans with folk art motifs back in the 1960s, if he prefers Japanese or Italian food to McDonald's, if he buys a Volkswagen or Toyota but keeps his old Trabant? When permitted by the communist authorities, he'd already traveled to the West in that car two decades before the collapse of the Soviet empire. Maybe he was a member of the *nomenklatura*, but his wife owned a flourishing firm in the fashion industry along the fine line between the formal and informal economies. They may have met at a rock concert organized by the Communist Youth League during the 1970s or at a yoga club (a cover organization of the Krishna movement) in the 1980s. What should we say about cultural globalization if she read modern French literature ten years ago but, put out of business by a multinational competitor and currently working for a Chinese merchant, the only luxury she can now afford is to subscribe to HBO? And finally, what if her husband remained a communist, now in national wrapping or, on the contrary, if he switched to become a human rights activist in an international NGO and in his leisure time, as an admirer of Giuseppe Verdi, downloads his operas from the Web?

In other words, (1) mass culture–based "penetration" of the West started in Hungary many years/decades before 1989; (2) one may also have been "globalized" in high culture under the old regime; (3) what is being imported today is not necessarily junk culture; (4) currently, Hungarians may follow quite a few non-American (Western as well as Far Eastern) patterns of culture—that is, they face rival temptations; and (5) most importantly, insisting on certain cultural practices of the past, they may mix local (communist and national), regional, and global components of culture for a long time to come. Eclectic reception of foreign cultural goods and bricolage seem to be the rule rather than an exception to it.

Based on these assumptions, our research group decided to handle the term "globalization" with extreme care to avoid connotations such as all-out homogenization and standardization. Unless we witnessed important cases of successful colonization, we preferred to speak of cultural opening up, rivalry, exchange, encounter, conflict, and cooperation ("creolization" and "glocalization" if you please)[23] rather than cultural occupation. This is how my attention turned to the concepts of cultural resistance and compromise, especially to their passive and spontaneous patterns.[24]

Accordingly, the notion of cultural vacuum was substituted for those of path dependency and friction. Our research question was deliberately simple: Let's suppose for a moment that there *are* global cultural goods and observe what happens to them after they've entered the country. How do these goods get transformed once they are transferred?

It was not our intention to celebrate local self-defense against global impacts because it can be based on rather controversial pieces of tradition, dubious forms of indigenous interest and the like, or even on an intervention by another external actor. The same applies to passivity: it too may include many different approaches to resistance, ranging from full apathy, through indifferent contemplation, to a spontaneous opting-out from the consumption of certain cultural goods.

As regards Hungary, I would stress the essential spontaneity and individual character of these choices. For the time being, there is no reason to suspect a comprehensive political conspiracy lurking in the background of these personal decisions. All the more so because resistance, among other things, may stem from inherently impersonal (external) circumstances such as the following:

- The inertia of the previous "globalizer" (in this case, resistance means that cultural entry is partly blocked)
- Competition between cultural exporters (in this case, the local importer resists, often instinctively, one cultural "provider" by choosing another)
- Controversial messages from the West (in this case, the incoming global cultures resist each other)
- Simulation (in this case, under the pretext of zero resistance, cultural importation may actually fail to happen)

DE-SOVIETIZATION?

In Eastern Europe, Western-style globalization is only one (albeit spectacular) aspect of a general opening up. In the first place, the revolution of 1989 resulted in de-Sovietization, a partial extinction of the so-called communist world system. This kind of deglobalization seemed to promise a rebirth of oppressed national/ethnic cultures—just the opposite of worldwide homogenization. According to the optimistic expectations of the dissidents in 1989, the collapse of the Eastern bloc would mean the sudden death of Soviet culture with its universalistic claims but semi-global reality, the survival of Russian high culture, and the birth of a mixed—national (but not ethno-nationalist) *and* truly global (liberal, cosmopolitan)—culture that would include both high and low components, without the latter's inhuman ramifications.

To put it simply, Leninist censorship would vanish, but Lev Tolstoy and Fyodor Dostoievsky would not. Béla Bartók, Frederic Chopin, and the Beatles would peacefully coexist. Although it would probably be difficult to find a decent bookshop in Warsaw, Budapest, or Bucharest, the nondecent ones would carry Walt Disney coloring books or esoteric literature, not hardcore porn and Nazi kitsch.

However, de-Sovietization led to a path-dependent development (or decline) of cultural life, rather than a revitalization of ethnic cultures.

Path dependency meant at least two things: either the cultural institutions continued to function in almost the same way as under communism (e.g., the Hungarian government kept on heavily subsidizing the movie industry without censoring the films) or precommunist patterns of culture resurfaced (e.g., plans for reintroducing religious education in public schools). Folk culture was doomed to stagnate. Although civic initiatives could already emerge without the risk of being stigmatized as irredentist, state subventions slowly dried up, the anticommunist charm of restoring national traditions disappeared, and authentic folk culture was outcompeted by its commercial mutant.

Paradoxically, in those fields in which de-Sovietization proved to be partly unsuccessful (e.g., political culture), ethno-national traditions did reemerge—under the aegis, for instance, of national-communist "red-brown" coalitions or, as in Hungary, neopopulism. "Let us rediscover our roots in ethno-politics!"—the current slogan of the populist right and left in postcommunist countries—did *not* feature in the dreams of a great majority of dissidents during the 1980s when they were meditating on the common cultural heritage of Central and Eastern European nations. Naively enough, they were talking about folk songs and cafés, urban jokes, grand novels, and the architecture of village churches.[25] Many of them were deeply convinced that the perennial conflict between the "populists" (ethnic traditionalists) and the "westernizers" would disappear once the last Soviet soldier left the region. Moreover, they assumed that (1) there were still many pearls of indigenous culture to be discovered and (2) the discoveries would be interpreted in a cosmopolitan spirit, free of national segregation.

Nowadays, following a long decade of repeated frustrations, many of these former dissidents who trusted in a cultural renaissance of the region are putting their faith in the European Union to block the revival of national junk culture and to keep out "cheap" Americanization. For them a kind of European-based, regulated, or filtered globalization of cultures seem to be the last remedy for losing quality from both directions.

The last Soviet soldier left Hungary many years ago, taking with him (along with all the lightbulbs from the barracks) not only Alexander Pushkin and Ilia Repin, who were Russian artists celebrated by Soviet cultural policy, but Mikhail Bulgakov and Kazimir Malevich, whose relationship with Soviet officialdom was more than controversial.[26] The teaching of the Russian language was abandoned and sank beneath the weight of economic rationality (Russia as a major business partner).

At the same time, a great amount of Sovietism survived the collapse of the empire in the satellite countries.[27] The most evident example is provided by the (ex)communist parties themselves and a political culture of general mistrust, irresponsibility, and aggression inherited from them by their rivals, even in countries with a long reform-communist past, like Hungary. The mafia (i.e., an institution that the Hungarians most often associate with present-day Russia without understanding that it was deep-seated in Soviet polity) is not an unrelated issue here.

However, a more exciting question is how official Soviet culture affected bureaucratic procedures, industrial routines, and everyday behavior among Hungarians. The culture of postponement reflected in a single phrase, *seitschas* (soon, but perhaps never), byzantine secrecy, the substitution of refined quality for primitive quantity, and the application of a brutal simplicity in many fields, ranging from military organization to the oversized concrete foundations of village lavatories—these are merely random references to a more than four-decade-long process of acculturation. Furthermore, the Soviets returned home but left quite a few articles of mass consumption behind. Although the Hungarians do not eat *borsch* or wear *gimnastiorka*, the Lada cars, the Saratov refrigerators, and the Raketa vacuum cleaners (or their rivals from the GDR and Czechoslovakia) still work and do not stop projecting their image of robustness and cheapness—while at the same time being incredibly energy inefficient and polluting the hell out of the air.[28]

No doubt about it, the recent durability of certain Soviet-style cultural practices in Hungary is also due to the fact that the four decades of communist rule followed a previous fourteen or forty decades (depending on one's reckoning) that had prepared the soil for Sovietization. In 1945, vodka was relatively new in Hungary, whereas alcoholism and a fatalistic approach to health and self-destruction had already permeated popular culture in my country during the nineteenth century.

AMERICANIZATION?

The one who comes first, who is strong enough and brings the most pragmatic, simple message to the citizens of Eastern Europe, who are sick and tired of overt indoctrination, can conquer the cultural world of the region. Therefore, most analysts stated in 1989 that the United States (who else?) had already won the cultural competition before it started. The terms "Coca-Colonization" and "Marilyn Monroe doctrine"[29] were originally invented to describe a transatlantic consumerist trend in the postwar history of culture in Western Europe; they are currently being applied throughout the former Eastern bloc without any reservation and with the same critical overtone.

Undoubtedly, many components of high culture (e.g., *belles-lettres*, opera, social sciences) acquired a rather strong position under communism because of state support or, paradoxically, because of state oppression (e.g., churches, censored art). In this respect, globalization may imply a substitution of one global culture for another, probably more global, one. To put it simply, Mozart for Spice Girls, Buñuel for Spielberg, Shakespeare for cartoon scriptwriters. At the same time, the all too evident features of pop culture–oriented globalization make many observers blind to a rapid increase in imported high culture from the West, much of it from the United States. These cultural goods, which are incorporated in scientific theories, skills, routines, legal procedures, and so on, are widely used in the framework of "blanket liberalization"; that is, in designing postcommunist government reforms, managing privatization, restructuring the universities, reshaping the society's communication systems. Aren't these fields at least as important culturally as the dissemination of fast food technologies? At any rate, global consumption goods may also carry "higher" forms of local or regional culture. The so-called Pepsi Island in Budapest is a case in point. This summer festival of progressive rock and world music has become *the* largest meeting place of Central European youth.[30]

Does the English language spread nothing but American mass culture? I apologize for this silly question, but it must be asked in a country in which an increasing number of cultural purists tend to forget that (1) a language, even if it is not your native one, is a high-quality cultural good in itself; (2) the English language not only provides vulgar slogans with dreadful spelling on T-shirts[31] but also helps the Hungarians learn the more subtle elements of Anglo-Saxon (that is, not exclusively American) culture, not to mention the non–Anglo-Saxon ones; (3) if, nevertheless, English did not carry anything more than the rules of baseball or the text of the last musical hit on Broadway, that would not be a tragedy either; (4) the challenge by English does not necessarily have to result in a low-brow "Hunglish" but can contribute to an ingenious refreshment of the Hungarian language; and (5) at any rate, English faces great difficulty in coping with Hungarian syntax and the revived tradition in the region of learning German.

According to our case studies, cultural importation followed some of the historical paths, and American cultural goods could not avoid competing with various Western European (and, with no historical precedent whatsoever, Far Eastern) import articles. Despite current U.S. hegemony[32] in cultural diffusion in many fields ranging from Hollywood to microeconomics textbooks and from NATO standards of military conduct to body building, it would be unwise to disregard the "subglobal" influences; that is, the traditional German/Austrian connection, especially in Hungary, and the ever greater impact of European integration on the cultural development of East-Central Europe as a whole. Moreover, with the steady inflow of Japanese and Southeast Asian industrial capital and the establishment of large commercial networks by Chinese entrepreneurs in the region, one can safely predict a series of cultural consequences (let alone an alternative mode of cultural globalization)[33] that may range from a radical change in work ethic to eating raw fish and singing in karaoke parlors.

Seen from a Hungarian perspective, Central Europe is a terrain of cultural turbulence in itself. With the collapse of communism, my country became a center of intraregional migration, including guest workers, refugees, and criminals, but also a great number of entrepreneurs and managers from Austria and Germany—not to speak of the citizens of these two countries who heavily invest in Hungarian real estate.[34] Among Hungarians, the German language still stands up to the competition with English. Since 1989, Springer and Bertelsmann, the Goethe Institute, the big German political foundations (Ebert, Adenauer, Naumann, Seidel), and so on, have all been extremely active in the media, cultural exchange, and political consultancy.[35]

In addition, the Yugoslav crisis recently left lasting traces of cultural change in the region by revealing the lack of solidarity between neighbors, stimulating corruption to cheat the embargo, and—a surprisingly salutary effect—moderating culture wars in other countries. Historical linkages reemerged in peculiar new forms; for instance, *K.u.K (Kaiserlich und Königlich)* nostalgia mixed with distrust toward an increasingly unfriendly Austria which fears "Eastern invasion" and Hungarian mini-expansion[36] (a sort of "Magyarization") in the neighboring countries with large Hungarian minorities. As regards cultural impacts from Asia, their scope ranges from Central Europe's largest Chinatown in Budapest with its Four Dragon Market, through a vast Suzuki factory near the Danube, to the South Korean manager in a provincial town who beats the employees if they do not work fast enough.[37]

To sum up, in Hungary today one can observe a unique mix of world-wide cultural homogenization, (re)emerging national/regional/continental features, cultural imports from the Far East, powerful remnants of a semiglobal culture, and the weakening (or restructuring?)[38] of old global patterns of high culture: an unprecedented carnival of cultures in a tiny little country in a very short period of time. Wouldn't it be an impatient simplification to call this "Americanization"?

CONTINUITY WITH ACCELERATION

The year 1989 does not really serve as a caesura in the change of this cultural mix. This year seems to sharply divide the current "age of globalization" from a previous "nonglobal" communist era in the region because the demise of the Soviet empire coincided with the information revolution, an upsurge in European integration, and worldwide business and communication in general, which made cultural encounters much easier. The opening up to international culture was really breathtaking in quite a few countries of the former Eastern bloc, such as East Germany and Romania, and there was no country or area of culture in the region in which communism's collapse did not impressively accelerate cultural change.[39]

The Soviet system, with its economic shortages and ideological controls, created the preconditions for this acceleration in mass culture in particular. If you had to queue up in Moscow or Sofia day and night to buy blue jeans in the 1980; if you saw no chance of ever riding a Harley Davidson in your lifetime and the movie *Easy Rider* was banned by the communist censors—then a simple pair of trousers becomes a powerful cultural good per se, symbolizing a much more desperate quest for freedom than that designed by the product's Western marketing strategists.

Hungary may serve here as a counterexample. In the framework of the post-1956 "live and let live"–type compromise, the communist regime led by János Kádár made a series of concessions in order to appease citizens through controlled, drop-by-drop westernization. These included loosening travel restrictions (e.g., the "every three years, $50" rule) and promoting incoming tourism; rehabilitating foreign trade and importing a growing number of Western consumer goods (e.g., "banana queues" on the eve of official holidays, selling the first bottle of Coca-Cola in the 1970s, opening the first McDonald's restaurant in the 1980s);[40] allowing semiconformist writers, scholars, actors, film directors, and rock bands to gain publicity in Hungary and to commute between East and West; expanding English language education in schools, publishing modern Western literature, and teaching "bourgeois" social sciences at the universities; ceasing to disrupt the transmission of Radio Free Europe in the 1960s; fraternizing with émigrés (cf. establishing the Soros Foundation in the 1980s), the Vatican, Israel, the champions of *Ostpolitik*, the Eurocommunists, and so on; borrowing heavily from the West, joining the IMF and the World Bank, and launching joint ventures with large Western companies (cf. opening the first Citibank office in the 1980s); making repeated macroeconomic experiments in deregulating central planning; encouraging informal business activities, individual coping strategies, private consumption, and embourgeoisement; replacing terror and mobilization with bargaining and tacit social contracts; showing relative tolerance toward the sporadic actions of dissidents and, in general, the initial moves of the civil society—one could go on and on listing the virtues of the "goulash communism" that saved many Hungarians from the culture shock of facing global capitalism during the past decade.

HOMOGENIZATION?

Even in seemingly unambiguous cases such as McDonald's, Coca-Cola, and pop music, it is hard to speak of uniform patterns of imitation and takeover. If fast food restaurants are predominantly middle-class meeting places, if Coca-Cola is often mixed with low-quality *pálinka* in seedy pubs, and rap rhythms can be combined with high-brow ironic text in the mood of the Austro-Hungarian cabaret tradition, then it is difficult to say that a massive diffusion of these global products carries standard cultural messages. In other words, if you consume fast food slowly, dilute hard spirits with Coca-Cola, and tell subtle jokes while playing aggressive music, then globalization will be fragmentary or even turn into its opposite: Pepsi without the *Pepsi feeling*.

The medium is *not* (or is not necessarily) the message, especially if the global message itself is ambiguous, because the West delivers not only itself but also its own critique to Eastern Europe: free market doctrines versus environmentalism, freedom of speech versus political correct discourse, the macho idols of Hollywood versus feminist values, health protection versus junk food, and so on. Eastern European citizens receive cultural packages filled with incompatible goods[41] such as these, before they can confront or mix them with their own. Strangely enough, the latter may often turn out to be incompatible with both kinds of incoming culture. For the majority of Hungarians, for example, the principles of classical nonintervention and affirmative action are in a number of cases equally unacceptable. If it comes to the "Roma (gypsy) question," I suspect that my fellow citizens would demand neither neutrality nor positive discrimination from the government, but sheer oppression—evidence of path dependency again.

The revolutionary project of blanket liberalization is sui generis controversial. One does not need to consider the extremities of Davos and faculty club cultures (imagining the dialogue between a fanatic money-maker and a dogmatic quota designer, for instance) to recognize potential clashes between simultaneous marketization/deregulation and democratization. The nearest example is, of course, cultural policy itself: Should public financing of cultural programs depend on their market success? Can governments have cultural preferences? Why not privatize the National Theater? Why subsidize the museums?

In the course of the past decade, governments in Hungary have swung back and forth between the "distributionist" French/Austrian model and the more "market-oriented" Dutch/American model in responding to these questions. Most recently, the latter suffered a humiliating defeat.[42] The regulation of public media, which has been a permanent battlefield of culture war in Hungary in recent years, poses similar questions: Should private television channels carry public programs? Can public channels carry commercials? Why not privatize the National Press

Agency? Do parliamentary elections authorize the winners to dominate the public media? Has the government the right to publish a newspaper?

In trying to solve these problems, Hungarian legislators, who in the early 1990s were discussing BBC-type regulations, have by now arrived in the world of the more interventionist Austrian/Italian model.[43] University reformers in Hungary have been confronted with the same "public versus private good" dilemma: they are seeking answers to the same question of whether or not the differences in the chances of citizens for getting access to cultural, informational, or educational services should be reduced through public action (and if so, to what degree, in what manner, etc.). Despite all efforts to partially marketize higher education, the reform attempts are currently stuck with the traditional German model.[44] Incidentally, the gravitation to more statist schemes of regulation in all three cases demonstrates the survival of old (communist and precommunist) cultures in public policy, as well as the dominance of continental patterns over Anglo-American ones. Unfortunately, in other fields of public policy, such as welfare reform and housing, not to mention banking and the capital markets, in which the United States has until recently exerted a greater (occasionally supreme) influence, the idea of strong government is gaining ground.[45]

Rival cultural patterns in the West imply rival temptations for Eastern Europe. If this is what one has to mean by homogenization, then I would rather talk about exporting and importing ambiguities.[46] And these ambiguities may in turn get further twisted locally. A good example is the Assembly of Faith, a neo-Protestant charismatic church, and the largest and richest new religious institution in Hungary. It preaches tough entrepreneurial spirit and conservative family values, cherishes pro-Judaist, almost philosemitic views, fights for the separation of church and state, supports the progressive and secular liberal party, the Free Democrats, and at the same time maintains a strictly hierarchical, theocratic structure bordering on what was called under communism a "cult of personality."

REVISITING THE COLONIZATION THESIS

If one describes the cultural opening up of the new democracies in Eastern Europe as spiritual capitulation, then in all probability one's vocabulary would include expressions that pertain to international *Kulturkampf,* with national heroes and cosmopolitan traitors, invaders and collaborators, war plans and "final solutions." In the framework of this discourse, cultural globalization would mean occupation, devastation and eradication, as well as the implantation of alien cultures in the deserted homeland.

Yet, if I run through Hungary's cultural history over the past decade, I am unable to mention a single important case of eradication, whereas there is an increasing number of obvious manifestations of cultural coexistence and compromise. Even in McWorld, the most celebrated example of the colonization thesis, in which incoming cultures are backed by Big Business, the inertia of indigenous cultures can be so great (and the purchasing power of the population so small) that the diffusion of import commodities usually slows down after a brief period of incredible acceleration.

For instance, following its first victories, the hamburger had to make peace with traditional pork sausages and the Austro-Hungarian *Faschiertes,* and it was unable to shatter the monopoly of Wiener schnitzel on the Sunday Hungarian lunch table. The same happened to pizza, although its current position vis-à-vis the *lángos* (a kind of donut) seems to be slightly better in urban areas.

To remain in the kitchen, we do not yet have a fast food restaurant chain specializing in goulash, the Hungarian national dish. The men and women (!) in Hungary still smoke strong cigarettes because this is what they got used to under the old regime, though the American tobacco companies monopolizing the Hungarian market sell lighter brands as well.[47] Decaf did not drive the strong espresso (a cultural import article from Italy) from the breakfast menu of the Hungarians. Similarly, cornflakes and muesli, as well as donuts and bagels, have not yet managed to make a breakthrough either. The same applies to most wellness fashions, which seem to remain a privilege (or an extravaganza) of the elite. Thus cultural globalization implies a series of compromises, including compartmentalization, rather than general diffusion, let alone occupation.

Even if the incoming culture succeeds in assuming a dominant position in important fields, this can be due to a lucky/unlucky coincidence. The cell phone is a good case in point. If the "Western" value of quick accessibility coincides with the verbalism of "Eastern" cultures *and* the communist legacy of a planned underdevelopment of communication networks (a crucial element of Soviet political culture) *and* with the extreme technological chauvinism of men in this region, then in present-day Hungary we can witness every second urban male walking on the street with a cell phone in his hand.[48] I really wonder whether we can apply the term "globalization" to a whole set of cultural encounters, when, for instance, techno music contributes to the rebirth of pseudo-folk songs called "wedding rock" in my country (which one can see every Friday in the Hungarian version of the German/Austrian television show *Musikantenstadl*) or when new, Western-mediated, New Age–style mysticism joins old, Eastern European witchcraft, the "global" effect is just a catalyst or partner.[49]

As mentioned before, external cultures have frequently been lured into the former communist countries by unsatisfied demand, not forced on the "innocent natives" as the smart colonization thesis would assert. The most spectacular example, of course, is the 1989 revolution itself. I still remember how often the sarcastic question "Why does nobody want to finally colonize us?" was asked during the last years of communism.[50] It reflected an extremely strong claim for an increased borrowing of anything with a Western label, ranging from free elections to private kindergartens to fashionable shoes.[51] Joining NATO and the EU is just a symbolic final act of "unilateral rapprochement" or, if I may coin another oxymoron, of "invited colonization."

Why mistake invitation for capitulation? Why not simply interpret cultural globalization as a massive appearance of foreign cultural goods that coexist in some way or another with the home products of a particular country? Of course, every act of cohabitation can result in fierce competition and conflict (with the dominant position, let alone, hegemony, of either party)[52] or in a marriage (with a large dose of cooperation and mutual adjustment); however, the likelihood of one party killing the other is fortunately not very great.

Soap operas in Hungary show an interesting blend of rivalry and cooperation. Viewers can currently choose from among a wide variety of soaps on public and private channels: imported and homemade, American, Brazilian, and German, urban and rural, brand-new and old regime. Deep down, they may all have North American roots, but their prolonged coexistence has resulted in a high degree of cultural interpenetration (the first weekly radio soap, the *Szabó Family*, was launched in the late 1950s and to date has aired more than two thousand episodes; the most popular Czech television soap opera, *Hospital at the City Limit*, was broadcast in Hungary in the 1970s). Not infrequently, localization occurs in the very consumption: two years ago, ordinary Hungarians who were fans of a Brazilian soap opera began collecting money for an eye operation for the main character, Esmeralda, who, according to the plot, would go blind by the end of the story. The viewers "naturalized" the Latin American actress to such an extent that they forgot the difference between fiction and reality. Well, is this the pinnacle of cultural globalization or just the opposite?

In any event, why do those who prefer to talk about U.S.–driven colonization not reveal the palpable cases of occupation failures? There are a couple of widely accepted items of potential cultural export from the United States that one cannot in good faith consider harmful, especially in their ideal versions. Contractual discipline, community spirit, civic patriotism, positive thinking, charity, respect for privacy:[53] in principle, each of these goods could enchant the natives, if their reception did not meet legacy-based resistance in the region and if there were strong vanguard groups to begin the cultural borrowing.[54] Or is the reception of these sophisticated cultural goods unavoidably slow, so that not even money and power can really speed up the acculturation process?

There are, however, commodities that are easier to import, even if the transaction costs are rather high. To use a down-to-earth example, would Hungarians switch from their favorite soccer to American football or baseball if vast investments were made in the latter? They probably would. The popularity of formula one auto racing, for instance, skyrocketed in Hungary during the 1990s, after a track was built near Budapest. Interestingly enough, basketball's recent success story in Hungary (among middle-class youth) seems to be primarily due to Eurosport (!), a satellite channel that regularly covers NBA games.[55]

As a matter of fact, a success story of "good" Americanization is still to come: according to most sociological surveys, there has been no significant change for the better during the past ten years in the high levels of corruption, egoism, ethno-nationalism, and pessimism that characterize Hungarian citizens.[56] Nevertheless, any one of them who is employed by a multinational company already has a strict work contract, is not allowed to snoop into the wage contract of colleagues, cannot use the office phone to call relatives in Buenos Aires, may be forced to observe diversity rules, and is squeezed into an optimistic corporate identity without actually having requested it.

HYBRIDIZATION?

In light of the above observations, let us put aside the concept of global-ization for a while to test that of hybridization (or glocalization or cre-olization). These terms suggest, however, that the combined cases have only two ingredients, whereas many of the post-1989 cultural products in Eastern Europe have more than one component with peculiar cross-effects on both the foreign and domestic territories.[57]

As we have seen, the incoming culture is not simply American and the native one is not exclusively "national." For example, many of the postrevolutionary constitutional amendments of the Hungarian Repub-lic have been imported from Germany,[58] business law increasingly fol-lows U.S. norms, the *acquis communautaire* of the European Union (which is also a cultural mix) is just being taken over in the course of the accession talks, while all parts of the legal system are permeated with major compromises between the various political forces, including those made with the communists in 1989 at the Roundtable talks. Or, to take another case, how could one understand the cultural preferences of the Soros Foundation, the largest philanthropic organization in Hun-gary, without taking into account the multiple identities of its president (e.g., a Hungarian Jew, a disciple of Karl Popper, a Wall Street tycoon, a recent critic of global capitalism) and the internal structure of the new political elite reflected in the foundation's various boards?[59]

Hybridization is an empty phrase if we do not specify the propor-tions between the ingredients of the cultural mix and the speed and quality of the mixing. If we do—that is, if we locate the combined cases in a continuum ranging from total replacement of an indigenous cul-tural good by a foreign one, to complete rejection—then we would probably find quite a few cases that actually lie closer to the former than to the latter extreme. Many NATO stipulations concerning internal hier-archies, principles of warfare, the language of command, or even the de-sign of the Hungarian army uniform exemplify the case of enhanced standardization. The culture of banking and other financial services is probably the paradigm case of recent success in homogenization.[60]

Furthermore, the EU has already begun to inundate Hungary with its legal requirements, which amount to almost a hundred thousand pages. I would not like to dwell on how the Union has already homogenized large segments of business practices, social legislation, or environmental protection in the member states by touching on long-standing cultural taboos such as British isolationism, French rural civilization; or, to cite a more banal case, the anonymity of savings in Austria. Let me just refer to the example of the euro, which will not only liquidate words like mark, lira, krona (and forint) and make most of the sayings and jokes that include these words fall into oblivion, but will also feature as the most frequent aesthetic experience of hundreds of millions of people when they open their wallets and look at the notes (which are rather awful, by the way).

Nevertheless, even these instances of intensive standardization bear witness to cultural globalization only if the powerful external cultural effect is of worldwide nature. For the time being, the European Union builds its legitimacy both on protecting the member states from the waves of globalization and on helping them ride these waves.[61]

SIMULATION?

Another criterion, which is easily overlooked, is that homogenization should work. Forcing every child in Eastern Europe to learn the Russian alphabet proved to be a disastrous pedagogical exercise. The same applies to teaching the history of the Soviet Communist Party, the anthem of the USSR, and so on. In Hungary formal acceptance and informal rejection of external cultures (e.g., official Soviet art) as well as formal rejection and informal acceptance (e.g., Western lifestyles) had long traditions under communism. Hence, it is no wonder that one of the trendy concepts in my country today is "simulated capitalism,"[62] which covers a whole series of cultural pretenses (i.e., the superficial, partial, fake reception of capitalist civilization/s). Our research group could not help joining this national outburst of self-irony while trying to avoid its "orientalist" overtones, which originate in an inferiority complex vis-à-vis the "Occident." To avoid misunderstandings, simulation is not equivalent with cheating: it can be exercised with a blend of self-delusion and a naive thrust for imitation. Both guarantee a clear conscience.

So, even though you may play tennis in a snow white designer dress, if you spit on the court and call "out" when the ball was probably in, you'd better know that you've not entirely mastered the game's culture. Similarly, if you constantly mix English financial terms with Hungarian but need an interpreter for your business lunch, at which you arrive in a drunken state, describing your behavior as "simulation" would perhaps be an understatement. The same applies to those members of the new political elite throughout Eastern Europe who employ the most advanced techniques of campaign management and are well versed in human rights and rule-of-law discourse, but when in government use the tax authorities and the intelligence agencies to frighten the leaders of the opposition, misuse public monies, cherish contacts with criminals, and upon returning from church, give their wives hell and beat up the kids.[63]

Quality matters. If we calculated the number of tennis matches and business lunches or, to take more serious indicators, measured the nominal size of private property or the number of laws passed by parliament, then Hungary would certainly represent an exemplary case of Western-led cultural globalization as compared with many Eastern European states—the supporters of any shade of colonization theory could then sit back and relax. However, I am afraid they would deceive themselves. Let us suppose that they counted the growing number of baseball bats owned by a representative sample of Hungarians year by year and come to the conclusion that this "fundamentally American" game will soon crowd out one of the native branches of sport. My guess is that their measurement would be distorted for a simple reason: in my country, these bats are primarily used to replace the knife in street fighting and the revolver in protecting one's home.[64]

For the sake of argument, let us assume for a moment that each and every indigenous and incoming cultural good is comparable and that the ratio between them has steadily changed in favor of the latter in both quantitative and qualitative terms in the whole society over the past decade. As years go by, more and more liters of Coke and fewer and fewer liters of wine roll down the throats of Hungarians, who smoke less, run longer distances in the morning, eat smaller doses of fat in the evening, organize their work more efficiently, plan their savings with growing care, increasingly refrain from even innocent forms of sexual harassment, become more charitable, and so on. What about this sunny (though a bit boring) side of cultural globalization?

It would, nevertheless, be equally premature to be either enthusiastic or frustrated about these developments. Not having systematic empirical surveys, even the quantitative aspects of the globalization story remain in the dark. Thus we unfortunately do not know whether our poor Hungarians really jog more and more diligently every day and whether they secretly increase fat consumption at the same time—an ironic example of passive resistance.

EPILOGUE

For good or ill, ours is the first attempt in this country to find mosaic stones in a joint effort to construct a still nonexistent picture of cultural exchange between Hungary and the world. Understandably, we were not capable of mapping external influences in a comprehensive analysis ranging from poetry and church music to the ways in which people give names to their children or behave in broken elevators. In this regard, at least, the case studies conducted by our research group have left plenty of blank spaces in that picture.

Nevertheless, the empirical material we collected proved more than sufficient to make most of the conventional truisms reflected by the metaphor of the horseman questionable. The vast turbulence of cultural effects and the rivalry of external temptations prevented us from discerning unambiguous tendencies of irresistible cultural globalization in Hungary. I am inclined to think that, for the time being and apart from a limited number of fields, such tendencies do not exist. Instead, one sees a large repertoire of responses to the temptations, which reflect spontaneous/passive resistance, simulation, and balancing (compromises) in a continuum between the extremes of parochial isolationism and neophyte imitation of everything that comes from behind the former Iron Curtain.

Is the resulting balance healthy? If there had been a cultural vacuum in 1989, this would be a reasonable question today. I, for instance, could have imagined at that time a less parochial Hungary that imitated *certain* Western (and non-Western) cultural patterns more, while others less vigorously. I would gladly have abstained from the beauties of path dependency, especially if cultural innovation happened to slow down, due to the bumpy surface of old communist or even older national-conservative paths. However, choice is not arbitrary on the lending side either: high transaction costs, time-consuming operations, twin products, and other rigidities may occur in the international market of cultures. Could Hungary just import the culture of solidarity from Sweden without copying Swedish-style state interventionism? Could it follow the example of France in supporting elite culture without prompting French-style nationalism among its citizens? Or could it take over both the culture of self-reliance from the United States and the culture of nepotism from Japan?

Self-pity aside, I feel sorry for the enthusiasts of globalization too, especially since I have been told the following joke in Budapest, which ridicules time/space compression, a favorite concept of globalization theorists. It goes like this: How much time would Hungarians need to *not* stop littering? The answer is, seven centuries and one second. In the first five centuries we get rid of the Turks, the Habsburgs, and the Russians, who—as is well known—mercilessly forced us to litter. Then about one century is absolutely necessary to define the notion of "Hungarian rubbish" and another one to copy and then to approve the current German law prohibiting littering. And what about that additional second? Ah, that we need to learn how to cheat the new law.

NOTES

1. See J. M. Kovacs, "Turbulenzen im Vakuum: Anmerkungen zur kulturellen Globalisierung in Osteuropa," *Transit* 17 (1999).

2. I invited more than a dozen colleagues to take part in the Hungarian subproject. We established a research group, the Globus Circle, which organized expert discussions on the case studies during the past two years. Our circle is not a representative sample of the Hungarian intelligentsia. The members of the group are interested in cultural studies without being "official agents" of the discipline. With one exception, they work as social scientists and belong to a widely defined middle generation. Four of them served the Alliance of Free Democrats (a governing party between 1994 and 1998). No one in the group cherishes nationalist views or communist nostalgia. Otherwise, there are marked differences between the individual researchers within a broad spectrum of liberal thought. I owe special thanks to all authors: Judit Acsády, György Dalos, Miklós Haraszti, István Kamarás, Éva Kovács, Péter Medgyes, Attila Melegh, Pál Nyiri, Endre Sik, Ákos Szilágyi, András Török, Balázs Váradi, Violetta Zentai. Their papers have been published in the Budapest journal *2000* and are included in a volume edited by J. M. Kovács, *Studies on Cultural Globalization in Hungary* (Budapest: 2000–Sik Kiadó, 2001).

3. It would be difficult to find a more spectacular example of the (literally) unerasable handwriting in our day than the Russian national anthem. According to a recent decision of the Duma, the tune of the Soviet anthem was rehabilitated and the same

author who had written its original lyrics, Sergei Mikhalkov, was commissioned to adapt it to post-Soviet conditions.

4. For a critique of the balkanization concept, see Maria Todorova, *Imagining the Balkans* (New York: Oxford University Press, 1997) and, in a larger context, Larry Wolff, *Inventing Eastern Europe* (Stanford: Stanford University Press, 1994). For an analogy of balkanization in terms of resisting "West by the rest," see Benjamin Barber, *Jihad versus McWorld* (New York: Times Books, 1995). For accepting both the westernization and the balkanization hypotheses by dividing the region in two parts, see Samuel Huntington, *The Clash of Civilizations and the Remaking of World Order* (New York: Simon & Schuster, 1996); and Samuel Huntington and Lawrence Harrison, eds., *Culture Matters* (New York: Basic, 2000) (especially Ronald Inglehart's chapter, "Culture and Democracy"). See also Roger Burbach et al., *Globalization and Its Discontents: The Rise of Postmodern Socialisms* (London: Pluto, 1997) for a horror scenario of postcommunist evolution.

Cultural studies have not discovered Eastern Europe yet. In the literature listed in note 15 below, for instance, there are few references to cultural developments in the region. For a detailed analysis of *New York Times* coverage of the former Eastern bloc, see Attila Melegh, "New Bricks, Old Walls: Eastern Europe on the Civilizational Map of the New York Times," *2000* 6 (1999) (in Hungarian).

5. The Balkan version of this phrase in English-language journalism is "from plan to clan."

6. In Russia they are called *nuvorishi* or, in a broader sense, the "new Russians."

7. Absurdly, Eastern Europe as a whole would thereby follow the Czechs, who recently invented the slogan "Albright na Hrad!" (paraphrasing the revolutionary demand "Havel in the castle!") and elect Western policymakers who resigned in their home countries. Lately, populist politicians in Hungary had a hard time accepting a FBI office being opened in Budapest and German policemen protecting their co-patriots at Lake Balaton during the summer. See also Éva Kovács, "Occupants, Guests, Neighbors: The First U.S. Military Base in Hungary," *2000* 3 (2001) (in Hungarian).

8. Following a more tortuous route, Buddhism, for instance, arrived in Hungary from the United States through Europe; see István Kamarás, "Globality and Locality in New Religious Movements in Hungary," *2000* 5 (2001) (in Hungarian).

9. The chief PR officer of the U.S. military base in Taszár, a prison guard by profession, told us frankly that he did not know much about Hungary (except that it is an old nation, the land of Dracula [!], which was occupied by the Russians). But it was clear to him from the very beginning that the Americans must behave more politely than the Soviets, go to church with the Hungarians, show their weapons to local children, and be charitable to the elderly. He may be right but, as the case of unified Germany shows, even an extremely high degree of cultural affinity is not a sufficient condition for preventing Ossi–Wessi conflicts.

10. As to odd ideologies, an obvious reason why certain parts of faculty club culture fail to spread in Eastern Europe lies in their similarity with what the communists represented in words (e.g., feminism, multiculturalism) or in deeds (quotas, language rules, dogmatic interpretation of social doctrines). See Judit Acsády, "Did We Need Feminism? Hungary after 1989," *2000* 7–8 (2001) (in Hungarian).

11. To cite another example of confused images, according to a former chairman of the Hungarian Democratic Forum, which led the government coalition between 1990 and 1994, Budapest is as surrounded today by Western shopping malls as it was in 1956 by Soviet tanks (see *Napi Magyarország*, 24 October 1998).

12. Most of the new religious movements in Hungary are interpreted by the "historical churches" in this manner. The stubborn resistance by the traditionally radical nationalist Reformed Church to what it calls "sects" is a telling example (see Kamarás, "Globality and Locality").

13. Since 1998, Hungary has had a national-conservative government again. The following is a partial collection of its favorite cultural symbols: Christian middle class, the Hungarian *Bürger* (in contrast to the republican concept of citizen), Hungary of the countryside, the ideal family with "three children, four wheels, and three rooms," the Hungarian "body of the nation," the country of the holy crown, the Hungarian millennium, the brave Hungarian soldier, joining the EU with national pride (to use the words of Prime Minister Viktor Orbán, "there is life outside the union"). For the consequences of this ideological attitude to exporting culture by Hungary, see György Dalos, "A Success That Failed: Exporting Literature from Hungary (the Case of the Frankfurt Bookfair)," *2000* 10 (2000) (in Hungarian).

14. The weakness of organized resistance is demonstrated by a decade-long struggle by "language guards" (as some of the linguists in Hungary like to call themselves) to compel shopkeepers to translate (but not eliminate) the foreign names of their shops. The initiative has not yet been discussed by the parliament. See Péter Medgyes, "Very English—Very Good: Thoughts about the Expansion of the English Language in Hungary," *2000* 10 (2000) (in Hungarian).

15. In Hungary, academic debate on globalization is still in an embryonic stage. The first, rather bitter, contribution was made by sociologists who complained about the exploitation of their profession by Western academia, for example, György Csepeli, Anatal Örkény, and Kim Lane Scheppele, "The Colonization of East European Social Science," *Social Research* 63 (1996). For the time being, a dialogue of the deaf with high passions and strong political overtones could be an adequate description of the debate. By and large, the cast is this: incessant panicking, primarily by sociologists, about colonization as well as social and cultural decay, which is confronted by pragmatic arguments of economists who keep sending reassuring messages about the beauties of economic globalization. (Compare the influential discussion in *Népszabadság*, August-September 2000, which began with an article by László Antal, István Csillag, and Péter Mihályi, "Explaining Globalization," August 12). See also milder lamentations on global developments in culture by Csaba Gombár and Hédi Volosin, eds., *Civilization Questioned* (Budapest: Helikon-Korridor, 2000) (in Hungarian); Péter György, *Digital Eden* (Budapest: Magvető, 1998) (in Hungarian); Elemér Hankiss, *Proletarian Renaissance* (Budapest: Helikon, 1999) (in Hungarian); Ákos Szilágyi, "Imagined Place," *2000* 4 (2001) (in Hungarian); Csaba Gombár et al., *United States of Hungary?* (Budapest: Helikon-Korridor, 2001). For a harsh critique of globalization, see Géza Ankerl, *The West Exists, the East Does Not* (Budapest: Osiris, 2000) (in Hungarian); Erzsébet Szalai, *Postsocialism and Globalization* (Budapest: Új Mandátum,

1999). Expressly globalist views are scarce (see, e.g., László Seres et al., "Globalization: the Big Circles of Freedom," *Magyar Hirlap*, June 5, 2000) (in Hungarian).

Although in the debate references to current Western literature on globalization and culture are still rare, antiglobalist or globo-skeptical ideas in Hungary do not really differ from those represented by Zygmunt Bauman, *Globalization: The Human Consequences* (New York: Columbia University Press, 1998); Fredric Jameson and Masao Miyoshi, eds., *The Cultures of Globalization* (Durham, N.C.: Duke University Press, 1999); Serge Latouche, *The Westernization of the World* (Cambridge, U.K.: Polity, 1996); Robert Phillipson, *Linguistic Imperialism* (Oxford: Oxford University Press, 1992); George Ritzer, *The McDonaldization of Society* (Thousand Oaks, Calif.: Pine Forge, 1993); Saskia Sassen, *Globalization and Its Discontents* (New York: New Press, 1998); George Soros, *The Crisis of Global Capitalism* (New York: Public Affairs, 1998); John Tomlison, *Cultural Imperialism* (Baltimore, Md.: Johns Hopkins University Press, 1991); John Tomlison, *Globalization and Culture* (Cambridge, U.K.: Polity, 1999); Immanuel Wallerstein, *Geopolitics and Geoculture* (Cambridge: Cambridge University Press, 1997); Rob Wilson and Wimal Dissanayake, eds., *Global/Local: Cultural Production and the Transnational Imagery* (Durham, N.C.: Duke University Press, 1996).

16. A paradoxical example of using the Web to disseminate communist culture after communism is given by Digital Immortals, a program of the National Cultural Fund. In order to avoid a nationwide (and probably unfruitful) debate about the best writers and poets in Hungary, the minister for culture in the previous government decided to put on the Internet the works of all Hungarian authors who received the highest state award, the Kossuth Prize, established in the latter half of the 1940s. Thus the club of the Digital Immortals includes a great number of second-rate artists who excelled in loyalty to the old regime.

17. Empirical research in the Globus Circle relied on a great variety of methodological means: case studies, focus groups, expert interviews, media analysis, participant observations, and so on. However, we have conducted no new sociological surveys.

18. See Peter L. Berger, "Four Faces of Globalization," *National Interest* 49 (1997).

19. Liberalization may be conceived of as a combined borrowing of Davos and faculty club cultures if the faculty club carries classical ideas of economic and political liberalism as well, not just their critique.

20. The popular mind created a peculiar amalgam from some of the legendary cultural exporters of Hungary such as the father of the hydrogen bomb, Edward Teller; Albert Szentgyörgyi, who discovered vitamin C and received the Nobel Prize for it; composer Béla Bartók; soccer player Ferenc Puskás; and the movie star Zsa Zsa Gabor (all of them émigrés, by the way). In more recent times, it was only George Soros and the inventor of the magic cube, Ernö Rubik, who succeeded in joining them.

21. In Taszár the first American soldiers were challenged by nothing but an ironic graffiti: "You should have arrived earlier!"

22. While hesitating to divide the world into "strong" and "weak" cultures, I would not dispute the fact that Hungary suffers from actual weaknesses ranging from the lack of a larger ethnic family to geopolitical insignificance. However, these weaknesses do not necessarily breed direct subordination to "strong" cultures. On the contrary, they can lead to ingeniously elusive strategies of resistance to them, which are far from a direct collision or a culture war.

23. Compare Arjun Appadurai, *Modernity at Large: Cultural Dimensions of Globalization* (Minneapolis: University of Minnesota Press, 1996); Arjun Appadurai, "Grassroots Globalization," *Public Culture*, Winter 2000; Joana Breidenbach and Ina Zukrigl, *Tanz der Kulturen: Kulturelle Identität in einer globalisierten Welt* (Munich: Kunstmann, 1998); Mike Featherstone, Scott Lash, and Roland Robertson, eds., *Global Modernities* (London: Sage, 1995); Ulf Hannerz, *Cultural Complexity* (New York: Columbia University Press, 1992); Don Kalb et al., eds., *The Ends of Globalization: Bringing Society Back In* (Lanham, Md.: Roman & Littlefield, 2000); Mario Vargas Llosa, "The Culture of Liberty," *Foreign Policy*, January-February 2001; Roland Robertson, *Globalization* (London: Sage, 1992); Roland Robertson, *Globalization: Social Theory and Global Culture* (Thousand Oaks, Calif.: Sage, 1994); James L. Watson, eds., *Golden Arches East: McDonald's in East Asia* (Stanford: Stanford University Press, 1997).

24. Hungarians are proud to nurture the tradition of organized passive resistance to the Habsburg Empire between 1849 and 1867, which was allegedly repeated under Soviet rule following the defeat of the 1956 revolution. They did not give Russian names to their children and did not force them to learn Russian. However, only a small minority of public figures chose internal emigration and virtually nobody boycotted Soviet consumer and cultural goods. Although the memory of passive resistance is probably still alive in Hungary, the current case of withstanding global cultural pressures reveals much more spontaneity than organization. For the time being, the icons of cultural protest are lacking and its symbols are old-fashioned. Resistance is neither active nor organized.

25. See, for example, the contributions of Iosif Brodsky, Václav Havel, György Konrád, Milan Kundera, und Czeslaw Milosz to the discussion on Central Europe during the 1980s. See George Schöpflin and Nancy Wood, eds., *In Search of Central Europe* (Oxford: Polit, 1989); Timothy Garton-Ash, *The Uses of Adversity: Essays on the Fate of Central Europe* (Cambridge: Granta Books, 1989).

26. From the 1960s on, the Soviet art offered to the satellite countries went beyond the junk culture of "socialist realism." The most celebrated items of cultural supply from the USSR included the Bolshoi Theater, David Oistrakh and Mstislav Rostropovich, the Moiseiev dance troupe, the Obraztsov puppet theater, the Moscow Circus, Sergei Eisenstein and Andrei Tarkovsky, Iury Liubimov and Arkadii Raikin, Vladimir Visotsky and Bulat Okudzhava, Anna Akhmatova and Alexander Solzhenitsin, or the Russian folk songs taught in school, which received considerable publicity in Hungary. The same applies to certain kinds of sport in which the Soviets demonstrated almost artistic proficiency (e.g., chess, ice hockey, gymnastics). See Ákos Szilágyi, "Traces in the Ruins: Sovietization or Soviet-Style Globalization?" *2000*, 2001 (in Hungarian).

27. A leading political philosopher in Hungary remembers: "Some years ago I met an astronomer and mathematician of my age in Boston who had immigrated from the People's Republic of China. At a boring university party we realized how similar our childhoods were. We read the same children's books written by Gaidar, Kataiev, Kaverin, Marshak, and Charushin. We sang the same songs, the *Warsawianka* and the *Song of the Amur Partisans*. We spent our summers in the same pioneer camps at the sea. Our first doubts emerged when reading Milton, Spinoza, and Hegel, i.e., philosophers whose intellectual heritage, according to the communists, fell to the working class. We played volleyball because for one

reason or another this sport was favored by the directors of the communist high schools all over the world. Finally, as small children we mourned the tragic fate of Karl Liebknecht and Rosa Luxemburg. Yet Professor Huntington says that we belong to civilizations that are hostile to each other" (G. M. Tamás, "Huntington Is Mistaken," *Magyar Lettre Internationale,* Spring 1998) (in Hungarian).

28. Low-quality modernization (of which the export of Chernobyl-type nuclear plants to the ex-communist countries is a striking example) is only one of the specific features of Soviet cultural imperialism. This kind of colonization, especially in its last two decades, was imbued with the paradox of claiming to outcompete noncommunist cultures by colonizers who were nourishing inferiority feelings toward these cultures. The imperial strategy of the Soviet Union was defensive in terms of keeping its own citizens away from the colonies and holding the occupation forces behind closed doors to avoid cultural contamination. The fact that the Soviet military barracks became vast underground suppliers of color television sets, water pumps, and Kalashnikovs for the indigenous population throughout the states of the Warsaw Pact illustrates the ambiguous position of the colonizers.

29. Compare Richard Kuisel, *Seducing the French: The Dilemma of Americanization* (Berkeley: University of California Press, 1993); Kaspar Maase, *BRAVO Amerika* (Hamburg: Junius 1992); Richard Peels, *Not Like Us: How Europeans Have Loved, Hated, and Transformed American Culture since World War II* (New York: Basic, 1997); Reinhold Wagnleitner, *Coca Colonization and the Cold War: The Cultural Mission of the United States in Austria after the Second World War* (Chapel Hill: University of North Carolina Press, 1994); Reinhold Wagnleitner, "The Empire of Fun, or Talkin' Soviet Union Blues: The Sound of Freedom and U.S. Cultural Hegemony in Europe," *Diplomatic History* 23, no. 3 (1999).

30. A controversial example of the same phenomenon was provided by the Coca-Cola Company, which a couple of years ago planned to decorate the historic Chain Bridge in Budapest with its red and white brand colors for Christmas. On how the company failed to implement the plan, see Zoltán Fejős, "Coca Cola and the Chain Bridge," *Café Babel* 2 (1998) (in Hungarian).

31. One of the new business locations in the Pest half of Budapest carries the puzzling name of Pest Center (see Medgyes, "Very English—Very Good").

32. It is worthwhile to distinguish between direct and indirect hegemony, particularly the two kinds of indirect hegemony: (1) essentially North American cultural goods transported by non-U.S. carriers (e.g., Latin American soap operas) and (2) essentially non-American goods becoming American (and in this way global) cultural prototypes (e.g., Porsche as a yuppie symbol). As far as direct effects are concerned, I would suggest considering both genuine cultural imports from the United States (e.g., pop music) and economic/political import articles that imply cultural change (e.g., Hungarian soldiers learning English in NATO).

33. Similar to Soviet-style penetration, the expansion of the Chinese world system in Hungary is also state led (or at least utilized by the state) and presupposes the settlement of large groups of "globalizers" (albeit no soldiers) who, despite the fact that they represent a grand civilization, often have feelings of inferiority toward the natives. A huge difference between the two is the predominantly commercial character of Chinese expansion and

the extensive use of Western globalization techniques by the merchant networks and mafias. See Pál Nyiri, "Non-Western Globalization in Post-Communist Hungary: The Case of Chinese Immigration," *2000* 10 (2000) (in Hungarian).

34. The Audi Works of Györ in western Hungary recruits labor in Slovakia; harvesting in eastern Hungary is contingent on seasonal workers from Romania; the Yugoslav wars forced many deserters, dissidents, businessmen, and tens of thousands of displaced persons to resettle in Hungary; thousands of Third World refugees are returned from the Austrian border to Hungary every year; hundreds of Austrian farmers cultivate cheap Hungarian land along the same border illegally; Russian big business invests heavily in future EU member state Hungary; Budapest is a favorite meeting place (and battlefield) of the big Eastern European mafias, a junction of the drug trade and prostitution, and an infamous production site of pornographic films. Finally, to cite more peaceful examples of coexistence, currently many multinational firms, international agencies, and NGOs are headquartered in the Hungarian capital; by now, the Central European University founded by George Soros has become a major international center of higher education in the region. For its "glocal" features, see Violetta Zentai, "Gifts of a Mercurial Donor or How the Idea of Open Society Becomes Localized and Globalized," *2000* 4 (2002) (in Hungarian).

35. What is nowadays called "fascism tourism" (repeated neo-Nazi demonstrations in Budapest) also has Austrian and German roots.

36. The Hungarian government sponsors Duna Televízió, a satellite television channel for Hungarians in the neighboring countries; recently, the Hungarian state-owned oil company, MOL, bought out its competitors in Croatia and Slovakia; a Hungarian university is being established in Transylvania, Romania; the ethnic Hungarian parties in Slovakia, Romania, and Yugoslavia are strongly supported by Budapest, and so on.

37. Suzuki advertises its cars with megaposters using the red-white-green Hungarian tricolor and the patriotic slogan "Suzuki is *our* car."

38. Another interesting dimension of research could be the mapping of changes in "concert hall culture" (a metaphor of high culture) that stem from its new global features (cf. the Three Tenors; Harry Potter, supported by the Internet; and the *Millennium Day* worldwide television show celebrating cultural diversity). In Hungary there are only a few protagonists of elite culture who would regard these examples as evidence of restructuring rather than decline.

39. In the beginning, cultural change was amazing in areas that had formerly been blocked by the most severe communist taboos (e.g., citizenship, property rights, media, religion, sexual representation) or by economic barriers (e.g., lack of purchasing power). After 1989 the spectacularly fast arrival in Eastern Europe of selected cultural icons of Western capitalism such as *Playboy*, the joint stock company, and the Visa card impressed most observers as an unstoppable cultural revolution.

40. The inflow of these commodities was ironically accelerated by their clones (some of the Hungarian products were Star Cola, Trapper jeans, City Grill fast food chain, etc.), which were unable to carry the same symbolic meaning as their Western counterparts.

41. A recent example of the "West against the West in the East" conflict was provided in Belgrade during the Kosovo war by rock concerts organized on the bridges of the Danube,

which were targeted by NATO bombers. The audience at these protest concerts wore targets depicting bull's-eyes, which were expected to reach viewers in enemy countries through Western television stations. Actually, this proved to be a strong weapon in the public relations war.

42. A first step of the current national-conservative government to counterbalance what it called "alien cultural influence," it recentralized the system of public grants, purged the grant committees, and defined their ideological priorities minutely. See András Török, "The Rise and Fall of the National Cultural Fund in Hungary," (unpublished manuscript) (in Hungarian).

43. In Hungary even the liberals considered BBC-type arrangements as *non plus ultra* in liberalizing public electronic media after communism. Although consistently backing privatization up to a point to create a competitive environment for the public channels, they proved reluctant to advocate the U.S. model because they feared "too much" commercialization. See Miklós Haraszti, "Democratizing the Media: Post-Communist Paradoxes in Hungary," 2000 3 (2002) (in Hungarian).

44. Satisfied with an attempt by the government to merge state universities in Hungary, the World Bank did not demand their privatization; the previous government introduced a Dutch-style public financing scheme based on the number of students and resisted (as its successor does) a voucher system. See Balázs Váradi, "The Impact of Globalization upon the Universities in Hungary, 2000 3 (2002) (in Hungarian).

45. The resistance to "Americanization" is partly due to the fact that many German traditions were reinforced by the communists, especially in party organization, military culture, public management (including schools, hospitals, theaters, etc.), and science administration. At the same time, many of the neoliberal guiding principles of the recent pension reform in Hungary were imported through Chile (with the help of a Hungarian émigré and the support of the World Bank). The new rules of bank management originated in the United States; for example, the extremely low share of public housing is reminiscent of American standards. For the proliferation of American textbooks of mainstream economics in Hungarian universities, see János Mátyás Kovács, "A Copy or a Parody? The Dubious Breakthrough of Mainstream Economics in Hungarian Economic Thought," 2000 2 (2002) (in Hungarian).

46. Obviously, conflicting principles can be reconciled. While in the West political correctness may have a market value (e.g., the multicultural messages by McDonald's, Benetton, and Ikea), in Hungary there has been no rapprochement between the two spheres. For instance, the recent emergence of the first black persons in Hungarian soccer, television, and theater cannot mislead the observer: the country's largest minority, the Romas (5–8 percent of the population) lack real and symbolic representation not only in government and elite culture but also in commercial campaigns.

47. However, no effort has been made to bring in, along with the lighter brands, the cultural fashion of "abstinence with middle-class pride."

48. A similar coincidence can be observed in the case of credit cards (which enable the clients of the ex-communist banks to avoid slow and unreliable transfers), shopping malls (which provide excellent opportunities for money laundering), and expressways (which give a superb opportunity for the government to strengthen its local networks and channel public funds in financing the ruling parties).

49. For the Native American and satanist contacts of the Hungarian "*sámán* (wizard) drummers," see Kamarás, "Globality and Locality."

50. Ironically, the scenario suggested by the old joke, according to which the only chance for Hungarian citizens to ever live under capitalism is to declare war on NATO, thereby forcing it to occupy the country, has in a way been implemented in Yugoslavia by Slobodan Milosevic.

51. Even in the late 1980s, the word "foreign" served as a brand name in Hungarian shopwindows. Symptomatically, the campaign clip of the ex-Communist Party in the first free elections was based on the pop hit "Go West."

52. For the images (often humiliating ones) of the "Eastern inviters" developed by the "Western invitees," see Attila Melegh, "Maps of Global Actors: Narratives, Identities, and the Representation of Eastern Europe," *2000* 2 (2002) (in Hungarian).

53. The unpopularity of positive thinking comes as no surprise after so many years of forced optimism under communism. But the continuing low respect for privacy in Hungary, despite the terrible memory of communist terror and surveillance, is puzzling.

54. The embryonic typologies of the "early borrowers" under postcommunism include the new-rich middle class, yuppies, celebrities, and, needless to say, television as the chief mediator of demonstration effects. This is no essay in the sociology of globalization. Nevertheless, I suspect that quite a few global cultural goods (the cheaper ones, of course, such as soap operas, rap music, tattooing, body building, video arcades, etc.) are imported, directly or via television, by lower-status groups of the society. As regards the old regime, researchers thus far have missed the pioneering role played by the émigrés and the *nomenklatura* in mediating Western lifestyles.

55. Valentine's Day is a great success in Hungary, owing to support from florists and chocolate producers and the innocent message of the ritual. However, some controversial U.S. cultural practices (e.g., loose control of guns, the death penalty, litigiousness, the role of psychiatry in everyday life, wrestling, etc.) have not been transplanted to my country yet.

56. For new forms of corruption, see Endre Sik, "Path Dependency and Network Sensitivity: A Culture of Corruption in Hungary?" *2000* 7–8 (2001) (in Hungarian). The following works offer insight into the changing value and belief systems of the Hungarian population over the past decade: Rudolf Andorka, Tamás Kolosi, Richard Rose, and György Vukovich, eds., *A Society Transformed: Hungary in Time-Space Perspective* (Budapest: Central European University Press, 1999); György Csepeli and Antal Örkény, "Social Change, Political Beliefs, and Everyday Expectations in Hungarian Society," in J. M. Kovács, ed., *Transition to Capitalism? The Communist Legacy in Eastern Europe* (New Brunswick, N.J.: Transaction, 1994); György Csepeli, Ferenc Erös, Mária Neményi, and Antal Örkény, "Political Change—Psychological Change," Collegium Budapest Discussion Papers no. 28, 1996; György Csepeli and Endre Sik, "Changing Content of Political Xenophobia in Hungary," in M. Fullerton, Endre Sik, and Judit Tóth, eds., *Refugees and Migrants: Hungary at a Crossroads* (Budapest, 1995); Zoltán Fábián, *Authoritarian Attitude and Prejudices* (Budapest: Új Mandátum, 1999) (in Hungarian); Tamás Kolosi, István György Tóth, and György Vukovich, eds., *Social Report* (Budapest: Tárki, 1999, 2001; Péter Róbert and Ildikó Nagy, *Redistributionist State or Self-Reliant Citizen?* (Budapest: Tárki, 1998) (in Hungarian).

57. In Hungary a great number of believers refuse to accept the conflict between the traditional churches and the new religious movements. Instead of making a choice, they opt for double or triple affiliation (see Kamarás, "Globality and Locality").

58. Among the checks and balances of government, the broad competence granted to the Constitutional Court and the weak intermediary position of the president of the republic were borrowed from the German *Grundgesetz*, whereas the institution of the ombudsman arrived in Hungary from Scandinavia.

59. See Zentai, "Gifts." An interesting example of mixing cultures in Hungary is provided by the "Krishna valley" of Somogyvámos. The religious community became so deeply embedded in the world of local farmers that the original (?) English text of the Krishna rituals was combined with the melody of Hungarian folk songs popular in the village.

60. Nonetheless, the recent involvement of the respected consulting firm Deloitte & Touche with the biggest corruption scandal in Hungary after 1989, the suspicious bankruptcy of a state-owned financial institution, Postabank, demonstrates the vulnerability of agents of Western business culture that are allegedly immune to contagion. For dubious business practices and cross-fertilization between economic cultures in the privatization process, see Sik, "Path Dependency."

61. Compare the official EU rhetoric claiming European cultural superiority and celebrating its unique welfare model, "unity in diversity" style pluralism, and so on.

62. The basic reference is a long forgotten paper by Lajos Leopold, "Pretended Capitalism," written in 1917; see *Medvetánc* 2–3 (1988) (in Hungarian). For an interesting comparison, see Oleg Kharkhordin, "The Soviet Individual: Genealogy of a Dissimulating Animal," in Featherstone et al., eds., *Global Modernities*.

63. Of course, such ambiguities belong to normalcy on the home territory of the cultural exporter as well. Bad manners, including hypocrisy and dubious taste, are also offered for global consumption. True, they tend to become localized. Without any intention to construct an East–West dichotomy, let me mention a few cases from the recent past: Chancellor Helmut Kohl in Germany broke the tax law for his party's sake whereas the late President Franjo Tudjman in Croatia expropriated public money for his own family. Furthermore, the former prime minister of Slovakia, Vladimir Meciar, has not been indicted yet for having the son of his rival, President Michal Kovac, kidnapped by the intelligence service a couple of years ago. It is hard to imagine that Bill Clinton, who weathered the Lewinsky scandal, could have survived such an accusation. Or could he have remained in office if Lewinsky had given birth to a child? Recently a Hungarian minister (in a government venerating Christian family values) had an extramarital relationship with his secretary, who subsequently bore his child. As of this writing, the minister is still in office.

64. There are, however, plenty of more serious examples for the transformation of meaning. While in the West most members of the new religious movements turn their back on consumerism, in Hungary many of them escape into consumption. While in the West multiculturalism normally protects the emancipation of ethnic minorities, it can justify their segregation as well, if multicultural ideas are interpreted by ethno-nationalists in Hungary (or, more aggressively, by ethnic cleansers in Serbia).

PART THREE

Globalization on the Periphery

7

Globalization, Culture, and Development

CAN SOUTH AFRICA BE MORE THAN AN OFFSHOOT OF THE WEST?

Ann Bernstein

A warning to those Africans who think of a culture as an anthropological thing that belongs in the past and must be reconstructed as a mere landmark or a monument: the here and now of its struggle to come to terms with modern technology, with the confrontation of other ways of life, must give as valid a definition of our culture as its historic past.

—Ezekiel Mphahlele[1]

While anthropologists and historians tend to think about culture as immutable core values, these can be manipulated. Ancient beliefs can evaporate or revive and become real.

—Peter Berger[2]

Unlike many other developing countries, South Africa has long-standing, close connections with Western countries and has long been subject to globalizing forces emanating from Britain, the United States, and elsewhere.[3] In many respects, the apartheid era in South African history can be seen as a hiatus of determined resistance to many global

185

Figure 7.1   Call for You on the Mobile

Source: "Geeks of the Bushveld," *The Economist*
15 April 2000, p. 66, *www.economist.com/display
Story.cfm?Story_ID=302619.*

but predominantly Western ideas, attitudes, and technologies emerging in the rest of the world after World War II. Instead of moving toward racial equality, the apartheid government entrenched and strengthened discrimination and segregation practices; instead of integrating and adopting new technologies and management practices, South Africa isolated itself, introduced television only in the 1970s, and failed to modernize many aspects of the society. But the introduction of democracy in South Africa helped reestablish the country's place within the global community and Western sphere of influence, once again revealing a country that is remarkably open to many kinds of globalizing forces.

Economically, South Africa's government and vibrant business community are leading the country's full reentry into international trading systems and competitive corporate practices. Politically, the country is acting swiftly to establish a leading position in African and north–south bilateral and multilateral organizations and relationships. Culturally, South Africa is now fully part of the international cultural circuit of theater, dance, music, and art and is in turn making its contribution on that global circuit with homegrown productions. All these dynamics reflect and have an impact on cultural developments in the country.

South Africa, as will be demonstrated in this chapter, is a society that is remarkably open to international cultural forces and has been so in many different ways for a long time. It is important to remember that the opposition to apartheid was shaped and fought with language, style, and forms that emerged out of Western influences rather than any traditional or atavistic approaches. From the formation of the African National Congress (ANC) early in the twentieth century by urban, missionary-educated, and mainly middle-class Africans, to the socialist ideologies of the liberation movements in exile, to the Western trade union–inspired domestic opposition forces, the impact of Western ideas, culture, money, and influence is strikingly apparent.

There has been very little opposition to these powerful cultural globalizing forces. In fact, South Africa has and will increasingly play a role as a subregional center, spreading Western consumer, cultural, political, and other forces into the wider African region. The country (and Johannesburg in particular) is becoming a place where larger global forces get a South African and sometimes larger African spin and are then transmitted into the continent.

There has been little resistance to this openness to global, mainly Western, mainly American, cultural forces; quite the reverse, in fact, with the vast majority of South Africans exhibiting remarkable eagerness and speed in adopting as much as they can of the new mores, technologies, music, fashions, and ideas emanating from the United States and elsewhere. However, the spread of global cultural forces takes place more easily at some levels than others, and South Africa lags far behind in adopting what might be called the "economic production culture" that underlies the successful and fast-moving entrepreneurial global economies.

The new democratic state led by Thabo Mbeki, South Africa's first deputy president and now its president, has on the one hand encouraged and assisted this process of "cultural assimilation" and on the other attempted to put an "African" twist on what is happening. Whether there can be any real traditionally African content to this African contribution to the core of emerging global culture remains to be seen. The final section of this chapter includes speculation about what this might be.

In this chapter we focus on the globalizing forces at play in South Africa and explore their interaction with indigenous cultural dynamics. First, we examine the impact of South Africa's historical exposure to global culture: Western colonialism, Christian missionaries, and their effects on indigenous culture. We look at the impact of commerce, Christianity, civilization, and conquest. After a brief historical description, we examine the question of whether South (and southern) Africa is a cultural ghetto of the West.

Berger has suggested that a key component of the process of globalization is the interplay between global and indigenous cultural forces. As Schlemmer observes,

> Much of the interest and conceptual challenge in approaching the effect of globalization on culture, values and economic development lies in the creative tension and interaction between the vigorous expansion of Western economic culture and the national and regional cultures of the non-Western world. Broadly, one has a picture of cultures and value systems, some older in origin than European civilization, either resisting, adapting to or becoming displaced by the models and styles of post-industrial economic culture. . . . This picture, however, assumes a 'contest'. It assumes the presence of sustaining cultures or cultures of origin of some tenacity in the regions of the world exposed to the waves of global influence from the West.[4]

Is this in fact the case in South and southern Africa? Looking at Africa and in particular South Africa makes it clear that this assertion begs the question of the existence and tenacity of indigenous cultures in the country. In the first section of the chapter we will briefly examine the evidence concerning cultural interplay in South Africa before turning to explore the hypothesis that there is and has been for some decades a receptivity to Western culture in this country.

In the second section we describe a "map" of the impact of globalizing forces. We focus on Davos culture but also look at popular culture, the impact of global cultural elites, and evangelical Protestantism in the country.

The third section examines President Mbeki's concept of the African renaissance—how he understands this term and how he is trying to use it. We look at the possibilities this might provide for South Africa to be a bigger player in the global arena affecting culture and development.

Finally I conclude with some thoughts on culture and globalization, suggesting that there may be two additional "faces of global culture"— underclass/ghetto culture and international criminal culture. The question also remains of the differential speed and timing of the absorption of international consumption versus production cultures. We briefly examine the relationship of cultural diffusion to power and then explore the possibilities of increasing global cultural influence emanating from South Africa.

IS THERE A CONTEST IN SOUTH AFRICA?

Brief Historical Perspective

According to Delius, the societies that existed prior to the colonization of the subcontinent ranged from hunter-gatherers through pastoralists to mixed farmers. Each was marked by distinctive political, social, and religious systems.[5] When white settlers arrived in 1652, these societies were subjected to profound processes of economic and cultural transformation; their capacity to weather these processes varied considerably.

Hunter-gatherer and herder communities were comprehensively dispossessed: they ended up as laborers/clients on white farmlands or as refugees on mission stations; many were pushed to the far periphery of an emerging colonial world. Given the comprehensiveness of this transformation, it is hardly surprising that very little survived of their values, way of life, or language. "They survived only in small pockets, in the clicks in the speech of the more southern mixed farming communities and in the rich cadences of Afrikaans."

SOUTH AFRICA'S NEW COAT OF ARMS AND MOTTO

On 27 April 2000, Freedom Day, South Africa's new coat of arms was unveiled by President Thabo Mbeki. It has an African look about it and replaces the coat of arms the country had used since 1910. Its elements include pairs of elephant tusks, a spear and knobkierie, a stylized protea, a secretary bird with outstretched wings, a rising sun, and a shield depicting two figures in greeting, derived from the famous Khoisan paintings on the Linton stone. At the base of the coat of arms is the motto: *!KE E: /XARRA // KE.*

President Mbeki said that this motto, "written in the Khoisan language of the /Xam people, means 'diverse people unite' or

Figure 7.2   South Africa's Coat of Arms

Source: *www.gov.za/symbols/ coatofarms.htm*

'people who are different join together.'"[6] He added, "We have chosen an ancient language of our people. This language is now extinct as no one lives who speaks it as his or her mother tongue." (The Khoisan were the original inhabitants of this country and the /Xam have ceased to exist as a people for centuries.) He went on to state that we should remember those exterminated by others and "by inscribing these words on our coat of arms—*!ke e: /xarra //ke*—we make a commitment to value life, to respect all languages and cultures and to oppose racism, sexism, chauvinism and genocide." The motto's purported meaning is not much different from the previous one, *Ex Unitate Vires*, Latin for "There is strength in unity."

The *Star* newspaper carried a phonetic transliteration and a guide on how to pronounce the motto: "(CLICK)-EH-AIR-(CLICK)-gaara-(CLICK)- . The first click is produced by flicking the tongue against the front of the palate. The second is produced by pressing the tip of the tongue against the front teeth. The third is made by sucking air through the side of the mouth. The 'g' is guttural."[7]

Figure 7.3   Cartoon Lampooning South Africa's Coat of Arms

Source: *Mail & Guardian*, www.mg.za/mg/madameve/2000/05/me20000506w.htm.
Accessed 6 May 2000.

One commentator cheekily describes the motto as "not the secret formula for something toxic that Dr. Wouter Basson [apartheid's Dr. Death] dreamed up in his apartheid laboratory. Neither is it a bad typographical error or even the work of a malevolent subeditor. That gallimaufry of seemingly random letters and jumbled punctuation marks is the country's new motto." He continued, "I think it's safe to assume that the country's new motto will go largely unappreciated by the majority of the population, most of whom speak one of our 11 official languages, which don't happen to include the language of the !Xam people, beautiful and lyrical though it may be. This is a great pity because I would have thought that the whole point of a country having a motto is that it should be pithy enough for all its citizens to remember and quote in times of exigency."

He also said that we only have the academics' word on the meaning of the motto: "The !Xam language is even deader than Latin, and for all we know the cunning linguists may have played a practical joke on us, and we could be walking around with the equivalent of a [dumb] blonde joke on our new escutcheon."[8]

Confusion arose when the chairman of the Khomani San Association of the Northern Cape, Gert Vaalbooi, said the motto in fact referred to the act of urinating! Yet University of the Witwatersrand Professor David Lewis Williams, who did the translation, said Vaalbooi was wrong: Williams's translation was based on transcriptions of the vanished language taken down in the 1870s; he also said that Vaalbooi's language would not be the same as /Xam, as Vaalbooi called himself a Khomani. In the end it appears that only two people in the whole world, both South African language experts, are "in any position to comment on any allusions in the new motto."[9] South Africans will be united in not being able to pronounce or understand their motto.

The popular daily cartoon strip *Madam and Eve* produced a satiric version of the new motto. Its comment: "Since there are eleven official languages, we have chosen a motto (in Danish) that nobody can pronounce, thereby promoting equality for all."[10]

Mixed farming communities proved considerably more resilient. If a wellspring of indigenous culture flowing into the present were to be found, this would be its principal source. These societies also shared a broadly common culture: they all spoke related Bantu languages and had political systems focused on the institution of chieftainship. Ancestors and other spirits played a pivotal part in their religious systems.

There were significant discrepancies of wealth, particularly in terms of cattle holding, but the wealthy were expected to show considerable largesse. Instead of being dominated by a communal and egalitarian ethos, as some have suggested, it seems clear that these tendencies existed in combination and sometimes in tension with elaborate hierarchies, individual accumulation, and competition among households. This was not a world of maximizing individuals, nor dominated by the suffocating communalism that some proponents of *ubuntu* and African socialism invoke.

The eventual military defeat of these mixed farming communities did not bring demographic catastrophe. Instead, colonial conquest was a prelude to a period of sustained population growth that made continued white domination increasingly improbable and ultimately unsustainable. The military tenacity and demographic resilience of these societies were not, however, matched by their long-term cultural cohesion. Part of the explanation for this lies in the genesis and influence of a westernized elite and in the particular processes of industrialization and urbanization that constituted the core of the making of modern South Africa.

There is a long history of evangelical Christianity in relation to the indigenous cultures of South Africa. Missionaries penetrated African societies with increasing intensity in the nineteenth century. The message they brought did not stop at proclaiming the power of a new God but went on to demand the fundamental transformation of the way of life of their converts.

> They denounced polygamy, initiation, bridewealth and other cornerstones of African culture. They enforced new dress codes and new forms of architecture. They introduced literacy and Western education and they celebrated the improving impact of commerce and wage labor. At first they attracted no more than a handful of followers. Their demands for radical transformation alienated the vast majority of Africans and their chiefs but a minority responded to the brave new world the missionaries offered.

In the view of Monica Wilson (1968), one of South Africa's preeminent social scientists, these converts were the radicals within African societies—the individuals ready to embrace change. Others castigated them as collaborators and colonial stooges. Notwithstanding this, it was these groups of converts who provided the basis for the development of an educated African elite that dominated leadership positions within African society in the twentieth century. Their experience of alienation and exclusion with the colonial order persuaded some to attempt to rebuild their connections with traditional society, but these attempts were made across the considerable cultural chasm that their initial immersion in missionary Christianity had opened up between them and their societies of origin. Their struggle to force open the doors of colonial society were predominantly couched in terms of the values of the Western discourses of liberalism, nationalism, and to a lesser extent socialism, rather than in any appeal to indigenous political and cultural forms. As a result, members of the educated African middle class have remote if sometimes ambiguous relationships to traditional culture.

While the educated African elite retained some connections to rural society, their most important reference points were the new urban centers with their rapidly expanding African populations. If indigenous cultural forms had retained popular legitimacy and vitality in this setting they might have asserted a stronger influence on the identity and aspirations of the elite. But the particular processes of urbanization that took place in South Africa ensured that colonial cities were far from hospitable to traditional culture. The dominance of a system of migrant labor, the resilience of rural communities, and the impact of segregation and pass laws (controlling movement into the cities) ensured that it was rare for entire segments of African societies or even extended or nuclear families to relocate to urban areas. More commonly, those who settled in towns were individuals whose relationship to rural communities and traditional cultures had been ruptured in various ways. They were migrants sucked into urban life and separated from their families in the rural areas: young men who became disenchanted with the patriarchal order on white farms and fled to the towns in defiance of both the farmers and their fathers; African women who defied prohibitions to leave rural communities and severed the relationship with their former homes when they departed for the city.

Cities became dynamic zones of interaction between individuals from a wide range of backgrounds, but they were also arenas in which African families struggled to establish themselves on a stable footing. Urban African families had to contend with harsh socioeconomic conditions, the countervailing pull of rural responsibilities, the absence of properly constituted political authority, and the buttressing role of lineage and clan. The capacity of these insecure urban families to inculcate a strong sense of tradition into new generations was undermined by the fact that the socialization of youths in rural communities was based on structures in which clearly defined and organized age cohorts played a central role in educating and disciplining young men and women. These processes culminated in most African societies in formal initiation in which youths were prepared for their roles as adults by groups of elders. In the burgeoning urban cities and townships, ethnic diversity, frail and fragile family structures, and the absence of processes of initiation militated against effective cross-generational cultural transmission. Urban youths still clustered together in age-based groups ranging from loose forms of street corner society to more organized and menacing gang structures. But this was a world whose primary cultural references were Western. Hollywood films, for example, provided models for modes of dress and sources of names, and those that were not submerged in the world of gangs were increasingly drawn into Western forms of education and culture (see the text box on Sophiatown, and the intersection of local and global culture in a segregated, discriminatory world).

SOPHIATOWN:
THE "LITTLE PARIS OF THE TRANSVAAL"

Sophiatown—the legendary racially mixed South African township destroyed in the late 1950s through the implementation of apartheid laws—was, at the time, one of the most culturally vibrant urban areas in Africa, and some of the best African writing in the twentieth century emerged from this period in South Africa.[11] As Hannerz observes, to the people of the township, a cosmopolitan aesthetic became a form of local resistance: accepting New York could be a way of rejecting Pretoria, of refusing the cultural entailments of any sort of "separate development."

> We are inclined to think of local cultural resistance as something that draws its symbolic resources from local roots and undoubtedly Sophiatowners could use such resources as well. As things stood however, it seems to have been in the logic of the situation rather to reaffirm the links between Sophiatown and the world.

A few quotes from novels and other books produced about that place and time are illustrative of the complexity of the emerging South African culture and the interplay between global and local forces:

> In a dance hall a jazz combo is creating . . . music taken from American Negro jazz and hammered out on the anvil of the South African experience: slum living, thuggery, police raids, job-hunting, shifting ghettos and so on. The penny-whistle takes the key melody. . . . the musicians grope their way through the notes, expressing by this improvisation the uncertainty and restlessness of urban life. . . . And so an urban culture has evolved. It is an escape route for people on the run; but it is the only virile culture in South Africa.

After portraying township culture ("a fugitive culture: borrowing here, incorporating there, retaining this, rejecting that"), Mphahlele goes on to argue the importance of migrant labor in extending the continuum into the rural areas. The migrants would bring back to their country homes new gadgets, gramophones, radio sets, concertinas, mouth organs. They would bring cloth and styles of dress and stories of industrial life. In such ways, the township was a center with its own periphery. Yet in Sophiatown it would be the connections with the outside world and particularly with metropolitan ways of life that would draw one's attention and capture one's imagination:

> You don't just find your place here, you make it and you find yourself. There is a tang about it. . . . You have the right to listen to the latest jazz records at Ah Sing's over the road. You can walk a Coloured girl of an evening down to the Odin cinema and no questions asked. You can try out Rhugubar's curry with your bare fingers without embarrassment. . . . Indeed, I've shown quite a few white people "The Little Paris of the Transvaal"—but only a few were Afrikaners. (*Can Themba*)

It seemed that one would leapfrog over white South Africa and involve oneself more directly with what we thought of as

interesting attractive or superior in more distant places . . .
"because with us virtually everything South African was always synonymous with mediocrity." (*Nat Nakasa*)

The well-dressed man about Sophiatown was exclusively
styled with American and English labels unobtainable
around the shops of Johannesburg; the boys were expensively
dressed in a stunning ensemble of colour: "Jewished" in their
phraseology; in dress items described as "can't gets"; clothes
sent for from New York or London. Shoes from America—
Florsheims, Winthrops, Bostonians; Saxone and Mansfield
from London; BVDs, Van Heusen, Arrow shirts; suits from
Simpsons, Hector Powe, Robert Hall, Dobbs, Woodrow, Bor-
solino hats. The label was the thing." (*Bloke Modisane*)

Sections of rural communities viewed with alarm the forms of culture
and society that developed in African urban communities in the twentieth century. Many saw the absence of chieftainship, initiation, dilution of
authority of elders, undisciplined youth, and relative independence of
women as profoundly undermining of a proper moral and social order.
In most rural areas, a tenacious struggle took place from the late nineteenth century on, to sustain a rurally focused culture centered on chieftainship, patriarchy, respect for ancestors, initiation, access to land, and
cattle. The migrant labor system came to be seen as one vital means of
sustaining this world, discouraging as it did the movement of whole
families to the towns; ensuring that at least a portion of migrant income
accrued to rural areas; and allowing the construction of a homestead
and a herd, and ultimately retiring to a rural community to remain as
central ambitions.

Rurally oriented migrant culture represents the most widespread,
holistic, and tenacious attempt to sustain indigenous African cultural
forms in twentieth-century South Africa. From the late 1950s, however,
circumstances conspired to undermine—although by no means entirely eradicate—this form of cultural resistance. Perhaps most important was that the ballooning population in rural areas, partly produced

by apartheid-inspired forced removals from "black spots" in "white land" and more effective influx control in the cities, overwhelmed a residual rural economy based on land and cattle that had previously helped to sustain this defensive rural culture. Attempts by the apartheid state to incorporate chiefs into structures of government chipped away at their legitimacy in the eyes of many. Expansion of schools in rural areas from the 1970s and growing interconnections between youth in rural and urban contexts, especially in the 1980s, helped shape new forms of youth culture that were far less amenable to the authority of chiefs and elders and focused on imagined futures remote from the limited possibilities that existed in most rural areas.

This is not to suggest that a rurally focused culture had been entirely extinguished. There are areas of the country in which chieftainship retains broad-based support and land and cattle continue to play a significant role. However, in most areas it is safe to say that this cultural adaptation is on the wane, despite the attempts of some interest groups—most notably traditional leaders in KwaZulu-Natal—to resuscitate forms of traditionalism.

The profound processes of transformation that have taken place in South Africa since 1652, and especially in the last two hundred years, have made it extremely difficult to sustain any cohesive and clearly distinctive form of indigenous culture. However, some elements of indigenous culture, while by no means static or unchanging, have proved resilient and highly adaptable to vastly changed circumstances; for example, the payment of bridewealth and a worldview that assumes an interpenetration of secular and spiritual worlds. It is dangerously misleading, however, to suggest that some cultural elements represent the tip of a powerful if partly submerged cultural substructure, just because their lineage connects back to precolonial societies.

Bridewealth and beliefs in ancestors and witches represent only two elements of indigenous culture that have survived and evolved in the "vortex of modern South African history," but it would be difficult to argue that these elements add up to an indigenous culture that shapes South African responses to the processes of globalization in significant ways. They represent evidence that the processes of transformation that have been unleashed in South Africa over the last two hundred years and more have not swept all before them. At the same time, the evidence indicates that, by the end of the twentieth century, "they represent sub-ordinate clauses in a political, economic and cultural order which has emerged out of a transformation of a precolonial way of life which has been uniquely comprehensive in Africa."

Is Southern Africa a Ghetto of the West?

The critical question to be posed about cultural globalization and South Africa is whether there is a cultural and symbolic value system in the country that offers a substantial contrast to the continuity of colonial European values and social influence over the past two centuries.[12] Schlemmer asks, "Does southern Africa not perhaps confront and inter-act with the current spread of global values as a cultural adjunct of the West itself. . . . Was the only thing that prevented the complete assimila-tion of southern African culture into a mix of (predominantly) Euro-pean influences—racism, apartheid and social segregation?"

In many parts of Africa, different schools of thought argue that an African personality and value system has survived in less manifest forms and underlies the surface effects of colonial domination. Only when this suppressed African cultural identity is revived will Africa be able to throw off the shackles of inferiority and loss of confidence that colonialism has caused. This can be seen in the concept of "negritude" and the particular notion of an African renaissance in certain circles now. Many African intellectuals believe strongly that some fundamental content of African culture exists in contrast to Western or European values and economic practices. If this latent African cultural identity does indeed exist and holds possibilities for either an alternative mode of development or some kind of motivational basis for development, then it could very well be at risk of attenuation under the impact of spreading global influences and forces.

In fact, considerable energy is now being expended in South Africa and elsewhere on the continent on the notion of an African renaissance (more about this later). An institute devoted to studying the African renaissance has been established in Botswana with branches in South Africa and else-where, with the purpose of the "further liberation of Africa from its colonial heritage and the application of African thought systems to de-velopment challenges."[13] Among its aims, it lists the following: problem-solving research in priority areas (e.g. human resource development, governance and peace, health and cultural affairs), building relevant research databases, assisting African governments to undertake economic recovery and reforms, facilitating job creation, advising of impending serious economic developments, facilitating discussion on economic recovery, and "work[ing] toward not feeling sorry for ourselves."

Many conferences have been held and considerable energy devoted to discovering and developing an African alternative to Western values and approaches. A recent conference jointly hosted by the African Renaissance Movement and the South African Department of Arts, Science, and Technology (held at a distinctly nonindigenous venue, Caesar's Palace Casino) focused official attention on this topic. The title of one of the papers captures the flavor: *Reviewing Indigenous Knowledge Systems: African Thought and Wisdom and the Issue of African Identity.* Some papers deviated from this theme by challenging the global economic system and the IMF/World Bank policy viewpoints, not from any particularly African perspective but rather from an adapted Marxist perspective.

> One rather impassioned speaker from the floor virtually demanded that the South African Broadcasting Corporation replace the bulk of its religious broadcasting with programs based on African ancestor workshop and religious philosophy. Another speaker argued that African traditional architecture should directly inform housing policy, the design of low cost housing developments and technology policy. Occasional interjectors from the floor insisted that African science predated Western developments in the field.

South Africa's president, Thabo Mbeki, has placed the idea of some form of mobilization of African developmental energy at center stage in South African politics. His addresses, while eloquent and important from a variety of policy perspectives, have not identified any particular content to be revived in modern African economic or political culture; rather, he has tended to stress the need for macroeconomic reforms and democratic governance. Schlemmer argues that perusal of much of the literature on the topic of an African cultural system or mode of development does not produce much by way of specific content. There are abundant claims that such content is there to be found, but very few are actually finding it. Very little with specific rather than merely suggestive arguments or hypotheses about African alternatives has been written down. He notes,

> If there is no substantive consciousness of an African way then one might have to debate whether or not the deep symbolism and value systems linked to original cultures of southern Africa have not been effectively displaced by colonialism and conversion by missionary Christianity. If this is the case more recent waves of global Western influence are exercising their effects within either a *receptive and pliable cultural milieu* or in an environment which has been defined by differentiation within the Western model itself.

Propositions along these lines would not necessarily be contradicted by the survival of some modes of cultural expression derived from earlier cultures (e.g., particular rituals, superstitions, traditional herbal medicine, particular choral harmonies). After all, thoroughly Western and global ethnic categories, like practicing Christians, Jews, Irish, Scots, Basque nationalists, and so on, all tend to cultivate older rituals and practices without anyone believing for one moment that they are less modern and Western because of it. Thus, if on the basis of the evidence available one were to conclude that any distinctive values and symbolic systems were displaced by early Western influences a long time ago, then one would have to debate whether modern African culture is not a subtype of Western culture—perhaps similar in status to African American culture. "The distinctiveness would lie in the extent to which racial differences and past discrimination have created a sense of cultural solidarity but the culture itself would be a Western off-shoot—hence, is South Africa a Western cultural ghetto?"

SURVEY EVIDENCE

A number of questions relevant to this topic were attached to a broad nationwide survey of 2,250 people conducted in South Africa in March 1999.[14] The findings are revealing. Respondents were asked, "What do African people in southern Africa have in common with one another which might help them catch up in development?" The number of people who mentioned *ubuntu* (a Zulu word denoting notions of being human or "humanness"—see the next text box), traditionalism, or ancestor worship was no more than 2-3 percent in replies that could be associated with something essentially "African." These results do not mean that Africans do not have a sense of cultural origin or do not have a respect for traditional beliefs; they simply mean that these aspects are generally not seen to be relevant to current problems and their solutions.

Another question asked was, "What is the special African way in which [then] Deputy President Mbeki's notion of an African renaissance will be achieved, or is there no special African way?" Here again the most frequent response (more frequent among Africans than among other races) was to sweep all notions of some African destiny aside and to concentrate on practical suggestions and priorities (33 percent) and pragmatic cooperation (12 percent). Some 4 percent said outright there was no African way and that the developed countries of the world or the policies of the previous (white) government should be copied. Only 2 percent referred to Africanization, African unity, and empowerment; 7 percent referred to a return to traditional beliefs and 3 percent to *ubuntu*. Religion received almost no mention. The top socioeconomic status groups certainly exploit African identity in jobs and career strategies, but it is against a background of an almost totally Eurocentric political ideology predominantly concerned with power and opportunity. The Africanists are a much less influential political-cultural deviation— they appear not to be in the black establishment.

If one accepts that there is no apparent contest between any particularly African worldview and that of the major global modes of confronting the world, then the way in which the future development of South Africa will occur should be fairly straightforward: class mobility to narrow the gap between white minorities of European origin and the emerging African middle classes, coupled with narrowing the development gap in respect of economic growth and per capita GNP. But is it so straightforward? To what extent do the newly educated Africans (the emerging South African middle class) appreciate and understand the challenge of competition and development success—fast, innovative, highly competitive, idea based—in the new global economy?

Forty qualitative interviews were undertaken with university-educated Africans to explore some of the nuances in the way they see the challenges of competing and catching up. Their ages ranged from the mid-twenties to the fifties, and all live in and around Johannesburg/Pretoria, the economic core of the country. Direct questioning coupled with conversational probing yielded very predictable types of answers. There appears to be "no barrier of traditionalism to cross, and the existing orientation is to become like Western role models as quickly as possible." For the vast majority of people, the only barriers to success are discrimination, occupational backlogs, rights, and opportunities.

One of the issues explored concerned the awareness and concern with the kind of human resource characteristics that the new economy requires. Respondents were asked what sort of values parents should encourage in their children "these days, to prepare them for the future?" Essentially the results followed a conventional pattern—what some would describe as the rather stuffy morality of the "respectable poor," surprisingly stereotyped for a group with this level of education, with a minority of responses "rather more appropriate to the challenges of success in a contemporary economy," incorporating independence, self-respect, commitment to goals and ambition. However, analysis of these results indicated a response of considerable concern:

> Our African respondents cannot begin to think of the kind of achievement values which they would like to instill in children. This is a luxury which is more or less completely displaced by the imperatives of sheer survival in a social world in which life-threatening conditions exist around every street corner and in every teenage hangout.

According to Schlemmer, what is exceptional about South and southern Africa is the extent to which the conditions of the spatially restricted inner-city ghettoes of the United States, United Kingdom, Netherlands, France, and others have become almost the dominant condition of southern African towns and cities outside of the established middle-class areas. To understand this one has to understand the effects of apartheid. Schlemmer argues that if apartheid were the only explanation, then the same conditions would not exist say in Botswana or Swaziland—but they do, particularly as far as the threat of HIV/AIDS is concerned. He concludes, "Therefore, to understand modern southern African society in a global context one has to understand social dislocation as a dominant feature of modern urban life. One has to examine the more general consequences of early inter-cultural contact between Africa and the global influences of an earlier era."

In his 1983 study of an African middle-class elite in the eastern Cape, Thomas Nyquist concluded that the upper stratum in the black community was reasonably cohesive and an important reference group for other Africans. He noted, however, that

> in many senses the ultimate reference group for urban Africans is actually the European community. . . . This upper stratum is in an acute position of sociological marginality. . . . there is a white-imposed barrier to upward mobility which prevents the able and the ambitious from attaining social, economic and political equality with Europeans but which does not prevent the distribution and acceptance of European values.[15]

Mia Brandel-Syrier reached the same conclusion in her analysis of an African elite on the Witwatersrand in the late 1970s (supported by the famous French scholar Georges Balandier's 1955 analysis of cultural and psychological "estrangement" in Central Africa). Brandel-Syrier concludes that the elite she studied "understands things only in the language of their own racial awareness" and finds that at that stage, the emerging middle-class elite was what many other authors had described as cultural "transitionals." One of its most dominant characteristics was what Balandier had described for the Congo as cultural "availability" and the disposability of the original culture. Crudely stated, Brandel-Syrier argues that the emerging elite faced at least two major challenges: the determination to escape from the "dark earth and tradition-boundedness of a tribal past" into the light of "civilization," individual dignity and freedom, powerfully supported by the missionary–led conversion to Christianity; and the struggle to deal with racial rejection by the very people who symbolized the elite group's most deeply held aspirations, the white middle class.

In her view, the stress of both challenges led to a rootlessness and lack of integration of identity to the extent that they were, as Balandier put it, supremely available to adopt new styles and manners, revealing in the process sharp discontinuities in their self-images and cultural identification. Brandel-Syrier's assessment was blunt: The problem was not one of cultural maladjustment but rather of "cultural immaturity"; this is akin to adolescence, with its rejection of roots, which results in few value anchors remaining—only dreams of great and unrealistic possibilities. This produced an open cultural "availability" to the promise of transformation that lay beyond the racially based educational constraints and technological disadvantages caused by segregation and apartheid.[16]

The overall point being made is that Nyquist, Brandel-Syrier, Balandier and others (including Frantz Fanon) were able to demonstrate the depth of alienation from their own sense of continuity and cultural heritage that colonialism, in the absence of a countervailing "high culture," had produced. This is illustrated in South African literature, in, for example, the words of Can Themba in his 1972 novel *The Will to Die,*

> I think the rest of African society looked upon us as an excrescence. We were not the calm dignified Africans that the Church so admires (and fights for); not the unspoiled rural African the Government so admires, for they tell no lies, they do not steal and above all they do not try to measure up to the white man. Neither were we *tsotsis* in the classical sense of the term, though the *tsotsis* saw us as cousins. . . . We were not "cats" either; that sophisticated group of urban Africans who play jazz, live jazz and speak the township transmigrations of American slang. We were those sensitive might-have-beens who had knocked on the door of white civilization (at the highest levels that South Africa could offer) and had heard a gruff "No" or a "Yes" so shaky and insincere that we withdrew our snail horns at once.[17]

And in 1965, Bloke Modisane wrote in *Blame Me on History:*

> I was encouraged . . . to develop and cultivate an appreciation for my own culture of the shield and the *assegai,* of ancestral gods, drums, mud huts and half-naked women with breasts as hard as green mangoes. . . . But I am a freak, I do presume an appreciation for Western music, art, drama and philosophy; I can rationalize as well as they, and using their own system of assumption, I presume myself civilized and then set about to prove it by writing a book with the title, *Blame Me on History.*[18]

The analysis of the celebrated East African philosopher Professor John S. Mbiti (1969) is useful here. He confirms the view of many other African writers in describing the typical traditional African worldview as a highly integrated concept of living beings, departed spirits, and natural phenomena as constituting a seamless whole, a "communion of souls." The intense reality of social and supernatural affinity and association has given rise to the concept of *ubuntu*.

Yvonne Mokgoro, a judge of the Constitutional Court, quotes Professor Kunene of the University of Natal in describing *ubuntu* as the "quality that guarantees not only a separation between men, women and the beast but the relative quality of that essence . . . the potential of being human." Mokgoro summaries it as "a humanistic orientation . . . the morality of cooperation, compassion, community spiritedness, and concern for the interests of the collective, for others and respect for the dignity of personhood"[19] (see text box below).

UBUNTU AND AFRICANNESS?

A number of South African anthropologists have observed there now seems little cultural basis upon which to define an "original" Africanness.[20]

For example, it has been suggested that an effective and particularly African management technique based on the concept of *ubuntu*—exemplified in historical, mainly rural, examples— needs to be developed as an alternative to Western management techniques. Hammond-Tooke (1998) notes that "the very prevalence of the term *Ubuntu* in contemporary discourse would seem to point to a deeply felt lack among many of an important moral element in the Western way of doing things."[21] However, as one interviewee noted, *ubuntu* provides no value system in terms of how one functions in a company situation. For example, with *ubuntu* one cannot fire an employee, which, although always unpleasant, is sometimes necessary. The interviewee went on to note that the "lack of parameters about where ubuntu begins and ends is problematic," underlining the point that *ubuntu* has not translated well into the radically different setting of a modern company.[22]

Reflecting on these problems, a prominent black businessman and member of the ANC national executive noted, "One of the problems I have with *ubuntu* is that it has been packaged for consultants to peddle to companies that are at a loss as to where to go. Largely what I see defined as *ubuntu* is a very reductionist use of the concept as it has existed historically. We are trying to develop the concept because we have been so denuded of our historical base that we are trying to find something common out there, which is largely mythological—and there is nothing wrong with that—society flourishes on mythology."[23] It is therefore unsurprising that, in South Africa, the most substantial alternatives to Davos culture and liberal democracy are rooted in alternative Western discourses of socialism/communism rather than in any substantial appeal to indigenous culture.

Hammond-Tooke captures the implications that flow from this. He argues that the most successful "Africanism" in a globalized world is likely to be one that can create bridges between the residual characteristics of African traditions on the one hand and the ethical bases of Western culture and its materialist economic forms on the other. He observes that "there seems to be no doubt that those Africans who have most successfully managed to succeed in a globalized world have in fact come from backgrounds in which the Protestant ethic was inculcated by Christian parents or educators."[24]

This concept of *ubuntu* is presented by Mokgoro and many other African intellectuals today in an idealistic way and without one vital qualification that Mbiti emphasizes. He describes the concept as a powerful spirit of mutual support and accountability but *one that applies within face-to-face traditional communities.*

Hence, for Mbiti, the norms and rules of behavior do not exist as discrete abstract principles to which people develop a commitment; nor are they akin to "commandments" or formally codified moral principles and dogma which can be extended beyond their original community context. Mbiti goes so far as to say that in many traditional societies

"God has no influence on people's moral values." God is seen to be the ultimate upholder of the moral order but is not immediately involved in keeping that order; the social order rests on the consensus within the community of the living and the departed. This means that the moral order and norms of behavior are not general principles—morality, as Mbiti describes it, is "societary" rather than "spiritual"; it is situational rather than absolute. A person is not evil or good; his actions in relation to the consensus within the community define the degree of sin or virtue: "Murder is not evil until a person kills another person in his community."[25]

This does not mean that moral norms are weak. The moral dynamic is powerful, but its props and dimensions are derived from the interaction and the relations of authority and status within the closely integrated kinship structure of the face-to-face community and not necessarily to strangers. Moral strictures will apply to the extent that a community of consensus has been established and is embodied within a system of affiliations, statuses, and relationships.

> This accords with observable reality. There is little in the behavior of Africans in history or in contemporary settings to suggest that they are more humane and sympathetic toward strangers than the typical European or Asian. Africa has demonstrated that it is just as prone to massacre and cruelty across groups and community boundaries as the historically warlike Europeans, Arabs, Chinese or Japanese. Mbiti's qualification locates *ubuntu* within the solidarity of the local close-knit community.

This pattern implies that the norms and values, family cohesion, and the work ethic of the traditional community will all be very vulnerable under conditions in which the close integration of community life is broken. This would particularly apply in the case of urbanization, the intermingling of peoples from different backgrounds, and the atomization of the modern mass townships.

The patterns of traditional behavior are not carried into the modern setting and applied to it as a code or as an internalization of abstract values—their grip evaporates, hence cultural availability. Modern urban African communities have therefore had to confront the stresses of interracial conflict and socioeconomic change in an exceptionally atomized and culturally dispossessed condition. The liberation movements for a time reestablished some community authority, but after independence or liberation from apartheid, community-based structures tended to dissipate.

Urban African communities were therefore doubly disempowered in terms of social and cultural coherence. Moral authority had collapsed; the sustaining original culture had lost its community props. Worse still, among the emerging elites, core aspects of the original culture were until recently quite devastatingly discredited among the leading urban black classes. Writing in the 1960s, sociologist Leo Kuper echoed the findings of many other observers and writers when he drew the following conclusions about the reactions of the educated African elites to traditional leadership: "Among the educated in particular there is a strong repugnance for tribal society, a sense of cultural shame, a feeling that tribalism is a return to the past, to barbarism to the primitive."[26]

At the same time, he and other prominent anthropologists, such as Mayer, have also established that at rank-and-file level in the urban areas, tribal identities and practices were remarkably persistent, particularly among non-Christians.[27] This contrast between the educated and the rank and file in effect meant that the potential for some kind of cultural continuity from rural to urban circumstances was effectively "decapitated" by the determination of the educated elites to renounce their cultures of origin.

The period before the commencement of the liberation struggle was therefore characterized in urban African society by the symbolic dominance of the educated elite, which was in fact a self-conscious cultural enclave located precariously on the edge of the social order defined by white settler–colonial society. As such, it conformed to the observations in the wider sub-Saharan setting. Masolo, for example, contrasts the active educated elites with the passive rank and file and says that the former "has done little if anything to establish a meaningful relationship with the large number of peasants living and working in the remote countryside."[28] The same could be said of the relationship between the early educated elites and the urban mass proletariat before the latter came to have a strategic utility in trade union organization and the political struggle for liberation.

Today, African elites are mindful of the importance of workers, peasants, and "the poorest of the poor," as it is from the condition of the disadvantaged that the elites acquire their leverage. Even traditional leaders have acquired some respect not unconnected to the votes they may be able to deliver. However, the persistent use of English with the poorest of the poor is probably indicative of real attitudes.

Conclusion

Urban Africans emerged out of a history in which their intellectual elites had broken the continuity with their sustaining cultures of origin and were marginalized by racial segregation. It is not surprising therefore that urban Africans in Southern Africa are among the most atomized and disorganized populations in the world today.

The rediscovery of African values and culture is largely an elite reinterpretation of residues of what used to be. *Ubuntu* is the prime example, and the major feature of its current definition is boundless idealism and the failure to reconcile it with the everyday reality of crime, violence, and brutality of life in urban concentrations. One gets the uneasy feeling that the fashionable celebration of *ubuntu* is intended more for white consumption or to display a badge of (Africanist?) honor than as sincere moral reconstruction.

While by no means conclusive, the empirical material reviewed suggests that when asked to contemplate what culture might contribute to meeting the challenge of Africa's development, the local black population responds like the "settler minorities," whether Indian, English, African, or Coloured. There is an alternative Africanist conception, but at this stage it is weak and inconsistent.

The dominant response suggests that South Africa is a "fragment" of the West in which the major commitment since the eighteenth century has been and still is to draw level with the West in the West's own terms. In a sense this is to assert the African renaissance mission as a competitive "Western product." Cultural globalization involves no contest in southern Africa.

CONTEMPORARY SOUTH AFRICA AND GLOBAL CULTURE

In this section we focus on current South African experience. We look at both Davos and popular culture, the influence of international cultural elites, and evangelical Protestantism.

Davos Culture

In the mainstream South African business community, Davos culture is patently widespread.[29] By their own and external observers' accounts, business executives are in many respects almost exact clones of those in either London or New York. We explored what makes South African-based corporate business culture similar to or different from U.S. or British corporate culture, through twenty interviews with multinational corporation (MNC) executives, asking them to compare their South African experiences with those in other countries.

These executives agreed that at their work level, South African business culture was most similar to that of the United States, followed by Britain and Australia. One said, "In all our partnerships and relationships it has been easiest to communicate with the Americans. It's not just because we share a language but a business culture." Another said, "South African business is not distinct. . . . you can see the corporate culture permeating. There is no real differentiation—just a time lag."

South African business culture is being heavily influenced by a "country-free" globalization. An MD from a medical supply MNC elaborates:

> The multinational company is replacing the country as a concept of what 'home' is. [Young] people in my field . . . are more company citizens than they are South Africans, English, Americans, Australians or whatever. . . . Citizenship of a multinational for them is much more important than national citizenship—it gives them more sense of security and identity, more material reward and less pain. . . . In the modern age . . . there is much less reason to identify with a particular country, especially in IT, finance and marketing.

Executives saw South Africa's business climate as unusual, one of labor militancy, crime, and maverick business practices—"a wild or untamed substructure." While not uncommon elsewhere, militant unions and crime seemed far more pronounced and unpredictable in South Africa. "Our American partners say . . . there is no work ethic here. They come from a hire-and-fire background in which such attitudes would not be tolerated. Our unions see it otherwise. . . . Unless your police, nurses and teachers take pride in their work and have a strong sense of civic responsibility reinforced by public respect for what they do and the services they offer, you can't build a society which people from outside find it easy to operate in."

The British Consul in Durban commented:

A British-owned company . . . took some of their employees over to Britain to see how the equivalent factory operated there. The South African workers' main reaction . . . was "Boy, can they work." It's the "speed" thing. South Africans seem comparatively slow and demotivated. . . . [The] . . . apparent lack of pride in one's work . . . is what British people find surprising about South Africa as a whole. . . . Whites in South Africa had the best standards of living in the world and even black South Africans had the best in Africa, but one senses that all of this is often not enough. . . . South Africans borrow and don't save; this indebtedness infuses economic life here.

Other illustrative comments include those from the following three interviewees:

There is an instability that makes ordinary people insecure and it definitely reflects upon the way staff perform at work. If your staff is being raped and/or beaten before work, they are bound to bring these problems to work. These kinds of problems hardly exist in Australia, Britain or Japan.

South African business . . . has had to adapt to avoid a combination of sloppiness and dishonesty. . . . The sloppiness borders on the immoral and we believe that it's the immorality that drives the sloppiness.

One international warehouse company . . . was shocked to find that stock "shrinkage" was ten times the level that they were used to, that their trucks got hijacked and so on. They are not here anymore. You can't blame them. Unless their previous experience was in running warehouses in Columbia, they were not to know what was about to hit them.

DAVOS SUPERSTRUCTURE, WILD SUBSTRUCTURE

Overall, the business executives emphasized superficial similarities but more fundamental differences with business cultures in their "First

World" homes. While top managers seem part of a global Davos culture, experienced American and British observers saw South Africa's broader business culture as anything but entrepreneurial, the sine qua non for the effective operation of MNCs in less developed countries.

Multinationals often fail in less developed countries due to an excess of "irresponsible or immature individualism" and a corresponding shortage of "responsible individualism" (equated with entrepreneurialism).[30] People exhibiting no self-restraint do not engender trust and are thus poor business risks. It is not excessive individualism in LDCs that is problematic, but too little "mature" individualism. Several interviewees believed that many South Africans suffer from this malaise in their attitudes to work and savings. The result is the conception of the South African employee/entrepreneur as "immature" and/or "irresponsible."

The portrait that emerges through the lens of multinational executives is of a South African business culture that exhibits "an upper veneer of emulation of an American-style model of Davos business culture, but this is superimposed upon a 'wild' and in some respects immature form of emergent capitalist social substructure." When viewed as a whole, South African business culture is quite different from that of Britain or the United States, but at the level of top management it is very similar. Over time it will become even more similar in style and content to its American equivalents; the great unknown is whether the country will be able to develop an equivalent mature individualism, entrepreneurship, and work ethic on a wider scale.

South African Davos culture is becoming increasingly deracialized, despite growing pains within corporate life. Significantly, racial issues within the economic elite were mentioned far less frequently than concerns about attitudes to work, social responsibility, and lawlessness. While the MNC is a powerful influence on the values and aspirations of the public at large, this impact is primarily felt at the level of consumer aspirations, not attitudes to work, self-discipline, and savings. Different forms of cultural change are occurring unevenly. The rapid adoption of globalized consumption patterns far outstrips the rate of adoption of globalized production values and attitudes to work and entrepreneurship. Within MNCs, employees are being rapidly socialized, but this only affects a fraction of the total population. The real challenges of coping with cultural globalization in South Africa pertains to those who may never in their lifetime enter formal jobs.

THE EMERGING "AMERICANS OF THE SOUTH"

Twenty successful members of South Africa's rapidly emerging black elite were interviewed to explore their degree of cultural globalization: seven women, thirteen men, all African, resident in Johannesburg or Durban.[31] All earned salaries or incomes equivalent to the top 1 percent of the South African population and worked in a range of professional and managerial fields.

These individuals do seem to be "conscious members" of Davos culture, but they have a residual sense of misgiving about loss of traditional "African values." This is not seen as a fundamentally contradictory or stressful dualism, as the dominant approach seems to be a pragmatic accommodation of cultures. Moreover, this generation of successful black people tends to fraternize socially within a racially defined subsector of the South African elite, hardly socializing with whites outside of work. There are now *parallel* elites in South Africa that share most values and aspirations but interact socially in largely separate domains. This seems more to do with a comfort zone of cultural pragmatism than racial hostility.

Education, family background, personal drive, and ambition were mentioned as the primary factors contributing toward personal success. These interacted with the broader *contextual* environment, including chance and exposure to international experience. Few people explicitly mentioned religion.

ARE AFRICAN BUSINESS PEOPLE DIFFERENT?

Responses to the question, "Are African business people different?" were mixed: 40 percent gave "an unambiguous yes," 40 percent "a qualified yes," and 20 percent said "no." The latter maintained that "business was business" and that personal rather than racial or cultural factors were paramount in business. The others perceived a number of distinctive aspects to the way in which Africans did business, amounting to either self-critical observations (lack of experience, problems of time management), or the (alleged) greater degree of community orientation among Africans.

Only 15 percent felt that being African made no difference in business. None saw their Africanness as being an unambiguous advantage. Most (54 percent) saw only disadvantages in being African, mainly because the perceptions of others (e.g., whites and Indians) required above normal performances in order to achieve recognition. A sizable minority (46 percent) had mixed views: many felt affirmative action and black economic empowerment policies were now favoring them. Fifteen percent saw their different worldviews regarding communalism and respect for elders as a mixed blessing in the work environment. There was no attempt to develop an ideological Africanist alternative to the way South African business currently operated. In sum, most respondents see Africans in business as different, and this is mainly construed in negative terms. The central challenge is to overcome others' views of them, but little anger was expressed about this.

Most interviewees rejected the notion that they themselves had been fully westernized, but all conceded that a wider process of westernization and Americanization was occurring, especially among young people. There was a sense of potential cultural loss associated with this acknowledged transformation. Some of the thoughtful responses included those from the following three interviewees:

> We studied through American books. We are influenced by the American media and its value systems. It's difficult to escape it. My anchor is Africa, nevertheless.

> We do not have our own identity as African people, because we have always seen ourselves in relation to other race groups. . . . The only good black people that we have known are successful black Americans. So it does not surprise me that people are adopting those ways because there is no one else that we identified with. . . . Everything that is taught [to our children in multiracial schools], from the language to value systems, is Western. There is no provision for African values. . . . They spend most of their time in school . . . being culturized differently so it also makes it easy for our children to aspire to other people than ourselves.

> I work in a Western environment, thus I cannot but fall prey to being westernized. I think I am a mixture of both. . . . For instance, when I go to my father's village I sit on the floor, rise when elders walk in the door, do not talk back to my elders, etc. But at work in the boardroom I am an equal. I am saying that as long as being westernized does not mean losing one's values and traditions, then it is fine.

The general recognition of the inevitability of westernization and Americanization is coupled with a sense of "quiet mourning" at what is styled as a loss of traditional values. This elite group understands the cultural dynamics at work. With respect to values and aspirations, there is an unabashed materialism. Most people wanted more money to give their children a good education and had a desire for international travel and exposure—it is unlikely that the desired travel is in the rest of Africa! None of the sample referred to the notion of the African renaissance.

Only a minority expressed the mildest forms of anti-Western cultural sentiments. Most clearly recognized that being African in South African business brought with it unique circumstances, mainly attributed to the supposed perceptions of Africanness by others. The rapidly growing black economic elite are cultural pragmatists with little attachment to particular cultural practices and symbols. They see culture as a means toward self- or family advancement in a competitive material world. These new elite South Africans could hardly be described as potential antagonists in any "clash of civilizations" on a global scale. They may well be the most American of the "Americans of the South" and may in time become the objects of envy and criticism by both fellow South Africans and others on the continent.

Popular Culture

To explore popular culture, tastes, and trends in South Africa, we interviewed members of the country's sophisticated advertising industry. We then studied the same phenomenon from the "bottom up" by examining urban hairdressers and hairstyles.

MARKETING AND ADVERTISING

> We . . . have noticed that places and countries don't matter to consumers any more. The media is the cultural glue that binds world society together and the media is selling brands. . . . Brands in turn represent a cluster of values—the BMW man, the Nike man—which define people, not places. (An advertising director)[32]

Marketers and advertisers are an important source of information on the culture of globalization. They, after all, "read the signs" of changing

tastes, preferences, and values on an ongoing basis and are therefore as-
tute observers and shapers of local cultural dynamics. We explored the
following issues through conversations with advertising executives: Is
South Africa a cultural receiver and/or sender, and if so, from/to where?
How much more "Western" has South Africa become as a result of cultural globalization and in what ways? To what extent has indigenous
culture been preserved or eroded through interactions with global and
Western influences?

In the late 1980s, leading South African advertisers Green and Las-
caris first asserted that racial/ethnic differences in consumer behavior
were becoming insignificant, with education and occupational status
being the most powerful determinants of consumer preferences. The
racial affiliation of consumers and advertising role models was rapidly
declining. Tastes, preferences, and consumption patterns were becoming
more unified, cosmopolitan, and internationally aligned. The role of
specifically African traditions in consumption patterns was rapidly
weakening. The old argument about Eurocentric versus Afrocentric advertising was becoming obsolete, and the positioning of world brands in
the South African marketplace was now effectively race neutral.

A comparatively recent trend in South Africa is the internationalization of the advertising industry. Almost all major local agencies now either have foreign partners serving as role models or are themselves
branches of multinational advertising firms. This reflects the lifting of
sanctions and an internal breakdown in the previously racialized and
"uniqueness-oriented" conceptions of the South African market. Many
locally promoted brands belong to multinational corporations (like
Coca-Cola and BMW), with track records of differentiated advertising
treatment in other countries. Local agencies will usually be presented
with a set of guidelines that have been tested elsewhere. In this way the
local ad agency is continually being educated into international best
practices and contributing to its "placelessness."

However, local ad agencies are generally staffed with South Africans.
They are not employed simply to be one-way recipients of best practice,
and they often add value through their local knowledge and creative capacity to translate international consumer culture into successful local
advertising. For example, a South African ad agency recently changed
Sprite soft drink's international positioning for the South African market. While Sprite commercials internationally assert "Image is nothing.

Thirst is everything," they felt that denying the importance of image in South Africa would be dishonest. The slogan therefore became "Trust your instincts. Obey your thirst." Sprite sales reportedly skyrocketed, with South Africans becoming the world's fastest growing group of Sprite drinkers.[33]

In three focus groups of advertising executives held in Johannesburg and Durban, three main areas of consensus emerged. First, South Africa is a cultural protégé of the United States, influenced by American television programming and the growing dominance of the English language. Discussants said,

> We are becoming more Americanized than anything else. McDonald's is the most obvious demonstration of this—an icon of America, and they present themselves quite unabashedly as such here and it works.

> Peter Stuyvesant cigarettes [are] only sold in South Africa. . . . yet all the ads have American voices and scenes of glamorous lifestyles led by affluent young white Americans.

Second, Europe and to a lesser extent Africa also strongly influence South Africa culturally. At this stage, Africa follows South Africa more than it leads:

> South Africans want to wear what the world is wearing. Italy is probably more influential in South Africa than America in this regard. So globalization in South Africa is not just about America. However, it is also possible that what happens here in most of the clothing fashion market is a reflection of the way the Americans interpret European fashions.

> South Africans in the five- to twenty-year-old age groups find nothing to aspire to in Africa. . . . there are no role models . . . in Africa . . . Their role models are American, and Americans are rich and Africa is a place of deep poverty [with the possible exceptions of music and food].

> The Alfred Dunhill products that we advertise . . . are products with the most upmarket Western symbolism you can imagine [British aris-

tocracy]. [Yet] 85 percent of the South African market for their products are black Africans.

Third, notwithstanding the leading roles played by American and/or European cultural symbols in South Africa, the market also has a significant "indigenous flavor." This is partly independent of international influences and sometimes draws upon more recent culturally unifying local symbols of prestige and aspiration in order to indigenize global trends:

Major ad disasters have resulted where local nuance has been miscalculated.

The debate between the African part of our culture and globalizing influences seems to be less about aspiration to the liberty and freedom aspect of American culture, which is not held in the slightest dispute. It's more about the American efficiency concept and its relationship to concepts of time and value.

South Africa selectively adapts American and other globalizing cultural influences and is highly porous to American popular and consumer culture. Race appears to have largely disappeared from the local industry's lexicon, apart from a recognition that black American role models may have facilitated the growth of American cultural influence and that Africa seems to hold few aspirational qualities.

Dated South African fashions can gain an extended life further north in Africa, and older South African chain stores are doing well there. In more conservative Zambia, men's suits sell extremely well, whereas South Africans have moved to a less formal, more individualized style. This theory of product markets is linked to innovative diffusion. Core–periphery relationships allow the testing of new products in core boutiques, their more widespread adoption in core-based chains, and later their diffusion to more retail networks, by which time the original demand has evaporated in the core in favor of later innovations. Thus South Africa emerges as the "America of the South."

Johannesburg is to Africa what New York is to the rest of the world. . . . Johannesburg is a brand name that could sell products throughout

Africa. It is a Brazilian-style melting pot which could lead fashions on this continent.

South Africa, as well as Chile and the Czech Republic, are seen by some MNCs as "regional entry points" into emerging markets—intermediate between developed market economies and emerging markets. Some South Africans disagree:

> In many respects South African marketers are way ahead in the global marketing game because they have long been mastering the subtleties of multicultural marketing.

South Africa certainly imitates a global popular culture with strong American influences. Local advertisers and marketers, however, emphasize Westernization rather than just Americanization, achieved mainly through television. South Africa has adapted American and Western models to its specific market needs, which in turn are role models for the rest of Africa. South Africa becomes a "second stage" transformer for the continent.

For example, advertising for Carling Black Label beer in South Africa replaces American images of cowboys wrestling calves, imbued with a sense of achievement and risk, with the parallel equivalent of miners tackling the rock face. A particular global concept of working-class masculinity is thus used to sell an "American" beer (brewed in South Africa) with indigenous imagery. In 1985 black South Africans founded a company in the remote township of Ga-Rankuwa, outside Pretoria, selling the Black Like Me range of hair care products. Colgate-Palmolive bought it and expanded it dramatically: the products are now marketed throughout southern and central Africa, and product knowledge has been transferred to the black American market.

The diffusion of global economic culture into Africa via South Africa is clearly what many South African political leaders and MNCs have in mind. Africa is South Africa's marketing hinterland. Despite the importance of the concept of "Africa" in the context of globalization, place seems to be waning as an influence on culture. Branded products are becoming much closer to the essence of different forms of cultural affiliation.

HAIRDRESSERS, HAIRSTYLES, AND POPULAR CULTURE

Hairstyles are an obvious expression of cultural affiliation, with women often spending a fifth of their clothing expenditures on hairstyles.[34] Most South African whites have long emulated North American and European counterparts. Among black South African women, there is an interesting mix between Afrocentric and Western hairstyle preferences. Hair straighteners, for example, have been used to emulate longer "Western" hairstyles. However, "black consciousness" advocates claimed that these styles denigrated African self-worth. The current situation is more complex, with many South Africans sporting a mix of African and Western styles: young white male environmentalists sport dreadlocks and young black soccer players dye their hair blond. While these apparent role reversals are extremes, it is more difficult to generalize nowadays.

American and African cultural trends and traditions engage creatively, with respect to hairstyles and hairdressers. There are hundreds of small, sometimes one-person hairdressing enterprises that cater to popular tastes on downtown sidewalks, railway terminals or inner-city premises. Our researchers interviewed seventy popular hairdressers in Durban and Johannesburg and seventy of their younger, black female customers. The implicit assumption was that urban black culture is probably the leading edge of current South African cultural change.

Sixty-five percent of those who use celebrity role models for their hairstyle choice chose Americans or those with obvious American connections. South African–American talk show host Felicia Mabuza-Suttle was the most mentioned individual role model, followed by black American singer Whitney Houston. Sixty-eight percent of customers believed American hairstyles were more influential than African ones, which is remarkable considering the interviews were mainly conducted in informal or black-operated hairdressing enterprises. The hairdressers were overwhelmingly black: 23 percent from Cameroon, Ghana, Nigeria, and the Democratic Republic of Congo (DRC), and 64 percent were black South Africans. While most inner-city hairdressers are black Africans, their clients have predominantly American tastes.

Some 30 percent of the hairdressers had received training financed by mainly American multinational companies. The company Black Like Me, owned by Colgate-Palmolive, had trained 20 percent of all hairdressers surveyed, while formal training institutions had trained 28 percent of respondents with considerable marketing of American-sourced brands like Clairol, Revlon, and Black Like Me. Thus American hair care culture is internalized at the trade-training level.

Hairdressers had more mixed perceptions of which styles predominated in South Africa. Some 51 percent believed American styles were more influential (including 27 percent who believed that "both African and American" predominated). Thus significantly fewer hairdressers perceived American influence than did customers, which was perhaps due to the number of non–South African hairdressers and that the customer sample was more Americanized than average.

Felicia Mabuza-Suttle's leading role model status is exceptional. Her TV talk show resembles the *Oprah Winfrey Show* in the United States (which is also televised in South Africa). She is a black South African who grew up in Sophiatown, emigrated to the United States, married an American, and worked for the Atlanta city council before returning to South Africa in the 1990s. Except for the slight residue of a South African accent, she dresses and presents herself mainly as an American. Obviously materially successful, she demonstrates a level of social concern that makes her audiences feel she is one of them.

Although her show has recently shifted to commercial television, when it was broadcast on SABC it was in the top five and was ranked number one among Nguni- and Sotho-speaking women. Consumer product ranges, including designer sunglasses, have been marketed locally using her name as the brand, South African magazines frequently feature her palatial Atlanta home, and she is regularly shown in the company of leading African American entertainers such as Diana Ross, Quincy Jones, and Natalie Cole. She has been described as "an African Princess Di," perhaps aptly, given Princess Diana's equivalent style role model function for white South Africans. But it is her combination of both South African and American connections that apparently confers special status. She claims she had to gain the trust of her audience after her absence from the country and has faced some hostility from South Africans who tell her to go back to America.

Twenty-three hairdressers identified her as by far the leading role model, chosen by 40 percent of their customers citing role models. This is remarkable, given that she is probably over fifty; nevertheless, she is still a favorite role model for young customers. Customer responses included: "Felicia is the best motivator in South Africa; she is a positive influence, looks professional, cool, hip and attractive"; "she accommodates old, young, everyone; I like her style—she's confident and her own person"; "the way she looks in her clothes and hairstyle makes her my model"; "Felicia lets me talk to the world"; and "she is a role model in this society. She is a multiculturalist."

Felicia is an enormously popular "crossover culture" role model embodying the best of South African and American culture for many black South African women. This model of global cultural transfer seems more successful at generating overall popularity than direct emulation or adoption of American popular culture. The hairdressers believe Felicia is used as a role model more frequently than four famous black American pop singers and Oprah herself.

It is an Africanist type of youth, older people, and males who tend to define the African hairstyle preference market, while younger people, professionals, and females tend to define the American equivalent. However, hairdressers indicated that "these young people who like the African renaissance" avoided American styles.

POPULAR CULTURE: CONCLUSIONS FROM THE EMPIRICAL REVIEW

Advertising executives believe that class aspiration explains the South African preference for American over African culture. American blacks may see themselves as relatively disadvantaged, but to South Africans they are wealthy and successful. At the same time, relatively few Africans can offer this model of material success. For many black South Africans, the ANC's real achievement is the creation of an open elite model in South Africa, where a black elite promotes the possibility of class mobility. In his book *An African Bourgeoisie* (1958), leading South African sociologist Leo Kuper argued that the ANC's rise as a popular opposition movement was attributable primarily to the "status incongruities" brought about by apartheid. The humiliation experienced by black professionals in having to produce their residence passes for poorly educated white policemen exemplified what (psychologically) led the ANC leadership to take political risks at the time.

Berger posits that common underlying values between Afrikaners and black South Africans facilitated the political negotiations; in particular, the perception that ANC leaders were not in fact communists but

people "just like us." American popular culture has traditionally ap-
pealed to both groups, perhaps because of their mutual experience of
British colonialism in South Africa, compared with the American model
of an open elite. Despite socialist language, militancy, and liberation
movement symbolism, American popular culture is ardently admired in
postapartheid South Africa, and its successful indigenization in South
Africa often requires innovative cultural interlocutors.

South African business largely views the African renaissance concept
as the desired penetration of African markets from a South African base.
(A continental franchise for Mabuza-Suttle?) Cultural globalization entails more than just indigenizing American popular culture in South
Africa; it also includes South Africa's growing influence in Africa, and
the addition of South African flavor to Western/U.S. popular culture.

Faculty Club Culture

South Africa has been influenced by Western cultural elites for decades.
The current influence of ideas, interests, and concerns from Western
cultures can be seen in academia, NGOs, media, and now increasingly in
government. We focus on one case study in this area.

WHY IS SOUTH AFRICA'S ANTISMOKING LEGISLATION
THE WORLD'S MOST DRACONIAN?

South Africa is a developing country with many pressing health care
problems.[35] An estimated 1.8 million South Africans were HIV positive
in 1995, a number that is predicted to rise to 6 million by 2005.[36] Tuber-
culosis (TB) currently kills more South Africans than AIDS, malaria,
measles, and murder combined. If unchecked, TB would infect 3.5 million South Africans by 2006. South Africa had eradicated malaria until
the 1980s; in 1998, over 23,000 cases of malaria were reported, though
the actual incidence is considerably greater. Many thousands of South
Africans suffer from malnutrition, lack of clean water, sanitary facilities,
and associated diseases.

Tobacco control issues occupied a surprisingly prominent position in
the country's first democratic government after 1994. The new minister
of health claimed that without changes in smoking patterns, 1.8 million
South Africans would die prematurely over the next forty years from

tobacco-related diseases. South Africa's new antismoking legislation is particularly stringent. The Tobacco Products Control Amendment Act (1999) bans cigarette advertising, promotion, and sponsorship; smoking in enclosed public spaces, including the workplace; and the free distribution of, and coupons or prizes associated with, tobacco products. It also regulates the maximum tar and nicotine yields and restricts tobacco-product vending machines to places inaccessible to those who are under sixteen.

The antitobacco campaign is an elite-driven concern that has assumed disproportionate importance and been shifted up the national policy agenda at the expense of other health priorities. Why this "developed world" policy in a "developing world" context?

There is evidence of international faculty club ideas spreading through global intellectual networks, which has an impact on local policymaking. The Tobacco Action Group (TAG)—a coalition of the National Council Against Smoking, the Heart Foundation, and the Cancer Association of South Africa (CANSA)—is the major antitobacco activist organization. While conclusive proof of a network of international ties remains elusive, the Department of Health has nevertheless relied on key advisers. They include Derek Yach, a South African now heading up the World Health Organization's Tobacco Free Initiative (TFI) in Geneva; Dr. Yussuf Saloojee, head of the National Council Against Smoking, with a University of London Ph.D.; Dr. Ian Roberts, a South African–born physician, previously in the British National Health Service; and David Sweanor, a lawyer from the Canadian Nonsmokers Rights' Association, who was brought out to South Africa at Yach's instance to help redraft the national legislation

It is difficult to trace the antismoking campaign's funding. TAG members can raise money from individuals and companies. The Heart Foundation recently received money from the Department of Health specifically to promote the new tobacco law. CANSA has a minimal government subsidy. Dr Saloojee expressed concerns that the tobacco industry might pressure his private donors and would not reveal names. His organization receives Department of Health funds for running the telephone Quit Line. All denied foreign funding.

The tobacco industry suspects more direct international linkages. In light of their vested interests, however, their "facts" must be regarded with caution. They believe the antismoking lobby receives funding from the pharmaceutical industry, especially those producing nicotine substitutes. They suspect WHO funding to the Department of Health, dedicating resources specifically to the antismoking campaign. Other possible international sources include Canadian NGOs such as the International Development Research Center (IDRC), the Canadian International Tobacco Initiative, and the Canadian Nonsmokers' Rights Association.

The international antitobacco conference circuit is financed through the TFI and other international organizations. Many international luminaries attended the WHO conference on the Economics of Tobacco Control in Cape Town, February 1998, which gave impetus, resources, and moral support to the South African antitobacco legislative process. The Tobacco Institute of Southern Africa speculates that South Africa is a guinea pig for the developing world and notes that since the Tobacco Bill was passed, similar initiatives have surfaced in Burundi, Kenya, Mauritius, Swaziland, Tanzania, and Uganda. It also speculates that WHO is making other aid contingent on antitobacco legislation.

The economic arguments advanced by the tobacco industry (e.g., aiding development, providing jobs, creating tax revenues) are ruthlessly dismissed by both the WHO and the local antitobacco lobby, which set out to deliberately delegitimize their opponents, portraying the tobacco industry as cruel purveyors of "cancer sticks"—as big business making money off an addictive drug that causes terrible diseases and kills people. The tobacco lobby is seldom adequately consulted on new legislation. The antismoking lobby has imbibed WHO statistics and arguments, and these infuse the local debate.

Dr. Saloojee claims that "South Africa has argued the tobacco control case *on its own merits.* Even if policymakers *are* reacting to international developments, they are trying to follow global best practice. It would be naïve and foolish to ignore what happens in the rest of the world and try to reinvent the wheel. *Any* legislation will adapt extant models."[37]

According to Saloojee, there was an estimated 20 percent decline in cigarette consumption in South Africa from 1994 to 1997, due to higher taxes and stricter advertising. He maintains that in South Africa between 1992 and 1997, the retail price of cigarettes rose by about 170 percent and that tobacco product sales declined nearly 20 percent. But there is a demonstration effect on South Africa's antismoking activists from their

international counterparts. Australian, Canadian, and New Zealand laws
have influenced local legislation. Currently, twenty-six countries have total tobacco advertising bans, including Botswana, Mozambique, Sudan,
Jordan, and Thailand, as well as the expected Scandinavian countries,
Australasia, and the EU. The number of countries in which smoking in
public places is controlled by legislation rose from forty-seven in 1986 to
ninety in 1991. Health warnings were mandatory in over eighty countries
in the early 1990s.

The Tobacco Bill drew tremendous popular opposition, including
over eighty submissions to parliament by varied organizations, including the Freedom of Commercial Speech Trust, the hospitality industry,
the media, advertising agencies, unions, tobacco farmers, and producers.
The government's transparency and openness was questioned. The law
was viewed as badly drafted, excessive, unnecessary, and unconstitu-
tional. "The tobacco bill, experts believe, offends the constitution on a
number of levels, but the most sinister is the ANC riding roughshod
over issues which are a matter of personal choice and freedom."[38]

While there are undoubtedly solid health reasons for wanting to reduce tobacco-related diseases in South Africa, the high priority given to
antitobacco legislation reflects a skewed ranking of health priorities and
suggests another agenda at work. Highly successful lobbying by the antitobacco movement, the ripple effect of international trends away from
smoking, and support from powerful international organizations (with
the WHO emerging as the government's chief ally) have all artificially
elevated the issue up the Department of Health's to-do list. Global cultural elites seem to have successfully driven the issue, despite widespread
opposition from strong elements within South African civil society.

Evangelical Culture

About 72.6 percent of South Africans now claim to be Christians, up
from about 46 percent in 1911.[39] The most dramatic growth is among
Africans: from 26 percent of Africans in 1911 to 76 percent in 1990.
Churches have had an immense influence on the development of South
African society. Until the 1950s churches and missions controlled almost all schools for Africans and sponsored social work, medicine, and
nursing.

From the arrival of white settlers in the Cape in 1652 until British conquest in 1795, the public expression of Christianity was mostly monopolized by the Dutch Reformed Church; thereafter, the country was exposed to "an explosive proliferation of Protestant movements." By the early nineteenth century, religion spread rapidly, chiefly due to the zeal of African converts. Africans continued to be the key agents of Christianization in the twentieth century especially through the African Initiated Churches (AICs), which went from a bare existence in 1890 to embracing nearly half of all black South Africans by the 1990s. Only the United States matches South Africa in the proliferation of Christian denominations and sects.

The six thousand diverse AICs have a distinctive African origin, and they are self-reliant and independent of foreign funding. Combined, they had an estimated 9 million members, including 47 percent of all black Christians in 1991, up from 40 percent in 1980. The development of these churches went through Ethiopian, Zionist, and Zionist-Apostolic phases. Ethiopian churches have kept the liturgies, hymnbooks, readings, organization, clothing, Bible interpretation, and much of the spirituality of the traditions from which they originated, and they are often more tolerant of indigenous custom than mainline churches. In 1995, the "Ethiopian" African Methodist Episcopal Church (AMEC) had over 125,000 full members, making it one of South Africa's largest churches among blacks.

Zionist churches arose to challenge the pan-Africanist vision of the Ethiopian leadership, especially in urban areas. They offer physical healing, supportive communities, and spiritual solace. The name is taken from Zion City, Illinois, which until 1935 was a communal society with a theocratic government. American Pentecostal groups arrived in South Africa in the early twentieth century, and this church movement mushroomed rapidly. The largest and best known is the Zion Christian Church (ZCC), founded by Engenas Lekganyane in 1925 at Moria, near Pietersburg in the Northern Province.

Zionist-Apostolic indigenous churches arose after 1945, mainly among the growing black working class. These churches were both urban and rural, influenced by the migrant labor system. Women are heavily influential in these churches. They dress in white and carry crosiers. In 1976 they were estimated to number at least 2 million.

At least six thousand South African churches with some 10 million people can be identified with some form of Pentecostalism. They are syncretic in their incorporation of traditional African religious concepts (ancestral spirits) into their worship, and they emphasize the Holy Spirit, divine healing, exorcism, prophecy, revelation, and speaking in tongues.

These churches have traditionally been seen as relatively apolitical. However, politicians began openly attending mass ZCC meetings in Moria in the 1990s. The ZCC (with an estimated membership of 2–3 million) urges its followers to be good citizens and to cultivate self-restraint, thrift, personal discipline, and industriousness. AICs have

wholly cut the umbilical chord with the churches of Western origin. They are the largest and potentially the single most important religious group in South Africa and in spite of weakness and divisions, their vitality their rootedness in African traditions and their capacity for innovation will most likely have a decisive influence on the history of the church and society in the changing South Africa.[40]

Pentecostal and charismatic churches are the world's largest Christian group after the Catholic Church and are the fastest-growing Christian movement, with an estimated worldwide following of over 372 million people in 1990. Many African Pentecostals remain in the interracial Pentecostal mission churches, such as the Assemblies of God, Apostolic Faith Mission (each with about 250,000 members), and the smaller Full Gospel Church of God. Together these churches made up over 10 percent of the South African population by the early 1990s. So-called Charismatic or neo-Pentecostal churches have emerged in South Africa, inspired by visiting American evangelists such as William Branham and Oral Roberts in the 1950s. The most significant are those in the International Fellowship of Christian Churches (IFCC), founded in 1985, and Rhema Bible Church. These churches are strongly influenced by American megachurches.

As *Time* magazine reported,

Christianity is growing faster in sub-Saharan Africa than anywhere else on earth. Adherents . . . are increasing at 3.5 percent a year in Africa . . . 2.5 percent in Latin American and Asia and less than 1 percent in

Europe and North America. The proportion of African Christians to all Christians has grown from one in ten in 1970 to one in five today. On current trends African Christians will soon outnumber European believers, leaving them second only to those in Latin America.[41]

This spectacular growth has come in two waves: the rise of indigenous African churches during the last years of colonialism in the 1950s and 1960s, and a more recent boom in Evangelical and faith healing churches. In place of the mainstream churches' offer of salvation in the next world for good deeds in this one, many newer African churches preach instant deliverance in the form of worldly wealth. It is this message, so-called prosperity theology, that appeals to the continent's poor and displaced.

Part of the message of Pentecostal church groups in South Africa is that wealth is a blessing to be enjoyed by the living. In the words of theologian Maria Frahm-Arp,

> The Pentecostal movement—[which] started in the U.S. in 1906— empowers people to have a belief in their own ability. What's happening in South Africa is that the biggest Pentecostal movement—the ZCC (with about 3 million members)—is teaching an almost Protestant work ethic . . . And the research shows that the positive results can already be felt. The research revealed that teachings were specifically aimed at financial independence. In fact, 80 percent of those interviewed said they were saving to start their own businesses. I believe we will start to see the power of three million people who are being told not to smoke or drink and that diligent work is a blessing.[42]

In conclusion, this is one of the few areas of South African life in which an effective hybrid between indigenous African culture and Western influences has developed.

QUO VADIS: THE AFRICAN RENAISSANCE

What will decide the outcome is not the strength of our opponents but our own determination to succeed.

—*President Thabo Mbeki*

In this section we will examine the idea of the African renaissance and its relevance for this exploration of culture and globalization. The president of South Africa, Thabo Mbeki, has been the initiator and leading spokesman for the African renaissance, and it is important to understand exactly what he says it is and what it should achieve. We will explore Mbeki's notion of the renaissance and whom he is addressing in propounding this idea. We will then look critically at this concept before exploring its possibilities in the context of a greater African and South African contribution to global influences in the future and, in particular, to its impact on culture.

Mbeki and the Idea of the African Renaissance

An examination of Mbeki's speeches reveals the following key components of his perspective on the renaissance:[43]

- *An Africa of poverty and backwardness.* Mbeki sees a continent which, "while it led in the evolution of human life and was a leading center of learning, technology and the arts in ancient times," has experienced three "traumatic" periods, "each one of which has pushed her peoples deeper into poverty and backwardness." Slavery robbed Africa of millions of healthy, productive inhabitants and reinforced racist notions of Africans as subhumans. Imperialism and colonialism resulted in the rape of raw materials, the destruction of traditional agriculture and domestic food security, and the integration of Africa into the world economy as a subservient participant. Neocolonialism perpetuated this economic system, and new elites in independent states joined in oppressing and exploiting ordinary Africans.

- *Recognition of the terrible legacy of "neocolonialism."* During this period Africa experienced unstable political systems dominated by one-party states, military rule, civil wars, genocide, and millions of displaced and refugee populations. Corruption was entrenched and predatory elites looted national wealth. The international debt burden combined with unfavorable terms of trade ensures negative growth resulting in declining standards of living and quality of life for hundreds of millions of Africans.

• *Continental renewal in the twenty-first century.* Mbeki believes the conditions for a continental rebirth finally exist: the "liquidization" of colonialism as a result of South Africa's liberation, the end of the Cold War, continent-wide recognition of the "bankruptcy" of neocolonialism, and accelerated globalization.

• *All African countries are linked.* He argues that "the peoples of Africa share a common destiny" and that each country is constrained in its ability to succeed unless "other sister African countries" are at peace and succeeding too.

• *The tasks of the African renaissance include*
  Establishing democratic political systems
  Taking into account African specifics so these systems, while being truly democratic and protecting human rights, are nevertheless designed in ways that ensure political and peaceful means to address the competing interests of different social groups in each country
  Establishing institutions and procedures that enable the continent collectively to deal with questions of democracy, peace, and stability
  Achieving sustainable economic development that continuously improves people's standards of living and quality of life
  Changing Africa's place in the world economy—free of its international debt burden, no longer a supplier of raw materials and an importer of manufactured goods
  Emancipating African women
  Successfully confronting HIV/AIDS
  Rediscovering Africa's creative past to recapture people's cultures, encourage artistic creativity, and advance science and technology
  Strengthening genuine African independence in their relations with the major powers and enhancing their overall role in the global system

Before moving on to analyze the African renaissance idea, we need greater insight into what Mbeki is saying, as it reflects directly on our interests in culture and globalization. Mbeki argues that:

- Africa is not different. He rejects the idea of "African exceptionalism" and the association of "black" with fear, evil, and death, claiming that the African royal court of Timbuktu was as learned as renaissance Europe. "As we speak of an African renaissance we project into both the past and the future. I speak here of a glorious past of the emergence of *Homo sapiens* on the African continent."

- Africa can change and reclaim African dignity and soul. He cites archeological evidence of Africa's primacy in the evolution of humankind as a mark of confidence for achieving "Africa's rebirth." Africa's leaders must destroy perceptions of the continent as eternal beggars. They must be inspired by great African achievements: Egypt's pyramids and sphinxes, Axum's stone buildings, Zimbabwean and Carthaginian ruins, San rock paintings, Benin bronzes, African masks, Makonde carvings, and Shona stone sculptures.

- Africans must take responsibility, acknowledge mistakes, and act. Success depends on Africans themselves formulating objectives and programs, acknowledging and learning from past mistakes, and taking responsibility for success and failures.

- Africa must banish shame. Africans were not always "children of the abyss" and must do what they can to ensure their renaissance. "We are the disemboweled African mothers and the decapitated African children of Rwanda we have to say enough and no more . . . and by acting to banish the shame, remake ourselves as the midwives of the African renaissance."

- Human rights and democracy must be respected and not understood as peculiarly "Western" concepts.

- Africans must be proud of their heritage but modernize to address present and future needs. Africa must contribute significantly to the development of economic activity, arts, science, and technology and transmit a new image of continental peace and prosperity.

- Africans must respond to a call to rebellion. In the cause of the African renaissance, Mbeki call for rebellion against criminals and for a war against poverty, ignorance, and backwardness as the mark of a true African.

What Is This All About?

The notion of the "renaissance" of Africa is a brilliant marketing concept. It performs many functions for South Africa and its political leadership at a critical juncture in the country's history. It builds on old sentiments (pan-Africanism, African unity, African solutions to African problems) and thus provides a link with an earlier and older set of leaders (revered for their contribution to colonial liberation), while communicating a very different set of messages from those of the past.

The concept provides a means of reintegrating a democratic South Africa back into the rest of the continent after its long isolation as "the white south." It can provide some protection for Africa's most powerful country to lead and assume its rightful place in the continent while promoting a larger "Africanist" message. The veneer of the renaissance concept enables its proponents to advocate economic reform and democratic governance. This is the U.S. and EU agenda for Africa (and that too, of course, of many critics in Africa) as actions to be taken in the interests of an African renaissance and as the prerequisites for the continent claiming its rightful place in the world. Essentially, the concept provides "face" while it promotes intrinsically Western ideas about change for the continent.

The notion of the renaissance provides a platform from which to engage the West and to try to secure continued positive interest in and assistance to the continent. It is a bold means to try and stave off growing African pessimism in regard to Western capitalism, and it provides South Africa's most westernized leader ever with some protection from Africanist sentiment within his country (both within and without his own political movement and circle of traditional allies) and an African "face" through which to push tough domestic reforms.

It provides camouflage in the growing relationship between South Africa and the United States, in which South Africa can be the continental champion for reform in Africa and the most reliable U.S. ally on the continent. It also provides an African tone to South Africa's role as one of the leading developing countries committed to market reforms, global trade, and institutions of global governance still dominated by industrialized powers.

It is an African base from which South Africa will try to lead its bid for an African seat on the UN Security Council (and other changes in international power dynamics), which South Africa would want for itself in the first instance. It provides an Africanist tone for South Africa's determined push for the reform of continental and regional organizations such as the Organization of African Unity (OAU) and the Southern Africa Development Community (SADC).

It provides a very useful vehicle for Mbeki and many (black) South Africans' views about the state of the continent. It is important to note that running through Mbeki's statements about the renaissance is a very personal and deeply held emotional anger and shame about the state of the continent, the horrors inflicted on its peoples, and the concomitant perception of Africa and Africans in the rest of the world. It also contains a knowledgeable and angry rejection of the sins that Africa's own leaders have inflicted on the continent through their corruption, greed, and bad governance. Africa's weakness in the global arena is now even more important because the impact of economic globalization is a barrier to the ambitions of both Mbeki and South Africa.

Critique

It is important to look critically at the African renaissance concept from a number of angles.

"AFRICA"

Although Mbeki has said that the "first contribution we must make toward the realization of the goals of the African renaissance is the accomplishment of these aims in our own country," he has nonetheless linked his and South Africa's future to that of the continent. By being the spokesman for the African renaissance (as a continental thrust), he is generalizing about a vast area of enormous diversity. It is hard to see what holds this all together, other than racism toward African people in general and some sense of geographic contiguity.

Most historical and economic research questions whether there is any coherence to the notion of an African culture or cultures. Certainly our research at the Centre for Development and Enterprise would indicate that the terms "Africa" and "Africans" are social constructs whose definition varies significantly according to the social purposes of those who construct them. It is very difficult to make generalizations about Africa. As one commentator noted,

> One final obstacle in the path of understanding the belief systems of African cultures is that it is very difficult to make generalizations about the continent. Both the highest and lowest divorce rate in the societies of the world are found there, the forms of political organization range from informal patterns of leadership in hunting and gathering bands to divine kings and bureaucratic states.[44]

McCarthy asks, "Why bother to generalize about Africa and why treat Africa as a construct with anything other than perhaps a geological coherence? Is it that there is an historical and racial association which unites Africa but which many are still too polite to confront?"[45] According to most analysts the answer to the question of African distinctiveness is often found in the political and institutional interests that have arisen around various forms of what might be styled the "Africanist project": a project that appears to have changed over time. Anderson (1983) argues that, looked at historically, pan-Africanist ideas ebbed and flowed, depending in part on their relationship with Western educational systems.

Anderson points out, for example, that the paradoxical concept of "negritude," the "essence of Africanness expressible only in French," was largely the product of the Ecole Normale William Ponty in Dakar, "the apex of the colonial educational pyramid in French West Africa." The best West African students came to this school from countries such as Guinea, Mali, Senegal, and the Ivory Coast, and, through mutual interaction, they developed their concept of a common Africanness there, in or around 1915. However, when similar institutions were later developed in the various individual West African countries (and communication between these countries was reduced), the concept of negritude subsided. The Ecole Ponty's "old boys" went home to become, eventually, Guinean or Malian nationalist leaders, while retaining a "West African" camaraderie, solidarity, and intimacy lost to succeeding generations.[46]

Freund observes (1984) that the African concept has become impossible to disentangle from the interests of those who have researched and written about it and from the political projects of a variety of stakeholders both within Africa and abroad:

> Stripped of racial determinism African history quickly loses the unity which common prejudices, positive and negative, assume for it. There is no foreordained African cultural oneness that has been convincingly defined that suggests otherwise. The broadest themes of African history do reflect continent-wide developments precisely because they are themes that belong to the basic stock of social and economic developments of mankind elsewhere.[47]

Commenting on one of the most discussed recent books on Africa, Mamdani's (1996) *Citizen and Subject: Contemporary Africa and the Legacy of Late Colonialism*, the experienced French anthropologist Copans was forced to observe that

> this type of historical approach is debatable because the historical unity of black Africa is a colonial chimera. Social history in the last fifteen years has tried to draw another picture, more detailed more empirical but also better documented of local and global interactions. *To view Africa as a significant social arena of comparison is an ideological choice and a methodological blunder.*[48]

WISHFUL THINKING OR PROPHECY?

Is it true that Africa as a whole is poised to begin a resurgence of development and democracy? For a brief period in the 1990s, there did appear to be signs of improvement. World Bank figures showed a handful of African countries achieving economic growth rates of more than 6 percent, enough, it was said, to lift the majority of their people out of poverty in years rather than decades. At the same time, varying degrees of multiparty democracy spread across the continent, and a new crop of leaders seemed to offer hope. In addition to Nelson Mandela in South Africa there was Yoweri Museveni in Uganda, Meles Zenawi in Ethiopia, Frederick Chiluba in Zambia, and Laurent Kabila in Zaire. This new kind of leader expressed a desire to make life better for people by providing basic health care and education and by attracting foreign investment. They talked of peace and good government and, although many had been (or still claimed to be) socialists, they were friendly toward markets and investors.

Now, in the first year of a new century, it appears that all this "was an illusion":

> The new leaders became embroiled in wars, some with each other and the cheerful statistics were the result of good rains and bad accounting. Sub-Saharan Africa as a whole had a growth rate of less than 3 percent in that period, which just about kept step with the rate of population increase. So no-one was getting richer. The figures—not to mention the recent crop of disasters and wars—now suggest that Africa is losing the battle. All the bottom places in the world league tables are filled by African countries and the gap between them and the rest of the world is widening. According to Paul Collier of the World Bank, only 15 percent of Africans today live in an "environment considered minimally adequate for sustainable growth and development." At least 45 percent of Africans live in poverty and African countries need growth rates of 7 percent or more to cut that figure in half in 15 years.[49]

It is much harder to talk plausibly of an African renaissance at the beginning of the new millennium than ever.

Renaissance in South Africa First

The one country (and perhaps some of its neighbors) that can be associated with a "renaissance" is South Africa. Although the ultimate fate of South Africa will be affected by its "weak" neighborhood, a South African renaissance is a more achievable objective than a continent-wide one. Achieving such a renaissance will be hard enough and will require considerable political will, hard work, and some luck. In the economic sense, at least, it is possible to think about the word "renaissance" in relation to the country's economy: whatever its moral and other flaws, the South African economy has in the past been a modern powerhouse of sorts, and it is conceivable that this could be the case—relatively speaking and compared to other middle-income developing countries—again.

One of the consequences of Mbeki's continental ambitions is insufficient attention being given to the strengths of South Africa and its real possibilities for greater renewal. A focus on the continent and its problems could require too much time and effort from the president and his cabinet, compromising the attention they can devote to South Africa itself. A concentrated focus on South Africa might allow Mbeki to put his grander ideas into practice. For example, what would be required of government and the country's other key players for South Africa to become a "new Florence"? Really looking at South Africa and its cultural intricacies and how these relate to our prospects for success requires resources of time and effort.

Few commentators talk about the devastation of the African family and its relationship to the idea of an African renaissance. Mongane Wally Serote, convener of the African Renaissance Conference 2000, talked about some of the South African specifics that need to be discussed: "We also support the liberation of women, which must involve men so that they begin to address something that was devastated by apartheid and colonialism: the African family, the basis of our society."[50]

Serious attention needs to be given to the difficult issue of relations between men and women. Although Mbeki and the ANC are firmly committed to the liberation of women (a rather untraditional concept), there has been considerable unease about discussing sex and the inevitable frankness that must accompany any serious attempt to come to grips with AIDS and its devastating spread throughout the country. Respect for authority, age, and a tendency for political leaders to centralize and be "big men" remain, and these could be inhibiting factors.

Most important of all, South Africa has to look to the growing inequities in black society and the imperative of sustained economic growth, effective education, and training and expansion of opportunities to deal with this. Like many other countries, South Africa has a small (albeit expanding), nonracial elite, which is ready to act and think as full-blown members of a highly international and mobile Davos culture. Left behind are millions of urban and rural people with little exposure to the culture of efficiency, rule playing, and meeting deadlines. For many, especially those in the urban and periurban areas, life is a daily struggle against violence, disorder, and poverty.

South Africa is a country that is enormously "receptive" to Western cultural ideas. The impact of the fundamental processes of change and transformation that have taken place in the society since 1652, and especially in the last two hundred years, have made it extremely difficult to sustain any coherent and clearly distinctive form of traditional indigenous culture. Thus the dominant culture of South Africa's new ruling elite is a Western one. South African opposition to the apartheid regime was led internationally by people who spent considerable time in non-African countries and in the process lost touch with many aspects of "home." They also spent time in African countries, but this seems mainly to have made them feel angry about the failures in those countries and determined to do better in South Africa.

Thus the exile leadership fought against apartheid with mainly Western ideas and tools and brought the latest Western thinking back into the country. For example, they have pioneered the country's need to catch up in the world of telecommunications, and it is interesting that one area in which the ANC has excelled has been its use of the Internet as a means of communication—not to its millions of supporters, some 40–50 percent (or more) of whom are illiterate, but to its mainly foreign "Western" audiences. Leaders against the apartheid state who remained inside South Africa throughout the 1960s and 1980s have forged a more indigenous approach to resistance politics and, later, to negotiation politics.

Within this Western mode, however, it is important to appreciate the unusual circumstances of particularly urban African life in South Africa since the 1950s onward. This is without doubt a different kind of urban culture from that found in Western cities. The particular circumstances of urbanization under the apartheid regime and then the impact of the struggle against "white rule" has led to some specificity in South Africa's urban areas. On the one hand there is township jazz and other forms of music, dance, and song; on the other, there is violence, dislocation, instability, and a tremendous psychological complexity about black South

Africans' relationship to whites, to their own culture (as it has evolved), and to other Africans.

South African Africans are generally not popular in the rest of the continent. They are perceived as "looking down" on other African countries as "backward" in services, infrastructure, and other areas. It is significant that Mbeki talks of "shame" with respect to what has happened in the rest of Africa. If we were to probe South African Africans' attitudes of superiority toward other Africans on the continent would we find, "We are proud of the country we and the whites have built in South Africa, which is so much better than what you have done"? And if so, how would a proud South African–African nationalist put that together?

South Africa is already a source of global emissions. In the past some were negative cultural additions; the global use (in the English language) of the words "apartheid" and "veld" are two examples. Since 1994 there have been some more positive emissions, and our "negotiations culture" is widely recognized for producing the miracle of the political transition and has already been "exported" for use in peace negotiations in Northern Ireland. Although "Madiba magic" is centered on one very special man, it is another form of the "negotiations" culture that was used in resolving the Libyan/Lockerbie situation.

There is some truth in the idea that South African managers are well suited (better than most) in dealing with many different cultures and levels of education in the workplace, and this too could become a South African cultural export. South African leadership in and into developing countries has also been remarkable since the country's democratization. South Africa is head of numerous international organizations such as the Commonwealth and the Nonaligned Movement, and here again its particular approach, as an inherently Western and confident developing country but with certain sensitivities, history, and peculiarities, can contribute to a different form of engagement by developing countries with the more powerful developed economies.

South Africa has already started "emitting" management, culture, products, and people into the African continent. Johannesburg is seen as a highly desirable "brand name" by advertisers, and South African sports stars are becoming well-known across Africa. It is possible that not only will South Africa become the "Hong Kong/Taiwan" of the continent (that is, providing the capital and expertise for economic development), but it could also be more than that. Fashions and trends that are American or Western in initial provenance are then translated into South African fashions with a local flavor and then spread into Africa.

All these globalizing influences can and will grow. If South Africa can become an economic success, then its influence too will expand. The critical question concerns whether there is sufficient understanding in South Africa about the nature of the new global economy and the ingredients required for success in that tough world. In Schlemmer's words, "South Africa has not only to catch up with the current economic development of global Western society; it has to do this while aiming at a rapidly moving target of development."[51] The pace of innovation, technological development, and the new culture of success in these societies severely test the resources of even the most competitive of North American, European, and developed eastern economies, let alone those of the developing societies of Latin America and Africa.

Has this new value system and mode of economic behavior and enhanced competitiveness permeated the African mission of fuller liberation and transformation? It would be tragic indeed if Africa aimed at excelling in an economic system that has already passed.

> If South, Central and East Africa fail in their attempts to "catch up" or succeed only to find that they have caught/bought a model due to be phased out, the stage will be set for the politics of reaction and the rebirth of ideological dissent. A new battle for liberation might emerge with concepts which could further weaken the motivation to understand the essence of the new globalization. Without international Marxism to drive a new struggle, the reaction will probably have to be ethnic or racial. If that does happen, then South Africa's small margin "of old and new traditionalists will grow in the ashes of frustration."[52]

It should be noted in relation to the above that South Africa's response to the Zimbabwe situation has been worrying in this respect.

The sleeping giant of South Africa concerns religion and the impact that the spread of evangelical and African Independent Churches could have. Religion is everywhere one of the most potent forces of cultural transformation, and the experience of Latin America is instructive. As David Martin put it in his seminal book on the spread of evangelical Christianity in that region of rapid urbanization and dislocation,

Pentecostalism renews the innermost cell of the family and protects the woman from the ravages of male desertion and violence. A new faith is able to implant new discipline, re-order priorities, counter corruption and destructive machismo and reverse the indifferent and injurious hierarchies of the outside world. . . . millions of people are absorbed within a protective social capsule where they acquire new concepts of self and new models of initiative and voluntary organization.[53]

We do know, if only impressionistically, that there is a different "Protestant work ethic" among at least some of the AIC and evangelical churches in South Africa. Many, especially the AIC, appear to be an effective hybrid between Western influences and indigenous African culture—the very element we have struggled to find evidence of elsewhere in modern South Africa. The ironic possibility is that an African renaissance in South Africa may be more Pentecostal than anyone suspects. While this is a rather different notion of the renaissance from what is currently discussed, the cultural dynamics of this should not be underestimated. As Peter Berger has argued with respect to the evidence from Latin America,

The social and moral consequences of conversion to Protestantism are important. The ethos of (what Weber called) "the Protestant ethic" shows itself to be remarkably helpful to people in the throes of rapid modernization and of the "take-off" stage of modern economic growth. The same ethos also continues to evince its time-honored affinities with the "spirit of capitalism," with individualism, with a hunger for education and (last but not least) with a favorable disposition toward democratic politics. . . . These affinities are in the main unintended; they are the result . . . of the unanticipated behavioral consequences of both doctrine and religious experience.[54]

CONCLUSION

In reflecting on the cultural impact of globalization at the beginning of the twenty-first century, it is important to place the discussion in historical context. Some of the current enthusiasts of globalization forget the scale, range, and impact of earlier periods of global trade, migration, and settlement. The first half of the twentieth century saw

> world-girdling maritime empires, world wars and the global spread of ideas. No better example of the last can be found than the communist revolution in China. In that most enduring of empires, Mao Zedong won in the name of an ideology developed just a century earlier by a German of Jewish origins. That was a possibility nobody—certainly no Chinese—could have imagined two centuries before.[55]

With respect to South Africa, powerful examples of the impact of global forces from an earlier period include Christianity, the urban culture associated with industrialization, and the opposition to apartheid as influenced by Marxist ideology.

The current spread of globalizing forces and their impact on culture is a multifaceted and complex process. The South African case gives rise to some broader thoughts and insights concerning culture and globalization.

- This globalization project was built on the notion of four "faces" of global culture. It seems worthwhile to consider at least two other cultural dynamics. The first is what might be called an international underclass culture perhaps originating and being shaped initially by the American and European underclass (as portrayed and glamorized by Hollywood, TV, and music) but with clear counterparts in South Africa and elsewhere. The second is what might be called "the dark side of Davos culture": the emergence and global spread of an international criminal culture. One thinks here of "the Russian Mafia," "Nigerian drug dealers," international money laundering, and so on. South Africa's isolation prior to 1994, coupled with authoritarian systems of control with differing effectiveness over immigration and other international influences, made the country unprepared for and therefore vulnerable to these criminal activities as it became a more open, democratic state.

- In thinking about globalizing cultural forces, it is important to distinguish between different types of cultural influence that spread around the world in different ways and at different tempos. Consumer culture has spread very fast and comprehensively—everybody seems to want certain global products and global brands. These are predominantly American but not always. On the other hand, the cultural values underlying American, European, and Asian productivity, which sustain the enormous wealth and diversity of choices inherent in "global consumption," are not marketed very much and certainly diffuse less easily than the consumer images flashing on television screens in almost every home on the globe. It is harder for the productive and work values underlying American economic success, for example, to be communicated and then adopted in very different societies.

• The flow of global forces is not one-way. The most powerful dynamics are certainly American and Western, but the South African case shows the possibility and reality of two other kinds of "cultural emission," even from the periphery of the global economic system. South Africa has contributed certain ideas and concepts (e.g., apartheid, "negotiations culture," "rainbow nation") that now have global currency and impact. In addition, South Africa is a subregional center in the global system. Its culture, strongly influenced by America and Europe, but often with real local content or a particular South African spin, has impact and influence on its own regional sphere of influence, and this is now expanding beyond its own borders, and even those of southern Africa, into the wider African continent and possibly into non-African countries in the developing world.

• Countries outside the West that are strong enough economically (Japan) and/or culturally (India) are able to influence global culture; this will happen more as the technology improves and the pace of globalization increases.

It seems reasonable to predict that South Africa will only become a *growing* source of *globalizing* influences if it is an economic success. It's the South African mix that is a potential winner: the mix of a powerful, vibrant, predominantly Western, English-speaking culture, coupled with African leadership and the best of the values and culture that have emerged from our complex history and can still emerge from the dynamics of a successful multicultural democracy. Clearly, South Africa can become an African success story and a bigger player in contributing to global culture and developments.

NOTES

1. E. Mphahlele, quoted in U. Hannerz, "Sophiatown: The View from Afar," in K. Barber, ed., *Readings in African Popular Culture* (London: International African Institute, School of Oriental and African Studies, 1997), p. 167.

2. Peter Berger, as quoted in notes from the Globalization Study research team meeting, Bellagio, Italy 1999.

3. The research on which this chapter is based is a collective effort. The following reports were commissioned by CDE. Professor Jeff McCarthy produced *Review Article— Globalisation and Africa: The Concept of Contemporary Africa and Africans in the Humanities and Social and Economic Sciences with special reference to South Africa; Globalisation and Business Culture in South Africa* (October 1999); *Successful Black Business People: Background, Culture, Aspirations, and Values; Globalisation, Marketing, and Advertising in South Africa; Hairdressers, Hairstyles, and Popular Culture: South Africa and Cultural Globalisation.* These are all unpublished reports, produced in 1999, commissioned by the Centre for Development and Enterprise, especially for the South Africa study/ chapter in the book. Professor Lawrence Schlemmer produced *Globalisation, Culture, and Development: Is Southern Africa a Ghetto of the West?* (2000), and Professor Peter Delius wrote a think piece, *One Hand Clapping? The Interaction of Global and Indigenous Culture in South Africa* (2000). Additional research and assistance was provided by CDE staff: Judith Hudson, senior research coordinator, and Steven Gruzd, researcher.

4. Schlemmer, *Globalisation, Culture, and Development,* p. 2.

5. Delius, *One Hand Clapping?* p. 1. Subsequent quotes are from this report and are not individually referenced.

6. President T. Mbeki, address at the unveiling of the coat of arms, Kwaggafontein, 27 April 2000. Subsequent quotations are from this speech.

7. E. Jayiya, "New Coat of Arms Brings Diverse People of SA Together," *Star,* 28 April 2000.

8. D. Bullard, "It's unutterable. It's unintelligible. You guessed: It's SA's new motto," *Sunday Times,* 7 May 2000.

9. "Confusion over Translation Puts Damper on SA's Motto," *Business Day,* 15 May 2000.

10. S. Francis, H. Dugmore and Rico, *Madam and Eve,* cartoon for 6 May 2000, at *www.mg.co.za/mg/madameve/2000/05/me20000506w.htm.*

11. The quotations in this text box are all taken from Hannerz, "Sophiatown." In some cases the quotes cited by Hannerz come from other sources.

12. Schlemmer, *Globalisation, Culture, and Development.* Unless indicated, subsequent quotes are from this report and are not individually referenced.

13. See the African Renaissance Institute, *Executive Summary,* published by the African Renaissance Institute, P.O. Box BR330, Broadhurst, Gaborone, Botswana, in August 1998.

14. Two open-ended questions were included in a nationwide sample survey in March 1999. This survey, the Markdata *Omnibus,* is a syndicated (multiclient) personal interview–based research instrument based on a multistage stratified sample of 2,250 South Africans eighteen years and older. It offers complete coverage of all types of residential areas including deep rural traditional areas, commercial farming areas, areas of informal residence, townships, hostels, suburbs, and inner city areas in all sizes of towns from metropolitan complexes to small villages. Interviews are conducted in the home languages of respondents by very experienced interviewers. The number of African respondents included in the sample was 1,525.

15. T. Nyquist, quoted by L. Schlemmer, *African Middle Class Elite* (Grahamstown: Institute for Social and Economic Research, Rhodes University, 1983), p. 260.

16. M. Brandel-Syrier, quoted in L. Schlemmer, *Coming Through: The Search for a New Cultural Identity* (Johannesburg: McGraw-Hill, 1978).

17. C. Themba, *The Will to Die* (London, 1972), p. 110, quoted in Hannerz, "Sophiatown," p. 167.

18. B. Modisane, *Blame Me on History* (London, 1965), pp. 183–184, quoted in Hannerz, "Sophiatown," p. 167.

19. Y. Mokgoro, "Ubuntu and the Law in South Africa," Konrad Adenauer Foundation, The African Renaissance, Occasional Papers, May 1998.

20. One possible exception to this is Chief Mangosuthu Buthelezi's assertion that African democracy is based on the principle of consensus rather than the typically international forms of proportional representation and multiparty political contest. Buthelezi goes on to say that this tradition has to be accommodated in a devolved system of local administration in rural areas in which the consensus-based democratic form could reassert itself in modern government. This argument is certainly serious enough to warrant debate. Other arguments seem to be more about possibilities than tangible patterns.

21. W. D. Hammond-Tooke, quoted in McCarthy, *Globalisation and Africa,* p. 7.

22. Gillian Godsell, interview by Judith Hudson, 17 March 1999.

23. S. Macozoma, in "Africa and Asia: Issues for South Africa," *Development and Democracy 9,* December 1994, p. 67.

24. Hammond-Tooke, in McCarthy, *Globalisation and Africa,* pp. 7–8.

25. J. S. Mbiti, quoted in L. Schlemmer, *African Religions and Philosophy* (London: Heinemann, 1960), p. 214.

26. L. Kuper, quoted in L. Schlemmer, *An African Bourgeoisie* (New Haven: Yale, 1965), p. 84.

27. P. Mayer, cited in L. Schlemmer, *Townsmen or Tribesmen* (Cape Town: Oxford University Press, 1961).

28. L. Schlemmer, quoting D. A. Masolo, "Ideological Dogmatism and the Values of Democracy," in W. O. Oyugi et al., eds., *Democratic Theory and Practice in Africa* (London: Curry, 1988), p. 29.

29. McCarthy, *Globalisation and Business Culture in South Africa* (October 1999). Subsequent quotes are from the interviews conducted in this study and are not individually referenced.

30. J. McCarthy, citing P. J. Buckley and M. Casson, "Multinational Enterprises in Less Developed Countries: Cultural and Economic Interactions," in P. J. Buckley and J. Clegg, eds., *Multinational Enterprises in Less Developed Countries* (London: Macmillan, 1992).

31. J. McCarthy, *Successful Black Business Persons: Background, Culture, Aspirations, and Values* (July 1999). Subsequent quotes are from the interviews conducted in this study and are not individually referenced.

32. McCarthy, *Globalisation, Marketing, and Advertising.* Subsequent quotes are from the interviews conducted in this study and are not individually referenced.

33. M. Kuzwayo, *Marketing through Mud and Dust* (Cape Town: Ink inc., 2000), p. 104.

34. J. McCarthy, *Hairdressers, Hairstyles, and Popular Culture: South Africa and Cultural Globalisation* (July 1999). Subsequent quotes are from the interviews conducted in this study and are not individually referenced.

35. This section draws largely on remarks by Dr. Yussuf Saloojee of the National Council Against Smoking and Mr. Edward Shalala of the Tobacco Institute of South Africa, interview by Steven Gruzd of CDE, March 2000.

36. *South Africa Survey, 1999–2000,* millennium ed. (Johannesburg: South African Institute of Race Relations, 1999), p. 205. Most of the other statistics in this paragraph are from this source.

37. Y. Saloojee, National Council Against Smoking, interview by Steven Gruzd, 1 March 2000.

38. W. Hartley, "Steamrolling of Contentious Laws Calls Up Ghost of NP," *Business Day,* 23 October 1998.

39. This section draws largely on three chapters in R. Elphick and R. Davenport, eds., *Christianity in South Africa: A Political, Social, and Cultural History* (Cape Town: David Philip, 1997). The chapters are R. Elphick, "Introduction: Christianity in South Africa"; H. Pretorius and L. Jafta, "African Initiated Churches"; and A. H. Anderson and G. J. Pillay, "The Segregated Spirit: The Pentecostals."

40. Pretorius and Jafta, "African Initiated Churches," p. 226.

41. "Praying for Success," *Time,* 7 February 2000, p. 26.

42. "Preaching Prosperity on Earth," *Finance Week,* 21 April 2000, p. 20.

43. The following section draws from Mbeki's speeches, found on the Mbeki page on the ANC Web site, www.anc.org.za. The insights come specifically from President Thabo Mbeki's speech at the launch of the African Renaissance Institute, Pretoria, 11 October 1999; Mbeki, "The African Renaissance, South Africa and the World" speech at the United Nations University, Tokyo, Japan, 9 April 1998; Mbeki, inauguration speech, Pretoria, 16 June 1999; Mbeki, African renaissance statement to the SABC, 13 August 1998; Mbeki, statement at the African Renaissance Conference, Johannesburg, 28 September

1998; and Mbeki, speech at the Gala dinner of the Union of Orthodox Synagogues, Cape Town, 27 January 1999.

44. I. Karp, quoted in J. McCarthy, "African Systems of Thought," in P. M. Martin and P. O'Meara, eds., *Africa,* 3d ed. (Bloomington: Indiana University Press, 1995), p. 211.

45. McCarthy, *Globalisation and Africa,* p. 5.

46. J. McCarthy, quoting B. Andersen, *Imagined Communities: Reflections on the Origin and Spread of Nationalism* (London: Verso, 1983), p. 113.

47. W. M. Freund, quoted in J. McCarthy, *The Making of Contemporary Africa* (London: Macmillan, 1994), p. 6.

48. J. Copans, quoted in J. McCarthy, "Review of Mamdani's Citizen and Subject," *Transformation* 36 (1998), p. 102.

49. "The Heart of the Matter," *Economist,* 13 May 2000, p. 23.

50. "Towards the Birth of the African Century," *Financial Mail,* 7 April 2000, p. 20.

51. Schlemmer, *Globalisation, Culture, and Development,* p. 24.

52. Schlemmer, *Globalisation, Culture, and Development,* p. 25.

53. D. Martin, *Tongues of Fire: The Explosion of Protestantism in Latin America* (Oxford: Blackwell, 1990), p. 284.

54. P. Berger, foreword to *Tongues of Fire,* p. ix.

55. M. Wolf, "The State in the Global Economy" (paper delivered at the EOMT Colloquium on Globalization, South Africa February 2000), p. 2.

8

Trends toward Globalization
in Chile

Arturo Fontaine Talavera

Is there a specifically Latin American manner of participating in the globalized world? There are sufficient indications that allow us to confirm that there is. Of course, this may only be a transitory phase that will end up flowing into a European model, as has occurred in Spain. This option should not be discarded, as there is much to say in its favor. However, at this point it seems more appropriate to investigate the possibility that a way forward may be emerging that essentially implies the acceptance of an open and pro–free market socioeconomic order that must live side-by-side with a conservative socioreligious order.

This is not a rejection of globalization per se in Latin America, for this very ethical-religious renewal is itself fed by globalized religious movements. We have, then, a sort of conservative globalization that competes with other globalizing forces, which can include, among others, feminism. The principal benefit that is sought is the strengthening of the family, conceived of as an institution that requires lasting hierarchical ties that are cultivated in the intergenerational proximity—at least that is the way it is conceived today.

While the case in Chile is extremely unusual, it is also very important. Not only has Chile been the pioneering country in the region—successful socioeconomic reforms have produced a strong economy—it is at the same time the country in which the new international conservative movements have the most vitality and power.

The Chilean socioeconomic model is permeated by the principles and mechanisms of the free market: competition, private companies, deregulation and privatization, market prices, an economy that is open to the outside, low tariffs, rational business administration, and so on. These principles and mechanisms have also been incorporated into the services provided by the national welfare system, including subsidies to the poor. For instance, the construction of subsidized housing involves private-sector competition and management, while private companies also carry out municipal rubbish collection.

The Chilean economic experience has made it the new paradigm in Latin America. Between 1984 and 1998, Chile doubled its per capita income; between 1987 and 1998, the proportion of the population living below the poverty line dropped from 44.4 percent to 22.2 percent; the poorest of the poor, the destitute, fell from 16.5 percent to 5.6 percent. Despite this, however, the enormous inequalities of income in the country have not diminished, probably because they are caused by sharp educational differences whose correction appears neither easy nor rapid. In any case the new economic consensus in the region has been very marked by this successful experience. And even though the reforms that brought about this tremendous growth took place under the military regime (1973–1990), the case of Argentina has shown that analogous reforms can be carried out under democracy.

It should be noted here (and will be described later in this chapter) that Chile's modernization and economic transformation came about in large part because a previous globalization that occurred in the academic world: in relationships that began in the 1950s between economists at Universidad Católica (Catholic University), Universidad de Chile (University of Chile), and the University of Chicago. Many of the Chilean graduates of Chicago have since gone on to occupy very relevant positions in higher education and in the management of the Chilean economy.

The impact of this partnership has been particularly felt in business. Most senior executives have the stamp of having been formed either by disciples of the Chicago school or by the disciples' disciples. The business heroes of this period are those who have made Chilean wine drunk in Berlin, London, and Tokyo, who have brought Chilean fruit to the New York and Riyadh markets, and who administer the private pension systems in different countries. These are men who love the global world (they are comfortable using key terms in English), modernity, technocracy, sports, efficiency, state-of-the-art computers and electronics, sudden travel, money, and the future. But they also love religion and the traditional family.

From the point of view of consumption, Chilean society is now completely integrated with international commerce. In the popular world, people wear used clothing imported from the United States and Chinese or Korean parkas; they watch television on Japanese sets, go to shopping malls, and include Italian and Chinese food in their diets. Young people, especially, seem to be the same as those in any developed country, but they prefer Cuban or Latin music and Latin American soap operas.

Parallel to this, evangelical Christianity, mainly of Pentecostal origin, has expanded notably among the poor and now represents about 20 percent of the urban poor. Of the poor who go to church at least once a week, one in two is an evangelical.

The evangelicals are characterized by their dedication to work and by their rejection of alcohol. The man who converts transforms his life, especially his family life, abandoning liquor and "the lads." The formerly absent father makes himself responsible for being in the house and providing for his family; he accepts the marriage and the paternity of his children, stops beating his wife, and goes to church with her and his children. His wife, who was the first in the family to convert, gains a new self-image and self-respect through the Dorcas Sisters, a Christian relief agency that offers aid to poor women, along with courses on health, running a home, cooking, sewing, and other ways of improving family life. This transformation of the male and female roles betokens an extraordinary reform of the family.

The reformed family that emerges, however, is not one that would satisfy the aspirations of feminists. The father is the head, but there can be no doubt that the woman gains in participation, respect, and emotional and economic security as well as equality. Evangelism helps the rise and development of an order similar to that of a classic bourgeois family: the predominant ethos favors work, honesty, and personal effort, which, with the help of God, will translate into economic progress. Around moral issues such as divorce and abortion, the evangelicals are more conservative than the Catholics.

The expansion of evangelicalism among the poor has a correlation in the world of the company: the revitalization of international conservative Catholic movements. Notable among these are Opus Dei, Legionarios de Cristo (the Legionnaires of Christ, a movement of Mexican origin), and the Schoenstatt community. These are religious movements with a global or international character that give a special participatory role to laymen, emphasize the cult of the Virgin Mary, oppose liberation theology and socialism, cultivate a strong presence in professional circles, are interested in education and the means of social communication, and follow the line of Pope John Paul II. The penetration of these movements has been particularly successful in the areas of business and journalism; their ideals are transmitted through instruction circles and institutes, colleges, universities, and the communications media. Their concepts, processes, and organization are international, with global aspirations.

As already indicated, I believe that the central point in this respect is the family. The businessman wants to act in the global world of business but not at the cost of changing his concept of the family, which is seen as running the risk of becoming dispersed if, for example, the path of the United States is followed. The businessman wants to protect and preserve the physical closeness between distinct generations in Chile and the sense of familial permanence.

The intellectual world is a world in tension. Today, intellectual groups that favor the market economy coexist with sectors that are interested in other types of global agendas, such as feminism, critical cultural studies, environmentalism, and supporters of indigenous peoples. Many among these latter groups resist economic globalization, though they of course belong to networks and movements that have global characteristics. There are also other sectors that promote conservative ethical-religious agendas.

It is too early to know the outcome of all this for Chile. Many of the processes that have been planted have not managed to crystallize and become established; as such, they only represent phases and momentary compromises. But what there can be no doubt about is that, day by day, either consciously or unconsciously, a coexistence is being sought in Latin America between socioeconomic globalization and a strong family-based, ethical-religious conservatism that in turn aspires to become globalizing.

THE GLOBALIZATION OF CONSUMPTION
AND ITS SOCIAL EFFECTS

It seems easy to fix a date. Until the mid-1970s, Chile's economy was largely closed to international commerce; from then on, the situation changed rapidly. This transformation is reflected overall in the trade figures, but they fail to give any idea of the modifications in lifestyles and expectations that were produced by this change. For many of the goods that became available—televisions, stoves, radios, refrigerators, parkas, jeans, sneakers, watches, cologne, deodorants, cosmetics, scotch whisky—had been status symbols, which gave rise to an interesting sociological phenomenon: even before any great change in real per capita income, significant segments of the population felt that they had moved up in status. Social change in this case did not result from economic growth itself but rather from the globalization of commerce and the new availability of these highly symbolic goods. This perception of social mobility was particularly intense during the transition period, before some of these goods became virtually universal, as has happened now with watches, televisions, and shoes, for example.

In 1970, the volume of Chile's international trade as a proportion of GNP (the most generally accepted manner of measuring the degree of an economy's openness) was 38 percent;[1] by way of contrast, the figure for a number of the East Asian economies was already more than double this. But between 1974 and 1979, the average for tariffs dropped from about 105 percent (with a range of 0 percent to 750 percent, depending on the specific product) to a flat rate of 10 percent. This opening of the economy, along with other liberalizing market reforms, put the vast and complex process of integration of the Chilean economy in motion. By 1999 the volume of international commerce as a proportion of GNP had reached 90 percent.

When the economy was still closed, one could find authentic Lee jeans for example—but only people who traveled had access to them. The same was true for foreign cigarettes and whisky. In 1970 you could

Table 8.1   Availability of Durable Goods in Chile (by Proportion of Homes)

	1970	1980	1990	1999
Cars	7.3%	15.4%	21.3%	33.7%
Washing machines	17.1%	33.6%	48.2%	78.1%
Refrigerators	14.4%	30.9%	44.9%	77.6%
Telephones	15.1%	18.6%	23.4%	54.8%
Televisions	10.3%	24.7%	78.6%*	91.4%

*   Includes 29 percent of homes with a black-and-white television. The data for 1970 and 1980 refer to black-and-white televisions—there were as yet no color televisions.

Source: Banco Central de Chile, *Indicadores Económicos y Sociales 1960–1988* (Santiago: Banco Central, 1989); Centro de Estudios Públicos, "Estudio Nacional de Opinión Pública: Junio 1990," *Serie Documentos de Trabajo* 136, August 1990; Centro de Estudios Públicos, "Estudio Nacional de Opinión Pública: Septiembre–Octubre 1999," *Serie Documentos de Trabajo* 300, November 1999.

buy a national or Argentinean whisky, but the price of real scotch was prohibitive. From this point of view, in terms of what could be consumed, an international employee of the United Nations' Latin America Economic Center (CEPAL), for example, appeared to live like a millionaire.

Table 8.1 demonstrates the evolution of trends in some of these symbolic goods.

Of all these products listed above, the automobile industry has been the slowest to liberalize and retains its privileged protected status. The increase in the number of telephones is due to a new regulatory system established after the return to democracy in 1990, which permitted competition and privatization of the industry and brought Spanish capital to the country.

But the case of televisions is especially revealing. In 1970 only 10.3 percent of households had a television. Chilean televisions (Japanese ones were not available due to their high cost) were expensive and of poor quality; having a television, therefore, automatically placed people in the richest 10 percent of the population. In 1977, however, over 300,000 televisions were imported, four times the total brought in throughout the 1960s. Although per capita income in 1977 was 11 percent less than what it had been in 1970, by 1980 one in every four homes had television, in 1990 one of every two homes had color television, and toward the end of the 1990s more than 90 percent of households had color television. Thirty

years ago, owning a black-and-white television placed a person in the upper middle class; twenty years ago, possession of a color television placed
a person in the middle class. Today it means nothing.

The social effects of the mass ownership of televisions are multiple.
Here I would like to emphasize that, in Chile's case, the "standard"
Chilean Spanish spoken on TV has decreased differences in regional and
class accents. Social distinctions as reflected in speech are no longer as
noticeable as they once were, as the two most important networks produce national programming. For many, television has also meant real
access to a more articulate language. Chilean society has never achieved
the level of effective literacy of, say, the United States, so the impact of
television has been strong in a society with an extended oral tradition.
One result has been that young people from different social strata speak
a more similar language than their parents or grandparents did—which
is also to say that the generation gap has in some ways become wider.
However, the class differences that were much more noticeable and significant in people's lives have now lessened.

The extraordinary popularity of radio stations that use young people's colloquial speech, such as *Rock and Pop,* the radio program *Rumpi,*
or the film *Chacotero Sentimental* by Cristián Galaz, are possible thanks
to the emergence of a generational slang that cuts across social classes.
Chacotero Sentimental has become the most watched film in the history
of Chile. It covers three successive stories which, we are told, come from
the *Rumpi* radio program, a sentimental phone-in for young people
known for its lack of inhibition and its host's juvenile slang. Although
the film moves between different social environments, the young people
in it appear more similar than one might expect, in particular through
their language.

This goes hand in hand with the consumption habits that now mark
young people of all strata and follow a universal model: jeans, baggy
trekking pants full of pockets, T-shirts, sweaters, drinks, chewing gum,
pizzas, sports, sneakers. The world "universal" however is misleading. To
be more exact, we should talk of the model of the United States and of
the most developed European countries. By the end of the 1960s, only
young members of the Chilean elite had the consumer habits of those in
California, London, and New York; since then, this style has become
widespread.

At this point, television began projecting images of young people in TV serials produced in the United States and dubbed in Mexico or Los Angeles, which are now often Chile's top-rated shows. TV series from Mexico and Venezuela also show this type of middle-class youth, who, despite certain Latin traits, is largely depicted as a gringo. But then, in certain moments, he or she is no longer a pseudogringo but becomes simply a standard Latin American guy or girl. Perhaps this coming and going back and forth between pseudogringo and more traditional Latin American values and traits is at the heart of what young people believe—or imagine—they are confronting in their lives.

During the 1970s middle-class youth came to revalue the traditional poncho and with it the style of the Che Guevara bearded *guerrilleros,* just as Spanish language protest music tried to revitalize indigenous musical instruments such as the *quena.* Foreign-inspired rock music followed a parallel course: it was popular, but the musicians who copied it were "gringofied." This was the moment in Latin American history when nationalism, antiimperialism, Marxism-Leninism, Castroism, the *aggiorniamento* of the Catholic Church introduced by John XXIII, the May rebellion in Paris, the struggle against injustice and misery, rejection of dictatorships and capitalist consumer culture, and opposition to the Vietnam War were all confounded into one wide and contradictory movement of revolutionary socialist aspirations.

The socialism of those days embodied a double promise: modernity (the socialism of the future, the vanguard) and, at the same time, to use Berger's expression, "the promise of a new home."[2] It is not possible to understand this Latin American socialist phenomenon, which the authors of *The Homeless Mind* understand so well, without setting it against the background of the threat of capitalist modernization which, despite its achievements and opportunities, uproots many people and leaves them helpless. Socialism, on the other hand, offered a different model of modernization, which included state-led industrialization and mobilization of the masses.

The protectionism of the development model based on import substitution penetrated Chile without encountering any real resistance. It found fertile soil in the Spanish mercantile tradition and created a capitalist sector that enjoyed the comparative advantages it generated. The socialist critique of private monopolies has a real basis: mercantile capitalism is not only unfair and inefficient from an economic point of view, it is extremely vulnerable to organized political pressure. The nationalization of the economy under the socialists was therefore presented as a necessary step for an alternative modernity that was both anti-American and anticapitalist.

This promise was violently destroyed with the collapse of Salvador Allende's socialist government and the military coup of 1973. The dramatic bombardment of the government palace and the suicide of President Allende within the building closed a chapter in the country's history. The subsequent repression and the task of founding an open and competitive modern economy were the hallmarks of the military regime, which governed until it lost a referendum and peacefully handed over power to a democratically elected president. The military regime, including its civilian ministers and aides, had felt called on to "modernize" the country, but the free market model of an open economy has now gained legitimacy.

At some moment under the military regime and the opening of the economy, patterns of consumption based on imported goods became generalized. For instance, by 1980 the parka had already replaced the poncho on farms and clogs had given way to imported Wellingtons. In the material it consumed, the Chilean population proved to be highly imitative.

One of the revolutions with greatest impact on the poor was the abolition of regulations prohibiting the import of used clothing, which had of course favored the producers and importers of new clothing, who for their part maintained that used clothing was unhygienic. No sooner had these regulations been withdrawn than tons of clothing, used but in excellent condition, began to arrive from the United States. Within three years, no one was walking barefoot. The poor districts filled up with parkas, authentic Wrangler and Lee jeans, and brightly colored T-shirts emblazoned with tropical palms or legends in English. Women began to wear trousers.

The overall contrast with the more traditional forms of dress (a simple white or dark-colored shirt or blouse) was striking. It wasn't unusual to see, for instance, a shantytown dweller, who was probably semiliterate at best, dressed in shorts and a T-shirt that read "University of Michigan" or "Make Love Not War."

There were many examples of this. A television program might interview a peasant from the south. The man cannot read or write; even so, he sports a Gap cap, jeans, and a parka, all of which are in good condition. Then the camera switches to Peñalolén, a district that still has pockets of poverty. Fifty-four homeless families are installed on a plot of land where their houses will be built; one of the young men wears an Adidas tracksuit that looks new.

Figure 8.1 summarizes the importance of the used-clothing market in recent years. The used clothing is imported in bales: both outer clothes and underwear are imported, and the graph compares equivalent items. It is clear that at the beginning of the 1990s, imports of used clothing were far greater than those of new clothes. Since then, strong economic growth has been responsible for the reversal in their positions, as has been increase imports of clothing from China: it is reasonably priced, similar to brand name clothing, and new.

According to interviews with sellers, the preferred used clothing is "seen on television" and is what "everyone uses": jeans, T-shirts, parkas,

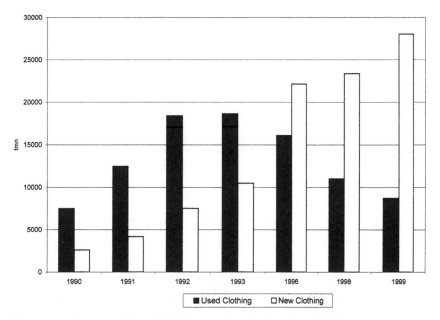

Figure 8.1   *Imports of Used Clothing and Equivalent New Clothing*

Source: Banco Central de Chile, "Indicadores de Comercio Exterior," 2000.

and tracksuits. The mass ownership of television has thus served as a vehicle to translate clothing styles, and there are clear indications that what is sought is assimilation with social groups that are perceived as mainstream. Here, globalization has an equalizing effect: people with high incomes wear brand name clothing, which the poor can only access secondhand. The result, however, is that the child of a poor family is visually seen in a manner equal to the child of a middle-class family—their differences are reduced, at least on a symbolic plane.

Used clothing forms part of the globalization of consumption. Without it, in a country like Chile, a smaller percentage of the population would be participating in the process. This was the situation before economic and commercial opening when, to use Toynbee's expression, only "Herodian" elites could share in this phenomenon. However, a certain type of high-end, old-fashioned used clothing is valued by sectors with higher income levels that are bored with the usual brand name clothing. In this case, the objective is differentiation rather than equalization.

Between 1984 and 1998 the Chilean economy grew at an average annual rate of 7 percent. The years 1977 to 1979 also saw high growth, but the depressions of 1975 (−13.3 percent) and 1982 (−13.4 percent) broke this continuity and lowered the overall growth rate. However, in 1984 and the fifteen years that would follow, growth was high and sustained. What is more, life expectancy increased from sixty-four years in 1970 to seventy-five years in 1997, while the infant mortality rate dropped from 82.3 per thousand in 1970 to 10.3 per thousand in 1998.[3]

In the ten years between 1988 and 1998, the consumption of the poorest 20 percent increased on the order of 6.5 percent annually. There are also some areas where this increase is significant from a social point of view: between 1987 and 1996, for example, the poorest two-fifths of the population increased their consumption of soap, shampoo, deodorant, cologne, and cosmetics almost tenfold. The globalization of consumption is also expressed in areas such as food and hygiene products.

I am writing this just after returning from La Pintana, the district of Santiago with the highest concentration of poverty. It is a precarious world of narrow streets devoid of people until dusk, when those who work return and the unemployed and the dealers of various types of contraband emerge. The streets then fill up with gangs of glue-sniffing adolescents and children on makeshift bicycles that are adorned like airplanes. The people live in narrow modular housing made from a variety of materials linked to each other like layers of skin. These houses were originally huts, but thanks to better times, extra rooms, kitchens, and bathrooms have been added, as well as a tiny gardens in which families from the countryside plant flowers, herbs, and trees.

Today is Sunday and I have come from lunch at the home of Hernán Quinteros, a housepainter and active member of a local evangelical church. The invitation was made more than a week ago: it is something special, and the whole family has come together. Everything goes well. The only curious thing for me is that instead of the traditional barbecue or casserole, which is what I was expecting, I was offered pizza. They tell me they bought it semiprepared nearby. It is obvious that they are proud to be able to offer this food at their table.

Through the conversation I learn that the people of La Pintana today are eating things that would have been unthinkable five years ago. Next time I come they will serve Chinese food. "Chinese food?" I ask incredulously. Yes, the entire family likes Chinese food. They even go out to eat in some of the new Chinese restaurants that are appearing in the popular districts of Santiago. There are now around sixty of these, with new ones starting up all the time. The owners are usually the chef and his wife, who manages the money, and they are the only Chinese in the place: local women wait at the tables, never male waiters who would be more expensive.

Despite being totally foreign to the Chilean culinary tradition, the food is appreciated. People find it tasty, cheap, and abundant. This last feature is very important, and McDonald's, by way of contrast, appears stingy in this regard. Each portion is rigorously measured out, so the restaurant cannot express the festive generosity that characterizes the ritual surrounding traditional Chilean cuisine.[4] Nor is the McDonald's atmosphere, bright and devoid of intimacy, much suited to conversation or the commemoration of special moments. In Santiago, most people don't eat at restaurants every day. In this city of 5 million inhabitants, there are only thirty-two McDonald's, and only one of them is located in a popular area.

Chileans, of course, are fond of Latin American soap operas. Local products of this sort have even been exported, but with less success than, say, Venezuelan, Mexican, and Brazilian soap operas. Soap operas are a type of Latin American emission. I remember visiting Israel with a group of writers a few years ago, and a Venezuelan woman in the group was extremely critical of the low cultural level of Latin American countries: popular taste had been debased, she claimed, by soap operas. She had also been told that Israel had the highest cultural levels. When we met the cultural officials, however, they all started asking her about Venezuelan soap operas. "Here in Israel," they said, "they are very, very popular." Our Venezuelan writer was absolutely appalled.

Why this talent for soap operas, I asked a Mexican friend. "Well," he said, "a Mexican, from the moment he wakes up in the morning to the moment he falls asleep at night, goes through more love and hate, more hopes and disappointments, more triumphs and defeats, more laughter and more pain than a Japanese goes through in his whole life." He was joking of course, but still.

One could argue that soap operas, together with Cuban and Brazilian music, are the most popular Latin American emissions. It is amazing what the Wim Wenders documentary, *Buena Vista Social Club*, has done to market Cuban music around the world. Latin rhythms today compete with rock, and for the first time in perhaps four or five decades the young prefer to dance to music that was not born in North America.

Despite all these changes during the last decades, the Chilean economy has not been able to reduce inequalities in income. All sectors have improved their economic situation, but the distribution of income is approximately the same as it was thirty years ago: the top fifth receives 13.5 times more than the bottom fifth. In most industrialized countries, this relation is on average 6.4 times. In the United States, the most unequal of the richest countries, the relation is 8.7 times; among the Asian Tigers, it is scarcely 5 times. Chile is today a richer society, but economists agree that it remains as unequal as before.[5]

As I have already stated, these figures reveal nothing about the symbolic and qualitative aspects of these phenomena. In general terms, the opening of the economy permitted a rapid globalization of consumption, which has in turn produced an equalizing effect from the point of view of status symbols. Marked differences in class that revealed a person's social origins through clothing and speech have become less evident. This is particularly true in the case of young people.

From the point of view of income distribution, therefore, Chilean society is as unequal as it was thirty years ago; but from the point of view of social stratification, things appear more egalitarian. More goods are within the reach of everyone. The difference between having a car and not having one are infinitely greater than the difference between having a BMW on the one hand and an old Lada or Trabant on the other, or between having a refrigerator either with or without an icemaker and having no refrigerator at all. In sum, status barriers have lessened to some degree in Chile, and even the poor have benefited from economic growth through the trickle-down effect; nevertheless, great disparities in income levels remain.

THE EVANGELICALS

In the popular world of Santiago—in La Pintana, for instance, which we have already visited—evangelical faith is boiling over. The phenomenon is visible at a glance:[6] small chapels, sometimes merely a shed adjoining the pastor's home, with names like Evangelical Army, The Torch of Faith, The Emmanuel Temple, Truth Will Free Us, or Heaven's Dew Congregation, are everywhere. Our studies indicate that around ninety chapels were in regular operation in La Pintana in April 2000.[7]

According to the latest census (1992), evangelicals represent 13.6 percent of the population; in 1920 they represented 1.14 percent and in 1970 they were 6.18 percent. Among the urban poor, this figure has increased to 20 percent, and among poor churchgoers there is one evangelical for every Catholic. A survey of evangelical pastors carried out by the Center for Public Studies (CEP) found that 44.7 percent had converted to Pentecostalism from Catholicism.[8]

Some 25 percent of evangelicals "started on the road" during the 1980s.[9] These were the years when Televisión Nacional broadcast a long weekly evangelical program by Jimmy Swaggart that became very popular. The loss of this television time has been a strong blow to the evangelicals, and its effects still remain to be seen.[10] These broadcasts were made during General Pinochet's government with, surely, the intention of punishing the Catholic Church hierarchy, which was concerned with human rights and looked critically at free market policies. Government therefore played a role in the spread of evangelicalism.

The above figures indicate two things: first, that evangelicalism (mainly Pentecostalism) now represents a significant percentage of the population, which implies that Catholicism is no longer the only religion; second, that Pentecostalism is expanding at a rapid rate. Since the data indicate that the phenomenon is mainly concentrated among the urban poor, we must examine the effects of conversion there. Our studies, which were carried out in La Pintana, Santiago's poorest district, show that evangelicals are the poorest of the poor, and religion has expanded among the least educated, the weakest, the most vulnerable.

La Pintana, which is on Santiago's periphery, has been called the garbage district because the poor from all parts of Santiago were relocated there in the 1970s in a rapid and massive operation organized by the military government. While districts near the center of the city experienced negative population growth, La Pintana's population more than doubled between 1982 and 1992, from 73,932 to 152,586 inhabitants. It is in this world of uprooted immigrants who occupy unsafe public housing that Pentecostalism has expanded. Conversion has increased in the ever present face of unemployment. Religion here is part of the hard daily struggle against alcoholism, drugs, and crime.

Special censuses carried out by the CEP in extremely poor communities reveal more on this phenomenon. In the poorest sectors of La Pintana, such as the Jorge Alessandri and Gabriela Mistral communities, Catholics effectively represent 57 percent while evangelicals are 31 percent of the population. Of the latter, 49.6 percent have converted since 1985. In terms of active worship, however, there are twice as many evangelical churchgoers as Catholic churchgoers; in fact, considering the overall figures of churchgoers (defined as those who go to church at least once a week), 67 percent are evangelical while 27 percent are Catholic.[11] In other extremely poor communities, such as the Estrecho de Magallanes community, Catholics account for 60 percent while evangelicals are 37 percent. However, of these figures only 10 percent of Catholics are active churchgoers, while the figure is 66.7 percent among evangelicals. Around one-third of these evangelicals have converted in the last ten years.[12]

The most renowned effect of conversion is reform of the family, which has been observed in a number of studies.[13] In her work on the women of La Pintana, Sonia Montecino found a "mixture of traditional and modern elements" in respect to the representation of women by themselves.[14] Most important in her opinion is that the evangelical woman places greater emphasis on the couple and on the running of the home.

One can exactly detect the change of emphasis that Evangelism produces in the definitions of the feminine. Maternity, for example, while having a very important place, is combined with the ideas of virtue, wisdom, domestic life, savings, and the rational administration of the home. Here we can see that Catholicism's traditional Marianism, which sets up the woman, the mother, the protector and bestower, as the center of the family, is transformed into a model in which the conjugal condition has a higher priority than motherhood and where value is accrued in the good economic upkeep of the home.

In another part of her work, Montecino observes,

From our vision, those who most "win" from entering the Evangelical movement are the women, and for this we think that their commitment and militancy are more permanent than that of the men. They gain in dignity, knowledge, the increase of gifts (such as the Word, the Reading, prophecies, dreams etc.), new spaces . . . There is without doubt the transition toward an "other" masculinity, but the move toward a new femininity is even stronger.[15]

All said, this redefinition of the genders does not imply feminism. To be sure, machismo is criticized, opening "a space" for the woman is talked about, the men are asked to share domestic chores, and it is often hoped the woman will go out to work—but at the same time, the role of the man as "head of the household" is recognized. According to evangelicals, this distribution of functions is given by God and is testified to in the Bible. "Being a man is something important because being first is an honor, because God made man first." Montecino also notes that "the existence of a masculine 'neo-machismo' that replaces the power classically exercised through violence and ritual virility (the conqueror, the most valiant, the biggest drinker, etc.) with a legitimacy in conventional and established values: being a good father and a good provider, but not losing the reign of power over the women."[16]

Investigations in La Pintana confirm time and again the thesis that evangelicalism produces reform in the family. It is testified to, for example, by Rubén Urrutia, a forty-five-year-old construction worker who converted to Pentecostalism: "The change is that instead of spending money on stupidities, it is invested in the family, to have a better life. To fear God is to be a responsible person like the Son of God, like husband, like the father of a family and like a human being."[17]

This is also the case for Eloísa Palacios, who lives today in the Santo Tomás community of La Pintana:[18]

> It happened that I began to live with a young man from there. I have two sons in the north, the father of the children beat me a lot and I wanted to change my life. He hit me so many times that my head split open. Then I went to dance in homage to the Virgin [of La Tirana] for more or less six days, because it's long, it lasts for days. . . . I did it to beg for a favor, to get out of this. My girl is three years old now. I danced like that in the clothes I wear now, not with the clothes that they use, they use costumes, so I started to dance. There I began to realize how the people dance who go about dragging themselves along the ground, arms cut to shreds, knees. I saw so many things that really left an impression on me, and I danced and danced. Before the dance finished I heard a voice from above telling me to leave, it was a sweet voice, a voice I had never heard before, and I felt that voice when I had to leave.

Looking to change her life, Eloísa had gone to the Virgin of La Tirana, participated in the festivities, mixed with the people, and done the traditional dances whose origins are lost in the pre-Colombian indigenous world. However, there she found people "dragging themselves along the ground," people wounded with their "arms cut to shreds." It is a terrible spectacle. Although she didn't mention it, one must also understand there was a great deal of drunkenness and that it was highly degrading. She went to a religious festival but only found everything she was trying to leave behind. Eloísa then heard a voice ordering her to leave, to get out.

Later she abandoned the man she was living with, a miner, but had to leave her two sons, although she took her daughter. She had no money, but she could not go on living with him, so she came to Santiago in search of work. She lived with her mother, herself in a precarious situation (twelve children plus Eloísa and her daughter), and got occasional jobs cleaning and washing clothes. One day she went into a church and "confessed straight to God, the Lord above, and said, Lord, I don't want to go on suffering, I don't want anymore of this life, this life is killing me, I want to start a home and have my own house."

Sometime later, one of her brothers, who had also come down from the north, took her to a "well hidden" evangelical church without telling her where they were going. "The Lord appeared to take him, something like that . . . And there I began to pray." From then on she began to "feel the impulse of the church itself, I knew nothing more than the church, the evangelical church."

The evangelical brothers took her in. They even "gave me a bed, bedside table, nightdress." She met her present husband in the market where he worked. She had gone there to buy pumpkin. He, Florentino Castro, was an evangelical who preached. He was single and had asked God to give him a wife so he could avoid fornication. He had prayed for a wife "even with children . . . even if she is a prostitute." The wedding took place in less than a year.

From then on, Eloísa's life changed completely. She and her husband have had two children. They are poor. At night, for example, they usually take nothing more than a light tea; for lunch they eat tinned fish and tinned peaches. They don't have a refrigerator, but they do have an orderly life. He respects her, doesn't take her for granted, worries about the children who attend school, and they love each other.

Eloísa had originally turned to the Madre misericordiosa, the Virgin Mary, looking for redemption, but she didn't find it—at least this is the way she sees it now that she is an evangelical. At the time, she was probably not looking for clemency, forgiveness, or comfort. Popular religion is fundamentally Marian—it is the religion of the Mother. According to Octavio Paz, it is linked to the conquering Spanish soldiers and their relations with the indigenous women who, accustomed to a polygamous regime, had children with Spanish men who did not understand this tradition and did not accept polygamy as a system of compromises. The Virgin Mary, who herself has a son whose father is absent, therefore becomes a key figure.[19] This model of an absent father who does not take responsibility for his children[20] is still very much present and forms the background against which evangelicalism has flourished.

Conversion to evangelicalism presupposes the change from a religion of the mother to one of the father, who represents severity, discipline, and authority, as well as economic support. For Catholics he is a far-removed figure: the Virgin mediates between the absent Father and the sons and daughters—she is "kind" and "our advocate" before God. For evangelicals, the situation is perhaps more demanding: it is necessary to reconcile oneself directly with the father—but theirs is a caring father. This image of a father who takes care of everything touches a deep nerve in the popular world and goes hand in hand with the redefinition of the role of the physical father that takes place in the home.

More common than the case of Eloísa Palacios is the tendency for the woman to convert first and bring her husband along later. That is the case of Isabel Calderón, who lives in Teniente Barahonda Street in La Pintana.[21]

> Eleven years ago I went to the evangelicals. My life before Evangelism was sad, stressful, it was an empty life, I had nothing, I didn't have purpose, I possessed nothing. . . . And, well, after I got to know the Lord, my life changes. I was on the point of suicide with my children and, well, when I got to know the Lord everything changed. Even my husband changed. He looks at our marriage in a different way. He used to see me as a housewife who did the washing, the ironing, all those things.

> Before, he was just like the rest. "I knew that husbands came to sleep, nothing else. They could go a fortnight without appearing, off drinking here and there, never worrying about the children. All this seemed normal." They married because she was pregnant; later, a second child came. They lived with Isabel's mother and sisters. Isabel's husband did not treat them well, and he ignored her. Money was very short. He spent long periods out of work. When he did have money, he went out on drinking sprees with his friends. The climate in the house was one of tension and violence.

> My life before I knew the Lord was chaos; it had a horrible aspect, horrible language, horrible thoughts. And having all this in the home is chaos. Life with the children was chaos. There was no respect or communication with my husband. He did not pay attention to me or the children. But after we got to know the Lord, He put our life in order, He taught us to order our life. He took away the bad language, the bad thoughts, the bad things we had in our life. He taught us the path we should have followed since the day we were born—this is the life of the Lord.

Isabel had fallen into a state of depression that made her consider suicide with her children. There was nothing to eat. When she went to the corner shop and begged for credit, they told her that her husband had given explicit instructions not to give her credit because he was about to leave her. But then when she was about to kill herself and her children with some sleeping pills she had kept, she suddenly prayed and the Lord changed her life.

A neighbor had spoken of the Church, the Lord, of His Word. Isabel began to go with her to the church and joined the Dorcas group. The affection of the sisters, their conversation, and, above all, the Word of the Lord, deeply moved her. She began to dress up to go out to the church in the afternoons. She felt supported. With the backing of the Lord and her new sisters, she was able to confront her husband and tell him that he had to change or she would throw him out. It seemed he didn't understand until he saw she had put all his clothes into a bag to take away once and for all. He decided to stay and promised to change. But he couldn't do it until the Lord changed him. One day, on his birthday, his two small children invited him to the church. He went just to please them but he left a changed man. He has not become Pentecostal, but he is a new man. According to Isabel,

In my case I have always worked . . . now that I'm old and ugly without a tooth in my mouth, he doesn't let me work. For sure, before he let me do whatever I wanted to do; now he looks after me. I don't understand it. It doesn't make sense. Why now? Now that I'm fat! Well, it shows that God does do miracles. Before, when I was younger, he never used to look at me; now he does. That's the difference. . . . God has done great things with him. He has changed him as a person, his thoughts. He drank and drank, was a womanizer. . . . God has changed him. My husband is not *machisto*. If I'm poorly or expecting, he does the washing, ironing, cooking, bathes the children, polishes the floors. When he is here on Saturdays, he helps with the housework. . . . He is a new man.

The example of Adela Amaya is similar: an irresponsible husband who drank heavily, womanized, had children by different women, spent all his money outside the home, coming and going as he pleased, with no time for her or the children. But after she converted, he did too, and now he is a deacon at the church. Conversion has made them start loving each other again, as if they were "dating" for the first time. The atmosphere in the house has changed completely: the bad language, the shouting, the beatings have all stopped, and he has given up liquor and women. At first his friends thought he was going to church to chase some woman that he fancied. It was difficult to convince them that he actually went to pray.

Conversion is linked to belonging to a group. For a woman it means getting out of the house three or even four times a week to meet up with the evangelical sisters. If she is part of the Dorcas group, she will pray and talk. Conversation generally revolves around the problems of the home, children, the husband. Frank confession is also possible, and problems are proposed and articulated in the discourse. The group is formed by women who have probably experienced similar situations, and deep friendships are rapidly forged. The pastor's wife is a guide and counselor; her marriage with the pastor is taken as a model.

After the conversations, the women return to their homes with a new feeling of their own dignity. They have been listened to and respected; they have shared their suffering and humiliations. In place of rejection, they have awoken interest, love and, most importantly, hope. For the tales of the other women are also stories of hope. For Adela Amaya, it also meant returning with a mission: to convert her husband. Success depends in part on her and her witness, but more than anything it depends on "the call of the Lord." It is not a stressful mission. The present situation of chaos and violence can be explained as the work of Satan; the way out is a new life that depends on the Lord. Only "God can change us," but as she is already on the path, she has hope. He has already wrought the change in her.

Soon her children will join her in finding a new group of friends in the church. For his part the husband sees her going out well dressed in the afternoons and sees her return happy and relaxed. She has begun to dress up a little, with sobriety and modesty as befits the sisters. For her husband this is a novelty. Before, she never dressed up because she had no desire to do anything. Why is she getting dressed up if he isn't even looking at her? There are many accounts of women who say that their husbands began to feel curiosity and jealousy toward the pastor and the evangelical sisters.

Only after being on the right path does Isabel Calderón find the moral force within herself to confront her husband; she is even prepared to lose him. He understands this and doesn't leave. He perceives in her an inner serenity, a conviction, a sense of her own dignity that are new.

Of course, not all the men change as the husbands of Isabel Calderón and Adela Amaya have done, but this phenomenon, this transformation, is sufficiently widespread to keep hope alive. The most visible change is that they stop drinking, and in this it must be remembered that this is a habit that begins as they leave childhood and is practiced among a very close group of friends. It is a ritual that belongs to the masculine world; hence, breaking with alcohol is also breaking with friends and redefining oneself as a man. In this sense, evangelical conversion possibly represents a much more radical change for the man than for the woman,[22] for how can someone be a man and not go out drinking with his friends? How can someone be a man, go out and play football, and not go out for a "celebration" afterward?

Both our focus groups and in-depth interviews in La Pintana demonstrate that this is change is fundamental to conversion.[23] The convert stops drinking, orders his life, abandons old friends, partying, and women, stops spending wildly, renews his marriage on the basis of respect and love, becomes involved with the children, and takes part in domestic chores. The change is so complete that it is difficult to believe; the evidence is overwhelming, however. Of more than one hundred men and women converts we have interviewed over the years, not one has failed to mention this as the main effect their conversion.

What are the economic effects of evangelicalism among the poor? The answer depends on the definition of poverty. In agreement with the usual definitions in Chile, the evangelicals are among the most poor. The study by Fernando Flores[24] indicates they have fewer years of education and their homes have a somewhat lower level of durable goods. Given the interrelationship that exists between education and income levels, it is unlikely that as long as the evangelicals have less schooling they will be able to achieve economic superiority over the Catholics.

The most detailed studies of the poorest areas of La Pintana show that even among the poor, evangelicals are the poorest.[25]

Comparison between Catholic and Evangelical churchgoers shows that of the lowest two-fifths, 40% are Catholic while 49% are Evangelical, while in the highest fifth 23% are Catholic and 15% Evangelical. This is to say that, in agreement with this indicator [index of durable consumer goods], the Evangelical population has a lesser level of goods than Catholic churchgoers as well as a lower level than the population in general.[26]

Something similar happens in the quality of housing: "Evangelical churchgoers tend to be concentrated in the two lowest levels. In levels 3 and 4 there is an equal proportion of people, but in level 5, the highest level, there are proportionally many more Catholics than Evangelicals."[27] In terms of monthly income, the average earned by Catholic churchgoers at the time of this study was US$229.00: Evangelical churchgoers made $207.00, while the average income in the area was $214.00. Evangelicals in these communities are less educated than the Catholics, which is particularly clear in the case of churchgoers.

Are the evangelicals interested in becoming part of the modern consumer world? According to Sonia Montecino,

> The purchase of different electro-domestic products assumes a high level of debt given the precarious incomes that are received. If previously the houses of Evangelicals were characterized by cleanliness, fences and solid construction materials, today inside they typically have true "altars" of ostentatious televisions and stereo equipment as well as refrigerators, stoves and washing machines. In the churches themselves, the pastors preach in favor of saving and against excessive debt, but they themselves are trapped by the mechanism.[28]

Do the evangelicals believe there is some connection between their economic situation and their faith? The answer is yes: 60.1 percent believe that their economic situation has improved since their conversion; for churchgoers, the figure rises to 72 percent. Asked about the causes of their economic success, "faith in God" is the third reason most often cited (following only "personal initiative" and "responsible work").[29] In a survey of evangelical pastors in La Pintana, a similar but not identical question was asked and "thanks to God" emerged as the second most mentioned reason for economic success (following "personal initiative").[30]

Among Catholic churchgoers, 17 percent say that they have seen that converts to the evangelical religion improve economically.[31] How can this evangelical optimistic scenario be explained? The most probable hypothesis is that evangelical converts started off from an even worse position than the average of the poor, and while they have made progress, they are still numbered among the poor. Our surveys as well as the personal interviews suggest that evangelism acts like a crane to lift families from misery.

Evangelicals believe in an intimate connection between faith and economic improvement, while 31 percent of Catholics believe that an exemplary Christian will be rewarded by material goods. Among churchgoers the figure is equal; among evangelicals, however, the figure increases to 41 percent, and among evangelical churchgoers, 61 percent believe that an exemplary Christian will be rewarded by God with material goods.[32] This indicates a marked difference of attitude between Catholics and evangelicals in respect to the economy. Could this be functionally equivalent to the sort of thing that Weber wrote about predestination and Calvinism? Could this generate a similar "psychic anxiety and will to succeed"?[33]

The relation between a Christian life and economic success is central to the evangelical experience. This proposition is also widely shared by the pastors themselves; in fact, 74.3 percent of them answer that "It is the will of God that those who believe in Jesus improve economically."[34] Among the pastors of La Pintana, the same question asked several years later received almost exactly the same reply in almost exactly the same proportion (74.4 percent).[35]

At the same time, "none of those interviewed expect to get ahead economically with the help of the state. . . . The Evangelical expects nothing from the state to get out of poverty."[36] Is this hoped-for economic improvement really going to happen? The people we interviewed were revisited a year later and did show economic improvement. Several of them had ideas of starting small commercial businesses; one had doubled his income and had acquired a pickup truck for his business. [37] There are, then, indications that some evangelicals are beginning to make inroads into the business world, though it is too early to make general projections.

It is clear, as has been said, that the evangelical movement is a powerful crane that is lifting thousands of poor Chileans out of misery. But will it also prove to be a vehicle for social mobility that will allow many of its members to become part of the middle class? Will they in time achieve greater economic success than the Catholics?

The answer depends to a large extent on what happens in education. If the evangelicals can achieve a similar level to that of the Catholics, if they can equal the educational average, then it is probable that they will progress rapidly. At that point, their work ethos, rejection of alcohol, concept of the family and vision of their faith as linked to material success will place them in an advantageous position.

What is happening in education among young evangelicals? A study of twenty-nine schools in La Pintana shows no difference in performance between evangelical students, Catholics, and the average,[38] which is much to the credit of the evangelicals, as their parents have an inferior educational level. Personal interviews show that evangelical parents are concerned about the education of their children. As a consequence, there are indications that the new generation of evangelicals will reach an educational level that will put them in a position in which they will be able to compete and benefit more from their habits and convictions.

At the same time, while Chile's evangelical movement is strongly rooted in the popular world,[39] its origins in Methodist pastors and its links with international evangelicalism are undeniable. From this point of view what is present is the fusion of different traditions:

> A look at the syncretisms and reworkings proves that we can talk of a "Baroque" Evangelism in La Pintana in the sense that we can appreciate elements copied from the North American cults that are transmitted by television or through visiting foreigners. Thus the music, vestments, the aesthetic of the churches tend to imitate these elements but with a native interpretation.[40]

Music in La Pintana has also evolved rapidly. Inside the churches, traditional Spanish guitars have given way to the reverberation of electric guitars.

> But it is in the ambit of music where the incorporation of percussion, electric guitars and the styles of songs evidences the fusion of distinct traditions and popular creativity. It is not unusual that a church is formed of young "trash" or "punks" who consider themselves dispossessed and where "heavy rock" music is the key to set off hymns and canticles in praise of the Lord.[41]

The evangelical message arrives today through many radio stations that sell time for Christian broadcasts. The evangelicals control the Armonía radio station, which is dedicated exclusively to the evangelical message, and programming time is now being rented on an open television channel. However, I believe that this by no means compensates for the loss of programming on Televisión Nacional, whose ratings and audiences were on a much greater scale.

Nevertheless, the pastors and many of the brothers on these programs are inspiring, and even though the small churches are dispersed and decentralized, they maintain a tight doctrinal unity, which is forged in Bible studies attended by bishops of the church and other pastors. Also, networks are established through radio and television, where it is common to hear the words of foreign pastors, above all those from Central America and Brazil.

Of the pastors in La Pintana, 16.3 percent have been outside of Chile more than twice to attend courses or religious conferences; within Chile as a whole, the figure increases to more than 80 percent. Furthermore, 44.2 percent of the La Pintana pastors admit to having been influenced by foreign pastors; the most popular at the moment seems to be Puerto Rican evangelist Gigi Avila.[42] Overall, however, even at the most popular levels, this only demonstrates that while the Chilean evangelical movement maintains links abroad, it does so without ceding its autonomy. The Chilean Pentecostal evangelical movement is a vehicle of globalization for the popular world.

TRADITIONAL STRAINS: REJECTING GLOBALIZATION OR AN ALTERNATIVE GLOBALIZATION?

Lack of trust in people and institutions is typical of Chilean and Latin American societies in general.[43] Consider table 8.2.

According to Valenzuela and Cousiño, "the particular structures of sociability of Chileans and North Americans have been inverted. [Chile] in effect shows a high tendency for people to remain as acquaintances, which goes against the North American tendency to relate to outsiders, in other words, to make friends out of neighbors." This is explained in part by the relatively greater importance of cohabitation: "The proportion of

Table 8.2   Trust in Society

	Chile 1997	U.S. 1964–1996
You can trust in people	14%	42%
You have to be careful with people	86%	54%

Source: Eduardo Valenzuela y Carlos Cousiño, "Sociabilidad y asociatividad: Un ensayo de sociología comparada," *Estudios Públicos*, Summer 2000, pp. 321–339.

people who live under the same roof with their mother, father and/or brothers and sisters is 3 to 1 between Chile and the United States."[44] In Chile, "sociability" linked to the family and to relationships based on gifts is greater than in the United States, where "associativity," or belonging to voluntary associations, is in contrast much greater. Associativity implies the "ability to 'do things' with outsiders, to get together with unknown people for work and communal objectives." It is grounded in the personal responsibility of whoever makes a promise, accepts a contract, or joins a voluntary association; as such it is also outside the realm of social threat represented by lies and betrayal.

For its part, sociability, which prevails in Latin America, is based on reciprocity and not therefore on "the personal compromise . . . the promise made." Rather, sociability is grounded in "the linking power of the act of giving with obligations to receive and return." Its paradigmatic relation is thus the attachment "that rests on a principle of reciprocity that is pulled out of the received gift."[45]

In a recent International Social Study Programme (ISSP) public opinion poll of twenty-four countries, as well as in the World Values Survey, Chile appeared among countries having the least trust for people, the courts, and the legal system.[46] In the World Values Survey the countries that had a higher proportion of their population having no confidence in the police, government, and political parties were, with a few exceptions, Latin American. For example, out of six countries that had over 30 percent of their population revealing no confidence in the police, all but one of them were Latin American countries. (Chile in this sense is an exception in Latin America, something linked, probably, to the lack of corruption in the country as shown in the surveys taken by Transparency International). Out of six countries where over 40 percent had no confidence in their political parties, all but one were Latin American: in Argentina the figure is 49.4 percent, in Brazil 47.6 percent, in Peru 43.8 percent, in Colombia 48.4 percent, and in Venezuela 60.1 percent.

These figures are worrying. They indicate that political institutions are very weak and that there is a serious problem of legitimacy with respect to secular institutions in Latin America.

In contrast with this there is total, or a great deal of, confidence in the church and religious organizations. In the ISSP study, Chile is in this respect in second place, behind only the Philippines (though no other Latin American countries except Chile were sampled).

This lack of trust, as well as the confidence in religious institutions, has great significance and suggests that social connections in Chile are founded to a large extent through the churches or through church institutions (high schools and universities, for instance). One way of overcoming mistrust of others probably has to do with belonging to the same church, belief, or religious movement. The origins of this situation go back to the role played by the Catholic Church after the wars of conquest, which, in a thousand different ways, was the principal mediating institution in the emerging mixed and colonial society.[47]

In the ISSP study, Chile, together with Cyprus, the Philippines, and Poland, is among the top four countries with the most believers: 95.6 percent of Chileans believe in God; in the United States the figure is 91.8 percent, in Italy 87.5 percent, in Spain 82.1 percent, in Holland 58.5 percent, and in the Czech Republic, the country with the lowest numbers of believers after Japan, only 45.9 percent. Chile also ranks third from the top as the country where the most people believe in heaven (82.4 percent) and fourth from the top for belief in hell (58 percent). In Chile, 76.2 percent of the people believe in life after death; only in the Philippines and Cyprus are the numbers higher.[48]

Figure 8.2 shows the number of people who said they believed in religious miracles. In terms of abortion, if the family is poor, 83.3 percent of Chileans consider it always or almost always wrong. (See Figure 8.3.) The majority of Chileans also think that "the family suffers if the wife works" outside the home. (See Figure 8.4.)

The image that emerges from all this data is of a strongly religious country that trusts in church and religious institutions and strongly opposes abortion. A majority are convinced that a wife who works outside the

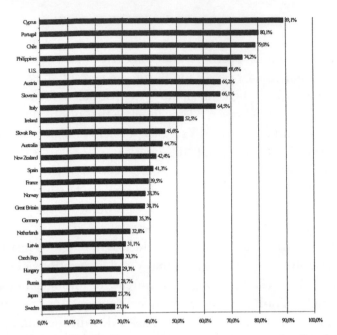

Figure 8.2   Belief in Religious Miracles: Percentage Answering "Definitely" Or "Probably Yes"

Source: International Social Survey Programme, "Religion Survey II," 1998.

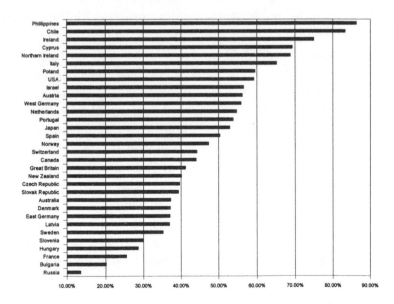

Figure 8.3   Abortion If Family Is Poor: Percentage Answering "Always Incorrect" and "Almost Always Incorrect"

Source: International Social Survey Programme, "Religion Survey II," 1998.

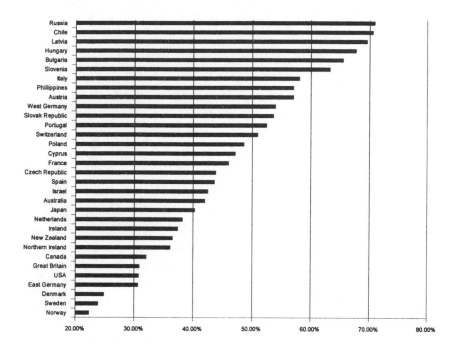

Figure 8.4   Family Suffers If Wife Works: Percentage Answering "Agree" or "Strongly Agree"

Source: International Social Survey Programme, "Religion Survey II," 1998.

home damages the family. In these areas, Chilean society appears to behave according to its own criteria and traditions, and globalization, at least for the moment, has only achieved the lowest level of penetration.

These data, therefore, show the other side of the globalization coin, the side that resists globalizing influences that spread secularism and encourage abortion and feminism, for example. While it is necessary to remember that the evangelicals themselves form part of a globalizing movement, they maintain and reinforce their faith and conservative positions on moral issues; something similar happens with the conservative Catholic movements, as well. All of them are international and, in a certain sense, represent alternative forms of globalization.

In Chile divorce and abortion are prohibited. Until May 2001, all cinema, including video and television broadcasts, were precensored in accordance with the political constitution. All these issues are surrounded by tension and criticism, as happened when the censorship board banned

Martin Scorcese's *The Last Temptation of Christ.* Even so, precensorship has been defended in the columns of prestigious newspapers. Chileans are deeply divided on these issues. In the case of divorce there is, through a loophole, the possibility of annulment, which is the equivalent of divorce through mutual consent. Chances are that a divorce law may be approved in the coming years. Illegal abortions are certainly frequent; nevertheless, it is strongly resisted by a wide majority of the people.

All in all we are confronted with a society that does not wish to legitimize behavior that is considered immoral, although there is abundant evidence that these rules are routinely broken or twisted. Resistance to adopting the laws originating in more developed countries primarily comes from the Catholic Church and the evangelical churches. As we have seen, these are the institutional links that inspire the greatest confidence in a society where widespread mistrust is prevalent.

On the other hand, the conservative position against divorce and abortion finds widespread support among the poor. Laws allowing divorce and abortion are the aspirations of the educated middle class. The owners of the most powerful communication media, however, tend to be conservative Catholics. One the country's two most successful television networks, one is owned by the Pontifical Catholic University, whose rector is appointed by the pope. The other, Televisión Nacional, depends on a council formed by the political parties on which the Right has a quota of influence, which it has handled well.

In terms of the newspapers and radio stations, almost all are controlled by conservative businessman or, directly or indirectly, by the Catholic Church or Church-related institutions. However, international consortiums have recently started getting involved with radio and cable television stations; one cable channel has even begun broadcasting a Playboy program, though it has been met with strong criticism.

Up to now, however, the lay sectors (represented mainly by the Left, which has a champion in current socialist President Ricardo Lagos) have been unable to match or counter the power conservatives wield in the communications media. Nevertheless, it is possible that President Lagos will manage to pass a law legalizing divorce (although he is opposed to legalizing abortion), but there are plenty of people who fear that this could end up being more restrictive than the irregular system of annulments currently in operation.

President Ricardo Lagos, who took office in March 2000, comes from a tradition of radicalism: a secularizing party with Masonic influences that lost importance at the end of the 1960s. His conservative rival, Joaquín Lavín, who came close to winning the presidential election, is a supernumerary member of Opus Dei trained as an economist at Catholic University (Universidad Católica) and the University of Chicago. He worked in General Pinochet's government and actively defended Pinochet's candidacy in the 1988 plebiscite that ultimately led to his defeat. Lavín was then the chief journalist in the business and economy section of the *El Mercurio* newspaper, by far the most influential of the media; he then took the number two position at the paper and then later distinguished himself as the most popular and successful mayor in the country.

Lavín's 1999 presidential campaign was marked by a closeness to the people. He avoided confrontation and positioned himself as a moderate who preferred to get things done rather than debate ideas. Neither Lavín nor Lagos gave critical importance to moral issues in their campaign, and the "cultural war" that some people had predicted did not materialize. Rather, the campaigns centered more on the social and economic matters, which, according to the polls, were of greater concern to the people.

Of course, the vigor of Chile's conservative tradition in all this could simply correspond to a stage in the transition towards a more permissive modernity in moral issues. In due course, practice and legislation may become more like that in the majority of the developed countries, The case of Spain is eloquent in this regard. Will Chile follows the same course?

So far, the data coming from the 1990 World Values Survey indicates that, for instance, Mexicans and Argentineans are more conservative with respect to issues like the importance of God and abortion than the Spanish people. Over 70 percent of Argentineans and over 80 percent of Mexicans declare that "God is important in their lives"; in Spain less than 50 percent do so. Opposition to abortion, divorce, and homosexuality is also much higher than in Spain.[49]

Consciously or unconsciously, the current conservative social actors are attempting to construct an alternative modernity: Western, family oriented, conservative in morals and religion yet probusiness. As Huntington maintains, modernity can adopt different forms,[50] and what many are seeking in Chile is not what happened in Spain. Certainly this is the predominant view among the most influential conservative religious, political, business and intellectual leaders of the country, and so far it is a fact that with the coming of democracy, nothing at all like the "Spanish *destape* (uncovering)" has occurred.

THE GLOBALIZED BUSINESS WORLD

The Chilean "Davos culture" is conservative on moral issues and free market in its economics. Valuing the family and "the new economy," it wants to be traditional in religion and advanced in technology. Is this contradictory? Difficult, certainly! And it may appear to be more in the style of Don Quixote—but it is not, I believe, inconsistent.

The global businessman circles the planet doing business. Nothing stops him from maintaining the religious beliefs and moral convictions that he has inherited from his parents, except for the danger of becoming infected with other visions of the world.[51] However, it would seem that, living in the midst of risk and uncertainty, sudden travel, technological change, merciless competition, the permanent transformation of his activities as well as Shumpeterian creative destruction,[52] the Chilean businessman needs to counterbalance this in the ethical-religious field, where "nothing changes and everything stays the same."

Not all businessmen and senior executives are active Catholics or conservative in morals. But the great majority are, and it shows.[53] This struggle to keep continuities and historical identities involves the most modern, globalized and competitive businessman of Latin America. This is why it catches one's attention.

But are these conservative businessmen truly globalized? From a strictly industrial, commercial, and financial point of view, there is no doubt that the answer is yes. Their machinery, for example, is imported, and they export their products to foreign markets: Chilean wine, for instance, is drunk in London, Tokyo, Caracas, Berlin, and New York, and Chilean fruit is eaten in Saudi Arabia, Japan, Mexico, Taiwan, and the United States. Furthermore, Chilean entrepreneurs obtain credit and capital from financial centers such as Wall Street, through the elaboration of American depository receipts (ADRs). They are continually interacting with consumers, producers, technicians, consultants, and international bankers. That 90 percent of the Chile's GNP corresponds to international trade speaks for itself. During the last fifteen years Chile has managed to double its per capita income, and this has been due foremost to these businessmen.

A significant section of them have obtained their MBA or MA in economics and business from Catholic University or from a U.S. university, ideally the University of Chicago. Before this, they studied business and economics at the Catholic University (the most in demand) or at the University of Chile (Universidad de Chile) or Adolfo Ibañez University. Their most prestigious professors are themselves graduates of U.S. universities, Chicago long being the most preferred.

According to a recent investigation, these businessmen (i.e., both owners and senior executives) never miss reading the *Economist* and they "recognize, without shame, copying customs and manners of dress of their New Yorker equals." They copy "working hours, eating routines, sports habits." The researcher speaks of a "recognition of belonging" among them.[54]

In effect the feeling is of belonging to a network and of a style of international work. One of the businessmen interviewed in the research cited above was confident that if

an executive could be moved instantly in some sort of tele-transporter from El Bosque Avenue in Santiago to the Stock Exchange . . . and then to the financial district of Kuala Lumpur, then to the Frankfurt Stock Exchange, then to the offices of Lloyd's of London and finally to Manhattan, it is more than likely that the executive would think he had only moved from one part to another of the same district where he started from, El Bosque in Santiago, now that the buildings, the clothes, the cars and even the manners are the same."[55]

There are sectors such as the fruit export or wine industry that have not only incorporated imported techniques, procedures, and forms of organization, but an aesthetic as well. The cellars of the vineyards are, for example, frequently redesigned in a California style. "It is not over-adventurous to say," noted Vergara, "that industrial and commercial establishments in general terms are the equal of their peers in the developed world and blindly follow their aesthetic models to the extent of convincing themselves that this is *the* style."[56]

In this business world, "political activity almost does not exist. . . . Every time there is a common line that we can identify, it is precisely that of not being active in political parties."[57] What this means is that as a rule they are not members in a formal sense of a political party. However, there is an undeniable contact with public issues, which is channeled in many different forms, including union activity, involvement in the financing and orientation of universities, in the financing of electoral campaigns and parties, and in benevolent works.

The evangelicals have not penetrated this local Davos culture. The most forceful Catholic movements on average tend to be conservative, papist, Marian, and tend to oppose socialism and liberation theology.

> Many of those interviewed were related in some way with the Jesuits, the Legionnaires of Christ [Legionarios de Cristo], the Schoenstatt movement and Opus Dei . . . Some recognize their links through the education of their children with the Legionnaires of Christ, in the practice of socially benevolent projects with some Jesuit priests, and receive spiritual assistance and their moral and religious formation from Opus Dei or from Schoenstatt.[58]

The four institutions mentioned own highly respected preparatory and high schools. English is becoming more important for the parents of these students, and this is an important matter. All, with the exception of Schoenstatt, own universities as well, and all are international movements. With the exception of the Jesuits,[59] they are relatively new organizations in which lay participation is much more active and key than was usual in the Catholic Church.

Ethical themes are not limited to the personal and family dimension; they are also touched on in business meetings. The efficient and successful business organization Generación Empresarial jointly organizes frequent and well-attended ethics seminars with the Legionnaires of Christ, in which well-known businessmen give speeches on, for example, "The Seven Deadly Sins." In one of these seminars a banner was displayed that read, "Ethics Are Profitable."

I should point out that some of the leaders of Generación Empresarial are influential columnists who address an audience of business and political elites. The Legionnaires of Christ is a religious order that was founded in Mexico a few decades ago. It is expanding very rapidly and can be considered an important Latin American religious manifestation. Along with Opus Dei, it is extending its influence outside the Hispanic world.

All this has a lot to do with family values, because what these people do not like about globalization is what they perceive as the disintegration of the family. Again and again successful professionals and academics return from the United States or elsewhere to protect their family life. Divorce is not the main concern: people fear movement from one town to another, and the separation of parent and child when the son or daughter goes to college. The "togetherness" of traditional families is meant to last in Latin America. Family life is full of social gatherings and rites like baptisms, first communions, birthdays, and so on. The old continue to live close to the young, and married couples with children maintain close contact with their parents.

This sort of social life also permeates the concept of friendship: to be someone's friend often entails being a friend of the family. Trust, then, as we have seen, is often related to family bonds. People prefer a brother or a cousin or an uncle as a partner, and family businesses are the rule in Chile. Even when it is a large corporation with many stockholders, the controlling group is a family. Behind every economic conglomerate, there is a family.

The questions is whether all of this is merely a transitory phase of capitalism or whether it will be consolidated in a business elite that is modern, innovative, and globalized in its commercial dealings while at the same time, thanks to the help of globalized, conservative religious movements, it is traditional in its ethical and religious matters.

THE INTELLECTUALS

Latin America is perhaps best known in the world of high culture for Gabriel García Marquez's magical realism and the intriguing and paradoxical stories of Jorge Luis Borges, who were "discovered" by Americans and Europeans during the 1960s. These writers, as well as others such as Mario Vargas Llosa, Carlos Fuentes, Julio Cortázar, and Alfredo Bryce Echenique, have captivated European and American readers. García Marquez has shaped the taste of readers to the point that one finds magical realism read and written all over the world, while Borges's influence has been so great that it would be difficult not to consider him at the "center." In fact, these two authors show the extent to which notions of center and periphery are relative in literature. Could one claim something analogous in the area of economic policies?

The globalization of the Chilean economy began under the military regime that came to power in 1973 through a coup d'état. The reorientation of the economy and the administration of the reforms were brought to a head by a distinguished group of economists who, in a sense, were initially formed at the University of Chicago and whose epicenter in Chile was the Faculty of Economics and Business at Catholic University. Looking back, everyone now realizes that Catholic University and its unique arrangement with the University of Chicago were crucial to the changes that have now taken place in the economy.[60]

The idea emerged in the 1950s in the economics department of the University of Chicago. The first steps were taken by Professors Aaron Director and Theodore Shultz, who were looking for an antidote to the economic development model put forward by the Latin America Economic Center (CEPAL), which, guided by the Argentine economist Raúl Prebisch, was recommending an import substitution strategy. In those days, Chile was a country with a solid democratic tradition and acute problems of poverty, low growth, and chronic inflation, whose single-export economy was one of Prebisch's favorite examples of an economy with a sound strategy for development.

The University of Chicago offered a number of scholarships to students from Catholic University's School of Economics and Business, as well as the University of Chile. Within a few years this resulted in the entire teaching staff and curriculum at the School of Economics and Business being completely renovated and adjusted to approximate the curriculum of the University of Chicago's MBA and MA in economics programs. In so doing, the school created an MBA with a strong economics background and a master's degree program in economics with some MBA training. So there was some originality in the ways in which the Chicago influence was adopted. The project also received the support of Agency for International Development (AID),[61] and for more than two decades, year after year, Chileans enrolled in Chicago's economics department. It should be pointed out that Professor Arnold

Harberger played a key role in all this by keeping his connections with young Chilean economists alive for many years.

The Chicago graduates not only occupied key positions in Catholic University, they also had posts in the University of Chile (albeit in less dominant positions), in the most vigorous economic groups, in the business organizations, and in the newspaper, *El Mercurio*. By the time of the 1973 coup, a high-quality technocratic elite had formed that was independent of the political parties and had a program of development clearly counter to that embodied by the Marxist-Leninist parties that supported Salvador Allende.

The country's economy was in terrible shape, and the military would be defeated if they couldn't control inflation (which was approaching an annual rate of 1,000 percent) and put the economy in order. The Chicago-educated technicians won their confidence (the export-led economic success of the East Asian countries gave their main tenets a great deal of credibility) and in effect governed Chile's economy for the next seventeen years.

The pillars of this strategy have been open markets, private property, and sound monetary policies. Indeed, privatization in Chile preceded that in the United Kingdom under Margaret Thatcher, and it included a voucher system of education, privately managed health care and pension systems, and flexible labor laws.

With the coming of democracy in 1990, this strategy for development "from outside," as it has been called, has put down roots. The economic growth of these years has been high and sustained. In some areas, such as telecommunications and infrastructure, new regulatory frameworks have been imposed that have freed up these sectors, opening the door for competition and private ownership. In education, parents today may add money from their own pockets in combination with the vouchers provided by the state.

What took place was a globalization of an academic type, whose vehicle in Chile would be one university that, after a series of historical transformations, eventually triggered a complete reform of economic institutions and globalized the economy. What did not form part of the original design was, of course, the military regime and its human rights violations.

The Chilean socioeconomic experience has served as a model for other Latin American countries, for example, with Peru under an authoritarian regime and Argentina under a democratic regime. Some claim that countries such as Russia should also follow the "Chilean economic model."[62] Could this be a political emission? Argentina has shown that democratic governments can undertake similar reforms, and the system of private social security designed in Chile has now been implemented with the help of Chilean advisers in Peru, Bolivia, Columbia, Argentina, Mexico, and El Salvador. It has even been considered as an option in the United States and Great Britain.

The systematic and continual program of scholarships offered by the University of Chicago to students coming from the Catholic University's School of Economics was a pioneering initiative. In those days international contacts with universities were rare; certainly there was nothing systematic about them. But by the 1980s the picture had changed, and a large proportion of Chile's teaching staff had completed postgraduate studies in prestigious foreign universities.

Today, regardless of whether they are in the natural sciences, the social sciences, or the humanities, Chile's academics have been globalized in terms of their academic training. They also belong to international networks that share areas or themes of interest, regularly attend international congresses and seminars, read international journals and publications, and maintain contact through e-mail. In the case of the social sciences "it is also possible to find networks whose origin and motive do not refer to a scientific interest, but rather to ideological or religious motivations. This is the case of feminist networks and some formed by Catholic intellectuals."[63]

However, neither research funds from outside the country nor publications by Chileans in specialized journals are as yet abundant. For now, globalization basically means direct or indirect support on the part of international scientists and intellectual, and this support helps obtain Chilean state resources for developing research.[64] On the other hand there are independent study centers and NGOs that in general have lost the importance they had in the years of the military government and during the transition to democracy.

"One of the thematic areas where the greatest number of NGOs are concentrated is environmentalism . . . finance comes, in respect to the private foundations, principally from the Ford and Weeden Foundations, although other resources also come from international cooperation agencies and foreign governmental organizations."[65] In the gender policy area, financing mainly comes from the "Ford Foundation, the MacArthur Foundation, and the Kellogg Foundation." La Morada, a gender study center, receives financing from the Ford Foundation as well as a special Italian financing to keep up its Tierra radio station. As one academic from the organization put it, "It can be said that the themes which are covered there are the same as the global agenda."[66]

One is also beginning to notice the presence of organizations and international networks interested in supporting ethnic movements that were, until recently, almost totally absent from the country. Different from the strategies of closure and self-referencing that characterized the academization process of the universities, the logic with which the NGOs have operates is the conquest of public space. Thus one of La Morada's projects proposes "to mobilize communications to incorporate these of class in mass media."[67]

According to Cousiño and Valenzuela, "there appears to be currently an ideal situation in Chile for the 'global agenda' to be diffused and financed by foreign foundations within the interior of the university world which until now has been relatively impermeable to them."[68] And it is a fact that radical environmentalists and ecologists, despite a lack of academic rigor and an inability to convince their opponents, are now making openings in formal academic channels.

And all of these globalizing factors coexist with an ever increasing number of university schools dedicated to business, whose model is Catholic University, and with successful—especially among the younger generation—conservative Catholic lay movements. On the whole, therefore, one can say that the global world is exercising pressure on Chilean academia through international requirements and academic standards, international accreditation of academic programs, and through intellectual trends such as feminism, environmentalism, free market economics and moral conservatism.

CONCLUSION

Chilean society has lived through a stage of accelerated changes, many of them traumatic. The opening of the economy has globalized consumption—this is evident in dress and eating habits—and international television programs are particularly important this regard. There are some sectors of Chilean society that favor an integration to globalization in habits, values, and customs that would lead to a secularization similar to that which has taken place in the most developed countries of Europe. Such a program is decidedly opposed by conservative sectors with influence and roots in the Catholic and evangelical churches, in the business community, and in the communications media.

The question is whether this is a transitional situation toward a European-style globalized modernity, or whether Chile, and perhaps Latin America, will develop an alternative modernity that is morally conservative and family oriented, but at the same time free and open in its economics.

We have not found any locally created antiglobalization forces in our investigation. The conservative Catholic and Protestant movements are themselves inscribed within global movements. For example, the conflicts between a globalized economy on one the one hand and the preservation of native forests and indigenous people's traditional lifestyles on the other cannot be translated into a simple conflict between globalization and those who resist it, because the resistance itself incorporates a global agenda, global organizations, and global networks. In the same way the conflict between radical feminism, which is in favor of legalizing abortion, and the conservative sectors that oppose it must not be constructed as a confrontation between globalization culture and conservative closeness: both forces are a part of globalized movements, networks, and circuits.

On the whole, family seems to me the crucial question. Family filters global tends, but it is clearly receiving the impact of powerful influences coming especially from the United States and Europe. Religious belonging plays an important role in providing a sense of continuity in the midst of change and, in general, attempting to strengthen the family.

In Chile, the family perceives itself as something that is meant to intensify and strengthen the proximity and sense of belonging of its members. Fathers and mothers and sons and daughters and uncles and nephews and cousins and grandfathers still meet, every week, usually on Sunday, and this is expected to continue throughout life. As mentioned earlier, the proportion of parents and children living under the same roof is three times higher in Chile than in United States. The moving from one place to another, the "early" separation of children from parents, and the divorce that are so common in the United States are viewed as dangers that could bring about family dissolution. This is the dimension of globalization that many do not want. They resist by joining global religious movements that support this point of view.

A World Values Survey asked what the most important thing to teach to children is. Typically in countries like West Germany, Norway, Sweden, and Switzerland, the majority answered "perseverance"; in most Latin American countries the majority answered "obedience." Tradition? Yes, but also anxiety.

This concern for the family is new, it is modern; it is not simply the inertia surrounding the traditional view of the family. In a plural world, you cannot assume that your children will inherit your form of life. They might choose to be Muslims or Buddhists, they might establish themselves as a married homosexual couple or marry in a heterosexual marriage but decide not to have children at all. They might join a New Age sect, they might decide to work on God knows what anywhere in the world. For someone raised in a conservative Catholic or evangelical home, these options are a serious matter: they mean that the line of religious and cultural inheritance is broken, and with it an entire sense of identity is lost.

On the other hand, this is undoubtedly part of what we understand as personal autonomy and freedom. Once the modern "virus" of choice settles in, it is no longer possible to expect that traditional values will effortlessly reproduce themselves. The self becomes, to a great extent, a personal project. In order for it to be passed on to the following generation, you must take proper care of your children, promoting the likelihood that they will invent their lives within the framework of your form of life—the life of your community. You want them to belong to the community within which your existential decisions were defined and made sense. Human beings do not want to transmit only genes but a certain way, mostly implicit, of inhabiting this world.

NOTES

I would like to thank Peter Berger, Ann Bernstein, Harald Beyer, Michael Hsiao, James Hunter, Samuel Huntington, Hansfried Kellner, Fuat Keyman, János Kovács, Marc Plattner, Tulasi Srinivas, Charles Taylor, and Yunxiang Yan for their helpful comments and suggestions on this work. I would also like to thank Sonia Montecino, Carlos Cousiño, and Eduardo Valenzuela for their excellent research and theories without which this paper would not have been possible. I would also like to give special thanks to Donald Halstead for his help editing this paper.

1. See Harald Beyer, "La Globalización como factor de igualidad social: El caso de las Importaciones de Ropa Usada," *Serie de Antecedentes*, January 2000, Centro de Estudios Públicos.

2. "If modernization can be described as a spreading condition of homelessness, then socialism can be understood as the promise of a new home." Peter Berger, Brigitte Berger, and Hansfried Kellner, *The Homeless Mind* (New York: Vintage, 1974), p. 138.

3. Larraín B. Felippe and Vergara M. Rodrigo, *La Transformación Económica de Chile* (Santiago, Centro de Estudios Públicos, 2000).

4. On gifts and festivities in Chile, see Carlos Cousiño, *Razón y Ofrenda* (Cuadernos del Instituto de Sociología, Pontifical Catholic University of Chile, 1990); Pedro Morande, *Cultura y Modernización en América* (Cuadernos del Instituto de Sociología, Pontifical Catholic University of Chile, 1984).

5. See Harald Beyer, Rodrigo Vergara, and Patricio Rojas, "Apertura Comercial y Desigualdad Salarial en Chile," *Estudios Públicos*, Summer 2000, pp. 97–130.

6. On this, see David Martin, "Tongues of Fire" (Oxford: Blackwell, 1990); and Arturo Fontaine Talavera and Harald Beyer, "Retrato del movimiento evangélico a la luz de las encuestas de opinión pública," *Estudios Públicos*, Spring 1991.

7. See "Encuesta Pastores Evangélicos, Comuna de La Pintana," *Serie de Antecedentes*, April 2000.

8. See "Resultados de Encuesta a Ministros Pentecostales," *Serie de Antecedentes*, March 1994.

9. See Talavera and Beyer, "Retrato del movimiento evangélico."

10. It would not be unusual for the loss of this television space to influence in a small way the growth of the evangelicals in the 1990s, but there is as yet no data to permit a methodological comparison. However, the rate of expansion is now slower.

11. See "Informe de Censo en La Pintana," *Serie de Antecedentes*, September 1994.

12. See "Pre-encuesta Masiva en La Pintana," *Serie de Antecedentes*, May 1994.

13. See, for example, David Martin, "Otro tipo de revolución cultural: El protestantismo radical en Latinoamérica," *Estudios Públicos*, Spring 1991; María Jesús Buxó, "Vitrinas, cristales y espejos: Dos modelos de identidad en la cultura urbana de las mujeres Quiché de Quetzaltenango" (Guatemala) in Lola Luna, ed., *Mujeres y Sociedad: Nuevos Enfoques Teóricos y Metodológicos* (Barcelona: University of Barcelona, 1991); Talevara and Beyer, "Retrato del movimiento evangélico"; Sonia Montecino, "Redefiniciones de lo femenino y de lo masculino en el mundo evangélico de La Pintana," *Serie de Antecedentes*, August 1977.

14. Sonia Montecino, "Redefiniciones de lo femenino y de lo masculino en el mundo evangélico de La Pintana," *Serie de Antecedentes,* August 1977.

15. Sonia Montecino, Alexandra Obach, and Marcelo Soto, "Caminar con el Espíritu: Perspectivas de Género en el Movimiento Evangélico en La Pintana," *Serie de Antecedentes* 29 (1999), Centro de Estudios Públicos, pp. 8, 10.

16. Montecino, Obach, and Soto, p. 7.

17. Montecino, Obach, and Soto, p. 28.

18. See "Entrevistas personales en La Pintana," *Serie de Antecedentes,* April 1994, p. 122.

19. Octavio Paz, "El laberinto de la soledad," in *Obras Completas* (Mexico: Fondo de Cultura Económica, 1999).

20. In this respect, see Sonia Montecino, *Madres y Huachos: Alegorías del Mestizaje Chileno* (Santiago: Editorial Sudamericana, 1991).

21. See "Focus no. 1," *Serie de Antecedentes,* April 1996.

22. See Talavera and Beyer, "Retrato del movimiento evengélico."

23. See, for example, "Focus Group no. 1," *Serie de Antecedentes,* April 1996; "Focus Group no. 2," *Serie de Antecedentes,* April 1996; "Focus Group no. 3," *Serie de Antecedentes,* May 1996; "Focus Group no. 4," *Serie de Antecedentes,* May 1996; "Entrevistas Personales en La Pintana," *Serie de Antecedentes,* April 1994.

24. "La variable religión en el censo de 1992," *Serie de Antecedentes,* January 1994.

25. See "Informe Censo La Pintana," *Serie de Antecedentes,* September 1994.

26. Miguel González, "Evangelismo y comportamiento económico: Conclusiones preliminares," *Serie de Antecedentes,* October 1995, p. 26

27. González, "Evangelismo."

28. Montecino, Obach, and Soto, p. 8.

29. Centro de Estudios Públicos, "Encuesta Nacional de Opinión Pública, 11 Marzo-Abril 2000," *Serie Documentos de Trabajo,* May 2000.

30. "Encuesta Pastores Evangélicos, Comuna de La Pintana, Santiago," *Serie de Antecedentes,* April 2000.

31. See "Informe de Censo en La Pintana," *Serie de Antecedentes,* August 1994.

32. "Informe de Censo en La Pintana."

33. I take the expression "psychic anxiety" from Lucan W. Pye. See "Asian Values: From Dynamos to Dominos?" in Lawrence E. Harrison and Samuel P. Huntington, eds., *Culture Matters* (New York: Basic, 2000), p. 248.

34. "Resultados de encuesta a ministros pentecostales," *Serie de Antecedentes,* December 1993. Also see Mathew Bonner, "El soplo del espíritu: Perspectivas sobre el movimiento pentecostal en Chile," *Estudios Públicos,* Winter 1994.

35. "Encuesta Pastores Evangélicos, Comuna de La Pintana," *Serie de Antecedentes,* April 2000.

36. See González, "Evangelismo," pp. 24, 30.

37. See González, "Evangelismo," p. 20.

38. See "Resultados de encuestas a colegios de La Pintana," *Serie de Antecedentes,* April 1994.

39. For a brief review of its history, see Talavera and Beyer, "Retrato del movimiento evengélico."

40. Montecino, Obach, and Soto, p. 9.

41. Montecino, Obach, and Soto, p. 9.

42. See "Encuesta Pastores Evangélicos, Comuna de La Pintana, Santiago," *Serie de Antecedentes,* April 2000.

43. In this respect, see Eduardo Valenzuela and Carlos Cousiño, "Sociabilidad y asociatividad: Un ensayo de socología comparada," *Estudios Públicos,* Summer 2000, pp. 321–339.

44. Valenzuela and Cousiño, "Sociabilidad y asociatividad," pp. 325–326.

45. Valenzuela and Cousiño, "Sociabilidad y asociatividad," pp. 327, 335, 337. According to the authors, the basis of the difference, in the last instance, is of a religious nature. "The foreignness of the Protestant God seems to favour relations of confidence between unknown parties in countries where this creed is predominant, while the closeness and familiarity with God which the Catholics have seems to counter the unfolding of these relations in the corresponding Catholic countries."

46. Harald Beyer, "Las opiniones religiosas y valóricas de los chilenos: Una perspectiva comparada," mimeograph, Centro de Estudios Públicos. This study presents the results of the International Social Survey Programme (ISSP) of 1998. CEP is one of the thirty-seven members of this program.

47. Pedro Morandé, "Cultura y modernización en América Latina," Cuadernos de Sociología, Pontifical University of Chile.

48. Beyer, "Las opiniones religiosas."

49. Ronald Inglehart, *Modernization and Postmodernization* (Princeton: Princeton University Press, 1997).

50. See this discussion in Samuel Huntington, *The Clash of Civilizations and the Remaking of World Order* (New York: Simon & Schuster, 1996).

51. See Peter Berger and Thomas Luckmann, *Modernity, Pluralism, and the Crisis of Meaning* (Gütersloh: Bertelsmann Foundation Publishers, 1995).

52. Joseph A. Schumpeter, *Capitalism, Socialism, and Democracy* (New York: Harper, 1942).

53. On this theme, see David Gallagher, "Chile: La revolución pendiente," in Barry B. Levine, ed., *El desafío neoliberal* (Bogota: Grupo Editorial Norma, 1992).

54. Nicolás Vergara, "El empresario chileno en un mundo global," *Serie de Antecedentes,* April 2000.

55. Vergara, "El empresario chileno."

56. Vergara, "El empresario chileno."

57. Vergara, "El empresario chileno."

58. Vergara, "El empresario chileno."

59. Many influential Jesuits in the 1960s, 1970s, and early 1980s followed the line of liberation theology, but this has now been left behind. For example, at the beginning of the 1970s, the priest Gonzalo Arroyo, S.J., was president of Christians for Socialism, an organization of priests who felt, in some way, Marxist. His article "Pensamiento latinoamericano sobre subdesarrollo y dependencia externa," *Revista Mensaje,* October 1968, was fundamental in the development of the celebrated book *Teología de la*

liberación by Father Gustavo Gutiérrez, as is borne out by the extensive quotations. Father Arroyo is today dean of the Faculty of Economics and Business Administration at the Alberto Hurtado University, a Jesuit institution, and is a firm advocate of the free market.

60. About this history, see Arturo Fontaine Talavera, "Sobre el pecado original de la transformación capitalista chilena," in *El Desafío Neoliberal.* Also see Juan Gabriel Valdés, *La escuela de Chicago: La operación en Chile* (Buenos Aires: Zeta, 1988).

61. According to Arnold Harberger, a key player in the process, the idea of the scholarships came from Alison Patrickson, the representative of AID in Chile.

62. José Piñera, "A Chilean Model for Russia," *Foreign Affairs*, September-October 2000, pp. 62–73.

63. Carlos Cousiño and Eduardo Valenzuela, "El impacto de la globalización en la universidad y en la intelectualidad chilena," *Serie de Antecedentes,* October 1999, p. 10.

64. In this respect, see Cousiño and Valenzuela, "El impacto de la globalización."

65. Cousiño and Valenzuela, "El impacto de la globalización," p. 20.

66. Cousiño and Valenzuela, "El impacto de la globalización," p. 22.

67. Cousiño and Valenzuela, "El impacto de la globalización," pp. 21–22.

68. Cousiño and Valenzuela, "El impacto de la globalización," p. 23.

9

Cultural Globalization in Turkey

ACTORS, DISCOURSES, STRATEGIES

Ergun Özbudun and E. Fuat Keyman

As we enter the new millennium, the rapid pace and the unpredictable direction of social and political changes in the world seem to be forcefully undermining "the established contours and the terms of politics." It is now increasingly difficult, if not impossible, to think of politics by situating it solely at the "national context," as the increasing interconnectedness of societies is making this realm increasingly vulnerable to both global/regional forces and local pressures. As a result, modern political referents such as the nation-state, national identity, and national economy have been losing their explanatory power for the analysis of social and political change.[1]

While economic globalization (that is, the globalization of capital as a powerful global force) is undermining the authority of nation-states by creating "a borderless global marketplace," cultural globalization is rendering the idea of national development problematic by giving rise to local reactions that pave the way for the emergence of "alternative modernities" and cultural identity claims. Thus it is not interstate relations or the national unit of analysis alone, but the interactions between universal Western values and the particular/local claims to authenticity that are framing the content and the direction of social change in our globalizing world.[2]

In this context it is necessary, if not imperative, to analyze critically and empirically the historically constituted interactions between the global and the local, not only to understand social change, but to imagine a democratic world vision as a foundation for a better world.

Turkey is no exception to this. On the contrary, during the last decade, Turkish society has undergone rapid social, cultural, economic, and political change, the manifestations of which have been felt in every sphere of social life.

We would like to offer three generally accepted points to make this suggestion more concrete: first, one of the sites at which such change has manifested itself is the resurgence of Islam; second, this resurgence has taken different forms, discourses, clashes, and attitudes; and third, the processes of globalization have, to a large extent, framed the way in which Islam has begun to play an important role in Turkey's political, economic, and cultural affairs.

In Turkey's political landscape, radical change has occurred as Islamic discourse was politicized and "political Islam" became one of the defining elements and powerful actors of Turkish politics.[3] This was also the beginning of the period characterized by polarization between secularism and Islamic traditionalism. In the economic sphere, we have witnessed the increasing role of Islamic discourse and values in economic organizations and the emergence of "economic Islam," with its actors, discourses, and strategies. Likewise, intellectual life, the activities of civil society organizations, and popular culture and consumption patterns have all been exposed to Islamic symbols and religious-identity claims to tradition and authenticity. Thus "cultural Islam" has also entered into and begun to characterize the formation of Turkish social and cultural life.

Globalization processes have played important roles in each sphere and have been "integral" to the operation of Islam's political, economic, and cultural discourses.[4] However, on the basis of our research, we argue that the impacts of globalization on the formation of economic and cultural life in Turkey, especially over the last decade, as well as the role of Islam in it, should not be understood as a cause and effect relationship in a linear causality. Instead, globalization's impacts vary and create different consequences, depending on which sphere of social life is being analyzed. In other words, polarization between secularism and Islamic traditionalism in political life does not directly reflect on economic life, where Islamic actors attribute a positive quality to cultural globalization and articulate it in their discourses as the necessary and indispensable element for new economic life.

Therefore, it is not polarization but coexistence between globalization and Islam that frames economic life. However, two additional points are worth making here. First, cultural globalization in economic and social life creates multidimensional impacts in the form of the coexistence between Western values and religious identity-claims to tradition and authenticity. Second, coexistence comes into being in different degrees and with different meanings, generating different discourses, strategies, and clashes, and thereby creating peculiarities in each sphere of social life. In this sense, we argue that cultural globalization is not a unitary but a multidimensional process that generates different impacts and consequences and makes possible the coexistence of modern values with Islamic traditional norms, symbols, and discourses.

We shall substantiate these arguments by documenting the findings of our research. We proceed from the commonalties that can be found among economic, civil society, and cultural actors, to specific characteristics, perceptions, and approaches that differentiate these actors in terms of their conceptions of globalization and its impacts on societal affairs in Turkey. In general, however, the ideas and arguments shared by almost all actors in economic life and civil society can be described as (1) the changing meaning of modernity, (2) the crisis of Turkey's strong-state tradition, (3) the end of the Cold War, and (4) the process of globalization.

SITUATING THE ROLE OF ISLAM
IN TURKISH MODERNIZATION

All the economic and civil society actors we interviewed agreed that the 1980s and 1990s have brought about fundamental changes in Turkish modernization. They also agree that this has created a paradox in Turkish society that can de found in the "increasing dominance of economic liberalization" in economic life, whose laws of motion are to a great extent dictated by economic globalization (i.e., the economic logic of Western modernity) and the concurrent resurgence of Islam as a powerful political and cultural force in Turkish social and political life. In other words, Turkish modernization since the 1980s has been increasingly marked by the coexistence of economic liberalization and the resurgence of traditionalism and its appeal to a "return to authenticity."[5]

This indicates that globalization is not confined to economic space and that cultural globalization is operating hand in hand with economic globalization, though it has different impacts on, and produces different results in, social and political life. This also indicates that in order to understand Turkish modernization, cultural globalization should not be taken as a reflection of the economic base, but as an object of analysis with its own peculiarities and specificities.

All the actors we interviewed also suggested that the historical context in which this resurgence of Islam has occurred is not only national, but global in nature. They also suggest that, since the 1980s, four distinct, but nevertheless interrelated processes have dictated the path and the direction of Turkish modernization.

The first process is "the changing meaning of modernity," or "the emergence of alternative modernities." Economic actors, civil society organizations, and intellectuals agree that the process of Turkish modernization has involved new actors, new mentalities of development, and new identity claims. These in turn point to:

- the emergence of the critique of secular-rational thinking as the exclusive source of modernity in Turkey;

- the increasing strength of Islamic discourse both as a "political actor" and a "symbolic foundation" for identity formation; and

- the need to think of modernity in terms of democracy has created a context for the upsurge of interest in civil society, citizenship, and the democratic self.

The second process is related to a "crisis in the legitimacy of the strong-state tradition." Our actors also agreed that since the beginning of the Turkish republic (1923), modernization has been characterized by and has given rise to a "strong-state tradition" in which the state has assumed the capacity of acting almost completely independently from civil society; it is the state, not government, that has constituted "the primary context of politics." This tradition functioned as the organizing "internal variable" of Turkish politics until the 1980s. Since then, however, the emergence of new actors, new mentalities, and the new language of modernization, as well as democracy as a global point of reference in politics, has made culture and cultural factors an important variable in understanding political activities. Thus the state now has a legitimacy problem in maintaining its position as the primary context for politics.

In order to understand these two processes, our actors all argued that we also have to refer to both "the end of the Cold War" and "the process of globalization" as constraining factors that have had important short- and long-term impacts on the interaction of politics, polity and policy in the Turkish politics of the 1990s. This suggests that the end of the Cold War has generated important consequences for Turkey in terms of its foreign and domestic policy initiatives. While Turkey's geopolitical and historical significance in the Middle East, the Balkans, and Central Asia has become increasingly apparent since 1989, the collapse of the Soviet Union has drastically changed its role as a buffer state in East–West relations. More importantly, the end of the Cold War created important changes in political culture and the sense of nationalism, so that the Turkish people "may now come to see themselves once again at the center of a world emerging around them, rather than at the tail end of a European world that is increasingly uncertain about whether or not it sees Turkey as part of itself."[6]

Our actors also agreed that, since 1980, Turkish society has been subject to "significant change" in which the processes of globalization operate and generate impacts on societal affairs. For them, globalization in general refers to the increasing interconnectedness between societies, so that events in one part of the world are increasingly having greater economic, cultural, and political effects on distant peoples and societies.

This understanding of globalization implies that in a globalizing world it is no longer possible to understand "change" only with reference to the national unit, since global/local forces have become as important as national actors. It also implies that culture can no longer be taken as secondary to politics and economics, for it is culture that makes it possible for new actors to emerge, for us to think about politics and political actors outside of the strong-state tradition, and for hitherto silenced identities to change the meaning of modernity.

According to our actors, however, the way in which culture becomes a main point of reference for the analysis of change does not constitute a single process but manifests itself differently in different spheres of social life. Cultural globalization creates both the universalization of Western values and cultural patterns and at the same time the revitalization of local values and traditions. While it brings about McWorld, in the sense of the worldwide standardization of consumption patterns and lifestyles in economic life, cultural globalization also provides a platform for the revitalization of tradition, the emergence of local identities, and the popularization of the discourse of authenticity.[7] To put it another way, cultural globalization is the process in which we can observe both the universalization of Western modernity and the emergence of alternative modernities— the clearest example of this in Turkey being the resurgence of Islam.

THE VARYING IMPACTS OF CULTURAL GLOBALIZATION ON TURKISH SOCIETY

The above four points regarding the role played by cultural globalization in the formation of Turkish modernization since the 1980s, to which all our actors concurred, should not blind us to the fact that cultural globalization is not a unitary process, but rather something that is "carried out by different institutions and processes that interact with each other." In order to understand the impacts of cultural globalization on Turkish society, therefore, we have to move to a more concrete level of analysis and explore the various ways (or various faces) in which globalization has brought about a number of coexisting cultures and alternative modernities in Turkish sociopolitical life.

Following Peter Berger's analysis of globalization's different faces,[8] our study has examined how it has played a constitutive role in the following:

- *The formation of economic life*, or the increasing importance of the global market and capital accumulation, and its articulation by both secular and Islamic industrialists. The main question we investigated in this context was the extent to which the logic of the global market creates the possibility for the emergence of Islamic capital and the coexistence of secular and Islamic cultures.

- *The formation of civil society and democracy,* or the impact of cultural globalization on the emergence of new discourses of identity, politics, and democracy, as well as its impact on the clash between modern and traditional values, which pronounces itself in the debates on both European integration and Islam.

- *The formation of cultural life,* or the extent to which Islamic identity, presenting itself sociologically and politically as anti-modern, is embedded in, and operates within, globalization's consumer culture.

CULTURAL GLOBALIZATION AND ECONOMIC LIFE

One of the sites of the greatest impacts of cultural globalization on Turkish society is economic life, whose scope, discourse, and actors have been enlarging since the 1980s. Its organizational structures are increasingly being extended beyond national and territorial borders.

Since the 1980s, and especially the 1990s, the Turkish economy has been exposed to the globalization of capital and trade and has been reorganized on the basis of the primacy of the global market over the domestic one. This in turn has led economic actors to realize that market relations require rational and long-term strategies, and that in order to be secure and successful in (globalized) economic life, it is imperative to gain organizational capabilities to produce and/or maintain technological improvement and strategic planning for production and investment. As a result, in the last decade, we have seen the increasing importance of free market discourse, the multiplication and the dissemination of economic actors, and the pluralization of economic organizations in Turkish society.

Until the mid-1980s, economic life in Turkey was mainly organized around national industries with no particular cultural identity. However, the 1990s witnessed the rise of what is called "Islamic capital" as a powerful economic actor,[9] and this has given rise to the introduction of Islam to the political economy of Turkish capitalist development, both discursively and organizationally. During this period, Islam began to operate as an economic code open to free market ideology and also created its own economic organization founded on the (Weberian) principles of rational, technical knowledge and expertise.

The establishment of the Association of Independent Industrialists and Businessmen (MUSIAD, in the Turkish acronym) was a clear sign of the articulation and coexistence of Islam with free market ideology. It should be noted here that the qualification of MUSIAD as "Islamic" is due to the fact that "a) it is affiliated with religious sects and communities; b) Islam appears as a significant point of reference in its activities; and c) it has close ties with political Islam mainly represented in Turkey" since the 1980s by the Welfare Party and then the Virtue Party.[10] MUSIAD's success lies in its ability to "bring together a large number of enterprises of different sizes located in different geographical regions of Turkey," and "to create a network within economic life on the basis of relations of trust among believers." It can therefore be considered an indicator of Islam's possible coexistence with the Western-rational model of organizational behavior.[11] Thus economic Islam, in addition to political Islam, has also put its stamp on Turkish modernity over the last decade.

Furthermore, the establishment of MUSIAD and the dissemination of its subunits throughout the country has ended the dominance of the Association of Turkish Industrialists and Businessmen (TUSIAD), which had been the country's primary economic actor of capitalist development since the mid-1970s. In this it is simply no longer possible to analyze the globalization of Turkish economic life without reference to MUSIAD, which has created a strong economic base for Islamic discourse. In this sense, we have seen not only the introduction of an Islamic imprint on economic life, but the pluralization of economic actors with different discourses and strategies.[12]

In addition to these two groups, since the early 1990s a third type of economic organization has emerged as a significant point of reference in understanding the formation of economic life and the impact of cultural globalization on it. This is the Association of Industrialists and Businessmen (SIAD), which gains its concrete institutional quality through its members' association with different cities and provinces in the Anatolian region. SIADs have been included in our research because they are important economic actors and contribute to advancing our understanding of the changing nature of Turkish economic, political, and cultural life. In addition, some cities in Anatolia, such as Gaziantep, Konya, Denizli, Çorum, Kayseri, and Eskişehir, have provided us with interesting economic success stories and exemplify an atypical model of what can be called "morally and culturally loaded economic modernization."[13] We shall now examine these three organizations.

TUSIAD

TUSIAD has undergone great transformation since its founding in 1971–1973. At one time known as "the biggest and most powerful business organization and pressure group in Turkey" and "the club of the rich," TUSIAD once viewed the 1961 constitution as too democratic and supported the 1980 military coup.[14] Now, however, it is the strongest voice in the call for the democratization of Turkey in accordance with European standards of democracy and argues for the need to protect civil rights and liberalization.

TUSIAD presents itself as an organization that "has changed over time." According to its president, Erkut Yücaoğlu, the changes the organization has gone through in the last two decades have to a large extent been framed by globalization: the changing nature of world economic and political affairs have not only made democracy necessary, but it is the required condition for modernization and development.

Three points emerged during the course of our investigation and our interviews with TUSIAD members. First, TUSIAD perceives globalization as a process that operates beyond the borders of national societies and is mainly concerned with the globalization of the market and the emergence of interconnectedness between countries, especially with respect to movements of capital, finance, and trade. Globalization is regarded as an "objective reality," a "social fact," that should be neither resisted nor celebrated, but viewed as the new context of economic development, as well as the historical context for national politics. Instead of the import-substitution industrialization practiced during the 1960s and 1970s, in which the nation-state was the major actor for national development, this is seen as a time when the globalization of market relations, which takes place beyond the reach of the nation-states, is the main point of reference for economic life and its actors.

Second, in their view, globalization brings about a new set of relations that are novel in context. These include the emergence of new trade relations that compress geographical distances; the increasing importance of supranational relations (with, for instance, the European

Union), which create new regulations beyond nation-state borders; and the fragmentation of domestic market relations into regions with their own transnational economic relations (e.g., the Black Sea Economic Co-operation Pact; trade relations with the new Turkish republics, such as Azerbaijan, Ukbekistan, and Kyrgyzstan; tourism for Turkey's southern and western regions).

Third, globalization brings about a new culture in economic life in that it forces economic actors to acquire a new economic rationality, in accordance with which they need to prepare economic strategies, take decisions, and act. Globalization therefore creates a new discourse on economic life that cognitively frames economic actors' strategies and decisions. This implies that the possibility of economic success lies in economic actors' mind-set, their ability to understand and articulate the new economic rationality, and their capacity to make long-term strategies to secure their position in global markets, which can only be possible by focusing on technological innovation and quality assurance.

Two points can be extrapolated from the above. First, according to one TUSIAD member, this new economic rationality also creates changes in the mind-set of economic actors whose identity formation now involves new values, such as technological orientation, the promotion of knowledge and information over tradition, the adaptation of a global network society, and the preference for long-term strategies over short-term gains.

Second, the adaptation to the new economic rationality brings about a new cultural platform for the creation of a cultural identity based on "a set of symbols" by which economic actors differentiate themselves from one another, as well as from earlier-generation industrialists and businessmen. In this sense, one of the impacts of globalization in economic life has been the creation of "symbolic capital" internal to economic actors' identity formation, involving postmodern references to lifestyles, tastes, outlook, consumption patterns, and the human body. This breaks with tradition and locality by privileging McWorld over the national culture of the past. Economic globalization therefore generates changes not only in economic organization but in the identity formation of the economic actors themselves.

TUSIAD members believe that globalization processes have given rise to two interrelated facts at the social level: cultural identity, which has taken the forms of the resurgence of Islam and the "Kurdish problem," and the need to protect civil rights, both of which require the democratic organization of state-society relations. They also think that Turkey's exposure to the globalizing world has two dimensions: (1) the problem of integration into the European Union and (2) Turkey's status and location in world politics.

Although they believe that Turkey has the potential to become what they call "a country that belongs to the first league," they also believe that to achieve its ends, Turkey has to solve the problems stemming from its lack of democratization and political liberalism: the violation of human rights, the protection of civil rights, and acceptance of the rule of law as the fundamental basis of state power. Globalization in this sense appears both as the process related to the emergence of the problems confronting the Turkish state and the primary point of reference for their solution through democratization.

For TUSIAD, therefore, the possibility of the realization of its economic interests embedded in the global market is directly linked to the democratization of Turkey—a clear indication of how much the organization has changed since the 1970s and 1980s. During the 1990s in particular, TUSIAD assumed a "democratic identity" with a vision of making Turkey a liberal, plural democratic society, proceeding not only as an economic actor but as a civil society organization that strove for what is good for Turkey as a whole and for democratization, the necessary precondition for the country's elevation to the first rank in world affairs.

In its social vision for a democratic Turkey, TUSIAD regards cultural globalization as creating both the universalization of democracy and the revitalization of traditional values and norms. However, while members value the rise of cultural Islam as a powerful symbol of identity to the extent that it functions within pluralistic and multicultural social formation, they are hesitant about the politicization of Islam with respect to democracy. In this context, coexistence between Western values and cultural Islam is possible as far as cultural life in Turkey is concerned, but this does not alter the clash between secularism and political Islam insofar as the latter remains both in discourse and in practice a "threat to liberal democracy."

In conclusion, the changing nature of TUSIAD during the 1990s cannot be understood without reference to cultural globalization, which functions as an integral element of the organization's discourse, strategy and activities, and in TUSIAD's identity formation as both an economic actor and a democratic civil-society organization. Globalization has also contributed to the enlargement of the scope and content of all TUSIAD activities, from an economic self-interested pressure group, to a collective identity striving for the realization of its vision of a democratic Turkey.

MUSIAD

There is no doubt that MUSIAD is the most important business organization claiming to carry an Islamic identity. Since its inception, it has played a crucial role in linking business organizations with the rise of Islam; supporting, promoting, and protecting their economic interests; and developing a societal vision on the basis of Islamic principles. By creating a "powerful network based upon trust relations" among Islamic economic actors, MUSIAD has become as significant and powerful as TUSIAD, even challenging the latter's dominance in Turkish economic life.

With MUSIAD, Turkey has seen the emergence of economic Islam with its actors, strategies, and discourses. We have also seen that a link between Islam and Western rationality is possible, and that the embeddedness of Islamic discourse in economic and cultural globalization can bring about coexistence between Islamic identity and free market ideology. Furthermore, *Homo islamicus*, which Islamic discourse derives from "Mohammed's rules to guide the exchange activity in the Medina market," defines Islam as compatible with exchange relations resting on market competition and a minimal state.

The following general account of MUSIAD has been extrapolated from our research of this organization. MUSIAD also views globalization as a process whereby exchange activities go beyond the nation-state's borders and operate within a global market. For its members, globalization creates interconnectedness among societies, economies, and cultures, and it sets "the rules of the game," which require rational thinking, long-term strategies, and organizational capacities. In this sense, globalization becomes the new historical context for economic development. MUSIAD also attributes a positive quality to globalization because it is as a result of the globalization of market relations that a suitable ground was created for the rise and the success of economic Islam.

However, MUSIAD is founded on Islamic principles, which include feelings of trust and solidarity, the primacy of community over the individual, the discourse of the just self over the self-interested actor, and the privileged status of ethical codes over individual morality. It argues that Islamic discourse is far more compatible with globalized market relations than the existing state-supported bourgeois class in Turkey, insofar as it creates relations of trust and solidarity.

In explaining the compatibility of Islam with the free market, MUSIAD cites the Asian model of development, in which it is believed success comes from "the strategic fit between the traditional institutions that regulate social relations and the requirements of global markets." MUSIAD's first (and former) president, Erol Yarar, explains the importance of the East Asian model with respect to Turkish economic development in the following way: "At the threshold of the twenty-first century, once again the western side of the Pacific—that is, the east of China—is becoming the dominant center of the world economy."

The crucial point here is that as opposed to the Western industrial model, this new model is based on the link between "small or medium-sized enterprises" and "the culture of traditional values" embedded in family and/or religion. The East Asian model's success relies on its commitment to cultural identity and its break with Western civilization, which gave primacy to secularism over religious morality and values. By following this model, MUSIAD presents itself as an alternative to nonviable capitalist development and centers its activities on *Homo islamicus*, which is the proper ethical basis for economic development, rather than *Homo economicus*, which has given rise to a self-centered individualistic morality.

In this context, MUSIAD argues that its discourses, strategies and actors create what is called the "proper Islamic discourse," which is neither backward, mystical nor solely traditional, but progressive, open to economic and technological innovation, compatible with free trade and capitalism, and able to create sources of wealth. This means that MUSIAD, like TUSIAD, promotes technology and quality assurance. Its actors prefer long-term, rational strategies over short-term interests to secure their success, and their entrepreneurial activities are embedded in capitalism and the economic rules of capitalist rationality.

Economic Islam, then, promotes capitalism as economic globalization but situates it in Islamic discourse as its cultural basis. As the representative of economic Islam, MUSIAD articulates Islamic religion with economic globalization, but at the same time creates a societal vision

based on the primacy of cultural/communitarian identity over individualistic morality. In other words, it represents a vision for Turkish sociopolitical life founded on *Homo islamicus* rather than *Homo economicus*,
which promotes self-interest over what is good for society.

This vision is directly derived from MUSIAD's positive view of globalization, which provides a basis both for the challenge that the organization has initiated against the existing political-economic order (i.e.,
statism and secularism) and for its promotion of *Homo islamicus*. Thus
MUSIAD sees globalization as a factor contributing to the development
of pluralism and multiculturalism, thereby creating a platform for democratization in Turkey. In this context, globalization is seen in relation
to the integration process in Europe, where Turkey wants to be a full
member of the European Union. It functions as both a conditioning and
an enabling factor: "conditioning" in the sense that it requires, and even
forces, the Turkish state to be open to democracy, creating a legitimate
ground for Islamic discourse as an element of pluralism and multiculturalism; and "enabling" in the sense that it facilitates the operation of
economic Islam beyond the borders of the nation-state.

Two points should be made here. First, MUSIAD's view of pluralism
and multiculturalism is not liberal, insofar as it accords primacy to the
community over the individual. For them, self-identity is discursively
constructed and defined not in individuality but in community. Based
on Islamic discourse, community comes before individual preferences
and morality, so that the references to democracy, freedom, and morality, and in this sense pluralism and multiculturalism, are situated in and
framed by communitarian ideology, rather than liberalism.

Second, this communitarian ideology, which also explains the link between economic Islam and its aspiration to the East Asian model of economic development, gives a clear expression of MUSIAD's view of
community-based economic organizations founded on an articulation
of Islamic cultural/moral identity and free trade that overrides difference
of class, power, and wealth between capital and labor. This means that Islam defines the identity of both the owner and the producer, makes them
part of the economic community, and masks the inequality, the uneven-
ness, and the differences between them in terms of power and wealth.

For example, the discourse of justice and fairness that economic Islam
uses never involves references to the organizational rights of producers

for unionization, the right to strike, security, health, or welfare. In fact, the communitarian ideology promoted by economic Islam acts against the principles of the welfare state and distributive justice in general and the organizational rights of the producers in particular.

Here, however, we can see that MUSIAD is in fact a class-based organization that uses Islamic discourse to "justify" its communitarian ideology and to "mobilize" its economic activities. We can see also that at the ideological level, MUSIAD and its Islamic economic identity differ radically from TUSIAD and its economic identity, which places a special emphasis on the language of civil rights as a basis for the process of democratization in Turkey.

SIADs

In recent years, Turkey has also witnessed the increasing importance (both qualitatively and quantitatively) in the province (city)-based and regional-based industrialist and business organizations known as SIADs, which have their own discourse and strategies. Even though they are not as strong or as influential as TUSIAD and MUSIAD, they deserve our attention for the following reasons: (1) they have created a dynamic economic life in Anatolia, especially with the emergence of the economically successful cities known as "Anatolian Tigers"; (2) because of their economic success, they have played an important role in changing our "orientalist vision" of Anatolia as an agriculture-based, underdeveloped, and traditional social totality; and (3) they have therefore shown us that there are different ways in which the global can be articulated with the local, creating different social forms and social visions.

In terms of their positive view of economic globalization, their adherence to free trade ideology, and their critique of the existing politico-economic order that privileges the strong-state tradition over economic and cultural activities, SAIDs appear similar to TUSIAD and MUSIAD. In terms of the scale and the scope of their economic organization, they represent (as in the case of MUSIAD) small and medium-scale enterprises located in different regions of Anatolia. They also promote a model of economic development in which the link between free trade and traditional/communitarian cultural identity defines the very basis of economic life. In fact their raison d'être and modus vivendi are founded on the promotion of community ties over individuality as the precondition for economic success.

However, SIADs differ from TUSIAD and MUSIAD in three fundamental ways. First, SIADs operate without state support and represent local development that depends exclusively on trade beyond the borders of the nation-state. In fact, SAIDs represent the clearest case in which the globalization of the local can be observed. SIADs therefore view economic and cultural globalization as "internal" to their emergence and development and as processes making a positive and valuable contribution to the protection of their local cultures.

Second, all SIADs give primacy to community over individuality, and they define community as an "organic social and cultural unity." In this sense, they prefer homogeneity, commonality, and sameness to pluralism and difference, and they promote conservative and communitarian societal visions over liberal individualism. SAID members maintain that success in economic life derives from the protection and the organization of cultural life as an "organic unity." However, their view of what constitutes organic unity differs from that of MUSIAD, in that Islamic discourse is not the exclusive source of cultural identity for SIADs: nationalism, family ties, traditional norms, ethnicity, and primordialism also play significant roles in creating the communitarian ties that make social and cultural life an organic unity.

Successful SIADs—Gaziantep, Konya, Kayseri, Çorum, Denizli, Aydın, Adana, and Antalya, for example—explain their economic development by emphasizing the importance of establishing organic organizational and cultural ties among powerful actors in their communities. In fact, our research found that one of the ideas commonly shared by SIADs is that the extent to which organic unity is produced and reproduced in a given community determines the degree of success in economic life. Therefore, while the success stories in Anatolia point out the value of organic unity in successfully linking the local and the global, in the provinces where underdevelopment remains, economic actors complain about the lack of community spirit necessary to creating this organic unity.

Third, this emphasis on organic unity explains the overarching power of nationalism and conservatism at the political level in most of the provinces and regions of Anatolia, where moral and ethical community as organic unity are seen as the unquestioned basis for the development of economic and cultural life. Therefore, while SIADs promote linkages between the local and the global, they also function as the "bearers of conservatism and nationalism" in their societal visions, which are limited in content, scope, and scale to the provinces in which they operate. SIADs therefore remain small-scale organizations both discursively and functionally, while the visions of both TUSIAD and MUSIAD address Turkish society at large.

Having outlined the main findings of our research concerning the linkage between cultural globalization and economic life in Turkey, we can conclude that this linkage takes the form of coexistence between the global and the local. However, the meaning that economic actors attribute to the impacts of cultural globalization vary in accordance with their economic discourses and strategies. While all of them see globalization as an internal element of the changing nature of economic and cultural life in Turkey, they differ in terms of their social visions. This manifests itself in the simultaneous promotion of both the universal language of civil rights and individuality and the protection of cultural/moral identity and the creation of a community as an organic unity. In sum, the ideology of free trade as an expression of economic globalization coexists with both liberalism and communitarianism in Turkish economic life.

CULTURAL GLOBALIZATION AND CIVIL SOCIETY ORGANIZATIONS

The 1980s and especially the 1990s saw an upsurge of interest in exploring alternative ways in which sociopolitical change in Turkey could be freed from the strong-state tradition. It is in this context that civil society organizations emerged and became important actors in Turkish politics. The sources of this interest in civil society are located not only in the general dissatisfaction with the strong-state tradition, not least because of its increasing independence from society and its concomitant failure to respond to social and cultural demands and to cope with social problems. Our research indicates that interest in civil society is also "global" in nature, as the emergence of a so-called global civil society has provided both a normative and an institutional basis for the call for a more participatory culture in Turkey. Thus civil society organizations value cultural globalization to the extent that it contributes to "the creation of the language of politics which is not associated exclusively with the state."[15]

During the 1990s, both the crisis of the strong-state tradition and the process of cultural globalization brought about a significant increase in the quantity and quality of civil society organizations. They were considered (1) an "indispensable element" of the democratization process; (2) a "necessary factor" in creating stability in the relations between Turkey and the European Union; and (3) an "important element" in the modernization and liberalization of the Turkish state, so that it can transform itself into a political organization whose power and activities are "accountable" to society.

The civil society discourse has been normatively supported and actively promoted in Turkish academic and public life, and civil society organizations have gained a "[political] actor-like quality" with normative and discursive power, which, through the globalized language of civil rights, has influenced the rethinking of state-society/individual relations beyond the strong-state tradition.

Furthermore, the tragic and devastating events of 1999—the Marmara earthquake on 17 August, which destroyed a large portion of the most industrial region of Turkey, causing almost twenty thousand deaths, and the Düzce earthquake of 12 November—have led many Turks to think about civil society organizations more seriously. These two disasters made it very clear that the strong state was in fact quite weak in its ability to respond to and cope with serious problems. Its failure to respond quickly and effectively to crisis situations has given rise to the belief that civil society organizations and a more participatory political culture are necessary for the efficient and effective solution to the problems confronting Turkish society.

At the same time, the role of foreign search and rescue teams and the global outpouring of help to those who lost their homes and families in these disasters have created a point of articulation between globalization and Turkish civil society. The large amounts of financial and moral help that came from various societies, institutions, and individuals has created a significant shift in Turkish attitudes and behavior patterns, from a more nationalistic view of the world to a more transnationalist and universalistic approach to social relations. As a result, the normative value of civil society organizations and their call for the global acceptance of the language of civil rights and participatory democracy has increased immensely in Turkey.

It should be pointed out, however, that our research indicates something of a paradox, in that most civil society organizations in Turkey actually view globalization as "a process to be resisted in the long run" or as "a problem to be seriously dealt with, in order to make its impacts positive for Turkish society." In other words, the general intellectual discourse of civil society, which sees globalization as one of the contributory factors for the development of civil society organizations in Turkey, does not correspond to the way in which civil society organizations themselves speak about the utility of globalization. Most appear to be "quite skeptical" in terms of how they consider the question of cultural globalization's long-term impacts.

This skepticism is sometimes quite strong, to the extent that globalization is seen as a new form of imperialism creating undemocratic power relations on behalf of rich countries. At other times, however, it can take the form of viewing globalization as an objective reality that produces both positive and negative impacts: *positive* in the sense of confronting the power of the strong-state and creating a platform for the protection of civil rights; *negative* in the sense of supporting the liberal hegemonic vision of the world, based on free market ideology.[16]

We think that looking at three effective human rights organizations will provide illustrative examples of this context. The Turkish Human Rights Association, which receives global support for its activities, takes a strong, skeptical position on globalization, arguing that although it supports the existing global discourse on the protection of human rights, globalization in the long run serves the interests of economically powerful countries. Globalization over the long term should thus be resisted in order to create democratic global governance.

The second organization, Mazlum-Der, which is associated with Islamic discourse, presents a softer skepticism, arguing that cultural globalization provides a platform suitable for its activities, although the liberal discourse on human rights it promotes is problematic in how it deals with cultural rights.

The third human rights organization, Helsinki Vatandaşlar Derneği (Helsinki Citizens Association), which was founded in Europe and operates in Turkey, views cultural globalization as generating both positive and negative impacts for both the nation-state and civil society. That is, cultural globalization cannot be rejected or celebrated but should be dealt with seriously, in order to take advantage of its positive qualities, such as its support for the universalization of the discourse of civil rights.

It is important to examine the differences between these three organizations, because they also illuminate a general problem that confronts all civil society organizations in Turkey and which determines, to a large extent, their approach to the question of cultural globalization. This can be called the "boundary problem"; in other words, the extent to which civil society organizations in Turkey actually operate as "civil society organizations" in terms of their relation to the state, the scope and content of their activities, and their normative and ideological formations.

The general definitional discourse on civil society in Turkey finds the institutional distinction between the state and society a "sufficient condition" for thinking of organizations taking place outside the boundaries of the state as civil society organizations. In fact, a large number of civil society organizations make use of this definition in describing themselves. However, this definition does not involve two important criteria used in the literature to define civil society organizations; namely, that they are issue-specific organizations that are *not* interested in creating or supporting ideological social visions.

But when we approach civil society organizations in Turkey on the basis of these two criteria, we see that the activities of most of them are in fact embedded in large social visions. These include Kemalism, the protection of contemporary civilized life, a secular-democratic Turkey, Islamic order, a modern Turkey, Islamic life, a socialist Turkey, and Kemalist Woman, to name but a few. Second, although some civil society organizations are institutionally outside the state, they can still have strong normative and ideological ties with state power. An example of this was the banning of the Welfare Party, in which strong ties had been established between some in the military, the state, and civil society organizations. In this case, we witnessed how the search for what is good for society at large could be a mission around which civil society organizations center their activities.[17]

Our research indicates that the way in which civil society organizations think of globalization is based on how normative their discourses and strategies are. Skepticism about the impacts of cultural globalization on societal relations in Turkey increases in those organizations whose activities are not issue specific but are closely tied with general ideological and normative social visions. On the other hand, this skepticism decreases in issue-specific civil society organizations, which conceive of globalization as creating a historical context for their activities.

In conclusion, we argue that there are differences between the intellectual discourse about civil society and the way civil society organizations perceive the impacts of globalization. The intellectual discourse locates civil society in a space that has occurred between the legitimacy/governability problem of the strong-state tradition and the changing nature of societal relations, partly because of the processes of globalization; it therefore views civil society as a necessary condition for democratization, pluralism, and multiculturalism. However, with their ideologically and normatively loaded discourses and strategies, most civil society organizations take a contrary view. So, even though their numbers are increasing and they are becoming important actors, how "civil" Turkish civil society organizations actually are remains uncertain.

CULTURAL GLOBALIZATION AND POPULAR CULTURE/CONSUMPTION PATTERNS

In addition to its impacts on economic life, civil society, and intellectual life, cultural globalization has also involved popular culture and consumption patterns in Turkey, where significant changes have occurred in recent years.[18] These changes have created two interrelated trends, the postmodernization of values and the globalization of the local, which have manifested themselves in our identities, lifestyle preferences, and consumption patterns. In French sociologist Pierre Bourdieu's terminology, these two trends have also functioned as "the cultural/symbolic capital" of the 1990s. Their role in creating and mobilizing identities has been as important as that of economic capital.

Thus, as opposed to the political arena, which has been characterized by the polarization of secularism and Islamic traditionalism, in the popular culture of the 1990s we witnessed the emergence of "calls for pluralism, the multiplicity of identities, the value of the local, increases in traditional symbols, and the emergence of consumerist culture." Cultural capital, therefore, has performed a double role: as a factor of differentiation, by giving meaning to the creation and the mobilization of different identities, and as an element of commonality among different identities, in terms of their tendency toward consumerism.

In the realm of popular culture, cultural globalization is seen as a process that enables coexistence, rather than clashes, between the global and the local. Three points are worth making here.

First, we found that coexistence appears to be most visible in the consumption patterns of different identities that have different political preferences, different economic status, and/or levels of well-being. This means that although the differences between these identities in terms of their choice of newspapers, magazines, and TV channels is noticeable and perhaps sometimes even significant, they vanish when it comes to their approach to consumption. In other words, while the choice of the newspaper or TV channels is still based on political or cultural identity codes, the significant increase in consumption patterns of different identities has brought about the "McDonalization of [Turkish] society." For example, whereas those who locate themselves in or near Islamic discourse usually prefer newspapers and TV channels associated with the Islamic movement, they nevertheless very much accept the universalization of Western consumer culture and its symbols. The same is true for those who define themselves as "Western" or "secular."

Second, cultural globalization can at the same time be seen as creating a suitable platform for the revitalization of tradition, not only as a political or economic movement but as a cultural movement with its actors and its discourses. As a result of globalization, therefore, Islamic identity no longer represents a backward self closed to change. On the contrary, we have seen the emergence of cultural capital used by Islamic identity in terms of fashion, music, art, and tourism, as well as an emergence of a consumerist Islamic identity acting as an economic citizen, integrated to shopping mall culture, making use of technology, and understanding the symbolic power of money. In this sense, Islamic identity is as much a part of the new consumerist culture as secular identity: it views this culture not as an evil emanating from the West but as a basis of social status and power.

Third, in this context, cultural globalization is viewed as a positive element for the revitalization of local art forms, cultural objects, and signs, thereby creating a cultural life that is more plural, democratic, and multicultural. Globalization ends the hegemony of secular culture, which aims at producing and maintaining a homogeneous cultural life by creating a platform on which marginalized and silenced cultural forms and objects can become both visible and marketable. At the same time, it makes an important contribution to the expression of differences through the discourse of tradition, locality, and authenticity, as it is through the globalization of the local that a more pluralistic and multicultural life has come into existence—a necessary condition for the process of democratization in Turkey.

In light of the above discussion and our exposition of the different impacts of cultural globalization on life in Turkey, we conclude that coexistence rather than clash is the form that delineates the interactions between the global and the local. We believe that coming to terms with this fact is of the utmost importance not only for understanding the changing nature of Turkish modernity but, more importantly, for establishing democracy in Turkey.

NOTES

1. A comprehensive analysis of globalization and its political impact on the national context can be found in D. Archibugi, D. Held, and M. Köhler, eds., *Re-imagining Political Community* (Cambridge, U.K.: Polity, 1998).

2. See M. A. Bamyeh, *The Ends of Globalization* (Minneapolis: University of Minnesota Press, 2000).

3. For a more detailed explanation, see E. Özbudun, *Contemporary Turkish Politics: Challenges to Democratic Consolidation* (Boulder: Lynne Rienner, 2000).

4. Z. Öniş, "The Political Economy of Islamic Resurgence in Turkey: The Rise of Welfare Party in Perspective," *Third World Quarterly* 18, no. 4 (1997): 743–766.

5. This point has also been made by Heinz Kramer in his recent book, *A Changing Turkey* (Washington, D.C.: Brookings Institution, 2000).

6. G. E. Fuller and I. O. Lesser, *Turkey's New Geopolitics* (Boulder: Westview, 1993).

7. For an important source, see P. Berger, "Four Faces of Globalization," *National Interest* 49 (1997).

8. Berger, "Four Faces," 24.

9. The term "Islamic capital" is also used interchangeably with "green capital" and "Anatolian capital."

10. See also A. Buğra, *Islam in Economic Organizations* (Istanbul: TESEV, 1999).

11. Buğra, *Islam*, 11–12.

12. In our research, we extensively investigated MUSIAD and TUSIAD by conducting in-depth interviews, mapping their publications, and collecting data from the related literature on these organizations. Whereas TUSIAD and its members are mainly located in Istanbul, the organizational scope of MUSIAD extends toward Anatolia, so our in-depth MUSIAD interviews involved trips to Anatolian cities, where there is a strong tie be-

tween the development of export-oriented economic activities and MUSIAD organizational activities.

13. That is why these cities are sometimes characterized as "Anatolian tigers," referring to the East Asian model of economic development. Understanding the process that this model has put into practice in these cities gave us crucial insights that could help clarify the varying impacts of cultural globalization in Turkey.

14. Unless otherwise indicated, quoted material from this section on is taken from our research.

15. For details, see A. N. Yücekök, İ. Turan, and M. Ö. Alkan, *Civil Society Organizations in Istanbul* (Istanbul: Tarih Vakfı, 1998); A. Gönel, *Primary Civil Society Organizations* (Istanbul: Tarih Vakfı, 1998); and Turkish Economy and Social History Foundation, *Civil Society Organizations* (Istanbul: Tarih Vakfı, 1998). All these publications are in Turkish.

16. On the other hand, the leaders of some civil society organizations, such as citizenship initiatives, environmental organizations, and organizations that deal directly with the problems of urban life, think positively of cultural globalization as a process "internal" to their activities.

17. E. F. Keyman, "Globalization, Civil Society, and Democracy in Turkey," in D. Durst, ed., *Civil Society in South Eastern Europe* (London: Vertigo, forthcoming).

18. This part of our research was based on in-depth interviews and the reports of the DAP marketing research company, *Life Standards, Values, and Preferences in Turkey* for 1998 and 1999. We thank Akın Alyanak and Erkani Keyman for their time and suggestions.

PART FOUR

———————— • ————————

The American Vortex

10

In the Vanguard of Globalization

THE WORLD OF AMERICAN GLOBALIZERS

James Davison Hunter and Joshua Yates

A friend of mine told me a story very soon after the genocide in Rwanda. He was there as a military representative accompanying an NGO tour of the area. The situation was awful. There was also no infrastructure to get to the people in need. And so there were United Nations convoys that just couldn't get through. This delegation literally sat there on the road for hours going nowhere. By the time they finally reached their destination, they discovered that Coke had already been there for two weeks distributing what they needed. What a fascinating thing—Coke got there before the UN. It shows you just how powerful the global market is and this brand in particular. . . . I suppose if Microsoft needs to be there, they'll be there too.

> —A senior administrator for Porter Novelli

The United States has generated what one observer has called "a veritable avalanche of artifacts" that are now taken-for-granted features of life around the world. The ATM, basketball, hamburger, skateboard, cell phone, computer, computer hacker, sneakers, baseball cap, laundromat, candy bar, microwave oven, parking meter, camera, jukebox, the modern passenger airplane, convenience store, greeting card, ice cream, sports drink, blue jeans, rap music, chewing gum, credit card, skyscraper, and the like, are virtually everywhere. Indeed, so much of what we know as globalization is, in both source and character, undeniably American. Whether McDonald's (serving 20 million people worldwide each day), MTV (reaching half a billion people per year), Coca-Cola (serving 1 billion people worldwide every day), Hollywood (from which 85 percent of the most watched films in the world come), Michael Jordan, himself a global icon (generating over $10 billion just over the course of his playing career for an array of global commercial ventures), and so on, the popular culture, food, and status symbols of America are ubiquitous.

Yet the nearly universal fascination for things American is not limited to its popular culture. In philanthropy, U.S.–based foundations are prevalent in their patronage and generous in their provision of assistance. In 1994 alone, American foundations gave an estimated $966 million to philanthropic, educational, and other causes outside the United States. In the realm of finance, the top investment firms and multinational corporations are predominantly U.S.–based, and the elite professional schools that train their executives are again American. Of the top ten Fortune 500 companies in 1999, six are American, and the United States was home to thirty-one of the overall most profitable companies.

On most measures—total revenue, foreign assets, foreign affiliates, number of foreign employees, and so on—the United States is the undisputed global economic leader. And in religion, American evangelicalism, arguably one of the largest social movements in the world, provides extraordinary financial, educational, and technical resources to evangelicals the world over. The parachurch organization Campus Crusade for Christ, for example, has shown its *Jesus Film* in over two hundred countries, translated it into 446 languages, and presented it throughout the world to 1.3 billion people. Likewise, *Focus on the Family* boasts that its flagship radio program hosted by Dr. James Dobson is heard daily by more than 660 million people in ninety-five countries. It is small wonder that "Americanization" is often considered synonymous with the processes of globalization itself.

At the same time, it is also clear that globalization is not merely Americanization writ large. We know that societies and localities elsewhere in the world neither uniformly nor passively receive the wide range of material and symbolic culture derived from U.S. markets. The consumption of global brands, whether as actual products or as mediated images, is often an occasion for cultural elaboration as well as accommodation, for syncretism as well as homogenization, for resistance as well as enthusiasm. Thus, although goods, technologies, and symbols created within the United States certainly "carry" a great deal of cultural baggage as they cross borders, they are often, upon reception, subject to the forces of indigenization and hybridization. Sorting out what all of this means is a task that will preoccupy scholars for many years to come.

At the end of the day, however, we are still faced with the present reality of America's powerful if not dominant role in processes of globalization. How do we understand the inner workings of this role?

In this chapter we will explore what this reality means to those Americans actually generating a "world culture"—elites in business, popular culture, politics, and faith, who compose the vanguard of globalization. What is their experience on the frontlines of this world-historical transformation? How do they envision the world they are helping create? And what do these men and women, and the organizations they lead, tell us about the complex yet still emerging global order? They are, of course, "cosmopolitan" elites who are creating a cosmopolitan culture, but what is the nature of this cosmopolitanism?

By examining the ideologies informing their formal programmatic and organizational missions, the social practices sustaining their daily routines and deportment, and the governing cultural infrastructure framing their most basic normative assumptions and commitments, we can make important conceptual distinctions as well as attend to less apparent points of comparison. Their lives, experiences, and perspectives are one prism through which we can understand the monumental social and cultural transformations we call "globalization."[1]

ENDURING DIFFERENCES

On the face of it, the vanguard of globalization and the organizations represented are bewilderingly complex. What possible commonalties are there among MTV, the Sierra Club, the Ford Foundation, McDonald's,

Merrill Lynch, and Campus Crusade for Christ? Their administrative structures, the "goods" and "services" they offer, the beneficiaries of those goods, their various institutional motivations and mandates, as well as their corporate bottom lines, vary widely. Even more, they often confront, challenge, and contradict one another, clashing over ideology and the leadership and direction of globalization itself.

Consider, first, some of the ideological tensions. There are American organizations that actively *export* their moral and ideological agendas abroad in ways that mirror the conflict they wage at home. As in the United States, the main point of contention is over abortion, but it also plays out in broader issues surrounding sexuality, the family, and education.

The conflict over abortion is especially emblematic. Progressive and traditionalist special interest groups have established offices and staffs around the world to lobby foreign governments on behalf of their respective causes. The president of Focus on the Family's International and Marketing Division candidly admits that the American culture wars are being fought on foreign soil. "I think mostly people from the West—Western Europe and the United States—are playing out these battles in places like Peru and Guatemala and Costa Rica. At root, we're confronting one another over our respective philosophies." The acting director of International Programs for Planned Parenthood of America conceded the point. "It's a reality," she said. "These anti-choice groups have gone global and, thus, so have pro-choice groups."

The tactics are oriented toward influencing the legal, political, and educational institutions of different societies. Typically, they go after "that key decision maker," whether a head of state, a first lady, a minister of education, or minister of justice. "The anti-choice people of the United States," the executive from Planned Parenthood explained, "have a very targeted campaign influencing and reforming laws around the world. In Poland, for example,

> amniocentesis has just been made illegal, because it's considered to be a precursor to the possibility that a woman will choose to have an abortion. . . . This is directly financed by anti-abortion movements in the United States. You see these initiatives happening in Ireland and South Africa as well. They're very active. Where abortion is legal, they're working very hard to make sure that access is qualified.

Not surprisingly, Focus on the Family characterizes Planned Parent-hood's activities similarly: "They pull together global conferences to talk about overpopulation. Then, they argue the case for abortion services as a response to overpopulation. They're very aggressive." As in the United States, the hostilities among such groups are unyielding.

The Consequences of Global Capitalism

A second and more prominent source of conflict among global organi-zations and elites is over the effects of global capitalism. The manifesta-tion of this is most obvious in the December 1999 protests of the World Trade Organization meeting in Seattle, the April 2000 World Bank and International Monetary Fund meeting in Washington, D.C., and others. Led by a number of transnational associations, coalitions, think tanks, and international nongovernmental organizations (INGOs) such as the International Forum on Globalization, the Turning Point Project, Public Citizen, Friends of the Earth, and Global Exchange, a growing, well-organized, networked, and media-savvy movement has emerged. At is-sue are alternative ideas of how best to achieve the global public good under the conditions of contemporary globalization.

The heart of the criticism of institutions such as the IMF and the World Bank is that they are complicit in creating and maintaining a "hegemonic global economic order" that only serves the interests of powerful multinational corporations. As one movement pamphlet stated, "The IMF and the WTO are the first and foremost instruments of Corporate USA's drive to dominate the world and maximize its profits at the expense of the workers and oppressed peoples."[2] One activist charac-terized the United States, in this regard, as the "belly of the beast."[3]

From the perspective of these activists, the present global economic and political context is no different from that present at the height of Western colonialism. Indeed, the only notable difference is that what used to be called "colonialism" is now euphemistically called "develop-ment." While the push for the deregulation and privatization of national markets together with heavy-handed "structural adjustment" policies are done in the name of Third World development and the planet's poor and needy, they actually benefit only the world's rich and powerful elite. What is more, critics argue, these organizations are, for all practical purposes, autocratic: they may present themselves as democratic but are in fact mostly unaccountable to the public. As the president of the International Forum on Globalization put it, the WTO, the World Bank, and the IMF form an "unholy trinity" or "iron triangle" that "couldn't have done a more harmful job on people and the planet if they set out with those goals in mind."[4]

In their view, the bottom line for these world financial organizations and the multinational corporations that rule them is profit—without concern for the well-being of humanity, cultural traditions, or the planet's ecosystems. Although not an active participant in the recent protests, in addressing the differences between international nongovernmental organizations and multinational corporations, World Vision's senior vice president for International Programs asks:

> If you took the profit motive away from Coca-Cola, would they exist? If you took the profit motive away from McDonald's would they exist? They're not out there for value transformation, or for building a better society. . . . The bottom line is to make a profit.

It is the unqualified pursuit of profit that motivates global environmentalists to protest as well. The Sierra Club's director for International Programs put it this way:

> We don't want to take away anyone's jobs, but we also don't want to undermine the environment. We support those environmentalists in other countries who want to have the same quality of life and environmental protection laws that we have in this country. The reason we were in Seattle protesting the WTO is because these trade agreements fundamentally challenge environmental laws not only in this country, but in any country that restricts trade. We have a problem with that— and so do environmentalists in other countries.

Perhaps their greatest concern is for the ways in which globalization can exacerbate the gap between rich and poor in the world. The director of strategic leadership for Compassion International spoke to this problem as it plays out in South America. "In terms of economic globalization, that's a two-headed dragon. While it leaves some people more free from the burdens and drudgeries of daily life, it has also created slums in our cities. Just go across the border to Mexico. We couldn't pay Americans that way and get away with it."

The executive director for Greenberg, Quinlan Research, Inc. (a U.S.–based political consulting firm) agreed: "I fear that the distinction between 'haves' and 'have-nots' will become sharper in this country as well as around the world." A senior program officer of International Programs at Planned Parenthood echoed this sentiment. "The divide between wealthy and poor is escalating. It's at its very worst in Latin America, particularly in Brazil and in Argentina." The vice president of World Vision articulated the potential for serious conflict along these lines. In his view, "I think we're heading for a collision of rich and poor. We see this taking shape in different ways even now—refugee movements, internally displaced peoples, violence within urban environments, and so on. These problems are only going to increase. In these ways, the future doesn't look good for me."

In working through his strategies for the Carter Center, former President Carter himself takes the view "that the difference between the rich and the poor is the issue of the new millennium."[5]

Yet it is essential to note that even those factions most opposed to the effects of global capitalism are not typically against globalization per se. Their own global networks suggest as much. As the preamble of the World Economy Project states, "We the people unite by building an international movement to stop business interests from confining the economic gains of globalization to a select few."[6] These opponents desire a kinder and gentler globalization, one more economically equitable, authentically democratic, and ecologically sound.

Leadership in the international business and finance communities sees things quite differently. They tend to agree that those who resist free trade and the global flow of capital—whether protestors of the WTO or local-nationals boycotting and even vandalizing global franchises, brands, and goods—are responsible for causing greater harm to the people and the environment the protestors claim to champion. "Some environmentalists," contends a long-time executive and now consultant for Archer Daniels Midland, "impede the ability to feed people and feed them well." In his view,

These groups have hidden agendas that are detrimental to the global environment. Take, for example, the anti-science and technology movement. The wave of fear against biotechnology and genetically modified foods threatens our ability to increase food production. The alternative would be to plow down fragile lands and wildlife habitat for food.

The same line of reasoning, he contends, holds for those opposed to free trade:

Those against liberalized trade fail to realize that a free market system is the best way to ensure that people are fed at affordable prices and in environmentally sustainable ways. Some labor unions oppose trade liberalization but ignore the ways in which free trade increases exports, which in turn create jobs, and jobs associated with exports are higher paying jobs.

In these circles, the benefits of their businesses for the societies in which they operate far outweigh any negative impact. "I think it's pretty sad," said a vice president of Corporate Communications at McDonald's.

Take the case in France—I think that the anti-McDonald's activities in recent months were just very ill placed. The fact is that over 80 percent of our products and packaging in France are French. We're a French company there. We contribute an enormous amount to the French economy. We employ tens of thousands of French people. We support French farmers and buy French agricultural products. It's our point of view that anyone who needs to use violence just to grab headlines is off in the wrong direction—and, as it relates to France, really off in the wrong direction.

It is for this reason that executives in the world of international finance and business see the transformations of globalization in only the most hopeful terms. The prism through which they see these positive benefits is the market itself, where the average person is regarded as a global consumer whose economic choices are expanding due to liberated, interconnected markets and whose social and political freedoms are expanding due to the democratization of information. The net effect is a historically unprecedented empowerment of the individual—a consequence that, for AT&T's vice president for International Public Relations, "can only be good." From the vantage of one corporate executive, the future is a place of massive consumer choice when the global capital markets make fabulous product choices available, the accessibility of technology and information, virtual travel, and it's a place where the consumer as king is extraordinary. There'll still be a few places where the consumers are denied by backward states who try to deny access. . . . [but overall] I think the incomes for world populations will be better fifty years from now and the relative costs of services will go down. I think it'll be a better world by virtue of information accessibility. There will be more appreciation for differences than there will be for similarities.

Evangelical Christians are no less enthusiastic about the prospects for their faith under the conditions of globalization. "I think it's awesome," said the vice president from Focus on the Family. "I think that the Christian faith in the context of globalization has a tremendous opportunity." Their fellow believers at the Christian Coalition International attribute what they perceive to be the increasing democratization of the world to the impact and spread of their religion: "Christianity as a global movement is tremendously powerful. Its social effects—namely, freedom—are now being felt around the world."

Taking hope from the world's ability to solve a recent "global" problem, one of the executives from Porter Novelli stated,

I think where we're heading is we're going to be more effective. We're going to be much better communicators. We're going to be more efficient. I think the greatest example of that in the last year is just what happened with Y2K. The fact that we didn't have one major international incident. . . . that's the kind of thing that blows your mind. You can have a problem that can be dealt with on a global scale and not have a meltdown. It's just incredibly exciting.

These are but illustrations of the main vectors of tensions that are common within the vanguard of globalization. These elites differ in their aims and ambitions and, at various points, even clash over the substance of those ends. If these elites are a prism, then at first glance, the story they tell is anything but coherent.

As important as these disputes are, it is difficult to know how consequential they will be. The differences that animate these disputes seem, in fact, rather qualified in light of all that these globalizers culturally share in common.

UNCANNY SIMILARITIES

There is, however, a subtext in the lives these executives lead and the worldviews they articulate. For all the complex differences distinguishing various American globalizing elites and their organizations, one does not have to dig very deep to find important similarities among them. Beneath the surface of explicit ideological contention, there exist similarities rooted in their social practices, and in the perspectives, attitudes, and values that emanate from those practices.

Life in a Bubble

Consider first the basic and concrete features of their workaday experience. The executives we interviewed live and work in a world made up of constant travel, both physical and virtual. The amount of time they spend traveling the globe ranges considerably: as "little" as 25 percent of their time in some cases, to as much as 60 percent. But they rarely go to remote or primitive regions of the world; instead, their destinations are nearly always large metropolitan areas, foreign capitals, and regional centers of culture and commerce such as Tokyo, London, Hong Kong, São Paulo.

When they are not physically abroad, they are nearly constantly interacting with their colleagues, partners, and subordinates located everywhere in the world—for some, these dealings are hourly. This is not only true for elites in international business, but also for those in relief and development agencies, news and entertainment networks, and so on. One AT&T executive described his global travel this way:

> I go all over Asia, Latin America, Europe, Canada. Predominantly, London, Paris, Frankfurt, Hong Kong, Beijing, Shanghai, Tokyo, São Paulo, Rio de Janeiro, Mexico City, and Toronto and Ottawa. They're national capitals with the exception of Brazil and China, where there are other urban centers.

Coca-Cola's vice president of Strategic Marketing and Research Trends said,

I'm probably in the field seven working days a month, seven out of twenty. . . . I go all over the world. I'll go to the Middle and Far East five weeks a year. I'll go to Europe this year about fifteen weeks just because the Belgium issues are so hot for us this summer. I go to Latin America a couple of days a month. I go to Africa probably twice a year. Altogether, I've been to seventy countries in the world and worked in forty different ones.

World Vision's vice president for International Programs said,

Between October and December, I was in Kosovo, Sri Lanka, Brazil, Senegal—Seattle and California too, which I view as another world, another country. On a daily basis, I'm probably on the phone internationally at least twice in a day. This morning I was speaking with folks in Kosovo. I spoke with folks in Costa Rica yesterday.

The head of international news gathering for CNN described himself in an understated way as a frequent traveler. "I've been to North Korea nine times, nine times to Iraq, forty times to China, Somalia, and Bosnia, ten times to Cuba. And I am leaving this weekend to go to Belgrade. Yeah, I am a frequent traveler."

These executives travel so much and so extensively that it is not surprising that destinations begin to resemble one another. With this comes a curious sense of time and space: a feeling that they could literally be anywhere in the world and nowhere in particular. An Aspen Institute vice president described one experience this way:

I remember having a meeting in Miami, just in one day. I had a two-hour flight. I got out of the airport, into a taxi, went into a glass office building, had a meeting and went to lunch at some fancy restaurant within the same building, had a little bit more of a meeting, got out, got into the cab, went back to the airport. I could've been anywhere in the world really. Internationally, I've had similar experiences—though they obviously extend for more than just a day. I go somewhere, do something, and turn right around and come back.

Much of what creates this surreal experience is the physical environment itself; it rarely changes. These international travelers go from their home office in one of the larger U.S. cities to an international airport, fly to another international airport somewhere in the world, manage business, attend a conference, or conduct a meeting in office space similar to theirs at home, and then return in a matter of days.

Occasionally, the traveler gets an opportunity for some shopping or for taking in some of the local scenery and sights, perhaps a cultural or sporting event before concluding the business of the trip. Again, the executive from the Aspen Institute aptly portrays a common experience among the globalizers: "Frankly, when you go to a lot of these gatherings . . . you're in a hotel. A really big hotel. They all look the same. Then you're schmoozing with all these people from all over the world . . . You go out for dinner or something, and you're pretty much connected to the convention the whole time, so you can get out a little bit and maybe get a little shopping in or something, and then you go back."

The worlds in which these men and women move as they circle the globe share a remarkable resemblance to their places of origin with most of the same amenities, conveniences, and creature comforts—everything from health spas and fitness facilities to executive business services such as e-mail and faxing, to satellite television, fine dining, and Western-style rooms. Thus the senior vice president for research and planning at MTV remarked that "whoever's making the decisions on the kind of creature comforts available for business travelers caters to the American business executives. So, for example, when it comes to food, there are a lot of American-style restaurants or the equivalent in terms of service, layout, and comfort level."

The sense of familiarity and predictability within their life worlds carries over to the people with whom they interact. Indeed, those with whom they associate—whether other Americans or foreign nationals—are typically part of the global network themselves. Like those we interviewed, they too are highly trained, often Western-educated and credentialed: virtually all of those we interviewed, regardless of profession or organization, possessed advanced degrees in fields such as communications (e.g., journalism, public relations), the social sciences (e.g., economics, psychology, anthropology), the health sciences, business, and law.

As we noted, most of those we interviewed remained a few levels removed from ongoing face-to-face involvement with local cultures and peoples they serve. "We're dealing mainly with political leaders and governing officials and those are clearly going to be elites," admits a Carter Center program director. "We come closest to nonelites when we meet with indigenous human rights activists, but they too tend to be local elites."

Even in the field, most humanitarian practitioners interact primarily with local program directors and other field staff in order to set up, monitor, and evaluate various organizational initiatives for which they are responsible. Moreover, travel often doesn't involve fieldwork but participation in numerous practitioner conferences and meetings, which occur with astonishing regularity. For instance, the vice president for international programs for the Sierra Club described how he sometimes spends most of his travel going from one international conference to another. He explained:

> For a while there was a heavy set of UN circuit meetings whether it was on UNICEF down in Rio, a population conference in Cairo, a biodiversity conference down in the Bahamas. . . . I travel sometimes to visit other environmental INGOs. I went to Kenya and I was in Nigeria to tour an area there and I was in France this summer at a UNESCO meeting on world science. I'm traveling down to Costa Rica next month for a rain forest visit and then possibly to Jordan for an IUCN meeting in October.

Of course, there are exceptions. A number of these managers, administrators, and directors do move beyond this rather insulated world. Those working for international nongovernmental organizations whose organizational mandates focus on environmental protection, human rights, religious evangelization, emergency humanitarian relief, and the like, frequently have to engage in face-to-face interaction with and grassroots organization of the local populations they serve. While they too tend to stay in the larger metropolitan centers at the "bigger hotels where international consultants and others go," as the associate director of the Carter Center's democracy program points out, there are times "when you have to travel outside the capital city." A strategist from World Vision acknowledged that while he typically stays in some fairly comfortable hotels, he also visits less traveler-friendly locales: "In relief situations, such as Kosovo, there aren't any hotels . . . so you sort of end up rooming with the relief and development workers just wherever they are. It all depends on the reason for the trip."

In the world inhabited by global elites, these experiences tend to be the exception and not the rule. Even when there are exceptions, the less insulated among them nevertheless operate according to the dictates of their organizational and professional agendas, rather than terms set by local custom, tradition, or practice. It is not surprising that the rules of natural time and space in this world are suspended: in quite tangible ways, these globalizers inhabit something of a sociocultural bubble that is generally insulated from the harsher differences between national cultures.

This is only reinforced linguistically, as few find any need to speak a language other than English. With the exception of a small number of these executives, the overwhelming majority of those we talked with did not speak a language other than English. Many were quick to add that they recognize the tremendous asset of speaking another language, but they acknowledged that they had little practical need to do so: no matter where they traveled, they could usually get by speaking only English.

The response of the MTV vice president to our query was echoed again and again. "Do you speak another language besides English?" we asked. "No," he replied, "I do not." So, we followed, "Do you have others translate for you?" "Actually," he said, "what I'm finding is that it's even less a need . . . for the most part people are moving towards speaking English more. It's the preferred language." Sierra Club's international program VP responded similarly: "The international business language is English, and it's pretty much the same in our field. It allows Americans to be very lazy. I haven't needed to keep up with my Spanish, for instance, and so far I haven't been penalized."

A number of executives and managers pointed out how even colleagues from non–English speaking countries resorted to communicating in English when visiting places whose language they did not know. "I was pleasantly surprised," confessed Porter Novelli's vice president for International Account Development, "to discover that English becomes . . . the language that Europeans have in common, so anybody who is working internationally or working across borders is going to have some basic English skills." Although she went on to claim that this is true only for corporate executives who work internationally, the senior strategist for Compassion International explained that "probably half of our people at least are English [speaking], not out of mandate, but out of their realization that if they're going to be interactive with the organization, they better know English."

The same observation was echoed by a Christian relief administrator who added that English is not only the language of the partnership, "it's also the language which most information encoding and processing is conducted in." And so, while speaking only English is a luxury enjoyed by most of the American globalizers, *not* speaking English is a luxury that very few others around the world can afford to do without.

The Vocabularies of Global Speak

Yet another linguistic practice that forms a structure of shared experience and perspective is American globalizers' use of the vocabularies derived from social sciences, human rights, the market, and multiculturalism. These vocabularies provide the terms by which the authority of these global agendas are established and their particular instrumental ends are legitimated, and it is within these vocabularies that the deepest normative commitments take shape and become meaningful. In the words of one especially reflective executive, "Our words make our worlds, and as you begin to use language, you begin to mold mind-sets and ideals and mental models; that is to say, worldviews."

Consider first the discourse of social science. Whether for the purposes of public policy, consumer research, or program evaluation, all global elites employ the language and techniques of the social sciences to frame their agenda and to solve any administrative or programmatic problems. Whether it is Coca-Cola conducting "presearch," Nike using numerous marketing focus groups, the Planned Parenthood Federation of America and Greenberg, Quinlan Research Inc. conducting numerous public opinion polls and surveys, the International Center for Research on Women employing statistical analysis to evaluate the effectiveness of UN, USAID, and World Bank programs, or Campus Crusade for Christ using quantitative analysis within their "ministry tracking systems" in order to "keep up with everything that happens in and around the movement," the quantifying, organizing, and evaluating techniques of social science not only provide the authority by which action is justified but also supply an idiom by which "the work" is accomplished on a day-to-day basis.

It is not surprising to find among the INGOs, for example, professionally trained social scientists among its leadership, and social scientists within the employ of multinational corporations. A company as wealthy as Coca-Cola can boast of having fifty cultural anthropologists, sociologists, behavioral psychologists, and ethnographers on staff working on matters relating to strategic marketing.[7]

The ubiquity of the language of the social sciences is reflected in the way it frames the claims and missions of those organizations that are ideologically opposed to each other. Consider, for instance, the case of Focus on the Family and Planned Parenthood. When asked how they persuaded foreign governments to use their abstinence curriculum, Focus on the Family said,

> We share with them the data on the rising rates of teen pregnancy in the U.S. We show, over the last thirty years since the inception of liberal programs of social re-engineering, how teen pregnancy has gone up hundreds of percent. Our message is that you don't want to go in this direction. At the same time, we can show how we're having great success in pockets of the United States where abstinence is taught; that substantial decreases in teen pregnancy and promiscuity are taking place. With the data, the conclusion is just common sense.

Planned Parenthood likewise shares empirical evidence with the foreign governments that they are trying to persuade. "Look at the statistics on what happens when a woman is educated," the Planned Parenthood executive explained. "There's a direct correlation between level of education and number of children." Once again, the choice is "obvious" and so is the idiom.

If epistemological authority for these elites is grounded in the language of social science, moral authority is grounded in the *language of universal individual rights and needs*. Whether selling soft drinks, fast food, running shoes, hybrid crop fertilizer, or financial investments or providing technical assistance for Third World health clinics, environmental protection advocacy, or biblical principles for a strong family, the American globalizers all understand their efforts as a fulfillment of rights and needs basic to human existence. Archer Daniels Midland and McDonald's market their products and franchise their brands around the world because people have "the right to be well fed." Merrill Lynch can peddle financial investment opportunities to foreign governments because those governments have a "right to be able to meet the basic human needs" of their citizenry. Nike can market shoes globally because people everywhere have "a universal need for athletic footwear." Twentieth Century Fox distributes film in response to "the need for quality entertainment."

International nongovernmental organizations are no different in this respect. "I feel very strongly committed to the issue of women's rights and part of those are her reproductive rights," said the Planned Parenthood executive. "We've been in this work for a very long time, thirty years, and the issue is the right to choice. That's the basic mission of Planned Parenthood, the issue of choice." Their opponents, Focus on the Family, frame their arguments in similar ways. "There is," an officer said,

> a need to have a healthy home environment. That's something that all have in common, meaning that we have a home that's nurturing, it's loving toward the children, etc. I think it is a universal need. I think parents being committed to one another in a monogamous relationship of love and fidelity and likewise parents being committed to their children in all ways in terms of their education and that's something that you find around the world.

Even groups that oppose what they believe to be the "new colonialism" of the multinational corporations justify their global activism with an appeal to individual rights and needs. The staffer from the Sierra Club put it this way:

> What [is] right in the U.S. is not always right in another country. Even so, there are things that are universal or universally recognized. We believe that it's okay to go abroad and support the idea of democracy and an individual's right to speak out to protect the environment. That's something we think is universally supported.

Underlying all such claims about the universality of human rights and needs, and the freedom of the individual for self-determination, is a common anthropology that understands the individual as autonomous, rational, resourceful, and acquisitive. Reinforcing this anthropology is the *idiom of the market.*

The idiom of the market is, of course, ubiquitous. All of these globalizing organizations, not just the multinational corporations, operate in a world defined by "expanding markets," the need for "competitive advantage," "efficiency," "cost-effectiveness," "maximizing benefits and minimizing costs," "niche markets," "profitability," and the "bottom line." Thus, in the realm of popular culture, MTV is "not simply a hip arts network, but a business."

Though often hostile to the effects of multinational capitalism, INGOs also often speak of themselves as "selling ideas" or "selling services."[8] The goal, as they sometimes put it, is being competitive as world-class assistance providers. What the program director from the Aspen Institute said of his own organization was descriptive of others: "One of the reasons why I think that we have to be global and think of ourselves as global is because it's a niche that we can play that is open right now."

Religious organizations likewise model their evangelism around commercial marketing strategies. One evangelical leader declared, "We want to do business with the world and in so doing put ourselves out into the market. It's just how it works." In promoting Campus Crusade for Christ's New Life Training Centers around the world, President Bill Bright has made the guarantee that for every training center established, 100,000 people will hear the gospel and at least 10,000 souls will saved in the very first year of operation. As he put it, "I have never heard of an investment with greater spiritual return."

One could go on and on about the ways in which a market culture shapes the day-to-day world of all globalizers. Linguistically, the grammar of the market frames their identities and actions as competitors in a changing and fluid world defined by alternative possibilities—in consumer goods, political ideologies, religious truths and soteriologies, and identities.

Most significant from our perspective, however, is the way in which this idiom hides within it assumptions about human beings as pragmatic, acquisitive, self-directed agents. There are different ways of articulating the same sensibility about people. For global executives in the world of business and popular culture, the operative term is "consumer." As the vice president from Coke explained, "Consumers will not accept the constraints of the past, and the more they're exposed to freedom of choice, the more they want it, the more demanding they become of companies and firms and governments, and it's going to change the world quite rapidly."

For INGOs, the term is "individual empowerment." Thus, for example, the goal of the International Center for Research on Women is "the social empowerment and well-being of women." "The message we promote at ICRW," its executive vice president said, "is that women are key economic actors and fundamental to economic development. The problem is that their economic contributions are not rewarded as they should be." Thus, she declared, "I think one of the core values of this organization is to mobilize people, and the way to do that is by enhancing their agency."

Needless to say, this conception of the individual has consequences. In each realm of globalizing activity, it frames notions of organizational progress and, more generally, of human progress.

The desire to globalize a brand or a message or a service by appeal to a universal need or right cannot be made without qualification. The elites in the vanguard of globalization are aware of the historical heavy-handedness of American or Western organizations and are eager to temper both the image and reality of their work as a soft imperialism. Balancing the moral appeal to universal rights and needs, then, is a tendency to indigenize their brands, organizational identities, and constituencies. It is here where the vanguard of globalization employ an *idiom rooted in multiculturalism*, one that focuses on sensitivity to local cultures.

Coca-Cola is paradigmatic in this regard. As the vice president at Coca-Cola put it, "our business is fundamentally local, our principals are global." For most global organizations, this formula is the key strategy for survival in the brave new world of global capital and fluctuating markets. To explain, he uses the metaphor of architecture:

> Think about the architecture as the blueprint for your house. We operate with a "global brand architecture" in positioning our brands that are essentially the same everywhere. Depending on where we are, the roof shingles might be tile in one place and asphalt in another.

The need to be "culturally relevant" and "connected" to local cultures, as he put it, is essential.

Coca-Cola does business in many countries. Because they ingest our product, we have to be part of the fabric of those communities. We have interactions with the whole infrastructure of a country: local governments that set the standards of purity, local bottlers, and local people.

The same is true for MTV. "We're one of the very few brands who have nailed the notion of being able to be global and local at the same time," said the VP for MTV:

We play local music, local music videos, from a massive brand that borrows from its heritage of being American, but it is able to be local. Many of the younger ends of our audience don't even know that MTV is an American company because they've only known it as being locally Taiwanese or locally German, or locally Argentine or whatever.

In describing their global strategy, McDonald's vice president for corporate communications uses the term "multilocal":

We're over 80 percent owned and operated by franchisees or joint venture partners. We have people from the community who work in our restaurants and manage them. They are involved in our local marketing approach, our advertising approach, and in adapting our core menu to local tastes and local culture. We're not creating advertising in some big agency here in America or London or Hong Kong and then shipping it out with a 119 voice-overs. We absolutely believe that that brand needs to be portrayed as a Moldavian company in Moldova, as a British company in the U.K., as a Japanese company in Japan.

This multilocal formula is practiced among the INGOs and evangelical organizations just as faithfully. As the VP for World Vision explains,

The business of an NGO is about trust. Local communities won't trust us as if we're not local. So we have to be local. Thus, we have a World Vision-New Zealand, World Vision-Taiwan, World Vision-U.K., etc. But, on the other hand, if you're only local, you may not be trusted by donors and therefore will not be able to get the resources necessary to accomplish your mission.

A senior practitioner from Planned Parenthood concurs:

> Never in the two years I have been with PPFA has there been an instance where we at headquarters have said to those we work with locally, "This is what you are going to do." You can't. It's their project and telling them what to do wouldn't work. We offer funding and technical assistance, but if there is no buy-in, no program will be effective.

Whether real or imagined, moral sensitivity of this nature is good marketing, not just good politics. Diversity fits the logic of the market. For any transnational organization to succeed, it *must be* "global in orientation and local in execution."[9] In this way, the sun never sets on the Golden Arches—or on the other highly visible brand names of our emerging global culture.

The World They Are Creating

Another remarkable point of commonality we found among the vanguard of globalization was their perception of the world they are helping create.

A SHRINKING WORLD

First, the globalization strategists, administrators, and executives we spoke to were unanimous in characterizing the emerging world as smaller, more interconnected, fast-paced, and global. "I think of the world getting smaller," the program director from the Sierra Club said. The newsgathering executive at CNN echoed the point: "The world is coming closer together through technology and information sharing." As it does, the public relations executive from AT&T argued, it would "make geography ... [and] where you are in the world irrelevant." As the consultant for Archer Daniels Midland put it, "When politics, economics, trade, financial flows, and communications operate on a global level, what happens in one corner of the world will ripple back to affect the lives of each and every one of us."

One of the important consequences of this is the transformation of traditional lines of global political power. The nation-state in particular is viewed as a weakening, even vanishing, institution. In this view, national borders are increasingly transparent, porous, and meaningless when it comes to flows of information and global capital. Sovereignty is challenged from within and without—whether from the financial might of multinational corporations, which rivals the economic power of even some of the wealthier states; from the moral authority of nongovernmental organizations, which through various media can bring the weight of world opinion to bear on "domestic" problems; and from the increasing power of individuals to influence national and global affairs via fax machines and the Internet.

At each of these levels, the power of technology is transforming the function and flavor of politics. "With the incredible distribution of hardware, like computers and fax machines, printers, and satellites," said the senior administrator at Focus on the Family, "governments have ultimately lost control of what they can message to their specific community." The vice president at Nike pointed out how people as well as information are constantly crisscrossing borders and boundaries and, as a result, concluded that "the only people who will care about national boundaries are politicians. Even in America, only 30 percent of the people vote these days. People are caring less and less about politicians." The executive from World Vision agreed: "I do think states are in decline. You look at the evidence. States are in decline, yet they're trying to reassert their sovereignty over their local populations and they're doing all that they can do to do that."

A telling illustration of how these technologies embodied in the popular press were challenging the ability of nation-states to control the information that comes into and out of their borders was provided by the head for CNN International. Contending that national states no longer have a monopoly on information, he suggested that a measure of CNN's power can be found in the extent to which national governments rely on it. "There are numerous examples. The headquarters of the KGB in Moscow has a Department of Intelligence office dedicated to watching and deciphering CNN broadcasts on a twenty-four-hour-a-day basis. You find the same thing within the CIA and the State Department. We are closely monitored by the leaders of the world."

The eroding power of nation-states is not due to new communication and information technologies alone, but also to the financial power of multinational corporations. A leading strategist at Merrill Lynch boasted of the company's power in the world. "Merrill Lynch," he said, "is a big player in the U.S. and in many global equity markets around the world." In Britain, for example, it holds a 25 percent share of the activity in the London Stock Exchange. If there are problems, Merrill Lynch has the kind of financial muscle to "go to the London Stock Exchange and say if you guys don't fix it, we're going to take our 25 percent a year volume elsewhere. If we do, the London Stock Exchange could die." Their influence extends to American markets as well.

> It might be a little hubris, but we have a pretty important relationship to the workings of the U.S. economy. . . . We have a big influence, for example, on what happens to the New York Stock Exchange and what happens to the Nasdaq Stock Exchange. We're in a position to say, "Listen guys, if you don't change with the times, if you don't get your act together, if you don't create a structure that's going to help us and our industries as financial intermediaries compete globally, we're going to create the structure ourselves that suits our needs for the future."

The point was noted earlier. For those in international business, this democratization of power translates into empowerment of the individual—as individual consumer. "One thing globalization has done," said the consultant for Archer Daniels Midland, "is transfer the power of governments to the global consumer. It is the consumer who dictates what we produce, how much we produce, and essentially what price we get paid for our efforts."

The empowerment of the individual as consumer is also seen in what Thomas Friedman has called the "electronic herd." It is a virtual assembly of millions of anonymous investors who have no national loyalties but control the world's financial markets. The vice president from Coke provided a pointed example:

> We try to think about the likelihood that the countries that feel their sovereignty threatened can throw up barriers to us. I don't think they have much ability to do that, because their capital structures are opening up. Take France, for example. The reliance of an average French company on equity is increasing. They have shareholders to answer to. They are going to look for scale and those shareholders are

going to look for returns. The inexorable path for their senior executives and employees, who are paid by options, is to seek competitive advantage. And competitive advantage seldom comes from hanging on to that which is only unique to one people.

In this view, yet another factor contributing to the weakening of national sovereignty has been the expansion of local, national, and international nongovernmental organizations, such as Amnesty International and Greenpeace, and intergovernmental bodies such as the United Nations and the World Bank. Aided by the alliance of new information and communication technologies and the press, these organizations have been able to mobilize people and governments around issues that include environmental protection, human rights, women's rights, and so on. While posting no standing armies and having no direct impact on the world economy, these organizations understand themselves to be the moral conscience for world affairs, including multinational corporations and national governments. They see their moral authority extending not only to events taking place within national boundaries but increasingly to the decisions and policies being made in corporate boardrooms as well.

The program officer from the Aspen Institute put it this way: "The fact that the whole world is watching when a country does something domestically, impacts the sovereignty of the country and the power of a leader within that country. That's part of the loss of sovereignty." Activist organizations can, with the help of the Internet or a fax machine, mobilize sympathetic people and organizations for a given cause anywhere in the world. "[A] rumor can be started on the Internet by a single individual. It can catch fire and spread very rapidly," the strategist from Porter Novelli observed. The worldwide paranoia over genetically modified foods, she noted, began with a handful of individuals: "I don't know the full details of it, but I know that it primarily began in France, and it was a number of individuals raising a lot of questions in the early days. Now, there are a million advocacy groups that are very, very well funded on the front lines of this issue. But it was the speed of the information that generated global concerns almost immediately."

A WORLD OF UNSTOPPABLE PROGRESS

In some respects, the power of globalization is measured in the ways it shrinks the world through markets and communications technology.

The elites in the vanguard of globalization recognize that the effect of globalization on national life is one of the central ways it manifests this power. Another way they see this power is in what they consider to be an ineluctable progression forward. As we've seen, these elites differ in their views of the long-term effects of globalization, yet nearly all view globalization, or certain aspects of it, as inevitable.

This is particularly true in the realm of the economy and technology. Said one corporate executive, "Everybody's moving at sort of a different pace, but they're all headed in the same general direction." The consultant for Archer Daniels Midland described globalization simply as "a fact." "It is," he said, "a reality which must be recognized and dealt with. The forces of globalization have led to a process of creative destruction . . . a new global environment has emerged and we must learn to function in it."

The die is cast in so many respects. As a manager in a religious organization put it, "It's just never going to go backward." Even within an INGO as academically grounded (and therefore suspicious of sweeping generalizations) as the Carter Center, there is a recognition that globalization is the dominant trend. This is not to say that there couldn't be a setback to globalization, but that, a division head says, "would take some tremendous disaster." Still, "for the short-term forecast, you've got to say that globalization is only going to get stronger; that its effects are going to be felt in more places, by more people."

Two of their most striking points of agreement were in the necessity of adapting to the demands of globalization and their metaphorical view of it as a train leaving a station or a ship leaving its port. Regardless of whether they were referring to business, nongovernmental activity, or national governance, the sentiment remained the same: If you don't "get on board," you'll be left behind.

In this, whoever wants to be a "player" in the new world economy, whoever wants to capitalize on the putative benefits, opportunities and prosperity this economy affords, whoever wants to provide their citizenry with a decent quality of life and to move to the next stage of economic and social (and human) development, must, say our globalizers, "come up to speed," "get in the tide," "play by the rules," and "get with the program."

Economically, this "program" involves deregulating national and regional markets, eliminating restrictions on information, and implementing the necessary infrastructure needed to attract and facilitate foreign capital investment. Anything that gets in the way of this pro-gram—whether culture, creed, or politics—needs to be either adjusted or divested. Globalization will brook no obstacles. For example, AT&T's public relations director observed,

> I think that countries are beginning to recognize that if they want to be players in this global economy, they need to have the infrastructure in place, and they need to have markets that will allow them to suc-ceed. This means that they will need to open their markets to compe-tition, and they will need to eliminate some of the restrictions that currently exist in terms of information transfer.

In the world unfolding, he concluded, "there'll by only two kinds of telecommunication companies: those that go global and those that go bankrupt." Merrill Lynch's strategist illustrated the logic of this system in the case of contemporary Japan:

> In Japan right now, there are 5 trillion dollars in assets sitting in al-most zero-yielding bank deposits, just because the culture has had an historical mind-set towards safety, security, saving for the future, sav-ing for retirement. You ought to envy the Japanese for their respect of the elderly and their respect of teachers and their desire to support their parents in their old age, etc. At the same time, they're not going to be able to do what they want to do if they keep their 5 trillion dol-lars in assets sitting in less than 1 percent-yielding bank deposits. They will have no money in twenty years to support their grandparents. It won't be there. Merrill Lynch goes into this market and says, "Listen people, if you keep your 5 trillion dollars in these bank deposits: (a) all your banks are going bankrupt so the money might not be there; or (b), even though global inflation is at 2 percent, a yield of a half a per-cent in twenty years will mean that the purchasing power of your money is little to nothing." Yes, I think there are certain cultural prac-tices and cultural identities that are critical to maintain. At the same time, there are certain practices that need to come up to speed with the global economic realities of the current times. In the past, the Japanese could keep their money in the banks, because the banks were the safest place and the banks offered a reasonable rate of return. But today and in the future that's not going to be possible for them.

At the Carter Center, this logic has led to one person's conclusion that a nation just doesn't have a choice anymore. He pointed to Brazil to make this point. "A large country like Brazil tried to isolate itself. They found that they couldn't do that any longer. No one can. So how they're going to globalize is the question, and I don't know the answer."

How to globalize is the central issue facing many countries (and organizations). Indeed, many of the INGO executives we interviewed were either undergoing or had recently undergone internal discussion about how to go global. A number of poor countries (and virtually all of Africa) are generally considered unable either to recognize or to capitalize on the opportunities of globalization. Our executive from Merrill Lynch (somewhat ironically) acknowledged this fact:

> When I think of globalization, I think about the countries . . . who are sort of outsiders, who are outcasts, if you will, because of political reasons or religious reasons, or whatever reasons. Certain countries in Africa, certain countries in the Middle East, who aren't sort of coming on board with an accepted protocol or way of recognizing each other, and they're losing out on the further interlinking of economies.

Likewise, the vice president from World Vision argued:

> There are certain values that are going to be rewarded by globalization and others which are not. I came out of a context in Africa where they're not going to be rewarded by globalization because they're not able to get on the information highway; they don't have the infrastructure to do these things. They don't have the initial capital to do this.

He argued that without access to global flows of capital, they lose "the ability to grow and expand and educate their children and feed their people and essentially move forward to the next stage of development."

The Merrill Lynch strategist frankly maintained that those countries "who are not linking up to this new global economy are going to clearly remain behind with respect to all the fundamental needs and necessities that their population requires to have a decent quality of life." In their experience, however, the choice for most countries they deal with is obvious: They must globalize. As Porter Novelli's executive vice president pointed out, "there are countries that are very quick to see the opportunity. . . . we don't have to spend five seconds to convince them that it's a good idea. . . . It clicks like that."

A WORLD IN THEIR OWN IMAGE

This vanguard of globalization is self-conscious about America's prominent role in the processes of globalization. "Globalization is a fact of life," an administrator at Porter Novelli explained. "That it's being driven largely, almost exclusively, by Americans is also a fact of life. It is because of the nature of the technology and the global corporations that all came from and still do come from America." Her colleague concurred:

> I would have to put America in that category of driving globalization for the simple reason that the top global corporations are U.S.–based. The top institutions are U.S.–based and the business schools that are training people to be global executives are U.S.–based. Likewise, 90 percent of the Internet economy is U.S.–based, so there's no question that the U.S. is a critical force in helping to make this happen.

"For better or worse," the vice president from Nike said, "American companies and their brands are the ones who are most able to develop critical mass for a product. Because that's really all that being global is." It is the organizational power to operate at a larger scale that, in their minds, accounts for the immense influence and transnational reach of the U.S.–based multinational corporations, INGOs, religious organizations, and so on.

As self-conscious as they are of the global power of their organizations, they are equally sensitive to the morally and politically ambivalent position this puts them in. Yet all of the global elites we interviewed strenuously resisted the idea that they were carriers of anything other than their own product or message.

For example, all these elites, to a person, denied that they were in any way Americanizing the world. "Most Americans I know who are really involved in this," said the executive from the Aspen Institute, "are not really trying to conquer the world. They see the world as a market and as a playground and as a place where you need peace or policies that are prosocial." The manager from CNN put it this way: "Whether it is

Americanization or globalization, I imagine there is a bit of both. But there is no imperialist goal behind it by any means."

If they are offering anything to the world, they claim, they are offering a product or an idea that meets a universal need—something that transcends national borders and local cultures. Though it possesses global brand recognition, it is also thoroughly indigenized. Most interesting in this regard was the incredulity expressed by the marketing executive at Coca-Cola.

> It would not be in our best interest to give consumers a position that they don't want. It's just completely counterintuitive. . . . The cultural anthropologists who would suggest that we're advancing one way of life over the other, I would ask them to understand why it is that Coca-Cola would be able to broadcast an optimist point of view unless it exists already. Trying to change the nature of cultures is not part of our success criteria. I don't even understand what would be the motivation.

Consider as well the case made by the vice president from Nike.

> We always describe the brand as a person. So who is the person? A person that you would most like to hang out with. First and foremost, they would be funny. They would be honest and say the things that you think should be said. They would be a team player, someone who would do the utmost to go after the loose ball. So what we are really trying to do is build up a personality. It is more like building a person than building a brand.

Is that "person" an American, we asked? "No, No," he replied. "I think that personality can be English as much as it can be American." Even the evangelical organizations, whose own missionary heritage is littered with indictments of imperialist agendas, were baffled as to how they could be engaged in that kind of activity today. The press secretary for the Christian Coalition International put it this way.

> We're simply teaching them how to be more effective in the government than they already have been and how they can have a voice. In no way do we want to Americanize what they do, and who says we

ever could? We don't have a military force behind us. We don't have that kind of power. We're simply teaching people, individuals, how to be effective in their countries, in their own governments. I don't see how that can be threatening.

Likewise, the vice president from Focus on the Family argued that the Bible is universally valid across cultures and even across time. Thus "what Dr. Dobson [the head of Focus on the Family] is espousing are principles that are rooted in the Bible. These aren't specifically American things that we're talking about. As long as you stick to two people committed in marriage and to good parenting—which come out of Genesis—these are already global ideals."

"Besides the gospel," we asked the head of International Ministries at Campus Crusade for Christ, "are there other elements of American culture or the 'American way of life' that are somehow being carried along in the message you proclaim around the world?" "We hope not," he replied. "Any of our American staff who go overseas we put through a thirteen-week training course to sensitize them to local issues."

This naïveté extends to their reflections about technology. When we asked the respondent from AT&T about the larger impact of their communications technology on local cultures, he replied,

> The technology is an enabler. And we separate carriage from content, and we're not in the content business, so we would be providing a capability to anyone. . . . We are not in a position to dictate how that technology ought to be deployed, or what it ought to be used for, or what content ought to be provided on the technology.

In his view, both AT&T and their technology products are therefore neutral.

When pressed on these issues, some did recognize that they might be carriers of cultural packages that went beyond their own product or message. Yet they insisted that what they brought to the world was good. "To the extent that there is Americanization," said the executive from the Aspen Institute, "I think it's fairly benevolent." The vice president from McDonald's responded in a similar way:

Look at agriculture. If somebody is using an ox to plow a field and then they're introduced to the tractor, their lives will probably change. But they've made the judgment that this is good for them; that it gives them an advantage economically. I don't think you can argue with the fact these technology transfers are good at the end of the day for people.

The consultant for Archer Daniels Midland was even less tentative. "We are a positive force in the areas where we enter," he said, "because we create employment and generate more taxes as we upgrade assets, expand capacities, and bring other core businesses to the area."

In part because the INGOs have a higher level of personal exposure to the local situations, they tend to be more reflective and ambivalent about their influence in these settings. "It's true," confessed the respondent from Compassion International,

it's very conflictive sometimes. On the matter of the environment, you see that people in some societies are destroying their habitat and yet they are also just trying to survive. So what's the alternative? It's a real hard thing to say. Environmental intervention may be very good for their ecology long term, but is it progress if they don't feel that way about it?

The program director of the Carter Center's Democracy Program had similar doubts about his work abroad:

You know you are stirring something into the pot that wasn't there before. Is it a good thing or not? That's something that I think about quite a bit. It hasn't weighed so heavily on me that I would quit my job or think that I'm doing the wrong thing. It's one of those cultural relativism kinds of arguments. But there are definitely some question marks there.

As the individual from the Carter Center said, none of these doubts deterred him from continuing his work. In fact, none of these globalizers see the world brought about by globalization as bad per se; they simply want to make it more humane. Their work, in the final analysis, contributes to this goal.

In the end, all of the elites in the vanguard of globalization see themselves and their organizations through the lens of fate. "Things are going to change and we're just part of that process," the executive director for Greenberg, Quinlan explained. "I guess I don't think that much about the big picture, of how we're actually doing it. I mean, we're not going in anywhere people didn't ask us to come. We're just participating in a process that's already happening." The vice president at Coca-Cola concluded much the same thing. "I don't know," he said, "what would the alternative be: suggesting that we ought to deny consumers choice? What's the practical alternative? I don't know. It's an interesting question."

PAROCHIAL COSMOPOLITANS

In sum, the vanguard of globalization agree that the world through globalization will be increasingly electronic, individualistic, driven by the free market, and democratic. In this way they also agree that, for the time being anyway, the world will probably look more like the United States (or the West) than not. In addition, if nations, local cultures, organizations, corporations, and so on do not "get on board" with globalization, they are likely to lose out on its benefits and opportunities and become increasingly unable to provide for their constituents' basic needs, thus falling further behind, with little chance of ever catching up.

At the same time, they deny that globalization, especially the part that they themselves play in it, threatens or harms indigenous cultures, traditions, practices, or identities. Where it might be perceived as such, they defer all responsibility for the impact of their products and services to the national governing agencies and to the local cultural organizations themselves.

In all of this, they see no contradiction and experience little tension. The environment they inhabit only reinforces the lack of contradiction. For all practical purposes, the sociocultural bubble that makes up the framework of their working experience eliminates these tensions.

Yet there is a degree of unsettledness in their sense of the world. Some are *ambivalent* about their own role as globalizers. This is mainly a function of the extent to which they "leave the bubble" and are exposed to local and indigenous cultures. As we have noted, these elites vary along this line—some are more exposed than others. Yet even those who do operate outside of the physical environment of the bubble nevertheless approach local foreign cultures through the normative and analytical frameworks of their own form of global engagement. Beyond ambivalence, all of these globalizing elites are *defensive* about the accusation that they might be carriers of any cultural baggage that foreign cultures might not want.

It is through the vocabularies of *global speak* that they are reconciled to any ambivalence they might experience or to their defensiveness about the world they are creating. They believe that they are all responding in different ways to universal needs rooted in a conception of the individual as a rational, competitive, and acquisitive social actor. They have come to know those needs and establish their validity through the tools of social science, yet they have tailored their response by making the effort to indigenize the brand, the product, and the message to local settings.

Paramount in this process is the belief that a larger humanitarian idea undergirds their work and the work of the organizations they represent. Whether commercial, entertainment, religious, or educational, the organizational mission of their work is to meet a fundamental and universal human need, even if they happen to be creating that need. Thus, in ways they are not always reflective about, they want to believe that they and their work contribute to a moral good. In these ways, globalization's vanguard maintains a sense of moral innocence about the world they are helping create. Cynicism is simply absent; instead, guilelessness—about who they are and what they are bringing about— is the overwhelming sensibility.

Cosmopolitans: After a Fashion

If the lives, experiences, and perspectives of the vanguard of globalization are one prism through which we can understand the monumental social and cultural transformations we call globalization, it certainly speaks to the kind of cosmopolitanism that is coming to prevail in a global culture.

Surely these elites *are* cosmopolitans: they travel the world and their field of responsibility is the world. Indeed, they see themselves as "global citizens." Again and again, we heard them say that they thought of themselves more as "citizens of the world" who happen to carry an American passport than as U.S. citizens who happen to work in a global organization. They possess all that is implied in the notion of the cosmopolitan. They are sophisticated, urbane, and universalistic in their perspective and ethical commitments.

At the same time, there are distinct characteristics and important qualifications to the cosmopolitanism they experience and represent. The physical environment they inhabit is mostly uniform, antiseptic, homogeneous, and artificial. For all of their worldliness, they never really leave "home." In this, "locality" and "place" are not so much destroyed as transformed into abstract, fluid, and provisional realities. The parochial quality of this cosmopolitanism is also reflected normatively. They would not say that globalization per se is an unmitigated good, but they have no doubt that their particular take on globalization—what they specifically champion as agents of globalization and the technology that delivers their "product"—is good. They are cosmopolitan, to be sure, but in ways that are distinctly bounded and insular.

NOTES

1. To this end, we interviewed the senior management and executives of twenty-three transnational organizations and corporations, all global leaders in their respective arenas. Included were executives from multinational business and finance organizations such as Merrill Lynch, Archer Daniels Midland, Porter Novelli, and AT&T; global purveyors of popular culture such as Nike, McDonald's, MTV, Twentieth Century Fox and CNN; international nongovernmental organizations (INGOs) representing a vast array of special interests including the Aspen Institute, International Center for Research on Women, Carter Center, Sierra Club, World Vision, and Greenberg, Quinlan Research, Inc.; worldwide evangelical Protestant movements such as Campus Crusade for Christ, Compassion International, Focus on the Family, Christian Coalition International, and Christian Broadcasting Network; and finally even organizations such as the International Forum on Globalization, the putative opposition to globalization. These are among the key players shaping the emerging global order.

2. Tract from the International Action Center.

3. Anuradha Mittal, Institute for Food and Development Policy. Quoted at the Globalization Teach-In, 14 April 2000.

4. Jerry Mander, president of the International Forum on Globalization. Quoted from his introductory speech at the Globalization Teach-In, 14 April 2000.

5. According to President Carter's assistant, Dr. Steven Hochman.

6. Brochure from the World Economy Project on Globalization, no date.

7. This, according to our contact at Coca-Cola.

8. This is how the executive from the Sierra Club put it.

9. Nike's global marketing executive.

Index

———————— • ————————

Note: Page numbers in *italics* refer to photographs and illustrations.
Page numbers in **bold** refer to chapters.